Volumes previously published by the University of California Press, Berkeley, Los Angeles, London, for the Center for Chinese Studies of The University of Michigan:

MICHIGAN STUDIES ON CHINA

Alan P. L. Liu
Communications and National Integration in Communist China

Richard Solomon
Mao's Revolution and the Chinese Political Culture

Kang Chao
Capital Formation in Mainland China, 1952–1965

Martin King Whyte
Small Groups and Political Rituals in China

Edward Friedman
Backward Toward Revolution: The Chinese Revolutionary Party

Andrew Nathan
Peking Politics, 1918–1923: Factionalism and the Failure of Constitutionalism

Joseph W. Esherick
Reform and Revolution in China: The 1911 Revolution in Hunan and Hubei

NATIONALIST CHINA AT WAR

Michigan Studies on China
Published for the Center for Chinese Studies of
The University of Michigan

MICHIGAN STUDIES ON CHINA

*The research on which these books are based was supported by the Center for
Chinese Studies of The University of Michigan.*

Nationalist China at War

Military Defeats and Political Collapse, 1937–45

HSI-SHENG CH'I

Ann Arbor   The University of Michigan Press

To Ssu-wei Liang:
May her free spirit forever shine.

Library of Congress Cataloging in Publication Data

Chi, Hsi-sheng.
  Nationalist China at war.

  (Michigan studies on China)
  Bibliography: p.
  Includes index.
  1. China—History—1937–1945. 2. Sino-Japanese
Conflict, 1937–1945. 3. Chung-kuo kuo min tang.
4. Chiang, Kai-shek, 1887–1975. I. Title.
II. Series.
DS777.518.C45 1982   951.04′2   82-2857
ISBN 0-472-10018-1   AACR2

Acknowledgments

My fascination with the Second Sino-Japanese War began as I lived through its daily excitement in childhood. In later years, I gained deeper insight into the intricate relationship between the war and the nature of the Nationalist government from my late father, Mr. Cheng-hsing Ch'i, who was a keen observer of Chinese politics on both local and national levels. I also drew much support from the late Mr. Po-k'un Liu, whose moral rectitude, revolutionary dedication, and love for his country inspired me to pursue research and write about the political tragedy of the Chinese people.

A research leave and extensive travel in 1976 were possible due to a generous grant from the Committee on Republican and Contemporary China of the Social Science Research Council, supplemented by a grant from the Faculty Research Council of the University of North Carolina. While in Taiwan, my research was courteously assisted by the staff members of the Bureau of Investigation (Ministry of Justice), the Bureau of War History (Ministry of National Defense), Commission of Party History (Kuomintang Central Committee), and the National Archives (Kuo-shih-kuan).

I also wish to express my gratitude to several friends and colleagues who have read the manuscript either in whole or in part. They are professors Albert Feuerwerker, Robert Kapp, Lawrence Kessler, Andrew Nathan, Jeffrey Obler, Andrew Scott, Hung-mao Tien, Tang Tsou, and Ernest Young. Their constructive comments and suggestions were extremely helpful. Needless to say, I alone bear the responsibility for errors of fact or interpretation.

Mrs. Barbara Higgins has greatly improved the style and organization of the manuscript. Bridie and Bernard have shared the pains and anxiety through this entire intellectual enterprise; they are now stoically resigned to the hazards of being the offspring of an academician. To them all, I wish to extend my appreciation.

Contents

Introduction

Amidst the thriving expansion of China studies in the United States in recent years, one area that has conspicuously lagged behind is our knowledge of the crucial Nationalist era. The lacunae in the literature are readily visible to serious students of modern Chinese political history. Ch'ien Tuan-sheng's *The Government and Politics of China,* first published in 1950, has been reprinted several times and remains to this day the standard reference work on the theory, practice, and structure of the Nationalist party and government. Robert North's collaborative work with Ithiel De Sola Pool, *Kuomintang and Chinese Communist Elites,* originally published in 1952, is still the most comprehensive study of the Nationalist leadership.[1]

A few scholars have contributed to the study of the Nationalist regime, although their coverage has been quite uneven. Professor Tien Hung-mao offered a significant analysis of the Kuomintang's administrative and political institutions, and Professor Lloyd Eastman added a more philosophical assessment of the KMT regime, but both dealt only with the Nanking decade (1928–37).[2] Other works on the KMT's Nanking era include those on student movements, economic construction, and foreign aid, but many more important issues of the KMT regime have remained unexplored.[3]

One of these unexplored areas is the intricate relationship between the military and the government. The role of the military in shaping twentieth-century Chinese politics and society cannot be overemphasized. During the early Republican period, the militarists occupied the center stage of politics on both national and local levels. The militarists not only monopolized political and governmental powers, but they affected the economic well-being of the people, stimulated social unrest, accelerated

rural decay, and provoked an intellectual revulsion so violent and extensive that it significantly contributed to the birth of the Kuomintang (KMT)
and Chinese Communist party (CCP).

When one traces the revolutionary theory of the KMT, two features
are particularly noteworthy. In the first place, although Sun Yat-sen
legitimized the use of military power to seize political power for revolutionary goals, military dictatorship itself was to be a very transient phase.
According to Sun's notions of revolution by stages, military power was
meant to lose its salience in politics progressively through the stages of
political tutelage and constitutional democracy and to become subordinate
to civilian authority, as in the Western constitutional systems which Sun
wished to emulate in China. Second, Sun was one of the earliest advocates
of the mobilization model of politics in the history of modern Chinese
revolutionary movements. Even as his contemporaries (e.g., K'ang Yu-
wei, Liang Ch'i-ch'ao) were endeavoring to arouse the intelligentsia to
adopt a new ideology in order to restore their long-accustomed leadership
role in national rejuvenation, Sun recognized that it was imperative to
arouse the masses (*huan-ch'i min-chung*) on the broadest possible basis to
achieve a genuine revolution. Sun's final revolutionary objective was
to transform Chinese politics from a regime predicated on military coercion
to a regime predicated on the enlightened political consciousness, support,
participation, and mobilization of the masses. Such a transformation would
take place during the stage of political tutelage under the stewardship of the
Kuomintang. In other words, political transformation was to be a "historic
mission" for the KMT to perform.

As a study of the KMT, the main thesis of this work is that the KMT
failed in this mission during its existence on the mainland. The post-Sun
KMT came under the domination of a leadership that became increasingly
and excessively preoccupied with military power and acquired the belief
that the party's military predominance was a prerequisite for implementing
its political programs. In the KMT's search for military supremacy over the
country, it inevitably came into conflict with other political groups with
their own military power—the regional militarists and the Communists.
The KMT leadership believed that the only effective way to deal with these
groups was to suppress them with military might. Yet in reality the KMT
never acquired enough military muscle to accomplish this goal. Consequently, it evolved a peculiar pattern of relationships with these groups
that was a mixture of distrust, hostility, appeasement and compromise, and
limited collaboration. It was these relationships that overshadowed all as-

pects of the KMT's existence on the mainland from start to finish, and the
KMT's obsession with the strictly military connotations of such mutual
relationships caused it to delay, evade, and ignore the fundamental tasks of
the socioeconomic and political reconstruction of China.

Social scientists have long maintained that a regime's viability must
depend on two kinds of support—specific and diffuse.[4] But as the KMT
moved toward increasing militarization, the only sector from which it
could draw firm support was the party's own army, which remained a
minority in China's military makeup during the entire time. Meanwhile,
the KMT's persistent and willful neglect of programs related to the
socioeconomic welfare of the people denied it the capability to tap the
reservoir of diffuse support of the general population. Given the fact that
the KMT was an extremely narrowly based militaristic regime under the
guise of party leadership, it was not surprising that it would be particularly
vulnerable to stress. A second thesis of the present work is that the Sino-
Japanese War of 1937–45 represented a stress beyond the KMT's coping
capabilities and eventually forced it to collapse.

To test the validity of these two theses, the substance of this work will
be concerned with a number of issues and questions.

One issue is the origin of the KMT's politics of militarization. Chapter
1 will provide an overview of the KMT's strategy of military reunification
during and after the Northern Expedition and show how it laid the foundation for a pattern of relationships marked by both rivalry and appeasement
between the central government and regional power structures. The trend
toward militarization became manifest during 1927–36 as the KMT became obsessed with the pursuit of illusive military power, which resulted in
ten years of civil wars and the nonimplementation of promised revolutionary programs.

Chapter 2 discusses the military process of the Sino-Japanese War to
demonstrate the extent to which the government army—the single most
important supporter of the KMT regime—was crippled repeatedly and
decisively by relentless Japanese attacks.

Chapter 3 assesses the political impact of the KMT's military defeats
on the wartime coalition between the central government and other
political-military groups. As the KMT's military strength declined precipitously, the coalition also began to crumble, and the regime was increasingly
challenged by organized military revolts from both the regionalists and the
Communists.

How did the war affect the KMT's relationship with the people? As a regime unskilled in mass mobilization, this relationship was fragile to begin with. But the government's military defeats, coupled with the intransigence of the regional and local ruling elites, exacerbated the stress of the war and produced a near-total breakdown of organized political life in the government-held territories. Chapter 4 shows how the regime exhausted all residual diffuse support of the people by the gross mismanagement of critical wartime programs.

Chapter 5 attempts to offer an explanation of the process of the fossilization and paralysis of the KMT as a revolutionary organization and of the causes for its failure to perform its assigned historic mission to revitalize and transform Chinese politics. The work ends with a critical review of the various existing interpretations of the KMT regimes, and the author's own effort to relate the KMT's military defeats and political collapse to a broader theoretical framework.

Chapter 1

The Militarization of the Kuomintang before the War

One remarkable feature about the Kuomintang's revolutionary ideology is the underemphasis of the role of the military. While most other revolutionary ideologies either are highly concerned with laying a moral foundation for the right to revolt or with actually developing strategic guidelines on how revolutionary violence should be applied, Sun Yat-sen's revolutionary theory is basically a series of policy statements on socioeconomic, psychological, and political reconstruction. Sun's scant attention to military matters can be partially attributed to his unfamiliarity with them, but more fundamentally to his aversion to violence and his basic commitment to Western-style constitutional democracy. Thus, once the Republic was proclaimed in 1911, he was ready to let the KMT play by parliamentary rules.

It was only repeated warlord betrayals of the revolution that convinced Sun to organize his own army. He did so reluctantly, and during the last years of his life, he devoted far more attention to refining his theoretical construct than to assuming active leadership over military affairs.[1] It may be argued that the synthesis of Sun's theories is the *Chien-kuo ta-kang* (Outline of National Reconstruction), which he drafted in 1924. (Many of the ideas contained in the *Chien-kuo ta-kang* derived from the Tung-meng-hui Manifesto of 1905, but received their final and most elaborate articulation in 1924.) In this short document of twenty-five articles, Sun's priorities and the interconnections of the various components of his theories are clearly summed up. It is in this document that his theory of planned revolutionary progress received a concise exposition. As is well known, Sun divided the revolutionary process into three stages: military

5

dictatorship, political tutelage, and constitutional democracy. The ultimate goal of Sun's revolution was to realize Western-style multiparty democracy in China. Consequently, the KMT would play a dominant role only in the first two stages to bring about the transition.

Of these two stages, Sun's greatest theoretical contribution was made with reference to political tutelage. While other revolutionary theorists either insist on perpetual dictatorship of a particular class or group, or expect democracy to follow revolution immediately, Sun introduced the intervening stage of political tutelage, during which the revolutionary party was assigned the role of educating the people and training them to assume increasing responsibilities in self-government. It is indicative of Sun's own values that the stage of military dictatorship was discussed rather perfunctorily in two articles (arts. 6-7), while constitutional democracy was discussed in seven articles (arts. 19-25); but most important, political tutelage was discussed in eleven articles (arts. 8-18).

According to Sun, the KMT's major responsibilities during the stage of political tutelage included mobilizing people to participate in the political process, electing and recalling local officials, and legislating or abrogating local laws. The party should help local governments achieve fiscal independence through the promotion of economic reconstruction in industrial and commercial investment, exploitation of natural resources, the development of transportation, and land reclamation. Finally, the party should assist local governments in promoting social justice and social welfare, including such tasks as census taking, equalization of land tax, land reform, education, medical care, relief, and care for the young and aged.[2] Therefore, from Sun's point of view, the role of the KMT as a revolutionary party was that of a midwife to hasten the birth of constitutional democracy. There is no doubt that, although Sun sanctioned the use of revolutionary violence, he only conferred legitimacy on the revolutionary party if it succeeded in efficaciously performing the specified responsibilities of political tutelage to sustain the revolutionary momentum and remain faithful to the revolutionary ideals. Sun unequivocally stated that insofar as the objectives of national reconstruction were concerned, the most important was to improve the people's livelihood, followed by the promotion of people's political rights, national equality, and independence, in that order. To reverse this order or priorities would be tantamount to a desertion of the revolution.

This chapter will trace the development of the KMT regime in the first ten years of its existence to show that military activities became the dominant, and sometimes exclusive, concern of its leaders, in contrast to Sun's original revolutionary plans. The result of this preoccupation with military conflict was inevitably detrimental to the KMT's socioeconomic and political commitments. Therefore, after a brief discussion of the Northern Expedition, the main body of this chapter will concentrate on the Nanking government's attempt to build a modern army, and how this effort precipitated a pattern of rivalry between the KMT, the provincial military power structures, and the Communists in the 1930s.

The Legacy of the Northern Expedition

Sun Yat-sen's choice of Canton as the site of his revolutionary government presaged the launching of a Northern Expedition against the reactionaries and warlords in the north at an opportune moment. Shortly after Sun's death in 1924, the worsening of the warlords' position in North China, Wu P'ei-fu's invasion of Hunan, the deteriorating relationship between the KMT and the CCP, as well as the mounting military pressure exerted by the British in the Canton–Hong Kong Great Strike, all led the KMT leaders to the conclusion that the time was ripe to launch the expedition. As will be seen, this haste was to entail considerable cost to the party and the army in subsequent years.[3]

The KMT took quite a gamble with the expedition against its northern warlord adversaries who commanded overwhelming superiority in both manpower and firepower. The enormous disparity between the KMT and its enemies greatly narrowed its strategic alternatives. From the outset, the overall guideline for the expedition was to reduce the number of opponents to allow the party to tackle them one at a time. More concretely, two strategies were adopted.

First, the KMT made a distinction between southern and northern warlords and decided that while the former could be tolerated, the latter had to be liquidated. Consequently, once the expedition was under way, the KMT sent out many representatives to negotiate with the southern militarists on the conditions of their defection. Typically, the KMT would grant official recognition and sanction to whatever positions these militarists were already holding at that time, promising not to upset their territorial control, taxing powers, or the internal composition of their military force. These concessions were made in return for the militarists' promise to accept the official designations issued by the KMT government and to be loyal to that government alone. In this sense, the impact of the expedition on the military-political power structures in the southern provinces was minimal.

Second, in 1926, the KMT was also successfully completing an alliance arrangement with two northern military factions, Feng Yü-hsiang and Yen Hsi-shan, who both maintained ideological positions somewhat closer to that of the KMT than most northern warlords.

In facing the other main northern antagonists, the KMT deliberately adopted the policy of isolating them and handling them one at a time. The consequence of this strategy was that by the end of 1928, most of the armies under the former Chihli and Anhwei factions were defeated and disbanded, while those under Fengtien were driven back into Manchuria.

Therefore, taken as a whole, the Northern Expedition can be viewed as having produced a fundamental alteration of the political-military alignment in China, since it ended the domination of Chinese politics by northerners who derived their military power from the Peiyang group. However, it failed to eliminate warlordism.

In addition, at the outset of the expedition when the KMT-CCP united front was preserved (1925-27), the KMT leaders still viewed the development of popular movements as a coequal of military power to extend the revolution: peasant organizations were to transform the social landscape of the countryside and labor unions would challenge foreign capitalist-imperialists in the port cities. The popular movements were considered to be essential to the establishment of a new democratic order in China and to play a key role in the representative assemblies in local and provincial politics.[4]

But as the expedition progressed, the military demonstrated their preference to use military-diplomatic means to assimilate former enemies. When these recently co-opted warlords and the business classes in the big cities began to protest the extension of popular movements into their territorial domains, and when even some conservative Nationalist commanders and civilian leaders feared that they might not be able to control these popular movements, the movements were then suppressed.

As one of the KMT's more radical but non-Communist generals, Teng Yen-ta, complained in March, 1927, the party and the whole future of the Chinese revolution were endangered because military influences had outpaced the development of the party, the government, and everything else during the course of the Northern Expedition.[5]

Thus, the price the KMT paid to implement its strategy of achieving quick military success was to abandon the path of social revolution through mass participation from below and opt instead for a conventional military-diplomatic approach of building coalitions from above, as well as to infest the ranks of the National Revolutionary Army with nonrevolutionary and counterrevolutionary military units, particularly in the southern provinces.

In the most immediate sense, the strategy of the Northern Expedition left unresolved the tension between nationalism and regionalism and impeded the KMT's goal of achieving national integration, as reflected in the difficulties surrounding troop disbandment and military reorganization. In turn, this tension prevented the KMT from pursuing the political and economic programs that the revolution originally set out to accomplish, triggered incessant civil wars, and greatly impaired the country's capability to withstand foreign aggression.

Troop Disbandment, 1928–29

The issue that immediately confronted the KMT government in 1928 was how to deal with the sprawling semi-independent military structures in the provinces. While the desirability of military reorganization and reduction was beyond dispute, the actual implementation was fraught with hidden dangers and provided the first demonstration of the defect in the Northern Expedition strategy. At the Reorganization and Disbandment Conference on January 1, 1929, the government proposed to divide the country into six disbandment zones and to reduce the huge armies to about eighty-five divisions with a total manpower ceiling of 800,000 men. Military administration and command was to be consolidated in the central government.[6] The disbanded soldiers would be absorbed into local police forces, engage in road construction, water conservation, afforestation, and exploitation of frontier wasteland.[7] Yet despite its appearance of being a reasonable proposal, it was rejected by the participants to the conference.

The failure of disbandment must be understood in relation to the political-military system as a whole. The root cause of the difficulty was that the KMT leaders were trying to solve the problem of military reorganization as a prelude to achieving genuine national integration, while, in fact, no military reorganization would be feasible without first changing the political context. Even during the Peiyang period (1911–28), numerous schemes and actual negotiations on troop disbandment were attempted, but all ended in failure. The crux of the problem was that, inasmuch as military power was the only effective way to insure a leader's right of continued participation in the political process, it would be extremely irrational for him to negotiate away his military power. As long as political power was predicated on military power, the stronger party could not realistically expect to gain anything from the negotiation table that he was not capable of winning on the battlefield, and the weaker side could not be expected to voluntarily surrender anything at the negotiation table that his army could successfully defend on the battlefield. This logic produced numerous civil wars during the Peiyang period.

Thus, only two situations could be conducive to disbandment. One was the existence of predominance by the advocate of disarmament over his opponents, and the other was an alteration in the terms of the political game, making military power either ineffective or irrelevant to the political process.

A quick look at the growth of Chiang Kai-shek's army shows that although his First Army was one of the better equipped of the eight National Revolutionary Armies (NRA), it did not grow very fast during the Northern Expedition. At the time of the disbandment conference, Chiang personally controlled only three armies, or about 5 to 10 percent of the nation's total force.[8] In contrast, some other NRA units took full advantage of the fighting and expanded their forces to impressive size.[9] Therefore, by 1929, the Nanking government was obviously too weak to force a decision upon the large number of provincial units from south and north China.

The second alternative would lead the KMT to mount an ideological and organizational challenge to the militarists. The *Outline of National Reconstruction* itself had made clear (art. 6) that even during the stage of military dictatorship the task of national integration could not be achieved solely by the application of military force against the obstacles of the revolution, but must be accompanied by extensive political work. Presumably the party could employ propaganda to agitate the people, offer concrete programs to improve their livelihood, and send cadres to organize among the masses so that the traditional power base of the militarists would be endangered from below. Furthermore, according to Sun's theory of revolution, the implementation of political tutelage need not wait for military pacification and integration of the whole country. The *Outline of National Reconstruction* specifically stated that political tutelage programs should be put into effect in a province as soon as that province had been pacified. This means that in 1928–29 and thereafter, the KMT could have concentrated on the sociopolitical and economic reconstruction of the provinces under its control (Kiangsu and Chekiang, in particular) and competed with the militarists by "out-governing" them. The combination of these "revolutionary" methods might have created such a groundswell of popular support that the militarists' armies would not insure their political survival. When the gun was no longer the final arbiter in politics, the central versus regional problem would have been resolved.

The lesson of the disbandment failure is that the causes of China's disintegration were complex, but they were generally reflective of the underlying socioeconomic realities of the country. Therefore, an enduring solution must deal with these realities. Chiang seemed to believe that simple administrative exercises could solve the problem and reintegrate the country by fiat. Even Chiang's failure in this area could not sway him to abandon his formalistic approach toward politics. Instead, he and his associates drew an entirely opposite conclusion from the experience. The failure of the conference only stiffened their belief that they needed greater military strength to overpower the militarists.

This view was authoritatively set forth by Chiang in his address to the opening session of the Kuomintang's Third National Congress on March 15, 1929.

> If our party wishes to employ politics to improve the people's well-being, we must first of all put a thoroughly unified China under the control of the national government. All regions must obey the orders of the central government.... As long as the reality of feudalistic division of the country persists under the nominal unity of the national government, none of the central government's reconstruction programs could ever be implemented. [Author's translation][10]

Views like this veered the KMT leadership progressively away from the commitment to the sociopolitical programs toward a fascination with the utility of military might. The KMT leadership obviously concluded that only when it commanded an overwhelmingly superior force could it sustain its authority over China, and that only after the military problems had been fully resolved could it embark on the tasks of political tutelage. It is this quest for military predominance that would consume the Nanking government's energy for the next decade.

KMT Military Politics, 1929–36

Two issues dominated the Nanking government's military politics during these years. One was the attempt to create a modern fighting instrument and an elaborate support system in industry, commerce, and civil administration. The other was the evolution of a complex set of tactics for dealing with domestic military rivals, including the Communists. The interplay of these two issues not only dominated military politics of the Nanking era, but also shaped the KMT response toward the Japanese aggression.

The Effort to Build a Modern Army—The German Influence

The German influence began in 1928 when the German officer, Max Bauer, was invited by Chiang to organize a group of advisors to help modernize the Chinese army.[11] The general thrust of Bauer's approach was to emphasize the economic aspects of national defense as heavily as the strictly military aspects. Bauer believed that the existence of a sound industrial base was essential for building and maintaining a modern army.

With respect to the military itself, Bauer held the view that the process should begin with the creation of a modern air force and the drastic reduction of superfluous troops throughout the country in order to make way for the training of a small elite corps. This model could then be extended to other armies as they were reorganized. But, during these initial years, the multitude of functions imposed on a small number of advisors tended to overtax their ability and reduce their efficiency in advising on strictly military matters. Although they participated in military instructional programs, the overall impact was less than satisfactory.[12]

It was not until General von Seeckt and General von Falkenhausen joined the German mission in 1933–34 that its operation was infused with a body of coherent and comprehensive strategic principles. Von Seeckt had been commander in chief of the German Reichswehr from 1919 to 1926 and a renowned military theorist whose published works were widely read.[13] Von Seeckt once expressed the view that the war of the future would be predicated on the existence of a small, well-trained, highly mobile force supported by air power.[14] Such a force should be small because the rapid progress in armaments would make it prohibitive to attempt to arm a large force; the smaller the force, the easier to modernize.[15] Von Seeckt also suggested that a period of peace must be insured before meaningful training programs could be mounted, and that munitions industries must be developed.[16] Although von Seeckt was replaced by von Falkenhausen in March, 1935, his views on reforming the Chinese army were inherited by his successor.

In addition to continuing involvement in the training of cadets in national military schools and some participation in the training of a few elite units, the German advisors paid serious attention to improving China's capability in munitions manufacture, logistics, transportation, civil air defense, mechanization, etc.[17] In fact, the Germans seemed to place more emphasis on laying the foundation for the infrastructure to support a modern army than on training and equipping that army itself, which they viewed as primarily the responsibility of the Chinese government.[18] Von Falkenhausen remained head of the German mission until he was recalled by the Nazi government in May, 1938, by which time there was a total of forty German advisors serving under him.[19]

Although the Germans did not play a pivotal role in the central government's economic policy, their recommendations to increase China's industrial capacity during these critical prewar years coincided with the government's desire to build a territorial base in the lower Yangtze area. Systematic surveys of natural resources were conducted, plans to build up heavy industries were drafted, impressive improvements were made in communications and transportation,[20] and German arms became standard issue for Chiang's crack units.[21] By 1937, China had established specialty schools to cover almost every aspect of modern warfare, many of which either were staffed with German instructors or used German teaching materials.[22] Finally, the Chinese government revived the practice of sending military students to study in foreign academies under government stipends, Germany being the most popular country for these students.[23]

Beyond these obvious facts, however, the KMT's experiment with the Germans also provides us with some insight into certain aspects of China's military politics.

First, from the Nanking government's point of view, the Germans conducted themselves exemplarily. Unlike the Soviet advisors of the Canton days, most German advisors had little ambition beyond performing personal service in China. In the beginning, German advisors were all attached to Chiang's personal staff and had little chance to develop independent contact with other Chinese either in the army or in the government. Even though their responsibilities expanded after 1931 and particularly after 1933 when highly prestigious generals like von Seeckt and von Falkenhausen served as chief advisors, they were still treated as guests, and never given operational control. Even in terms of armaments, while German military hardware was extensively used, Chiang retained American and Italian aviation specialists to help build the infant Chinese air force.[24]

Second, the impact of German advisors on specific operational matters was quite substantial. Nanking's disbandment proposals of 1928–29 were literally carbon copies of those made by the German advisors. Starting in 1929, Nanking also relied extensively on the German advisors in conducting civil wars against domestic challengers. In particular, the Germans made a great tactical contribution in the fourth and fifth anti-CCP campaigns of 1933–34.[25]

Even in operational matters, however, the German advisors did not always agree with their Chinese hosts. German advisors in general wanted to employ the few well-trained units to serve as models for training other units yet to be reorganized, but Chiang was often tempted to employ them in civil wars during the 1930s, thus hindering the army-building effort. When civil war became unavoidable, the Germans advised hot pursuit to insure complete annihilation of enemy forces, but Chiang often chose to allow them to capitulate or escape and to patch up the feud. These differences indicated that while the Germans could afford to approach matters from a strictly military perspective, Chiang was subject to political pressures that sometimes defied military logic.[26]

Third, while the Germans' impact on China's army-building program was considerable, it should not be overestimated. They helped modernize the military organization, laid down the general principles, and established the priorities for creating an infrastructure to support a modernized army, but the Germans were not entirely immune to the frictions that usually develop between a host country and its foreign advisors. There was belief among some Chinese generals that the Germans' advice on many operational matters was impractical because they did not understand the psychology of Chinese soldiers, or the historical backgrounds of particular units, or the intricacy of power relations between the commanders. What appeared to be rational, scientific ways of handling things were often politically untenable in China. Therefore, not only did Wetzell finally give up his effort and resign, but even von Falkenhausen had his complaints.[27]

The German contribution was also significantly limited by the number of advisors, which peaked at around 100 in 1934[28] and was far from adequate to undertake a comprehensive program affecting hundreds of thousands of officers and men. Not only were the units directly trained by the Germans few in number, but the first large-scale manuever to test the combat effectiveness of the new force was not conducted until November, 1936, just eight months before the outbreak of war.[29]

In view of Chiang's strong personal interest in the German-supervised training program, why was he not more successful at creating a large modern army? There may be two explanations.

First, Chiang had great difficulty in establishing broad and sustained contacts with leading elements in Germany's army or defense-related industries. Even in the early 1930s, Sino-German relations continued to be handled through professional diplomats inherited from the Peiyang regime who had little aptitude for negotiating military and industrial matters.[30] Consequently, Chiang had to rely on private channels to identify and negotiate with Germans potentially interested in service in China. It was not until von Seeckt's second visit to China in 1934 that a large-scale army-building program began to assume a coherent, concrete operational form.[31] Only in 1936 was Chiang able to have his own confidant, Ch'eng T'ien-fang, appointed as China's ambassador to Germany and to place Sino-German discussions of military collaboration on a regular diplomatic basis.[32]

Second, the army-building program was an extremely sensitive issue in the volatile political environment of the 1930s. Not only was its implementation kept secret from the Japanese, but from other KMT leaders as well.[33] The need to maintain strict secrecy naturally placed considerable restrictions on the pace and scope of the program. Chiang could not fail to realize that if he pushed the process of building his personal military machine too openly and too aggressively, he might provoke a grand alliance of all of his rivals against him. In order to win the collaboration of the militarists and other KMT politicians, the posts of the chairman of the Executive Yüan and/or the minister of finance were usually conceded to his rivals. Even such concession could not mollify some domestic rivals, and the training program was interrupted repeatedly by challenges from Chiang's rivals.

After his resignation as chairman of the national government in December, 1931, Chiang only retained his role as head of the military and no longer exercised complete control over the bureaucracy of the Nanking government. Thus he had to finance the army program through covert, nonbudgetary means, which inevitably hampered the program's progress. These obstacles were appreciably reduced only toward the very end of 1935 when Chiang again became chairman of the Executive Yüan and succeeded in appointing his loyal supporters to serve as ministers of foreign affairs, military affairs, and financial affairs, respectively. For the first time since December, 1931, Chiang's control over the government was finally strong enough to put his military program on a routinized administrative footing. By then however, the outbreak of the Sino-Japanese War was less than eighteen months away.

Pattern of Civil Wars among Domestic Rivals

The great emphasis placed by the Nanking government on the army training program produced two different effects on China's military politics. On the one hand, it inevitably alarmed the regionalists and provoked them to respond by conspiring against the Nanking government. On the other hand, the Nanking government was anxious to avoid antagonistic relations with the regionalists both militarily and politically in order to buy more time to complete its army-building program. Over time, a peculiar pattern of interaction between the Nanking government and the regionalists became discernible.

For analytical purpose, the Nanking government's domestic rivals can be divided into four groups and their relations with Nanking will be briefly sketched.

The Kwangtung-Kwangsi Group

The first group included the military leaders from Kwangtung and Kwangsi who were originally Chiang's allies in the Northern Expedition. But by 1927, serious schisms had developed between them. In early 1929, a dispute between Kwangsi and Hunan and Hupei over taxes finally triggered a war in which Chiang took the side of Hunan and Hupei.[34] The Kwangsi cause was lost when the defection of some of its generals forced Li Tsung-jen, Pai Ch'ung-hsi, and Huang Shao-hung to flee from the province.[35]

In 1929, Li, Pai, and Huang again succeeded in seizing control over Kwangsi. Then, in 1931, the feud between Chiang and Hu Han-min led to the latter's house arrest in Nanking. This infuriated Kwangtung leaders and produced another coalition between Kwangtung and Kwangsi. Together they established the "southwestern government," which remained the virtual government for the region until shortly before the outbreak of the Sino-Japanese War.[36]

In 1936, relations between the central government and Kwangtung-Kwangsi deteriorated sharply after Hu Han-min's death, and Ch'en Chi-t'ang of Kwangtung began to plan military action against Nanking. Bound by their mutual defense pact, Kwangsi also declared its support for Kwangtung. In mid-July, however, Ch'en Chi-t'ang's camp was rocked by the defection of its entire air force and several leading generals to the government's side. Ch'en hastily fled and the rebellion ended.[37] Two months later, Kwangsi also put an end to its rebellion by accepting the nominal authority of the central government, although it in fact retained its autonomous status.[38]

The Northern Provinces

The second group of militarists, Feng Yü-hsiang, Yen Hsi-shan, and Chang Hsüeh-liang, were all survivors of the Peiyang warlord era. Of these three, Feng was the first to break with Chiang over the disbandment issue.[39] In April, 1929, Feng organized his forces for a showdown with Chiang;[40] however, Feng's plan was upset by the defection of Han Fu-ch'ü and Shih Yu-san to the government's side. Although Han was immediately rewarded with the governorship of Honan,[41] the feud was hardly over, for in October many of Feng's generals issued a joint denunciation of Chiang and requested Feng and Yen to lead a punitive campaign against the central government. In April, 1930, Feng and Yen formally organized another anti-Chiang coalition that now included the Reorganization faction and the Western Hill faction as well. Together they prepared vigorously for the convocation of a so-called enlarged congress of the KMT.

But when Chang Hsüeh-liang threw his support behind Chiang, the rebels' cause was doomed. By October, the Central Plains War was over and both sides suffered heavy casualties.[42]

The 1930 war broke up the Kuominchün of Feng Yü-hsiang, greatly weakened Yen Hsi-shan's force, and left the Manchurian Army as the only respectable military power in northern China.

Insofar as Feng was concerned, his days as an active powerful military figure were over, but his subordinates continued to rule over north China and continued to rebel against the central government or fight with other regional forces from time to time.[43] In either case, the most Chiang could do was to contain the crisis or to pacify the offender. The central government's tolerant attitude was of course greatly influenced by the Japanese occupation of Manchuria and her blatant efforts to attract regional armies into the ranks of the puppet army. Chiang was fearful of moving against unruly regional forces lest they defect to the Japanese side.

After the Japanese attack against Jehol and the Great Wall in 1933, Chiang was forced to accept the so-called T'angku Agreement (May, 1933) which required central government forces to withdraw from north China and effectively reduced the capability of the central government to intervene in north China politics. Instead, an ad hoc committee composed of regional political and military figures became the de facto government of this vast area. Politically, militarily, and economically, north China became quite independent of the central government.[44] Then, in June, 1935, even Nationalist party activities were banned in Hopei under Japanese pressure.[45]

By virtue of these developments, the regional army units in north China were freed from any interference from Chiang. After 1933, even efforts by Chiang to maintain political contacts with these units had frequently to assume nonpolitical disguises.[46] The Japanese scheme to endow north China with a special status was to eventually merge the provinces into another autonomous puppet region. At this time, many of the provincial leaders became the objects of Japanese overtures to win them over.[47] On the other hand, these leaders also adopted deliberately ambiguous responses to the Japanese, causing the Chinese general public great anxiety about their patriotism.

Nanking's relationship with the Manchurian forces took a radical turn when the latter were driven out of their home base in September, 1931. Between 1931 and 1937, these units were scattered around north China, and since the central government had no power to assign them territory in north China, and they were not welcome by other established military leaders anywhere, their situation was unenviable. Their frustration with the lack of prospects of going home soon and their defeats by the Communists finally precipitated the Sian Incident in December, 1936.[48]

The Southwestern Provinces

The relationship between Nanking and the third group of militarists remained remote for some years, during which its army and government were simply incapable of reaching the southwestern provinces. Besides making an occasional symbolic gesture to assert the central government's jurisdiction over these provinces, Nanking primarily was satisfied to leave them alone to go about their affairs as their own rulers saw fit. Of the three, Yünnan was under the virtual dictatorship of Lung Yün and its relations with the central government were kept at a bare minimum. Kweichow remained aloof from the central government until 1934–35.

On the other hand, Szechwan presented a more complex picture. As all Szechwan generals had defected to the KMT by the end of 1926, they maintained the basic pattern of confrontation with each other that had existed since the Peiyang days.[49] In addition, they continued to have their own defense districts (*fang ch'ü*) within which they exercised exclusive control over the civil government, taxation, transportation, economy, and the opium trade. Between 1928 and 1934, civil wars broke out every single year among these militarists to readjust their power relationship.[50]

Nanking turned its attention to Szechwan only when it was freed from the Communist threat in the lower Yangtze Valley. In late 1934, the Communists broke out of the blockade and escaped toward Szechwan and Kweichow. Responding to Liu Hsiang's plea for help, Nanking dispatched the staff corps and organized two armies to pursue the retreating Communists.[51] This marked the first time that central KMT forces had set foot in Szechwan.

The central government made slow progress in extending its authority into the province through the reorganization of the Szechwan provincial government and the introduction of a more rational fiscal policy.[52] It was also in March, 1935, that Nanking was able for the first time to name its own appointee to the governorship of Kweichow, although the appointee, Wu Chung-hsin, was a civilian and on good terms with the Kwangsi leaders.[53] Beginning in the summer of 1935, the KMT established a central training program at Omei, established a branch school of the Central Army Officers' Academy, and drew up plans for the reduction of Szechwan troops.[54] Yet even in 1936, Szechwan had close to 300,000 regular troops and 600,000 militia, while the central government was represented by only one army and one division in the province. Under these circumstances, the most Nanking could do was to maneuver the Szechwan militarists against each other.[55] It was not until June, 1937, that Nanking and the Szechwan generals arrived at a preliminary agreement on the need to reorganize the provincial military. But before anything was accomplished, the Sino-Japanese War broke out, and the whole plan was shelved.[56]

The Communists

The last group of military forces to pose a threat to Nanking was the Communists. Since the origin and general strategy of the Communists' armed struggle against the KMT have been ably analyzed in a large number of works, our main interest here is to relate the Communist insurgency to Nanking's effort to bring about national unification.

The Communists stepped up their armed struggle in 1929–30 with the goal of seizing central China from which to extend the revolution to the rest of the country. When this policy of armed struggle collapsed, the Communists retreated to the border area between Hupei, Kiangsi, Anhwei, and Fukien. In December, 1930, Nanking, using only a small number of Hunan forces, finally launched its first campaign of annihilation against the Communists. Operating in the typical relaxed manner of regional armies, and totally unfamiliar with the tactics of the Red Army, the Hunanese forces suffered serious defeat and the campaign ended in total failure in January, 1931.[57]

Concluding that the cause of the failure of the first campaign was insufficient strength compounded by poor coordination, lax discipline, and lack of caution, Chiang assembled a larger force for the second campaign in April, 1931. Some northern troops were brought in for reinforcements, and the government forces were instructed to proceed with caution, emphasizing the need to lay an economic blockade. Yet even though the government had a two-to-one advantage over the Red Army and was equipped with far superior arms, it still lacked the will to seek victory. The instinct for self-preservation led to the breakdown of coordination among friendly units, thus allowing the Red Army to attack them one by one. In May, 1931, the campaign again ended in defeat.[58]

In June, 1931, Chiang personally went to Nanchang to supervise the third anti-CCP campaign. For the first time, crack units under Chiang were thrown into the battlefield, and the government was tightening the noose around the Communists' base area when Kwangtung rebelled and moved its troops against southern Hunan and Kiangsi. This was followed by the Manchurian Incident of September, 1931. Faced with the pressures of internal rebellion and external aggression, Chiang decided to call off the campaign.[59]

In the next year and a half, the CCP took advantage of the mounting Japanese pressure, which diverted Nationalist troops to northern defense posts, to expand their own bases in Kiangsi and Hunan, and threatened to link up with Hupei, Honan, and Anhwei in one continuous zone of operation. Meanwhile, Chiang began to organize yet another anti-CCP campaign and in June, 1932, officially committed himself to the policy of achieving internal pacification before resisting external aggression.[60] In January, 1933, the fourth campaign began. Again, loyal central government units were assigned the crucial role; again, the Japanese operations against Jehol in April and the battles of the Great Wall forced Nanking to divert its attention to the northern front and call off the campaign.[61]

After accommodations had been reached with the Japanese in north China, Chiang returned to the Communist problem and began the fifth and final campaign in October, 1933. By this time, an entirely new set of strategies had been developed. Under the general guideline of conducting the struggle through 30 percent military effort and 70 percent political work, Chiang initiated such programs as census control, *pao-chia,* a militia system, the New Life Movement, improvement of rural life, and the institution of a strict blockade system whereby all essential commodities were forbidden near the rebel zones. Instead of the old methods of penetrating deep into enemy territory, Chiang now called for the establishment of pillboxes, the linking up of major arteries of communications to put pressure on the Communists from all sides and to tighten the ring of encirclement and eventually to suffocate the enemy. Major organizational reforms were implemented, and training on the basic level was strengthened. But most important of all, not only was a huge force assembled, but the brunt of the attack was to be borne by Nanking's crack units.[62]

By October, 1934, the fifth campaign ended in a resounding success for Nanking when over 80 percent of the Red forces were killed, wounded, or captured. But Mao and Chu escaped with the remnants and embarked on their epic Long March that took them to Shensi province almost a year later.

Some General Characteristics of Nanking Politics

The preceding discussion of the Nanking government's army-building program and internal pacification campaigns allows us to make several general observations about its relationship with non-Communist regionalists that will prove relevant to our forthcoming analysis of the Nationalist regime in the war years. The implications of the anti-Communist campaigns will be discussed later in this chapter.

First, the events of the 1930s suggest that the Nanking government's strategy of reunification was to create a strong military force first and to use it to overcome its domestic rivals eventually. In order that the army-building program would proceed smoothly, Chiang insisted on tight control over the central government apparatus and assured territorial control over the lower Yangtze provinces, which he deemed absolutely essential to the infrastructure in support of his army.

But beyond the lower Yangtze area, Nanking's policy followed a flexible path. There was no clear timetable set for the completion of reunification. In comparison with its Peiyang predecessors, the Nanking government adopted a relatively mild attitude toward the provincial militarists. Confident that its army would be invincible once it was fully trained, Nanking was primarily interested in placating the militarists to gain the necessary time to accomplish its military programs.

For this reason, Nanking was content to live with the reality of regional semi-independence as long as it could maintain the fiction of being the national government. Even as opportunities arose for Nanking to extend its territorial control, it showed a preference to induce provincial militarists to accept its authority by administrative maneuvers or material rewards rather than outright military invasion.

The regional militarists recognized, however, that if Chiang were allowed the time to consolidate the central party and administrative apparatus and to proceed uninterrupted with his military buildup the day of reckoning would soon arrive. Therefore, they had to stop Chiang. This explains why most civil wars of the 1930s were triggered by a regional power declaring war against the Nanking government rather than vice versa.

Second, whenever serious disputes developed between Nanking and the provinces, the former was willing and anxious to employ intermediaries to patch up relations, or to seek mutual accommodations. Even when persuasion failed and force was resorted to, Nanking seldom pursued a policy of ultimatum or of total annihilation of its opponents. The reason behind this policy was Nanking's conviction that time was on its side. If Nanking treated its opponents mildly for the time being, its opponents would remain hopelessly divided; but if it should adopt a very harsh policy toward them, it might actually alarm them sufficiently into forming a united opposition. Therefore, Nanking's general purpose was to show its opponents the futility of challenging the government, and to accomplish this, Nanking seldom needed to employ its crack units (fig. 1).

Third, precisely because Nanking preferred to maintain a relationship of nonconfrontation with the regionalists, it would rather conclude every war by means other than military. Consequently, a complex of nonmilitary methods was employed to defuse tense situations.

Personal relationships were extensively exploited to influence political attitudes. Chiang himself not only personally entered into sworn brotherhoods, but used school connections, locality ties, friendship, or institutional ties as diplomatic instruments. In provinces where his power could

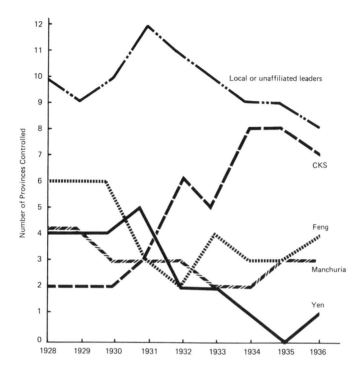

Fig. 1 Territorial control as measured by the factional background of provincial governors, 1928-36. In 1928 the CKS controlled 7 percent of the provinces and 25 percent of the provinces in 1936.

not reach, he also relied on secret agents to collect information and sow dissension.[63] Whatever money could buy in terms of support, Chiang would pay for it, often with handsome amounts. In the 1930 Central Plains War, Chiang's "silver bullets" diplomacy persuaded Marshal Chang Hsüeh-liang to throw his weight against Feng and Yen. Likewise, in the 1929 conflict against Kwangsi, huge sums were spent by Chiang to buy the defection of the troops of Li Tsung-jen and Pai Ch'ung-hsi.[64]

For those who were not content with money alone, arms, positions, and territories were offered. In almost every single case of challenge to Chiang, the corrosive effect of tricks on their own followers contributed more to the defeat of the rebel leaders than a crushing beating delivered by Chiang's army. Out of these maneuvers, Chiang gained the reputation of a consummate master of the game of "divide and rule," but these maneuvers also so seriously poisoned the interpersonal relationships between Chiang and some other military leaders as to preclude any possibility of entering into a genuine cooperative relationship based on mutual trust and respect later during the war years, even when national survival was at stake. Also we must realize that Chiang got no more than what he paid for in the Nanking decade. He did not obtain a fundamental solution to the problem of disintegration; he only bought temporary peace and a breathing spell in which his army could grow. The chemistry of regional sentiments and the logic of power politics was such that the weakened and divided opponents would soon regroup and mount another challenge, because the fundamental contradiction between centralism and regionalism had not been resolved once and for all.

On the other hand, throughout the prewar years, the regional leaders never succeeded in toppling Chiang from power, even though their collective strength was considerably greater than Chiang's. A curious pattern of confrontation recurred. In each case, a dissatisfied military leader would challenge Chiang single-handedly. Only when he was about to be defeated would other military leaders come to his rescue, producing a stalemate. The lack of an integrating ideology, the absence of a community of interests, poor organization, and mutual distrust all condemned the regional military leaders to repeated failures in challenging the central government.

Fourth, the corollary of Nanking's appeasement policy was that whoever left the Nanking government alone would be left alone in turn. There is no better proof of this point than the case of Szechwan. The utterly lawless conditions in the province and the feudal character of its leaders would make the province the most logical first target of the KMT's revolutionary attacks. Yet no serious attempt to touch Szechwan was made until Nanking began the pursuit of the retreating Communists in 1934–35. The same applied to Nanking's attitude toward Yünnan and Kweichow.

The Intellectual Genesis of Nanking's Militarization

There is no doubt that Chiang left a stronger imprint on the politics of the Nanking government than any other Kuomintang leader, yet to study Chiang's politics presents no easy matter. Ideally, we need to acquire a penetrating view into his psyche, for it is only reasonable to expect Chiang's political conduct to reflect his attitudes and personality. Unfortunately, while there are a large number of works on Chiang that are liberally sprinkled with clues and suggestions regarding his personality traits, there are few attempts to treat Chiang as the subject of a rigorous psychoanalysis.[65] Not surprisingly, Chiang, being a complex man, appeared to different observers in different and often contradictory light. Any attempt to psychoanalyze Chiang successfully will have to wait until we have freer access to the records of his private conversations, personal correspondence, and most important of all, his diaries.

For the time being, a more realistic way to assess Chiang's impact on Chinese politics is to trace his intellectual development, in order to identify the major beliefs and themes that guided his behavior. In this respect, we find that Chiang was exposed to heavily traditional intellectual stimuli during his formative years. Biographical sources on Chiang agree that his reading materials before the age of twenty were almost exclusively restricted to standard Chinese classics including *Tso-chuan, The Strategy* by Sun Tzu, and works by scholars of the Chou and Ch'in dynasties. Even in the 1910s and 1920s, the subjects of his self-study continued to show his preferences for such Chinese thinkers as Wang Yang-ming, Tseng Kuo-fan, and Hu Lin-i. These thinkers undoubtedly foreshadowed Chiang's lifelong espousal of traditional virtues such as the "four principles and eight virtues" (*ssu-wei pa-te*) and his moralizing tendencies reflected in his New Life Movement. There is little evidence to indicate that he ever had much familiarity with classical or contemporary political or social thoughts and institutions of the West.

In his early career, Chiang revealed himself to be a young man with an activist orientation. He was vehemently opposed to the Manchu regime because the latter was an alien race and brought humiliation to China in its dealings with the Western imperialists. In contrast to the intense pain he felt for China's disgrace, the youthful Chiang had little to say about the social evils of China and demonstrated little interest in broader ideological issues. Even in his association with Sun Yat-sen, Chiang was probably more inspired by Sun's daring revolutionary deeds than by the latter's ideological formulations. After he joined the revolutionary movement, most of Chiang's own revolutionary contributions were in terms of planning and executing sabotages and uprisings.[66] Consequently, in the few years that Chiang was constantly in Sun's company in the early 1920s, the latter relied on Chiang's counsel primarily on military matters.

There is another interesting contrast between Sun and Chiang. Both men had experienced several reverses in their revolutionary careers. Each time Sun was forced into retirement, he would devote himself to a searching investigation of the country's problems to refine his revolutionary programs. The intellectual productivity of Sun constituted a true mark of the man as a revolutionary idealist. In contrast, the years of Chiang's forced retirement in Shanghai were spent under very ambiguous circumstances, but definitely not in any way associated with revolutionary theorizing.

Outside of his classical training, Chiang's modern formal education was a narrowly focused professional military education acquired at the Paoting Military Academy and Japanese military schools. Chiang's only foreign contact was his years of study in Japan, and the features of Japanese politics and society that impressed him the most were loyalty, discipline, sacrifice, martial virtues (*bushido*), hierarchy, order, and the absolute authority of the emperor and his government over the subjects, all of which tended to reinforce his own neo-Confucian preconceptions about politics.

This portrait of Chiang's thinking can be corroborated by the tenor of his speeches and writings over the years. The earliest public writing attributed to Chiang can be found in the journal *Military Voice* (*Chün-sheng*). In the preface to the first issue in 1912, Chiang accented two themes that would reflect his political views for many years to come. First, Chiang advocated the Bismarkian policy of blood and iron as a guiding principle for the salvation of China. Second, he asserted that the overthrow of the Manchu would solve the "internal" problem and that henceforth China's revolutionary efforts should be directed toward solving the "external" problem of foreign imperialism in a predominantly military way.[67]

Other articles contributed by Chiang to the same journal articulated his preferences for benevolent dictatorship, national unity through political centralization and military solution, the predominance of nationalism over democracy, and political revolution over social revolution.[68]

A perusal of Chiang's writings and pronouncements of the 1920s reveals that his views changed very little. Between 1924 and 1928 when Chiang maneuvered to become Sun's successor, he continued to build his credentials on the one subject he was most equipped to handle—military affairs, especially the management of the Whampoa Military Academy.[69] There is no evidence that Chiang developed any astute insight into Sun's political theories, nor is there any sign that Chiang had impressed Sun enough to be designated as the latter's heir apparent.

What then constituted Chiang's conception of revolution? Reviewing China's history at the end of 1928, Chiang said that China's revolution had two enemies—feudalism as represented by domestic warlords, and foreign imperialism. However, Chiang regarded the completion of the Northern

Expedition as having ended the preparatory stage with the downfall of warlords. Hence the "true revolution" for the future was to be the overthrow of imperialism and the unequal treaties—this was to be the *only* revolution.[70]

Chiang was equally explicit on how this highest revolutionary objective was to be achieved. He said in 1928,

> If we wish to abolish the unequal treaties now, we must unify our ideology, solidify our will, prevent the armies from fighting civil wars, and forbid civilian groups and social classes from struggling against each other. All people must strive to realize the Three People's Principles and to abolish the unequal treaties. Worker strikes, student strikes, and public demonstrations without government permission must not be allowed to take place.[71]

The overthrow of foreign imperialism was such a paramount revolutionary objective that everything else had to be subordinate to it. Above all, Chiang wanted to create an obedient and disciplined citizenry who respected the prevailing social order and devoted themselves wholeheartedly to production. Since popular expression of protest for political or economic causes would disrupt production and sharpen class antagonism, such protest would be suppressed in the interest of anti-imperialist revolution.[72] In this sense, the defense of the domestic status quo had become the prerequisite for realizing the KMT's revolutionary mission.

Furthermore, since the fight against foreign imperialism was to be a test of military strength, it followed for Chiang that only a militaristic approach could save China.

> Whether in China or in foreign countries, whether in the past or at the present, whenever one wishes to organize a healthy and complete state and society, the only way to do it is through the militarization of the whole nation. . . . Therefore, the only way for us to achieve national salvation and reconstruction in the future has to be the militarization of all social groups and the organization and training of the entire population of our country.[73]

This view was strengthened after the Japanese invasion of Manchuria in September, 1931, which not only presented Nanking with a grave international crisis, but which might have presaged more imperialistic intrusion into China in the years to come. Addressing a national conference on internal politics, Chiang insisted that the most crucial method to save the country at this critical juncture was to militarize domestic politics and to manage all domestic political programs by military command.[74]

What was the role of the people in this revolutionary process? While acknowledging the government's obligation to take care of the needs of the people, Chiang made clear that this was not so much the ultimate end of the revolution as it was a means to a higher end—the abolition of foreign domination over China. Consequently, the increase of production and the economic well-being of the people were treated as functional requisites for creating a strong national army capable of challenging foreign armies. These requisites had to be achieved in an orderly and disciplined manner and were not to be allowed to interfere with the higher goal of nationalistic revolution.

Such views inevitably led Chiang to favor an authoritarian conception of the state. He maintained that officials had to learn about their localities thoroughly so that they could "scientifically control and manage" local population as a commander could his soldiers.[75] In this political universe, the people's role was to respond unquestioningly to the dictates of the state, rather than to initiate political demands upon the state.

Speaking in 1934 about the ways to revitalize and reconstruct China, Chiang argued that the foundation of local government had to be laid in three kinds of work—education, economy, and defense. Chiang made clear, however, that defense was to be achieved through the promotion of obedience and discipline by the people, education through the promotion of the traditional virtues of propriety, righteousness, integrity, and honor (*li, i, lien, ch'ih*), and economy through the promotion of a life-style of "uniformity, cleanliness, simplicity, and frugality."[76] Chiang identified these three kinds of work as constituting the ingredients of the vitality of a modern state, of which the ultimate goal was to transform citizens into functional components of the state to guarantee revolutionary success. This transformation could only be realized, Chiang elaborated, by instituting a wholesale militaristic education (*chün-kuo-min chiao-yü*)—the inculcation of the Bismarkian spirit of blood and iron combined with traditional Chinese martial virtues (*wu te*) and martial techniques (*wu i*).[77]

Despite his rhetoric about the importance of popular support, Chiang demonstrated little sensitivity to the people's real needs. For example, he was fond of admonishing local officials to "treat the people as if they were three-year-old children."[78] Basically, Chiang held the view that government officials should adopt a paternalistic attitude toward the people, and that their obligation toward the people should be prompted by their own moral standards. In the interest of preserving the status quo, the government was to do its best to improve the well-being of the people, and the people were to passively obey the government. The notions of constitutional democracy, political rights, redistributive justice, or social reform were almost never addressed by Chiang in the Nanking period. Chiang had its vision fixed on the creation of a modern state predicated upon a rigid and stable social structure, a disciplined and trained citizenry, and a thriving productive process under a unified central government. Once such a state was built, China would be able to wage an effective nationalistic revolution against her foreign humiliators.

The Implications of Nanking's Politics

Once we understand Chiang's views of the meaning, goals, and process of revolution it should become easier to appreciate the implications of many of Nanking's political actions in the 1930s. As many of Nanking's specific policies have been ably analyzed by scholars like Ch'ien Tuan-sheng, Tien Hung-mao, Lloyd Eastman, and Arthur Young, there is no need for this work to review them in detail. Instead, we will attempt to highlight Nanking's policies to illustrate the main thesis presented in this chapter. Several points deserve our special attention.

First, the most impressive accomplishments of the KMT government during the Nanking decade were made in the superstructure of the state. Numerous local currencies floated by warlords in the lower Yangtze were removed from the market, and currency was standardized within the areas controlled by the government. The national tax structure was rationalized and some central control was reestablished over taxes like customs, salt, and so on. The banking system was modernized as central-government-owned banks were promoted to a dominant position over private banks. The government drew up plans for industrialization and established control over certain defense-related industries. Telephone and telegraph services were extended to most major urban centers, and more mileage of highways were built in the 1930s than during any previous decade. Order was restored to rail traffic, which had been heavily damaged by warlords.[79] All these activities reflected Nanking's determination to accord the highest priority to the tasks of economic reconstruction that would have an immediate impact on improving China's military, strategic, and administrative capabilities.

In contrast, Nanking's achievements in the socioeconomic realm were far more modest or nonexistent. In structural terms Chiang's government never developed into an effective instrument to implement socioeconomic reforms. Yet Chiang saw the issue from a different perspective. In 1930–32, Chiang repeatedly complained that domestic political programs were going nowhere after the Northern Expedition because there was a lack of military discipline. His solution? Politics must be managed in accordance with the same principles as in the army.[80] Thus even as Chiang stressed the pivotal role of *hsien,* or county, politics in the 1930s, he was primarily concerned with increasing the efficiency of the *hsien* government as an instrument for extending centralized control to the local level, and not with using it as a catalyst of local socioeconomic rejuvenation or political democracy.[81]

A ray of hope was provided by the so-called model *hsien* or experimental *hsien* program. In the 1930s, less than a dozen *hsien,* including Tsou-p'ing and Ho-ts'e in Shantung, Lan-hsi in Chekiang, and Wu-hsi, K'un-shan, and Chiang-ning in Kiangsu, were designated as the sites to promote a new kind of politics—local self-government. Among these, the Chiang-ning experiment was the most important because it was established by Governor Ku Chu-t'ung of Kiangsu in 1932. Not only was General Ku a close associate of Chiang, but Chiang-ning was only a short distance from Nanking. By 1935, the Chiang-ning program was placed under the direct supervision of the KMT headquarters. The cadres for Chiang-ning were initially drawn from the best the KMT had to offer, the graduates from its political academy. Subsequently, a training center was set up to train party workers, *hsien* functionaries, and *pao-chia* chiefs to promote the new politics. Programmatically, the local self-government was supposed to achieve these goals: (1) government—simplify and streamline the bureaucracy, promote public health, rationalize the tax system, unify the *hsien* accounting system, train more teachers, and expand school enrollment; (2) economy—conduct land registration, promote irrigation, promote the cooperative movement, increase agricultural production, raise rural income, and stimulate general economic growth; (3) defense—upgrade the quality of police work, pacify the population, and protect the land.[82]

Between 1935 and 1937, Nanking and the provinces raced with each other to draft new regulations on local self-government, the number of which eventually exceeded 900.[83] But this flurry of paperwork only provided one more illustration of Nanking's knack of confusing abstract language with reality. Just as in so many other instances, the Nanking leaders preferred to deal with the issue with a sterile, formalistic, and bureaucratic approach by forming commissions, holding conferences, and producing high-sounding statements or rational-looking plans and regulations. But it was an act of self-delusion to expect these products of bureaucratic formalism and detachment to have any significant impact on the concrete problems of the people's livelihood. In the end, the experimental *hsien* movement never received the necessary support from the national government and simply withered. Even though Nanking had absolute control over Kiangsu, the Chiang-ning case was declared a failure by Ku's successor, Governor Ch'en Kuo-fu, and its experimental status revoked in 1936. By 1937, there was only one experimental *hsien* left. One extreme measure of the failure of the program was in cooperative work, which was supposed to have been the key to rural revitalization. By 1937, in the entire province of Kiangsu with its rural population living in over five million households, only 79,000 farmers had been enrolled into 1,870 rural cooperatives with total assets of a paltry $810,000 in Chinese currency.[84] As Ch'en Kuo-fu himself candidly acknowledged, whatever good was accomplished by the experiment in Kiangsu was too miniscule in scope, uneven, temporary, noninstitutionalized, and made no impact on local politics elsewhere during the Nanking era.[85]

That the experimental *hsien* program should come to such an unfortunate denouement should not surprise us, given our understanding of Chiang's views on politics and government. In a 1934 speech, Chiang told China's senior bureaucrats that the way to achieve political reform included centralization of administrative powers, adherence to the principles of scientific and rational management, and understanding the people's problems so that the bureaucrats could help them like parents help children.[86]

In 1936, Chiang instructed local officials that the methods for conducting politics were to be found in the ancient *Four Books* and *Five Classics*. He told these officials that they should study the works of Kuan-tzu, Shang Yang, Wang An-shih, Chang Chü-cheng, Hu Lin-i, Sun Yat-sen, and himself to acquire a sound grounding in politics.[87] Again, traditional Chinese Legalists and neo-Confucianist writings were praised for the political wisdom they imparted, but no single work of a contemporary or modern thinker of any political and philosophical persuasion was recommended except for Chiang's own works and those of Sun Yat-sen. That such an approach would result in an extremely rigid and parochial political perspective among the regime's officials was only to be expected.

Little wonder therefore that the record of socioeconomic policies of the Nanking era had extremely few concrete successes to show. The land tax rates and collection system were not revised to lessen the unequal economic burden placed on the poor. The organization of agricultural cooperatives received very spotty attention and failed to achieve its intended purpose of rejuvenating the rural economy. The rent reduction program was started in a few places but quickly suspended when confronted by loud protests by landlords. The problems of rural indebtedness, high tenancy rates, high interest rates, decline of rural handicraft industries, breakdown of irrigation networks, and banditry all remained unresolved. The public granary system was either nonfunctioning or poorly managed. Rural health service was extremely rare, illiteracy was widespread, and sharp class exploitation existed in many localities.[88]

Nor did the Nanking government have much success with the urban masses. The 1930s saw a continuation of the trend of diversification of China's urban life. New professional associations, occupational groups, students, industrial workers, and public utilities workers brought with them new problems and new perspectives into urban life. Their very existence required the government to expand its operations into the socioeconomic realm. They demanded more government responsiveness and new functions such as mediation of labor disputes, housing, medical care, transportation, education, and social welfare, none of which the Nanking government was in a position to provide.

As a revolutionary party, the KMT could have played a decisive role in restructuring the socioeconomic order in both the villages and the urban areas. It could have become more responsive to the new demands created by rapid social change or even become an active agent of social change, the agitator of a new political awakening, and the molder of a sense of participation and community.

But these functions were never undertaken by the Nanking government because they did not seem to be immediately related to their overriding goal of creating a modern state to combat foreign imperialism by military means. In fact, in both the rural and urban areas, the Nanking government was far more concerned about the preservation of law and order so that its militarization programs might proceed smoothly. This helps explain the unsympathetic attitudes of the Nanking government toward groups like students, union organizers, intellectuals, or educators who were at the forefront of social change. A key reason why these new political and social pressures did not threaten Nanking's viability was the military power the KMT controlled, which was overwhelming in proportion to the size of the territory and population of the lower Yangtze region.

Probably the best illustration of Nanking's preoccupation with military power and lack of interest in issues of broader social and ideological implications was its handling of the Communist threat. Here was a case in which the military power of an arch enemy was employed to promote a set of socioeconomic programs diametrically opposed to the values endearing to the Nanking leaders. Yet even in this case, we find Nanking initially had trouble grasping the implications of the challenge posed by the CCP's social revolution.

Even as late as 1928–29, when other Nationalist generals, including Li Tsung-jen, urged Chiang to eliminate the Communist "menace" in Kiangsi, Chiang replied that it was not necessary to fight the Communists because "they were only a bunch of native bandits who could not cause much trouble" and asked his generals why they were so paranoid about the Reds.[89] Chiang himself became interested in the extermination of the Communists only when the latter assumed the unmistakable form of a military challenge and when their growing power began to threaten the security of the lower Yangtze provinces. The impression one gets from observing Chiang's reaction to the Communist challenge is that his own bias rendered him incapable of appreciating the appeal of revolutionary ideology or programs other than in military terms. Thus, as long as the Communists were militarily weak, he had little respect for them. However, by late 1932, when the Communist movement had grown substantially, Chiang asserted that the secret of the CCP's success was because it had borrowed the Soviet model of "militarizing its land, grain, and cultural programs."[90]

In subsequent years, even though the anti-Communist campaigns had provoked the KMT into introducing some of the most audacious and innovative policies it ever attempted, the KMT seemed to treat the CCP revolution primarily as a challenge to Nanking's military and administrative effectiveness rather than its revolutionary ideology and programs. Thus, instead of offering fundamental solutions to the problems of rural decay, class antagonism, and other causes of popular alienation, the KMT's countermeasures were mostly of an anti-insurgency nature aimed at bringing quick military victories, such as pillboxes, blockades, and the *pao-chia* system.

Even when some of these countermeasures gave the appearance of being radical solutions, they in fact were not so. One case in point is the creation of the Special Administrative District (*hsing-cheng chuan-yüan kung-shu*), which was sometimes presented by the KMT as a great institutional weapon to combat communism. In fact, its main aim was to improve the efficiency of the local government to pacify the population, organize militia, protect local taxes, and support the army in its campaigns of encirclement and annihilation of the Communists.[91] As Ch'en Kuo-fu reported, Chiang himself claimed that "the concept of this institution was derived from military institution." The Special Administrative District commissioners were selected and appointed directly by the Bandit-Suppression Headquarters, primarily on their military qualifications in the hope that they would be able to set up a command system more effectively "with primary function in implementing the policy of cleaning the countryside (*ch'ing-hsiang*) and assisting the military suppression of Communist bandits." Thus, the commissioners were coordinators of the militia and other forces in the counties under their jurisdiction.[92] It was a bureaucratic answer to communism devoid of socioeconomic capabilities. Yet even this meager innovation was restricted only to areas immediately threatened by the Communists. In other provinces, this office was given sporadic attention.[93]

The same mentality was reflected in the much-publicized New Life Movement. Originally conceived by Chiang and his associates in February, 1934, it was intended to overcome public alienation from the government, to instill new values and new styles of life among the people, and to innoculate them against the "alien" and "subversive" elements embodied in the Communist social revolution. But from the inception of this movement, the government indicated that it wanted to achieve this goal by mechanical, bureaucratic control from above, rather than by encouraging individual initiative, voluntarism, and revolutionary change from below. The socioeconomic grievances of the people were hardly heeded. To the extent that it offered a vision of a new society, it was rigidly conventional, authoritarian, and sterile. Its ultimate goal of social transformation was the militarization of Chinese society marked by hierarchical social structure, uniformity, regularity, discipline, regimentation, hard work, obedience, but with no room left for democracy, social justice, and mass participation. In other words, it aimed at turning every citizen into a soldier, who would be ever ready to respond to bureaucratic dictates to perform specific functions required for the good of the collectivity.[94] Not surprisingly, the promoters of this movement offered military training and the inculcation of military attitudes as the key to social progress.[95]

The preceding discussion points out a striking parallel between the 1930s Nationalist modernization efforts and many modernizers of the late nineteenth century. Chiang's views echoed those of, for example, Yüan Shih-k'ai; the overriding concern for both men was to create a wealthy nation and a powerful army (*fu-kuo ch'iang-ping*). Despite its revolutionary rhetoric, the KMT under Chiang's leadership still clung to the very same assumption that a new army, modern arsenals, railways, telegraph lines, and airplanes were the only important ingredients of power. The etatist orientation and its militaristic manifestations inevitably produced casualties.

First, this policy produced a very unhealthy impact on the Nationalist party itself. It promoted complacency and accelerated the atrophy of the party. The party ceased to make serious efforts to penetrate the territories of the regional opponents to propagandize and organize the masses, to recruit party members, win over bureaucrats and soldiers, or incite discontent and unrest among the general populace against their oppressive rulers. Likewise, the KMT's basic-level cadres acquired the habit of doing party work only under the protection of the gun. In some cases, the KMT even insisted on obtaining a militarist's approval before setting up a party branch in the latter's territory. But in most cases, the party stayed well behind its own military shield.

Furthermore, the party was never accorded the dominant role promised in Sun's tutelage theory. In the 1930s, Chiang preferred to see the party as distinct and outside of the government, its role to educate the people and serve as an intermediary between the people and the government, but without any independent powers of its own.[96] Over time, the party simply lost its revolutionary appeal and political relevance for the majority of people in the outlaying provinces.

Second, it produced a top-heavy political structure in which leaders on the national level lost touch with the socioeconomic aspirations of the masses. Because Nanking in the 1930s enjoyed such an overwhelming command of military power in relation to the small territory it held, the masses in general remained silent and docile. This had the intoxicating effect of reinforcing the leaders' confidence in the correctness of their policies, policies that assumed that the masses could be kept in line by military discipline and that their needs could be met by bureaucratic pronouncements. As a result, the KMT denied itself ten precious years to search for effective ways to improve the livelihood of the masses.

Finally, the logic of Nanking's internal policy also ran into conflict with China's national security requirements. Nothing upset Nanking's strategy more than the Japanese invasion. Starting with the invasion of Manchuria in 1931, Japan's provocations escalated each year. But in 1932, Chiang enunciated the doctrine of "achieving internal pacification before resisting foreign aggression," and obstinately adhered to it for the next five years. Chiang's policy no doubt reflected the strong influence of the German advisors. Von Seeckt himself had told Chiang,

> The hypothesis of every reorganization of any army is, first of all, peace on the outer borders. That means several years of external peace and state of political stability. . . . Before these conditions are achieved, a successful military reorganization cannot be accomplished. Success cannot be attained while you are in a continued state of war.[97]

Thus, again, one can attribute the policy of nonresistance to the KMT's obsession with military power. As Nanking viewed it, since its conventional army was considerably inferior to the Japanese army, and since the regional armies were either unreliable or ineffective, there was no sense in fighting the Japanese. Chiang was determined to swallow the bitter humiliation of Japanese occupation to buy more time.

Unfortunately, this policy had at least three major flaws. First, the exclusive concern with conventional military power, strategies, and tactics unnecessarily excluded unconventional forces and guerrilla warfare from the range of possible Chinese responses. Second, the KMT completely misjudged the psychological interplays between Japan and China and believed that only appeasement could slow down Japanese advances. In fact, it is perfectly plausible that a more resolute Chinese reaction at an early stage might have deterred further Japanese aggression even though the Chinese needed to pay a high price for it. As it turned out, Nanking's appeasement only encouraged the Japanese to drop their restraints and escalate their demands against China. Third, in its rigid adherence to this policy, Nanking lost a golden opportunity to exploit mass nationalistic fervor to its own advantage. It could have greatly strengthened the moral foundation of the regime by acceding to the popular wish of resistance. It could even have put the regional militarists on the defensive by assuming the leadership in national resistance at an early stage. But the KMT chose the opposite course and provoked universal condemnation.

History shows that the policy of achieving internal pacification before resisting external aggression finally failed in 1937. The outbreak of the Sino-Japanese War in that year conclusively demonstrated that it had been an unrealistic policy all along. The KMT was nowhere near completing its internal military pacification at that point. And even after internal pacification had been achieved, how much longer would Nanking need to bring its own army to match the Japanese? The pace of Nanking's army-building program was repeatedly interrupted by civil wars that inflicted considerable casualties on its already trained units. It was, in fact, not until the spring of 1935 that it could contemplate a more comprehensive army reorganization program for the entire country. At this point, von Seeckt recommended that three hundred thousand men should be reorganized into crack divisions and the rest be disarmed and sent to man various construction projects.[98] Consequently, General Ch'en Ch'eng was put in charge of army reorganization by stages. The target was set to complete reorganization by the end of 1938.

Although the German advisors had originally set the target to create sixty modern divisions, by the eve of the war Chiang's total command of the army was only thirty-one divisions, of which my research reveals that no more than ten divisions could be considered elite units in the sense that they had been directly under German training for varying periods of time. The rest were mostly reorganized units of former regional armies (table 1). Even the best-trained units were equipped with light arms and lacked the ability to fight modern integrated warfare on a sustained basis as Chiang and his German advisors had wanted. Therefore, the logic of Nanking's policy would mean that China's military needed at least another decade before it could resist Japan in the conventional mode of warfare. The

TABLE 1
Distribution of Military Power, 1937

Background	Number of Divisions
Chiang's elite	10
Chiang's regular	21
Manchurian	18
Feng Yü-hsiang	12
Yen Hsi-shan	8
Kwangsi	6
Kwangtung	15
Hunan	12
Yünnan-Kweichow	9
Szechwan	27
Misc. northern provincial	30
Misc. southern provincial	8
Total	176

Source: Kuo-fang-pu, *Lu-chün ko pu-tui yüan-ko chi-yao* (Nanking, February, 1937).

Japanese military leaders were certainly in no mood to accommodate this timetable.

To sum up, the political-military strategy of the KMT in the first decade of its existence constituted a significant departure from the party's original revolutionary action program. Sun Yat-sen had emphasized political reconstruction over military conquest and instructed that political tutelage could start in a few pacified areas well before the whole country was pacified. The general thrust of this revolutionary plan would point to the possibility that the good performance of political tutelage registered in a few areas could considerably ease the task of military unification in other areas at a later stage. But Sun's successors gave clear preference to military might over political work and believed that political tutelage could be put off until military dictatorship had been firmly imposed over the entire country.

After abandoning the mass movements in 1927, the KMT became increasingly wedded to an etatist and bureaucratic orientation in coping with the problems of national reconstruction. It wanted, above all, to create the apparatus of a modern center, with a strong and efficient national bureaucracy, a professional army, and a modern infrastructure in finance, banking, taxation, communications, and so forth, in the urban areas. The passion of the KMT leaders was to achieve respectability and recognition as one of the modern nation-states in the world community.

As pointed out earlier in this chapter, Sun's action programs for national reconstruction gave top priority to the improvement of people's livelihood, followed by people's political rights, and national equality and independence in that order. But under the leadership of Chiang Kai-shek, the Nanking government went through a significant transformation. National independence defined exclusively in terms of the abrogation of unequal treaties now became the overriding revolutionary objective, while a heavy veil of silence and neglect was cast over the other two issues. The mass line approach was rejected, and the leaders were blind to the great potential of popular participation and social progress.[99]

The Nanking government severely narrowed its own options by showing a clear preference for militaristic solutions. In Chiang's perception of the modern state, citizens should be disciplined, responsible, know their assigned roles in society, uphold law and order, believe in the Three People's Principles, and guide their personal conduct by "military rules" and "traditional virtues."[100] Such a heavy dependence on military power to guarantee political control, the exaltation of martial virtues, the subordination of the political-economic-social management needs of the state to its military needs, and an authoritarian and hierarchial view toward the general population constituted the true marks of the KMT's militaristic system. Under this kind of system, the bureaucracy acquired a formalistic and arrogant style of work. Finally, the party was relegated to a subsidiary position in the Nanking bureaucracy and lost its revolutionary edge.

Clearly, by the end of the Nanking decade, the government had emerged with serious liabilities. Furthermore, these liabilities were all endogenous. Whether such a regime could have been viable under certain hypothetically ideal conditions is a moot point. But how a regime encumbered with these multiple endogenous liabilities coped with the new stresses of the Sino-Japanese War is the subject of the analysis in the following pages.

Chapter 2

Military Disasters, 1937–45

As the decade of the 1930s progressed, Japan's China policy evolved into a discernible pattern. Japan's primary strategic interests became increasingly tied to north China after the Manchurian Incident. After the establishment of Manchukuo, the Japanese Kwangtung Army overran Jehol in 1933, eastern Chahar in 1935, and annexed them into Manchukuo. The army also engineered secession-minded Mongol princes into establishing a regional government claiming sovereignty over Chahar, Suiyüan, and Ninghsia in 1936, and launched an incursion into Suiyüan in the same year. These moves signified Japan's intention to create a buffer zone between itself, Korea, and Manchukuo on the one hand, and the Soviet Union and central China on the other.

When the first shot of the war was fired at Lukouch'iao on July 7, 1937, north China had already been under the control of a semi-independent regime for over two years. At this time, Chiang promptly concluded that Japan was dissatisfied with the present arrangement and desired to place north China directly under Japanese control.[1] As a result, China was forced to react strongly.

Several pieces of evidence lead us to believe that Chiang had decided before July, 1937, not to allow the Japanese further dismemberment of north China. This evidence includes Chiang's prompt instructions to the commanders of the Twenty-ninth Army to retreat from Peking to Paoting and not to compromise with the Japanese field commanders, to insist to the Japanese that only central government approval could sanction any localized settlement, to dispatch four crack central divisions to north China, and to send a personal representative to Peking to firm up the local troops' determination to resist.[2] Ten days after the initial conflict, Chiang told a gathering of China's military, political, and intellectual leaders that

40

any more concessions to the Japanese would only lead to total surrender, and declared that China must be prepared to sacrifice and fight to the end unless Japan was willing to restore the status quo as of July 7, 1937.[3] With these words, the stage for a total war (*ch'üan-mien k'ang-chan*) was set.

It is not the purpose of this chapter to present a detailed chronological account of the war, but to select a few campaigns that represented the turning points in the war and subject them to a critical analysis. The Shanghai campaign of 1937, the winter offensive of 1939, and Operation Ichigō of 1944 will be the focus of this chapter. In between these campaigns, the Chinese army-building program and concurrent developments in international politics will also be discussed. The main objective of this chapter is to trace the evolution of strategic thinking on both sides, and to assess the military consequences the war imposed upon the Chinese army.

The Shanghai Campaign

The results of the Japanese attack in the north gave all indications in the early stage of the war of a speedy occupation of north China without serious resistance from regional troops. If this should happen, the Chinese leaders had to face the possibility that the Japanese might move down the Peking-Hankow or Peking-Pukow railway, cut China into two halves longitudinally, drive the main force west into the mountains, and finish off the troops stranded in the east.[4]

This early diagnosis of the Japanese war plan greatly influenced Nanking's decision to make a stand at Shanghai, since one obvious way to frustrate the Japanese design was to draw them away from the north, where the government forces were weak, and into the lower Yangtze where the government forces were well-entrenched.

On the eve of the Shanghai campaign, the Japanese strength there was quite modest;[5] in contrast, the best Chinese units were stationed along the Nanking-Shanghai railway. Consequently, the Japanese naval and diplomatic personnel in Shanghai chose to conduct themselves with considerable circumspection. On August 9, a Japanese officer, Lieutenant Oyama, was shot to death as he tried to intrude into the municipal airport; the Japanese consul general actually apologized. But the Chinese ignored Japan's conciliatory move and ordered their troops to pour into the demilitarized zones around Shanghai in violation of the 1932 agreement. As Western diplomats were making efforts to reach a local settlement of the

Oyama incident, they were rebuffed by the Chinese on August 12 when the mayor of Shanghai informed them that his authority to negotiate had been withdrawn by his government and given to the commanders of the Chinese army.[6] Thus despite Chinese official effort to depict the Japanese as the aggressor in this area, it was the Chinese who took swift, decisive, and well-coordinated action once hostilities started on August 13.[7] From the very start, the Chinese strategic directive called for the encirclement of the Japanese settlement and for the blockade of the coast against Japanese reinforcements, in order to "drive the Japs into the sea."[8]

Although the Chinese put relentless pressure on the Japanese, the Japanese gradually exhausted the Chinese offensive capabilities. By September 1, the town of Wusung fell into Japanese hands, thereby compelling the Chinese high command to direct its forces to switch to positional warfare and hold fast to their positions as long as possible.[9]

Both sides continued to pour more troops into the seesaw battle. By October, the Chinese had deployed about seventy-one divisions, five artillery regiments (nearly everything the Chinese had in artillery), and miscellaneous garrison units totalling half a million men, while the Japanese Shanghai Expeditionary Force under the command of General Matsui consisted of six divisions and five to six independent brigades, complete with air and naval support, totalling 200,000 men.[10]

On November 5, General Yanagawa's Nineteenth Corps of 30,000 men successfully landed at Chinshanwei about thirty miles south of Shanghai and immediately rendered the Chinese strategy entirely untenable. On November 9, the Chinese high command ordered its troops to retreat along the Nanking-Shanghai railway and to set up defenses around the capital. The Japanese air force destroyed most of the bridges in this canal-infested area and greatly impeded the speed of retreat. Under these conditions, the mechanized Japanese columns pressed on and turned the Chinese retreat into a slaughter.[11]

The Japanese assault on Nanking began on December 7, 1937. Under heavy artillery fire and tank assault, the Chinese defenders collapsed in five days. As the year 1937 closed, China had lost nearly all her important centers of culture, commerce, industry, and political power.

When we review the cost of the fighting, we should keep in mind that during the ninety-day defense of Shanghai, the heaviest fighting took place within the city and its suburbs where the Nationalist command deployed about 60 percent of its loyal forces, including practically all the elite units. The only cover these forces had were buildings that were grossly inadequate to protect them from enemy artillery fire or aerial bombardment. Because most of the central troops were assigned to the most crucial positions and because of their strict adherence to do-or-die tactics, their casualties were high throughout the campaign; some 300,000 men perished at Shanghai.[12]

Immediately afterwards, the defense of Nanking exacted higher tolls: 100,000 defenders were lost in four days.[13] In the north, more armies had suffered heavy casualties[14] and thus by the end of 1937, the Chinese side had lost a total of 370,000 to 450,000 men, or between one-third and one-half of her fighting strength.[15] In effect, the military machine that had taken the KMT a decade to build with German assistance was essentially destroyed, together with a number of regional forces that patriotically responded to the government's call to fight the Japanese.

An Evaluation of the Shanghai Campaign

The Shanghai campaign has since become a point of serious contention in the history of the war. While a few Western military analysts have maintained that the Shanghai campaign helped the war in the long run, most have regarded it as a disastrous event. Some also see the Shanghai campaign as a calculated scheme on Chiang's part to play with world opinion and to wait for foreign help to defeat the Japanese.[16]

Certainly, the attempt to arouse international sympathy was clearly conspicuous during the entire campaign. China's appeal to the League of Nations for justice, speeches by Madame Chiang and Hu Shih to the American public, and the dispatch of numerous emissaries to European capitals all gave the impression that China expected strong and swift foreign response. Yet it would be inaccurate to view every Chinese move as designed to achieve the single goal of foreign intervention. KMT leaders themselves should have been the first to realize that there was little historical precedent for foreign intervention. In the view of the KMT leaders, Japanese aggressive acts in China had been numerous since the founding of the Nationalist regime in 1928. Things took an ominous turn in 1931 when the Manchurian Incident occurred. When the Chinese government tried to mobilize world opinion as well as big power intervention by appealing to the League of Nations, the league was impotent to do anything beyond a censure, which promptly led to Japan's withdrawal from that world body. In 1932, a battle actually took place in Shanghai, raged for over a month, but again failed to produce foreign military intervention. Although the crisis was resolved by foreign mediation, it also gave the Chinese ample reason to question the reliability of the British or Americans as a countervailing force against the Japanese in China.

Furthermore, Chinese Nationalist leaders probably also gradually developed some awareness of the distinction between Japan's policy toward north and central China. While Japan's policy toward north China was governed by geopolitical concerns that could be best taken care of by military means, her policy toward central China was marked by a general willingness to accept the constraints of the framework of international treaties and concessions, to promote economic interests, and to rely on conciliatory legal maneuvers.[17] From the end of the 1932 Shanghai campaign until mid-1937, the Japanese never stopped creating armed conflicts in north China, which were supplemented by attempts to pry Chinese regional forces from the central government or to encourage the establishment of puppet regimes in various forms.

Although the KMT might have expected the Americans and British to intervene when Shanghai itself was the site of war, their intervention could be expected to take a diplomatic form only. But in north China, this did not occur. For once Japan's foreign policy in north China had been dictated by geopolitical considerations, foreign intervention would have had to take military form to be effective. Yet none of the big powers were in any mood in 1937 to challenge Japan on China's behalf.

In fact, Chiang's immediate assessment of the Lukouch'iao Incident as conveyed to the American ambassador was that the Japanese government "intended to use the Marco Polo Bridge Incident for the purpose of bringing about the complete separation of Hopei and Chahar provinces from the control of the Central government." Chiang expected that the Konoe cabinet would agree to a diplomatic settlement only if Nanking was prepared to recognize the Manchukuo and sign the Anti-Comintern Pact with Japan.[18] Chiang was willing to accept neither of these conditions.

If China had deliberately created a new front in Shanghai to provoke foreign intervention, she would have at best only obtained a local cease-fire in Shanghai, but what about the war in north China?

Therefore, the question really hinged on whether the government in 1937 was determined to offer just enough symbolic resistance to trigger foreign intervention or a resolute stand against Japanese aggression. The critics of the Shanghai campaign felt that the Nanking government was merely interested in symbolic resistance. Yet they failed to explain why China would risk all its military might in trade for a foreign intervention that almost certainly would produce a result no better than an antebellum status quo locally. Could China realistically expect the consequence of foreign military intervention to be the recovery of territories lost since the early 1930s? This question is unanswered by the exponents of the foreign intervention hypothesis. It appears that rational explanations will emerge only when we free ourselves from this single-factor analysis and begin to dissect the Nanking government's decision to take a stand in Shanghai from a political-military strategic perspective.

China's Strategic Options

If we view the foreign intervention motivation as relevant but not dominant, then we realize that the government had to face two really difficult choices: (1) Where it should make a stand against the Japanese and (2) What form the resistance should take. On both questions, the Chinese government seemed to have been influenced by several concerns.

First, the government had been under criticism for years for not resisting Japanese aggression, and by 1937, it suffered from a serious credibility gap. If it did not take a resolute stand at the very outset of war, but conserved its own forces and conceded the coastal areas to the Japanese,[19] it would immediately rekindle the suspicion that it was saving its own power for internal power struggles. Under such conditions, it would have great difficulty convincing other regional leaders to resist the Japanese. Given the long history of mutual hostility and distrust, the only way the government could win over the confidence of the regional forces and forge a united front would be to take a firm stand as soon as its forces were challenged by the enemy.[20]

Second, since the government's territorial control prior to the war had been in the coastal provinces of Kiangsu and Chekiang, the government had a paramount interest in preventing these provinces from falling into hostile hands. It could afford to lose any other province but these two, as its political and economic power were firmly planted there. By the same token, it was in these provinces that the government could most realistically prepare for a war. Since central troops were excluded from north China as well as the interior provinces in the west, it would have been infeasible for Nanking to plan major operations in unfamiliar terrain over whose governments it had little control, and the support of whose armies was by no means certain at this point.

In contrast, the central government had had nearly a decade to develop the coastal provinces and since the early 1930s had been preoccupied with the construction of fortifications there. By 1937, the Shanghai-Nanking-Hangchow triangle had become the best fortified area in all China.[21] This area also had the best support infrastructure in the civilian economy, in transportation, and in industrial capacity. These factors dictated that not only would the government choose the area for a showdown with the Japanese militarily, politically, and economically, but that in any case this area had to be defended to save the only economic resources in China to fight a long war. As it turned out, it was during the siege of Shanghai that the central government evacuated a number of factories that provided the backbone of wartime industries in the interior.

Third, since the early 1930s, the German advisors' primary strategic concern had been precisely in the lower Yangtze area. General von Falkenhausen was particularly interested in the area for its potential to engage the Japanese in full-scale battles.[22] If the Japanese invaders were allowed to move upstream along the Yangtze, they could cut the country latitudinally. North China would fall immediately and south China would not be able to stage meaningful resistance from its mountainous and industrially backward provinces.[23]

Fourth, Shanghai was also a favorable choice because a small number of Chinese had in 1932 fought the Japanese there to a standstill. At the outset of that conflict, the Japanese commander had confidently proclaimed that he would take the city in four hours. However, after repeated failures of Japanese offensives and four changes of commanders, the Chinese army held on for nearly forty days and forced the crisis to end in a mutual withdrawal of forces.[24] The 1932 campaign had been an exhilarating experience for the Chinese leaders. At the conclusion, General Chang Chih-chung was instructed to prepare a special report on the conduct of the war and the lessons to be drawn from it. The result was the secret report, *Experience and Lessons from the Wusung-Shanghai Anti-Japanese Campaign,* which made a comparison of the strengths and weaknesses of both sides. One important conclusion drawn was that city fighting was preferable to field operations because it would neutralize the Japanese superiority in firepower, mobility, and logistics,[25] a deduction which seemed to be borne out by the defeats of the crack Chinese divisions in the battles along the Great Wall in 1933-1935.

As the Japanese threat intensified in the following years, an opinion was gradually formed on how an anti-Japanese war needed to be fought. In 1934, addressing high-ranking military leaders in three crucial lectures entitled, "On resisting foreign aggression and revitalizing our Nation," Chiang argued that the basic strategy in the upcoming Sino-Japanese War would be to rely on regular troops to engage in active defense to frustrate Japanese attempts to seek quick victory, to bolster defense at every point, to defend fixed positions to the last man, to employ supplementary guerrilla warfare, and to organize the masses. Chiang pointed out that, given the Japanese superiority in air force and armored troops, any Chinese attempt to run away from a battle would turn into a suicide.[26] Chiang called the tactic of defending every post to the last man the "revolutionary tactic," and believed that it was the only way to exact a high price from the Japanese since China was in no position to plan an integrated national defense system.[27] It was also believed that although such a tactic would cause the Chinese to lose many initial battles, it would help them win in the end.

Although the eventual purpose of this strategy of attrition was to produce war-weariness within Japan or to invite foreign participation in the war, the strategists did not envision that one single battle would do it.[28] Instead, Chiang claimed that Japan would be forced to invade every one of China's eighteen provinces.[29] In this sense, the Shanghai campaign may be more accurately viewed as the first of a long attritional war rather than as a one-shot ploy to end the war immediately. In fact, in the two years prior to the war, the government had already been warned by its foreign advisors that it would be unrealistic to hope for foreign assistance early in the war. In August, 1935, General von Falkenhausen dismissed the Nine-Power Pact of the Washington Conference (February, 1922) as a scrap of paper and advised that China had to exert her utmost effort to defend herself before she could ever expect any form of foreign assistance.[30] In 1937, the highly respected Australian advisor, W. H. Donald, warned that China would do better avoiding war with Japan unless she had the determination to persevere for at least two years single-handedly, regardless of the course of international and domestic developments.[31] Such views from highly placed advisors should have disabused the government of any lingering illusion of using the Shanghai campaign to trigger foreign intervention.

Finally, the central government's decision to proceed with the Shanghai campaign must have been influenced by its long-term assessment of the military resources available to the two opposing sides. In July, 1937, Chinese intelligence indicated that Japan had an army of 500,000 men on active duty, and additional reserves of 2.4 million men, the world's third largest navy with over 1.2 million tons of displacement, and 3,000 aircraft.[32] In comparison, China's navy consisted of a dozen or so river patrol boats and no sea-worthy vessels and her air force had 100 planes. China's total military strength stood at 182 infantry divisions, nine cavalry divisions, forty-six independent brigades, twenty-eight artillery regiments with a paper strength of 2,000,000 men, but no trained reserves of any kind. In reality, barely half of these units could be used for front-line duties.[33] While some contemporary observers credited Nanking with a great degree of military control,[34] our discussion earlier revealed that it actually had firm control over no more than 100,000 elite troops and an additional 200,000 troops of mediocre combat capability. One must also realize that even at full strength, the Chinese infantry had about one-quarter of the firepower of its Japanese counterpart. Even more decisive, however, were the differences in armor, mobility, and logistic capability; while a Japanese division had twenty-four tanks, 266 trucks, and 555 horsedrawn vehicles, a Chinese division had none.[35] Unless everything went in China's favor, it was really doubtful as to what advantages the Chinese would gain by investing their limited military strength over time in a large theater.

Nanking's dilemma was not dissimilar to that of a gambler with little capital facing an adversary with a great deal. Basically, it had two strategies. It could follow a conservative strategy by betting in small amounts and hoping to accumulate a large number of modest wins to turn the strategic balance into its favor. Or it could follow a bold strategy by putting all its chips on what appeared to be its best hand. When translated into the realm of military reality, the implications of these two strategies were also very different. From the point of view of a game theorist, it would seem that on balance one would choose a bold strategy instead of a conservative one. The advantage of a conservative strategy is that it would delay enemy advances and buy the time necessary to create new forces or to enlist outside assistance. But if China had no strategic reserves to tap, if it would take years to train additional forces, and if no outside assistance were in sight, then the strategy had little appeal. On the other hand, a strategy of boldness would yield different results. If the enemy had not wished to enlarge the crisis, such a resolute posture might have brought a quick accommodation. If the enemy were determined to push for greater gains, such a posture would at least dampen its enthusiasm and still buy time so that valuable assets could be salvaged and evacuated to the interior to prepare for the inevitable protracted struggle.

Therefore from Nanking's perspective, while the strategy of evading an initial showdown in favor of mounting mobile warfare against the Japanese later on in the interior involved incalculable risks, the strategy of making an initial resolute stand had at least two apparent advantages. If the Japanese intentions in 1937 turned out to be as restrained as in 1932, China would have achieved a quick cease-fire and gained a few more years to build its army. If the Japanese had larger territorial ambitions, then China would have saved something to fight a long war with. This was of course a gamble of enormous stakes, yet the fault of the campaign was more on its execution than in its conceptualization. Had the government possessed more elite units to defend the southern coast against the landing of Japanese reinforcements, or if it had issued the order to evacuate several days earlier, it could have scored a significant political victory at acceptable military costs. But Chiang had always been convinced that many of his victories on the battlefield were owed to his perseverence and that "the ability to outlast the enemy in the last five minutes of a fight is the key to all success."[36] Unfortunately, in Shanghai, the temptation to hang on just a little longer in the hope of breaking the enemy's will finally turned a potential political gain into a complete military disaster.

The Defense of Wuhan

In the wake of the Shanghai defeat, it became amply clear that the Japanese would not only drive up the Yangtze River, but also resume the north China campaign which had been temporarily stalled. In late November, 1937, the Chinese central government made the decision to transfer its capital city from Nanking to Chungking, thus demonstrating its resolve to pursue a long war against Japan.

In January, 1938, the government asserted that China's political strategy during the past six months had paid off by denying the aggressor a quick victory, and that henceforth the Chinese would switch to a more mobile posture, seize the initiative whenever possible, and deny the Japanese access to Wuhan. It also acknowledged that the war had revealed serious shortcomings of the Chinese army, and therefore a period of intensive training and regroupment would be initiated.[37]

The Japanese, in the meantime, were not sitting idly by. In February, 1938, they mounted a new offensive against Hsüchow from Shantung along the Peking-Pukow railway as a prelude to attacking Wuhan. At this time, the Chinese army in the fifth war zone under the command of Li Tsung-jen totalled 200,000 soldiers. In March, the Japanese army mounted an attack against the town of T'aierhchuang to clear its path toward

Hsüchow. By the time the campaign concluded on April 8, the Japanese had suffered the most serious defeat since the creation of their modern army. In addition to heavy losses in equipment, 16,000 Japanese soldiers lay dead.[38] The Chinese casualties were also close to 15,000 soldiers.[39]

The T'aierhchuang victory was important not only because it was the first significant Chinese victory in the war, but also because it was brought about by a combined force of both central and regional backgrounds. Such a force clearly had its limitations; the diverse historical backgrounds of the units made it necessary to preserve their identities, which in turn hampered organizational unification. In some cases, the need to preserve the appearance of equality among regional leaders produced the phenomenon that a group army in fact had only a single division. Lack of sufficient equipment, absence of a sound logistic system, and low combat proficiency all created serious problems.[40] Consequently, when the Japanese retreated, the Chinese failed to engage in hot pursuit and lost the chance to wipe out the enemies entirely.[41] This allowed the Japanese a respite and the opportunity to remount their attack on Hsüchow a month later and seize it. With the fall of Hsüchow, the Japanese achieved the double purpose of linking up the Peking-Pukow railway for their own use, as well as cutting the Lunghai railway into two sections for the Chinese. They could now use Hsüchow to stage the next major offensive against Chengchow, further west on the Lunghai railway, and then turn south on the Peking-Hankow railway toward Wuhan. In early June, in desperation the Chinese broke the dikes of the Yellow River west of K'aifeng and flooded parts of Honan, Kiangsu, and Anhwei, which effectively delayed the Japanese advance for nearly six months.[42]

By every standard, Wuhan was an extremely important target in Japanese military planning. As a political center for central China, a control point for the traffic on the Yangtze River and the Hankow-Canton railways, and finally as China's only remaining industrial center, the fall of Wuhan would be no less a blow to Nationalist China than the fall of Shanghai. For these reasons, the Japanese organized vigorously for the Wuhan campaign and marshalled a huge force of 380,000 men under General Shunroku Hata.[43] The Chinese took the defense of Wuhan with equal seriousness. The basic force of 450,000 men in the ninth war zone under Ch'en Ch'eng was reinforced by another 340,000 men from the fifth war zone under Pai Ch'ung-hsi, making a grand total of 800,000 men—the largest concentration of Chinese combat troops since the Shanghai campaign.[44] To support such a huge force, the Chinese government mounted a campaign of logistic support, thanks largely to the good transportation system surrounding Wuhan,[45] never to be equalled in the following years of the war.

The Japanese army began its operation in early June, 1938, after having amassed several hundred pieces of heavy artillery, airplanes, a fleet of landing vessels, as well as cruisers and destroyers. Its plan was to seize a string of fortresses along the Yangtze banks leading toward Wuhan. But the Japanese move upstream was met not only by stiff resistance of the fortress defenders but also by harassment of Chinese troops operating in the hilly areas on both sides of the Yangtze River. Consequently, it was not until late September that the Japanese advance units entered Hupei province, after sustaining considerable casualties and equipment losses.[46]

Just as the Japanese were advancing toward Wuhan, they also made a surprise landing near Canton, overran the feeble regional forces, and marched literally unopposed into that city on October 21.[47] Since the fall of Shanghai, about 75 percent of China's import of urgently needed war supplies had entered through Canton and moved onward to the interior along the Canton-Hankow railway.[48] With the loss of Canton and the railway, the importance of Wuhan was diminished accordingly. Four days after the Kwangtung generals lost their capital, the government ordered the complete evacuation of Wuhan.

A New Japanese Strategy Emerged

As the Japanese saw it, the fall of Wuhan signaled the approach of the end of the military phase of the China Incident. Even the most radical among the officers of the China Expeditionary Army never seriously contemplated waging full-scale war in the interior of the country. During the first fifteen months of the war, the Japanese had repeatedly tried to escalate the war to bring the Chinese central government to the negotiation table, but to no avail. Once Japan had seized all the major military prizes and China continued to be obstinate, there was really little incentive for the Japanese to make any concessions. As far as the Japanese were concerned, the Chinese government could be allowed to rot in the mountainous and backward southwest forever.

On January 16, 1938, the Japanese announced that henceforth they would cease to accept the Chungking government as a party to any negotiated settlement of the China Incident. In the following months, the

Japanese stepped up their effort to promote various puppet figures in north and central China in the hope of creating a regime with some measure of respectability. In north China, the so-called Provisional Government of the Republic of China had already been in existence since December, 1937. On March 28, 1938, the Japanese installed a counterpart for central China, the so-called Restoration Government of the Republic of China at Nanking. The logical next step was to combine these two regional governments into one national government and to treat it as a partner to the Japanese design of a "New Order for Greater East Asia." At the time of the Wuhan campaign, the Japanese were already in regular contact with Wang Ching-wei to defect from Chungking. In late December, 1938, Wang finally broke with Chiang and found his way to Nanking.

From the Japanese perspective, Wang's defection was a clear sign that they could wind up their China involvement soon. Consequently, during much of 1939, the Japanese were preoccupied with negotiating with Wang to organize a central government in Nanking for the entire occupied area. Politically, the Japanese preferred to dismiss the Chungking regime as a local regime and to shift their sights toward the creation of the new order based on the close cooperation between Japan, Manchukuo, and China.[49] Militarily, their main objectives were to isolate and contain the Nationalists through continuous limited offensives in the hope that the latter would eventually collapse. The Japanese refrained from mounting massive attacks on the Nationalists because they judged such endeavors to be wasteful of their resources and not likely to achieve a decisive victory in the short run.[50]

Meanwhile, as the Japanese settled for the return of normalcy in occupied China, they found the time to be right to wipe out the many pockets of Chinese resistance they had by-passed in their earlier rush to seize the key military targets in north and central China. Therefore, in 1938, they exerted considerable effort to seize the few communications links in these areas and in general to drive remnant Nationalist forces from the lines of communications in the occupied areas. In lieu of ground assaults against interior positions, the Japanese initiated a massive air campaign against key population centers to demoralize the people and retard the process of reconstruction. By May, 1939, when the winter fog cleared up, Chungking itself became the prime target of systematic Japanese air bombardment. The Japanese air bombardment did not taper off until late 1941 when their aircraft were diverted to the Pacific theater.

China's Military Revitalization Programs

After the Shanghai campaign, China's continued effort in fighting the enemy was predicated on its ability to train a new force as quickly as possible. The miserable performance of many regional units and the nearly complete destruction of central government forces convinced the government that it needed a comprehensive plan for the rehabilitation and training of the Chinese armies. One immediate step was the introduction of a conscription system to put China's manpower supply on a regular basis.[51]

At the first Nan-yü military conference convened November 25–28, 1938, the first large-scale conference of the war, the government unveiled a comprehensive program for reorganizing and retraining the armies.[52] The basic plan called for the training of the nation's armies on a rotational basis to be completed in one year. One major purpose of the training was of course the upgrading of the soldiers' combat skills, but equally important was the retooling of the generals.[53] The machinery of military administration was revamped[54] and the command structure was simplified with the reorganization of ten war zones. Within each war zone, Chinese troops were organized into group armies (*chi-t'uan-chün*), armies (*chün*), divisions, and regiments.

Efforts were made to modernize the logistics system. From the outset of the war until the end of 1938, combat units in war zones were usually supplied with grain to meet their current need from a few depots, which involved a great deal of transportation cost and delay. Whenever the system broke down, the troops simply commandeered their needs locally. In view of the increased difficulties in transportation, starting in January, 1939, a new system of cash payment was instituted so that troops could purchase their needs from nearby areas. To improve military supplies, the rear services introduced a more elaborate system of depots to render direct support to combat units.[55] Finally, to improve the quality of officers, the government established several officers' training programs, including the Central Training Corps.[56]

It would be erroneous to interpret these concerted efforts by the central government as merely intended to increase the combat effectiveness of the armies. In fact, they should be regarded as reflecting a very fundamental reassessment by the Nationalist leaders of the momentum of war, as well as China's need for a new strategy.

Clearly, at the outset of the war, when the government referred to a long war, it never imagined that it would last eight years.[57] Once fighting began, a more coherent strategy also began to crystallize. In December, 1937, Chiang borrowed the metaphor of the whale and the silkworm in his analysis of the strategy of Japanese aggression in China and argued that the Japanese were anxious to bite off big chunks of Chinese territories like a whale and not nibble like the mincing of a silkworm. The appropriate Chinese counterstrategy then was to deny the Japanese the pleasure of taking big bites and to force them to mince, and the method for achieving this purpose was to "trade space for time." In this way of thinking, China had enormous territory, abundant human and physical resources, but backward technology and organization, while Japan had little territory, scarce human and physical resources, but advanced technology and superior organization. If China succeeded in absorbing the impact of the initial shock, it would cause the Japanese army to bog down in China's huge space while China was purchasing time to modernize and organize her own resources, and the victory in the long run would be China's.

This line of analysis gained currency after the Shanghai-Nanking campaign, and in time brought about a very pronounced change in strategy. Therefore, for example, in sharp contrast to earlier insistence on the need for making a death stand at every defense position in the Shanghai campaign, the government began to advise its generals to adopt mobile warfare and avoid fixed positional warfare, and to rely on flanking actions to offset the Japanese army's frontal attacks.[58] During the first Nan-yü conference, Chinese generals were told that the first phase of war had ended, a phase during which the Japanese advances had been stymied and their strength sapped. Henceforth would begin the second and final phase, which would turn Chinese strategy from defensive to offensive to achieve final victory.[59] The generals were urged to seize the initiative, to harrass the enemy in attritional warfare, and to conduct guerrilla warfare on all fronts against the enemy.[60]

This new strategy was more succinctly propounded by Ch'en Ch'eng.

> Henceforth the emphasis of our war efforts is not predicated on the gain or loss of cities, but on whether we can seize the initiative and conduct mobile warfare throughout the entire country, in order to harrass and disperse enemy force and thereby leading to their attrition and total destruction. Under the general principle of mobile warfare, our army must not only engage in frontal and flanking attacks, but also aggressively operate behind enemy lines. Such a strategy will make it impossi-

ble for the enemy to cover all points, put the pressure on it both in the front
and in the rear, and render it incapable of doing anything right.[61]

Insofar as the regular army was concerned, the implementation of this new
strategic thinking can be seen in the mobile warfare operations around
T'aierhchuang, the willingness to give up Wuhan without a bitter fight, and
the Chinese experiment with a trapping lure which produced a stunning
victory at Ch'angsha. In the eyes of the Chinese high command, all three
were confirmations of the correctness of the new strategy.

Equally noteworthy was the new emphasis on guerrilla warfare. Despite the lack of exposure to the theory and practice of guerrilla warfare in
his own traditional military education and the low opinion of his German
advisors,[62] Chiang finally endorsed a decision to incorporate guerrilla warfare into the new master plan in January, 1938. In the next two years, the
task of mass mobilization was assigned to the newly created Combat Area
Party-Government Joint Commission (*chan-ti tang-cheng wei-yüan-hui*).
The task of training guerrilla organizers and cadres was given to the newly
established Guerrilla Training Corps at Nan-yü under the directorship of
T'ang En-po.[63] In deference to the Communist expertise on this subject, Yeh
Chien-ying was appointed deputy director, and a number of Communists
were appointed instructors in the school.[64] Finally, two separate war zones
were created in the occupied areas to coordinate guerrilla activities.[65] Guerrilla activities were stepped up over the entire country.[66]

These changes were made with the conviction that they would contribute to the defeat of the enemy. Although the physical hardship of the
war had increased, the mood of most Nationalist leaders in 1938–40 remained optimistic, which was partly reflected in Chungking's steadfast
refusal to negotiate with the Japanese for anything short of the full restoration of the antebellum status quo as of July 7, 1937.[67] In their minds,
certain developments were interpreted as turning the tide against the
enemy. In January, 1938, the government already saw the Japanese as
having exhausted their reserves in the war, that the Japanese would never
dare to reduce their defense against the Soviet Union, and that the Japanese
had reached their upper limit in their deployable troops in China, which
could only decline in the future.[68]

After the fall of Wuhan, the Japanese decision not to push westward
was seen as a further indication of the exhaustion of their forces.[69] The fall
in January, 1939, of the Konoe cabinet, which had initiated the China war,

was seen as a sign of the impending bankruptcy of Japan's China policy and war weariness.[70] The floating of numerous Japanese domestic loans were interpreted as signalling the imminent collapse of government finances.[71] To further support this interpretation, it became customary for Chinese government documents to recite certain statistics purporting to show the narrowing of the Sino-Japanese casualty ratio and the slowing down of the speed of the Japanese advance from 1937–39.[72]

Chinese morale received a great boost in September, 1939, when the Japanese marshalled a force of 120,000 men in an attempt to take Ch'angsha, the capital of Hunan, but instead suffered a serious defeat; they lost large quantities of arms and ammunitions, and possibly as many as 40,000 troops.[73] The Ch'angsha victory represented a "decisive victory" for China and convinced the Chinese that the time had come to enter the second phase of war to mount aggressive offensives against the enemy as soon as the troop training program was completed.[74] The Chinese reaction toward these supposedly encouraging signs was the launching of the winter offensive in 1939.

The 1939 Winter Offensive and Its Impact

The 1939 winter offensive is largely ignored in most accounts of war history because it was such a military fiasco that even the Nationalists later tried to deny that it had ever occurred.[75] But the winter offensive not only did take place, it was for a while endowed with very high expectations by the Chinese leaders, and its failure, more than other widely discussed events, shook their confidence in the efficacy of the so-called new strategy and in the long-range prospects of fighting the war.

Between the time of China's enunciation of the beginning of the second phase of war and October, 1939, 82 of China's 308 divisions had gone through at least eight months of reorganization and training.[76]

On the opposite side, the Japanese deployment in China by late 1939 consisted of about twenty-five divisions and twenty independent brigades, and slightly over 500 planes. Of the 1.2 million soldiers involved, slightly over half were combat troops. But rotation of Japanese divisions back to Japan and their replacement by home-trained units without battle experience, which was a normal practice in the Japanese army, combined with the visible Japanese disinclination to engage in hard fighting in the battles of Kiangsi, Shensi, Honan, Hupei, and Hunan in the spring and summer of 1939, had led the Chinese to conclude that overall Japanese fighting capability had deteriorated.[77]

International developments at the time also had considerable impact on Chungking. In January, 1939, the United States announced its refusal to recognize the Japanese conception of a new order in east Asia, and the British government also indicated that it would not recognize any situation created by the use of force.[78]

During June and July, the Chinese government concluded the third loan agreement with the Soviet Union for the amount of $150 million, and received the first shipment of American aid.[79] American attitudes toward the Japanese stiffened with the announcement that the United States–Japanese commercial treaty would be void after January, 1940. Between late June and early September, 1939, the Japanese Kwantung Army clashed with Soviet troops and suffered defeats.[80] After World War II broke in Europe in September, Chiang confidently concluded that in the next three months the international situation would drastically alter the conditions in the Far East to China's advantage.[81]

Therefore, China's optimistic estimate of the increase of her own fighting strength, the corresponding decline of the strength of the Japanese army in China, and favorable international developments all played some role in pushing China toward attempting to conclude the war by military means. Last but not least, Wang Ching-wei's intensive negotiations with the Japanese toward the establishment of a competing regime in Nanking also had the effect of accelerating Chungking's timetable in order to forestall its establishment. The upshot was the decision to launch the winter offensive.

The directives to launch the offensive were issued on November 19, 1939. The entire Chinese force was to be mobilized. The armies in the second, third, fifth, and ninth war zones were to constitute the main attacking force, while those in other zones would mount supplementary attacks. In addition, the government released nearly all of the strategic reserve under central command to the war zones. The objective of the offensive was simple: to drive the Japanese back to the lower Yangtze River east of Nanking.[82] The importance attached to the campaign can be seen in telegrams to the commanders, in which they were repeatedly exhorted that this offensive was "the key to turn defeat into victory," "the beginning toward the final victory of the second phase of the war," and "our only good opportunity to completely annihilate the enemy.''[83] On December 18, the Supreme Military Affairs Commission instructed the commanders to attack the enemy in mobile warfare and to avoid investing a large amount of manpower to overrun strongly defended fixed enemy positions. In addition, they were cautioned against unnecessary sacrifices, as were made at Shanghai, and told to cut enemy supply lines in order to force the enemy to abandon their positions and come out to do battle.[84] Clearly, the government had changed from its earlier insistence on fixed-position, death-stand tactics to mobile and aggressive warfare.

The supplementary attacks began in late November, and the main offensive was launched in early December. According to Japanese military intelligence, between December 12, 1939, and January 20, 1940, the Chinese mobilized a total of 450,000 men and mounted 960 assaults and 1,340 engagements across the board, with the fiercest attacks directed against the Japanese Eleventh Army near Hankow.[85]

From the fifth war zone, a large number of Chinese units concentrated in southern Honan and central Hupei made several successful attempts to break the western end of Japan's defense perimeters, retook several important towns and inflicted heavy casualties upon the enemy forces. But more important was a series of aggressive attacks mounted by Chinese units under General Ch'en Ch'eng's ninth war zone. These attacks extended over a large geographical area from western Kiangsi to southern Hupei. In particular, several units had penetrated deep into Wuhan's surrounding counties and caused serious disruption in the enemy's logistic and communication system. The Japanese army's official report observed the high combat enthusiasm and fierce attacks mounted by some Chinese troops, especially those considered loyal to the KMT. The report also conceded that the offensive was quite costly to the Japanese army, which sustained over 8,000 dead and wounded as compared with 51,000 Chinese deaths.[86] But the Chinese war plan was disrupted by a Japanese diversionary attack against southern Kwangsi. This new campaign posed a serious threat for the Nationalists because, if successful, the Japanese might drive into Kweichow and Yünnan and cut China's only link with the outside world through the Yünnan-Hanoi line. In desperation, Chiang dispatched the very last of his strategic reserves into Kwangsi and the situation there was stabilized by late February, 1940.[87] But the Japanese attack against Kwangsi had also exacted a high cost: not only were the Chinese forces severely mauled, but the winter offensive was checked. By April, 1940, the offensive simply lost its momentum and withered to a halt.[88]

Reasons for the Failure of the New Strategy

What went wrong with the new strategy? What impact did this have on the Chinese government's management of the war in the subsequent years? No doubt one major factor for the failure of the winter offensive was that China simply overestimated the efficacy of the training program to restore the combat efficiency of its troops. One year was far too short to recreate a modern army.

Second, although the army reform program was fairly comprehensive in concept, its implementation was severely hampered by objective circumstances. In particular, equipment and personnel proved the most insurmountable difficulties.

Whatever modern equipment the Chinese had acquired prior to the war had been lost during the first six months of fighting. In ensuing years, supplies of arms and ammunition became a very taxing problem for Chinese military planners. The few arsenals that were salvaged and relocated in the interior were grossly inadequate to meet the demands of the war. Foreign supplies also became precarious. Under mounting Japanese pressure, the German government terminated all shipments of arms to China after March, 1938.[89] Bound by her neutrality status, American assistance remained very meager, and more private than public. The only country that rendered substantial assistance to the Chinese was the Soviet Union. Between 1937 and 1939, Soviet loans amounted to about $300 million,[90] Soviet military advisors soon numbered 500, and Soviet delivery of military hardware totalled about 60,000 tons.[91]

Yet even Soviet assistance was too meager to make a strong impact on the Chinese army. Thus by the time of the winter offensive, the Chinese army of close to 4.5 million men had only 1.6 million rifles, 68,762 light machine guns, 17,700 heavy machine guns, 5,885 mortars, and 2,650 pieces of artillery of all description.[92] Compared with 1937, there had been a pronounced deterioration of equipment of all categories for all Chinese units.[93]

China's problem in mounting an all-out offensive was compounded by serious logistic difficulties. Nineteen thirty-eight was the last time in the long war that China had available modern means of transportation in quantity. With the loss of Wuhan, the railway network was truncated and water traffic along the Yangtze was disrupted. At the end of 1939, China had only 1,532 military vehicles, a number so inadequate that human power, draft animals, and junks emerged as the primary means of logistic support.[94] Food alone posed a challenge that the government proved unable to cope with, and consequently, when the winter offensive got underway, eight of the ten war zones had less than one-third of the required ration.[95] The problem with fuel and ammunition proved just as intractable. The records of the offensive indicated that where serious fighting took place, logistics were often a major impediment to the combat effectiveness of the troops.[96]

Equally serious was the shortage of field-grade officers. China's assorted military schools had always been deficient in meeting the needs of her ever-expanding armies. After 1928, the country's military education had achieved a measure of standardization due to the central government's efforts. The Central Army Officers' Academy became the major producing ground for junior officers who, upon graduation, were usually assigned to the central government forces. Under the German influence, the quality of these officers was usually judged to be fairly high; yet between 1928 and 1937, this academy had produced only 10,844 cadets and another 15,278 irregular trainees.[97] In a single blow at Shanghai, as many as 10,000 junior officers, mostly from Chiang's crack units, had been lost.[98] This loss created a serious leadership vacuum in the lower echelons that the government was unable to make up for in the first two years of the war. The disappearance of a generation of competent junior officers inevitably reduced the effectiveness of the training program and directly contributed to the poor combat performance of the troops during the winter offensive.

Finally, the winter offensive and the entire war strategy up to this point bore the strong imprint of Chiang's personality. His earlier experiences had conditioned him to think that any odds could be overcome with will power. In Chiang's many exhortations to his army, he was fond of reciting how his small revolutionary army had defeated more numerous and better-armed warlord armies time and again during the 1920s and 1930s. His prescription for victory included, among other things: no fear of death, the capacity to outlast the enemy in the last five minutes of the fight, and the superiority of revolutionary willpower over modern weapons. As Li Tsung-jen testified, war plans were decided by Chiang personally at this stage and nobody dared to argue with him.[99] Just as Chiang confidently declared that he would drive the enemy into the Huangpu River in Shanghai, he insisted on the defense of Nanking on the ground that Sun Yat-sen's tomb there should not be allowed to fall into enemy hands without a fight.[100] This pride and blind faith in spirit and determination contributed substantially to the miscalculation of the winter offensive.

The Aftermath of the Offensive

The winter offensive was followed by a period of serious difficulty for China, both internationally and domestically. Internationally, the outbreak of World War II not only failed to bring about prompt American involvement but the Nazi's advances against the Western democracies created reverberations in the Chinese theater as well. Emboldened by the fall of France and the fiasco of Dunkirk (June 9–14, 1940), the Japanese pressured the Vichy government into closing the Yünnan-Hanoi railway on June 20. Meanwhile, Japan imposed a blockade around Hong Kong to prevent shipment of goods into China's interior, and forced the British to close the Burma Road for three months.[101] Although in August, the American government expanded its embargo of strategic goods to Japan to include scrap iron and gasoline, the Japanese had gained the right to land their army at Haiphong, Vietnam, and had concluded the Tripartite Pact with Germany and Italy in September.

The winter offensive also failed to forestall the installation of the Wang Ching-wei puppet regime. By November, 1940, Japan had normalized her relations with this regime by diplomatic recognition and the conclusion of a number of agreements on such outstanding issues as anti-Communism, troop stationing, consular rights, and economic cooperation, and gave the impression that the realities of a puppet regime were there to stay for a long time to come.

In the midst of a rapidly deteriorating situation for the Western powers in Europe, the Soviet Union and Japan concluded a treaty of neutrality and friendship in April, 1941, by virtue of which both countries bartered away China's rights over Manchuria and Outer Mongolia. The most immediate effect of the Soviet-Japanese pact was the evaporation of China's hope of obtaining continued Soviet military assistance, an issue which was soon rendered academic when the Soviet Union herself was attacked by Germany in June, 1941. This assured Japan a period of stability on its northern front and a greater degree of freedom to pursue her China policy. The American material assistance to China, although made official by President Roosevelt's inclusion of China in the Lend-Lease Act, was so disorganized and assigned such a low priority as to have little real meaning. Therefore, the combined effect of international developments in 1940–41 was to deepen China's sense of isolation from her potential allies, and cast gloom over the Chinese leaders that the war was to last much longer than they had recently projected, if victory would ever come at all.

The confrontation between China and Japan also underwent some important changes as each side reassessed the significance of the winter offensive.

From the Chinese perspective, the one single most influential lesson Chungking inferred was that the Chinese army was too weak to mount a full-scale offensive to evict the enemy and should revert to the earlier strategy of holding ground firmly against further Japanese advances.

From the Japanese perspective, the aggressiveness of the Chinese army throughout 1939 obviously surprised them and forced them to increase their troop deployment. This need upset an earlier Japanese plan to reduce troop strength in China to beef up their defense against the Soviet Union, a plan which was favored by the Operations Division of the Army General Staff. But the field commanders of the China Expeditionary Force argued for one more large-scale offensive against Chungking before the projected reduction of force level took place. The issue was resolved in favor of mounting the offensive in the fall of 1940, to be followed by a reduction in early 1941. Consequently in 1940–41, the Japanese initiated attacks against Hupei, Honan, Anhwei, and Shansi.[102] The Chinese fought hard and in many cases caused considerable difficulties for the invaders. But they also paid dearly. The Japanese reported that during this series of campaigns, they had completely destroyed twenty-four Chinese divisions, including most of the best KMT units.[103] The Chinese confirmed that they lost about 200,000 men.[104]

The only bright spot for the Chinese occurred in the ninth war zone where in mid-August the Japanese suffered another major defeat in their second attempt to take Ch'angsha. But even this victory could not conceal the fact that the general condition of the Chinese army was visibly inferior to previous years. According to a governmental review of the military performance from December, 1938, to February, 1940, the most common weaknesses of the army included unwillingness to exercise independent judgment or to fight independently, lack of coordination, poor staff work, poor intelligence, poor logistics, lack of equipment, poor control over troops, inadequate knowledge of the principles of field operations, poor discipline, and low combat effectiveness.[105] But at the third Nan-yü military conference in October, 1941, Chiang directed his harshest criticism against the generals and accused them of disinterest in training, arrogance, inexperience, and corruption. Chiang pointed out that in some war zones some generals even took advantage of the blockade and engaged in trading with the enemy.[106] Even as China continued her army reorganization and training, little comfort could be drawn from it in view of what happened before. In fact, the Japanese military intelligence estimated in 1941 that the combat effectiveness of the Chinese troops had declined by 20 to 30 percent in one year.[107]

Military Reorganization, 1942–44

Since the first wartime army reform program proved to be a failure, a more comprehensive program was put into practice between 1942–44.[108] Yet again, official claims notwithstanding, the program was in fact far less successful than anticipated for a number of reasons.

The lack of efficient logistic support for the armies continued to pose a serious problem. Due to limited military production capacity, the damage of war, and the general shortage of nonferrous metals and explosives, the total Chinese production in the war years amounted to 800,000 rifles, 87,000 machine guns, and 12,000 light mortars.[109] This production capacity simply was deficient even to keep up with war losses, not to mention improving the equipment of the army.

One factor that could have radically improved China's logistical difficulties was the American Lend-Lease Act. Whereas this program was subject to constant diplomatic bargaining before Pearl Harbor, after America's entry into the war, it was administered on a routine basis. However, China's exclusion from the Combined Chiefs of Staff and the Munitions Assignment Board meant that China's demands on lend-lease would be processed by Anglo-American strategists preoccupied with the war in Europe and that China would have to appeal for Roosevelt's personal intercession whenever it thought its needs were not adequately met. Whatever the amount of aid earmarked for China, after the closing of the Burma Road in the spring of 1942, the only way China could be supplied from outside was by the Air Transport Command (ATC), which was operating barely twenty-five planes from India, and the monthly delivery to China actually fell below 100 tons for some time.[110]

The American strategists shared Stilwell's view that the only long-term solution to China's needs was to reopen the Burma Road, for which plans were being drawn. For the short term, great efforts were exerted to increase the over-the-hump tonnage. Yet for the entire year of 1943, only 61,151 tons were flown into China by the ATC,[111] an amount that would have kept a single American infantry division in operation for only sixty-eight days *after* it had been fully equipped.[112] In fact, after the major portion was taken by the United States Air Force, very little was left for China's ground forces. It was not until October, 1944, that the monthly air delivery broke the 30,000 ton mark. By then, a large number of American support personnel had already arrived in China, and their share of the delivered materials had reached about 48 percent.[113]

Inevitably, the delivery of lend-lease aid became a matter of serious discord between the American and Chinese governments during the last three years of the war and in no small way contributed to the Chinese decision of asking for the recall of General Stilwell. During the Sino-American crisis of October of 1944, Chiang complained to President Roosevelt that "prior to June 1944, with the exception of the Yünnan Expeditionary Forces, the entire Chinese Army did not receive a single rifle or piece of artillery from American Lend-Lease," and that up to October, 1944, the Chinese army, again excepting the Yünnan Expeditionary forces, had received sixty mountain guns, 320 antitank rifles, and 506 bazookas.[114]

After the reopening of the Burma Road in late 1944, but more significantly due to the stepped-up air delivery, greater quantities of arms and equipment began to arrive in China.[115] In monetary terms, the amount of lend-lease aid for China was $26 million for 1941, $100 million for 1942, $49 million for 1943, $53 million for 1944, and $1,107 million for 1945.[116] The total tonnage airlifted into China was about 650,000 tons, or the equivalent of the cargo capacity of seventy Liberty ships.[117] But after allocations to Chennault's fighters and the B-29s, the shares of the Chinese ground forces and arsenals were very modest.

In comparative terms, lend-lease aid to China constituted only 1.7 percent of global American lend-lease apportionments in 1941, 1.5 percent in 1942, 0.4 percent in 1943, 0.4 percent in 1944, and 8 percent in 1945, or about 3 percent of total American lend-lease aid for 1941–46 inclusive.[118] But since the largest amounts arrived in 1945, they were too late to improve the Chinese army's position or to have any appreciable effect on the conduct of war within China proper.

Under these conditions, the armament of the Chinese army showed visible deterioration. By late 1943, the Chinese army of three million men was equipped with only one million rifles, 83,000 machine guns, 7,800 trench mortars, and 1,300 pieces of artillery of diverse description.[119]

Yet even when the materials were available, distribution often posed an insurmountable problem. At full strength, a division's monthly ration of provisions was about 270 tons. Since the modern means of transportation in east China had been lost, thousands of bearers had to devote full time to carrying supplies between the depots and the troops. Due to the shortage of storage facilities, complex administrative boundaries, difficult terrain, and lack of roads and vessels, troops often resorted to unauthorized seizure of supplies. In most cases, the wanton impressment of civilians and their draft animals to be bearers was a common practice. But in other cases, an army might have to devote so much manpower to logistics that it hardly had enough left to carry on combat duties.[120]

With such a rudimentary logistic system, it was not surprising that the army's combat effectiveness was sharply curtailed and that its often foraging soldiers posed more threat to the civilian population than the enemy force.[121]

The shortage of competent officers also worsened. Although the most important producer of field-grade officers remained the Central Army Officers' Academy, significant qualitative changes had occurred over the years.[122] Compared with the Nanking era, the quality of education declined precipitously after the academy moved to Chengtu. There the facilities were primitive, management was poor, and competent instructors were in short supply. Even after admission standards were lowered and the training for the overwhelming majority of cadets was reduced to twelve months, the Chengtu campus only turned out 34,430 graduates between 1937–46. After 1939, nine branch campuses were set up throughout the country and produced an additional 88,461 graduates during the war.[123] But their standards were even lower. When we include the 80,000–84,000 officers who had risen from the ranks and gone through some form of a refresher course,[124] the grand total of officers produced by the regular and auxiliary military educational institutions was 200,000 for the entire war.

It becomes immediately apparent that China produced a very small corps of officers in relation to the magnitude of the war—about 25,000 per year. After war losses and natural attrition, little if anything was left to upgrade the leadership and improve the officer-to-enlisted-man ratio. The officers were hampered by their lack of specialization as very few of them were trained in the special services.[125] As General Ho Ying-ch'in reported in August, 1943, of the 140,000 lower- and middle-ranking officers commissioned in all military units, only 37,587 (or 27 percent) had graduated from regular military academies.[126] In other words, over 70 percent of junior officers had been promoted from the ranks. This was almost exactly the reverse of the situation that existed in the KMT forces before 1937 when 80 percent of the junior officers in these units had been properly trained in the academies.[127] Such a paucity of qualified officers inevitably rendered any rotation system entirely academic, increased casualties among the soldiers, and impeded training due to their own professional deficiencies.

An even worse problem existed among the senior officers of the Chinese army. The senior officers usually came from one of four sources: the Paoting Military Academy and its affiliates, the Whampoa Academy, the Japanese military schools (particularly the Shikan Gakkō), or from the ranks. The Japanese-trained officers had the most solid technical training, but they were in a clear minority. The officers trained in Chinese military schools generally had insufficient knowledge to handle a modern war, while those who had risen from the ranks had almost no appreciation of the intricacies of a complex modern war, although combat experience and even courage were not in short supply among some of them. By 1944, however, only 10 percent of China's generals had received foreign education, but since most had received it during or before World War I, they did not really acquire a solid grounding in the new technology and strategies that had evolved since. Another 38 percent had received their education from either old-style provincial or local schools or had risen from the ranks. This group was definitely ill-equipped to fight the Japanese. The remainder had graduated from either Paoting or Whampoa. A most glaring deficiency among the general officers' corps was in the special services. The overwhelming majority of generals in logistics had graduated from the Peiyang Logistics School, a very poorly conducted school, and had long careers in Peiyang armies before 1928. Likewise, the cavalry and military communications services were dominated by old-fashioned generals from northern provincial armies, particularly the Moslem ones.[128]

During the Nanking era, the government had created the Staff College (*lu-chün ta-hsüeh*) to offer senior officers advanced training and prepare them for top leadership posts. Although this was the pinnacle of Chinese military education, the benefits that officers could derive from it were usually negligible. After the war broke out, the Staff College was in worse condition than most other military schools. Again the causes were shortage of funds, primitive facilities, lack of instructors, and obsolescence of teaching materials.[129] Quality aside, this school also trained a very small number of generals. Between 1930 and 1944, a total of 1,878 officers had been trained at the highest levels.[130] Not surprisingly, as General Wedemeyer commented in his capacity as Chiang's chief of staff at the end of the war, he had encountered very few senior officers whom he deemed "efficient or professionally well trained."[131]

The impact of all these interferences and disruptions was highly visible among the Chinese armies. Even the Chinese government conceded in 1942 that the most prevalent faults among Chinese soldiers included fear of airplanes and artillery fire, lack of patrol and intelligence work, fear of bayonet fights, excessive and undisciplined firing during night combat, no appreciation of basic firing principles among junior officers, and breakdown of control during retreat.[132]

Beyond these combat deficiencies, it is common knowledge that Chinese divisions continued to be understaffed. Embezzlement became more widespread as most commanders continued to mistreat their soldiers and pocket soldiers' pay.[133] As a result, manpower losses sometimes reached alarming proportions.[134] For instance, the American ambassador reported in late 1943 that under prevailing conditions, a division of soldiers might be entirely wiped out by disease, starvation, and desertion within two years' time without ever having participated in combat.[135]

Discipline within the army also deteriorated sharply. As Chiang himself revealed at the Sian military conference of September, 1942, problems included pervasive gambling, engaging in smuggling enemy merchandise, opium smoking and opium trade of major proportions within the army, and the dominant influence of secret societies (such as Ko-lao-hui) in many regional forces. Nevertheless, Chiang was not able to prescribe effective solutions.[136]

America's Role in Chinese Military Training

It was under the weight of these multiple deficiencies that the Americans were invited to play a major role in the revitalization of the Chinese army, and in March, 1942, the Chinese government initiated a request to the American government to help equip and train 30 Chinese divisions.[137] Subsequently, the 30-division concept became the basis for America's military program in China. General Stilwell presented his first comprehensive critique of the state of the Chinese army in the spring of 1942, right after the Burma defeat. In a lengthy memorandum, he took note of the fact that China's 300-odd divisions were probably 40 percent under strength but that it would be self-defeating to try to reorganize them all at once. He argued that a few dependable well-equipped and well-supported divisions would be worth far more than the large number of them as presently organized, and that they would simplify logistics and management. Therefore, guided by the 30-division target, he recommended the merging of divisions to bring some units up to full strength and the assignment of all available weapons to these divisions. He also recommended a thorough screening of officers on the basis of merit, rewarding the able ones with promotion and purging the inefficient ones even if they were high commanders. Finally, he recommended that a man in whom Chiang had confidence be given the command over the troops without interference from any quarter.[138]

Such a proposal soon ran into political complications (to be discussed in chap. 3), and the pace of the reorganization and training proceeded very slowly. By September, 1944, Stilwell had concluded that only a thorough reorganization of the Chinese command system could have remedied its major military defects. To achieve this objective, he demanded to be given the command over Chinese forces and the authority to reorganize the Ministry of National Defense, to consolidate units, to take over provincial troops, to inspect and reorganize replacement centers, and to have full powers over appointment and dismissal, promotion and demotion of Chinese officers.[139]

But these demands far exceeded the Chinese government's readiness to concede, and Stilwell was relieved of his duties in September, 1944. Thus, during his tour of duty in China, Stilwell succeeded only in partially training and equipping the Nationalist army force designated to participate in the second Burma campaign (code named by the Americans the Y-force), but had not introduced any sweeping reforms into the Chinese forces, in China proper, as he had wished.

Operation Ichigō

That such an army as the one possessed by the Chinese government could not fight should have been self-evident all along. Yet in the early 1940s, the Japanese were preoccupied with other problems. The invasion of Southeast Asia, the naval engagements in the eastern Pacific, the pacification campaigns in north and east China, all helped to reduce Japanese ground activities against the Chungking government. Few battles were fought and the front remained stationary over long periods of time. But this state of affairs could not last long. Finally, the acid test came in 1944, and when it did, it graphically revealed all the weaknesses of the Chinese army that had been concealed from the public view for a long time.

It is regrettable that Operation Ichigō of 1944 has received relatively scant treatment in the literature on the Nationalist government or the history of the war. Most authors prefer to make passing mention of the operation and to use it as one more proof of the military and political ineptness of the Chinese government. Those who accord more attention to this operation are primarily interested in analyzing its impact on Sino-American relations.

This is unfortunate for the very simple reason that no single military event in the second half of the war ever had a stronger impact upon Chinese politics and the Chinese military than this operation. For these reasons, Operation Ichigō deserves very careful scrutiny.

The Conceptualization of Operation Ichigō

Japan's China Policy

Four days before Pearl Harbor, the Japanese high command issued Continental Directive Number 575 (December 3, 1941), which laid down the guiding principles for conducting the China war in the future. This document conceded the existence of a serious morale problem in the China Expeditionary Army due to the stalemate, warned against contemplating any large-scale offensive against the Chungking government in the future, and instructed that major efforts be made to consolidate occupied territories in north China, by increasing pacification, building up its economy, and winning over public support.[140]

The Japanese decision was in line with the general strategy of concentrating their attacks against the British, the Americans, and the Dutch in the Far East at the beginning of the war. In the meantime, Japanese strategists decided to use northern Chinese politicians and foreign channels to explore the terms under which Chungking would be interested in stopping the war, and to create a favorable combat situation to induce Chungking to enter into negotiation.[141]

During the course of 1942, the new China strategy was incorporated into two separate campaign proposals. As the Japanese Imperial Headquarters saw it, Chungking would respond to Japanese peace overtures more positively if its will of resistance were demolished by significant defeats, preferably at the very beginning of the Pacific war when the superiority of

Japan's military might could be most convincingly demonstrated. To the Japanese high command, the termination of China's active role in the war would allow Japan to establish a separate route of communication through India to the Indian Ocean, thence to link up with Germany and Italy, which fundamentally would alter the global balance and hasten the day of victory for the tripartite powers.[142]

The first attempt to translate the new strategic thinking into concrete action was the drafting of Operation Number 51 in June, 1942. This operation envisioned the launching of a major thrust against Sian, complemented by another offensive from Wuhan, both to converge toward Szechwan. The Japanese projected the deployment of sixteen divisions to complete the mission in five months, and to seek to annihilate the central Nationalist forces as the main targets.[143] The operation remained in the planning stage and hit several snags. By late August, an alternative plan was being considered. Designated as Operation Number 5, it envisioned a westward general thrust from Hupei-Honan-Shensi directly against Chungking, bypassing Yünnan-Kweichow-Kwangsi completely. But the implementation of this plan was delayed because unfavorable developments in the Pacific compelled the Japanese to divert some air and ground units.[144] By the end of 1942, the operation had not materialized.

Japanese Defeats in the Pacific

The optimism the Japanese entertained at the beginning of 1942 gradually dissipated as they began to suffer reverses in the Pacific theater. In early June, 1942, the American fleet delivered a stunning blow to the Japanese navy at the Battle of Midway and demonstrated that American naval power had been restored. Japanese naval strength was progressively cut down in the two battles of the Solomon Islands of October and November, 1942, and the Battle of the South Pacific in March, 1943.

By then the United States had already committed itself to an island-hopping strategy in the Pacific area. In June, MacArthur was appointed commander in chief of the Allied forces in the south and southwestern Pacific and the Allied forces made a successful landing at New Georgia in the Solomon Islands. By December, 1943, American units had reached the Marshalls and New Britains.

This brief chronological review suggests that it was in the summer of 1942 that the United States went on the offensive in the Pacific and the Japanese navy proved incapable of stopping it. Since the beginning of the war, the Japanese logistic system had relied exclusively on the security of the sea lanes between the homeland and the Philippines which served as an entreport for distribution of war material to the Dutch East Indies, Burma, Thailand, and to French Indochina.[145] As long as the American navy was kept beyond the mid-Pacific, the fruits of recent Japanese overseas conquest were secure and the Japanese felt no need to seek an alternate supply route on the continent. But as the Japanese felt the increasing strain of the onslaught of the American navy on the western Pacific in 1942–43, the situation began to change.

According to Japanese projections at the outbreak of war, about 1.8 million tons of shipping would be lost to Allied attack in the first twenty-four months of the war. Yet in twenty-one months, 3.8 million tons had actually been lost, more than twice the projected figure. Allied aerial attacks accounted for only 24 percent of the loss, while submarine attacks accounted for 55 percent of the loss.[146] Therefore, the Japanese military data suggest that while the China-based Allied air force caused considerable difficulties to them since it stepped up activities in the spring of 1943, it was not as great a threat to Japanese shipping as Allied naval operations. The depletion of tonnage forced the Japanese government to institute the policy of pressing privately owned vessels into military duty. But this was no solution. The closer the Allied navy moved its operations westward, the more dramatic were the Japanese shipping losses.[147]

At the outbreak of war, Japan had a transport capability of about 5.5 million tons. By the end of 1943, even after herculean efforts to build new ships, the capability was reduced to about 77 percent of prewar level. In 1943 alone, the reduction was 16 percent, with the worst obviously yet to come.[148] These losses not only cast grave doubt on Japan's ability to supply her outlaying posts in Southeast Asia, they also seriously undermined her long-range survival as a nation. For Japan used the sea lanes not only to supply her troops overseas, but to extract strategic raw materials from Southeast Asia.

Particularly crucial to Japan's entire war effort was the supply of petroleum, a resource considered important enough to lead Japan into war against the United States. At the Imperial Conference in November, 1941, it was estimated that petroleum imports from Southeast Asia would rise steadily and that by 1944 they should supply 84 percent of her needs.[149]

But difficulties began to mount after mid-1942 when more and more oil tankers were destroyed. In 1943, Japan was already forced to turn to synthetic fuel in the volume of 760,000 liters to make up for the shortfall. Yet oil tanker losses continued to mount and by February, 1944, the total reached 111,000 tons.[150] The fuel shortage in turn severely affected the production of such critical items as steel, airplanes, general ordnance, warships, merchant ships, and motor vehicles which all began to decline sharply after mid-1944.[151] Thus as the Pacific war entered its third year, Japanese strategists were already under enormous pressure to find an alternative to the logistics system by the sea.

The speed of Allied advance in the Pacific and the logistic difficulties it created were not entirely unforeseen by the Japanese strategists. Even as early as December, 1942, the Operations Department at the Imperial Headquarters was already engaged in drafting a long-range combat plan, which directed attention to the feasibility of establishing a continental corridor to supply Southeast Asia. Continued deterioration of the Japanese position in the Pacific and a much-feared confirmation that Japan's sea lanes had become even more vulnerable, finally produced a formal plan drafted by the chief of operations on November 22, 1943, that called for the linking of Japanese occupied territories from north China, through south China, down to Indochina to offset the Allied superiority in the Pacific. Three days later, the Hsin-chu airfield on Taiwan was raided for the first time by American planes—a big shock to the Japanese.

Under the close guidance of the chief of staff, General Sukiyama, the continental war plan quickly took shape. Specifically, it called for Japanese occupation of important cities along the Peking-Hankow and Hankow-Canton railways, marching into Kwangsi and Kweichow, stripping the rails from the Liuchow-Tushan section, and laying a new railway from Liuchow to Liangshan (Longsam) on the China-Vietnam border. If this plan worked, the Japanese would have seized one-half to two-thirds of the railway stocks in China's interior provinces. The Japanese also planned to supplement them with an additional 200 locomotives and 2,500 freight cars. This operation would insure the Japanese an uninterrupted supply line of 3,000 kilometers between Peking and Hanoi. Finally, it was hoped that in the course of opening this corridor, the Japanese would have demolished the KMT's main forces and destroyed the big airfields at Hengyang, Liuchow, and Kweilin. The Japanese strategists believed that once this plan was successfully implemented, Japan would be able to maintain its 600,000 troops in China proper and 500,000 troops in Southeast Asia and continue the war against the United States indefinitely.[152]

All these strategic considerations were reflections of a much larger change in Japan's attitude toward the war induced by the adverse developments of late 1942 and early 1943. By late September, 1942, the Japanese were already talking in terms of "insuring a posture of undefeatability" and not unqualified victory any more. During the following year, the Imperial General Headquarters became increasingly resigned to the fact that no amount of effort would reverse the Japanese defeat in the southwestern Pacific, and began to contemplate where best to meet the expected Anglo-American counteroffensive.[153]

On September 25, 1943, the Japanese government finally agreed on the so-called absolute national-defense sphere whose boundary started from the Kuril Islands southward to the Bonin Islands, Mariana Islands, Caroline Islands, and then westward to west New Guinea, the Philippines, Dutch East Indies, Malaya, and northward to Thailand, Burma, Indochina, China, and back to Japan's homeland. Obviously this was the last line of defense, or minimum sphere of influence, the Japanese were willing to accept. The purpose of setting up this absolute sphere was to protect the sources of physical resources for the Sphere of Greater East Asia Coprosperity, to insure the safety of transportation between homeland and the various parts of this sphere, and to gain the advantage of an internal line of combat and support against the Allies.[154]

The Meaning of Operation Ichigō

It is clear that if one restricts one's examination of Operation Ichigō to the language contained in the headquarters' directive to the China Expeditionary Army, one would gain the impression that the destruction of the air fields was the paramount objective.[155] But then it was rare for any operational directive to contain a thorough exposition of the full range of strategic considerations that led to the decision to launch a particular operation. One would commit an elementary mistake by not putting the particular operation in its proper perspective.

It is recalled that even when the Japanese went to war against the United States, they did not entertain any illusion of defeating her singlehandedly. The decision to attack Pearl Harbor was made on the assumption that it would delay full American reprisal by several years, by which time Japan would have consolidated her new possessions in Southeast Asia, and probably even have linked up with the Axis allies in order to shift the balance of global power in their favor. Unfortunately for the Japanese strategists, the recovery of America's naval power in the Pacific was surprisingly quick, and by late 1942 the Japanese already sensed that the tables had been turned against them. But while the Japanese were unable to make up for their losses with new construction, the Americans seemed to have an inexhaustible capacity to replace their losses and then add some more.

After mid-1942, the Japanese simply had no way of stopping the American march toward Japan's home waters. Therefore, from Japan's perspective, as long as the American strategists were determined to advance toward Japan from the Pacific and threatened the lifeline of imperial defense, Japan would be compelled to establish the continental corridor, even though the Chinese ground forces posed no real threat to it at this time. The increasing harrassment caused by the China-based United States Air Force only strengthened the Japanese decision to carry out the attack as soon as possible.

The Honan Phase

In December, 1943, the Japanese Imperial Headquarters designated the forthcoming campaign as Operation Ichigō and instructed the China Expeditionary Force to make the necessary preparation for its implementation. The campaign would consist of two stages. The first stage would link up Japanese-occupied territory north of the Yellow River with Hsinyang in Hupei along the Peking-Hankow railway, and the second stage would secure the territories between Yüehchow (Hunan) and Liangshan in Vietnam (map 1). Even under the difficult conditions of 1944, the Japanese allocated 70,000 horses and 12,000 vehicles to support a ground force of 400,000 men in this operation.

On April 18, 1944, the Japanese opened the first stage with 140,000 men and crossed the Yellow River in central Honan.[156] The Chinese defense along the Yellow River consisted of twenty-one divisions, of which only eleven were combat-worthy, most from the armies under T'ang En-po. Faced with the need to defend a long line with such meager force, Chiang instructed that one division be assigned to defend a particular area.[157]

The Japanese used the Twelfth Army as the main attack force against Chengchow while sending their First Army to attack Loyang from the west to confuse the Chinese. Taking advantage of the flat terrain, the Japanese relied heavily on tanks, long-range artillery, and mechanized units to spearhead their offensive. Without air cover or sufficient ground support, the poorly trained and poorly equipped Chinese troops simply melted away under the withering attack.

The absolute superiority of Japanese firepower was attested by the fact

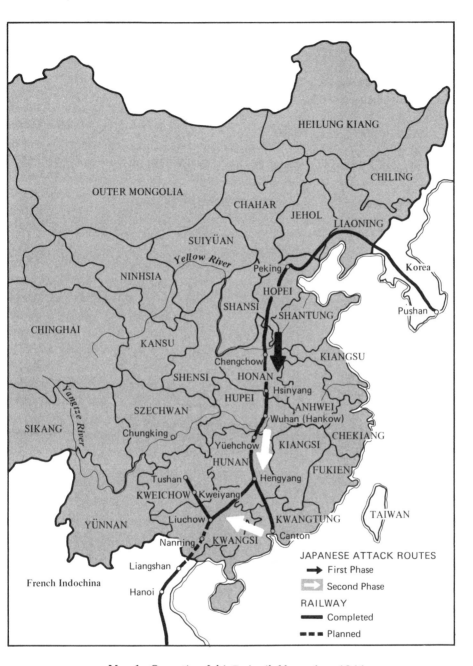

Map 1 Operation Ichigō, April- November, 1944

that between the crossing of the Yellow River on April 18 and the occupation of Loyang on May 26, the Japanese killed 21,643 Chinese soldiers and
a large number were wounded at the cost of only 1,061 killed and 2,866
wounded among their own troops—a kill ratio of twenty to one. The
situation worsened when even less well-trained Chinese units from the first
war zone were sent in as reinforcements. Between May 9 and 20, some
32,390 Chinese were killed, while the Japanese lost only 760 dead and
2,032 wounded,[158] thus improving the kill ratio to forty-two to one. As
Chinese war historians admitted afterward, the defenders' poor training
and equipment were simply no match for the speed, armor, and firepower
of the Japanese force operating on a flat terrain.[159]

The most devastating damage of Japan's attack was not so much the
number of casualties inflicted upon the Chinese as the destruction of the
command structure of many Chinese units. Under the lightning speed of
the Japanese advance, the Chinese were sent on a rout and discarded their
weapons in large quantities. Thus, for instance, before the attack, T'ang
En-po had twenty-eight to thirty divisions of the central government's best
troops. After the Japanese attack, its remnants were driven into the
mountains of western Honan, where it was instructed by the government to
take up "garrison duties," to "conduct guerrilla warfare," and to engage
in "regroupment and training," all familiar Chinese euphemisms for the
simple fact that this force had lost its combat-effectiveness.[160]

The Hunan Phase

The second phase of the operation got underway as soon as the Honan
campaign concluded. The First and Twelfth armies were shipped to central
China, the Thirteenth Army was dispatched from Nanking. Additional
units were drawn from Mongolia and Manchuria to reinforce the Eleventh
and Twenty-third armies already poised in the staging area around Wuhan.
Anticipating more active Sino-American air activities, some air force units
were even sent from the Japanese homeland. This force of eight divisions
and one brigade of over 360,000 men represented the largest concentration
of troops of the Japanese army in the entire history of the Sino-Japanese
War.[161]

The Chinese defense in the ninth war zone under Hsüeh Yüeh consisted of forty-eight divisions, half of which belonged to the central government. With a total of less than half a million men, the Chinese only had
a numerical advantage of less than 1.4 to 1 in relation to the Japanese.

Again troubled by the problem of defending a large territory with insufficient force, Chiang reiterated his demand to adhere to the death-stand
tactics in defending every point independently and separately.

The Japanese attack force faced a tougher task in the Hunan campaign. Between Wuhan and Ch'angsha, the terrain was crisscrossed with
numerous rivers and lakes. Below Ch'angsha, the terrain was mountainous
all the way down the Sino-Vietnamese border. Both were less favorable to
large-scale troop movement by mechanized means and restricted the fighting to the railways and their vicinity. The Japanese avoided the costly
mistakes made on three previous occasions in attacking Ch'angsha and
resorted to an encircling action with a very large force and took the city on
June 18. To demonstrate its seriousness in demanding the death-stand,
Chungking executed the commander of the Fourth Army for failing to hold
Ch'angsha.

The next major target for the Japanese was Hengyang, which was
defended by the Nationalists' Tenth Army under General Fang Hsien-
chüeh with 16,000 men. Hengyang was not only a crucial point on the
Hankow-Canton railway, but also the site of the largest air base in Hunan.
Here the Japanese met unexpectedly strong resistance. Making excellent
use of the terrain and strong defense works there, the men of the Tenth
Army remained faithful to the death-stand policy and held the city for
forty-seven days. When the city finally fell on August 8, 1944, all but
1,200 of its defenders had been either killed or wounded. The Japanese
also paid dearly: 19,380 men and 910 officers were killed or wounded in
the campaign.[162]

End of the Attack

Since the inception of the operation, international developments had turned
increasingly to Japan's disadvantage. The Normandy landing of June 6,
1944, almost coincided with the beginning of Operation Ichigō and made it
clear that after the fall of Italy, the days of Hitler's Germany were numbered. When that occurred, the Allied powers would be in no mood to
compromise on the harsh terms of surrender agreed upon at the Cairo
Conference (November 23–26, 1943).

In the Pacific area, the Japanese found the developments to be more
ominous. The seizure of the Marianas by the Americans at precisely the
time the Japanese were fighting a fierce battle against the last defenders of
Hengyang would take much sense out of Operation Ichigō had it been

intended only to destroy Chinese air bases in the southwest. The Marianas had given the United States a better base of operating the B-29s against the Japanese homeland than any Chinese bases, because bases in the Marianas could be easily supplied from the continental United States and were beyond the range of Japanese counterattack.

In July, 1944, however, Imperial Headquarters in Tokyo was plainly worried primarily about linking the railways on continental Asia from China to Indochina in light of the increasing difficulty of maintaining the supply lines by sea. Imperial Headquarters began to consider mounting two offensives at the same time, one from Hunan against Kweilin-Liuchow, the other one from Canton toward the Sino-Vietnamese border, so that rail connections with Indochina could be completed by January, 1945.[163] This concept was incorporated into a larger plan of imperial defense called Operation Sho, which was activated on October 18, 1944, when the United States task forces were sighted heading for Leyte.[164]

Yet by the time the Japanese had carried out the last leg of Operation Ichigō they were plainly near exhaustion. Stiff Chinese resistance in Hunan caused Japanese casualties to mount. According to Japanese sources, between early August and early September, they had suffered 7,602 dead, 13,174 wounded, 20,183 sick, as well as 1,804 horses dead and 31,602 horses sick or wounded.[165]

At the conclusion of the Hunan campaign, Chinese casualties had reached such an alarming level, particularly among the elite units, that the government had trouble organizing for the defense of Kwangsi. When Japanese advance units crossed into Kwangsi in early September, the Chinese finally scraped together only ten divisions of 60,000–70,000 men, mostly from the defeated units evacuated from Hunan, for the defense of Kweilin.[166]

But as the Japanese pressed on, logistics had become an even more

TABLE 2
Japanese Mobilization for Operation Ichigō, 1944

Items	Honan Campaign	Hunan-Kwangsi Campaign	Total
Manpower	148,000	362,000	510,000
Horses	33,000	67,000	100,000
Artillery	269	1,282	1,551
Tanks	691	103	794
Motor vehicles	6,100	9,450	15,550

Source: Bōeichō, *Ichigō Sakusen (2) Konan no Kaisen* (Tokyo, 1967), pp. 48–49.

serious problem. Japanese records show that during the operation 3,500 tons of supplies were sent from Japanese depots in Wuhan each month. By the time they reached Hengyang, they could still receive 2,500 tons per month through the railways and highways. But when they arrived at the Hunan-Kwangsi border, their force could only receive 600 tons a month, and only 300 tons when they reached Liuchow.[167]

Nevertheless, the Japanese advance continued. More reinforcements were drafted from Manchuria, central China, and the homeland (table 2). These forces crossed into Kwangsi on September 10 and occupied Kweilin and Liuchow on November 11. In the meantime, the Japanese force in northern Vietnam crossed the border into China and succeeded in meeting with the Ichigō force on December 10, 1944, finally linking up Hunan, Kwangsi, and Vietnam. In late November, the Eleventh Army had ignored the restraining order of the Sixth Area Army and made a rapid thrust toward Kweichow. The farthest it went was Tushan, a town about 100 kilometers from Kweiyang, but there the momentum of Operation Ichigō was spent,[168] for China had thrown in its last resources, including Chungking's own garrison units to make a last-ditch defense. In early December, these units reached Tushan and forced the Japanese offensive to stop there. At this point, the Japanese force was still 300 kilometers from Chungking and 500 kilometers from Chengtu where the largest number of B-29s were based, but the terrain of northern Kweichow and southern Szechwan would have been much more difficult for the invaders to negotiate.

The Impact of Ichigō

On the eve of Operation Ichigō the Chinese National government had a paper strength of 3 million soldiers in combat formation of 300 divisions. During the early phase of the Honan campaign, Japanese intelligence took cognizance of the Chungking armies' propensity to avoid hard battle in order to minimize losses, to steer away from the enemy's strong units and jump on its weaker ones, to send inferior troops to the front and keep the elite units in the rear in order to attract enemy forces into penetrating deep and then releasing the elite units to annihilate the enemy in one blow.[169] But the Japanese strategists were determined not to play the Nationalist Chinese game and instructed the troops from the very beginning of the operation to seek out the Chinese elite units as the main targets and to destroy them first. As Japanese directives repeatedly pointed out, once the Chinese elite (central) units were broken, the rest (regional) would melt away. Consequently, wherever Japanese armies went, they concentrated on attacking the strongest Chinese forces in sight.[170]

In eight months of fighting, Operation Ichigō had inflicted enormous damage on the Chinese government forces.

According to Japanese Imperial Headquarters' estimate at the end of 1944, the Chinese lost over 23,000 tons of weapons and ammunition, or the equivalent of the equipment for forty divisions (table 3). Seven hundred fifty thousand troops had been put out of action through casualties or the destruction of their units. The loss of Hunan, a rich rice-producing province, together with other areas, had deprived the Chinese government of the capability to support about 500,000 troops. China's own war records reported that over 310,000 casualties had been sustained (table 4). This was nearly twice the casualties of 1943 and made 1944 the most costly year for the Chinese army in personnel loss since 1941, and possibly the most costly year in equipment loss since 1938.

In light of the Japanese strategy of deliberately seeking out and destroying the elite units, those that were loyal to the central government and those regional units that were more enthusiastic and competent in fighting (e.g., the Fourth Army of Kwangtung) were the most devastated. The only Chinese troops that escaped the wrath of Operation Ichigō were those stationed in China's northwest, including some central divisions under the command of Hu Tsung-nan.[171] By the end of 1944, the government no longer possessed an effective fighting machine for the defense of China proper, and the Japanese were probably correct in predicting that none could be revived in the next two years.[172]

The only bright spot in China's military performance in 1944 was the expeditionary force in Burma. After much wrangling and foot-dragging, the Chinese government finally placed six elite central armies under Gen-

TABLE 3
Japanese Estimates of Damage of Operation Ichigō to Chinese Forces (divisions)

	Honan Campaign		Hunan Campaign	
Damage Level	Central	Regional	Central	Regional
Completely destroyed	10	2	12	13
Seriously damaged	4	3	9	10
Total Chinese units participating	23	19	21	26

Source: Bōeichō, *Ichigō Sakusen (1) Kōnan no Kaisen* (Tokyo, 1967), pp. 377–78.

TABLE 4
Chinese Estimates of Damage of Operation Ichigō to Chinese Forces

Total Manpower	Honan Campaign (300,000 in 52 divisions)	Hunan Campaign (286,000 in 43 divisions)	Kwangsi Campaign (100,000 in 32 divisions)
No. of divisions in combat	45	34	27
Central government	26	15	12
Regional forces	19	19	15
Casualties[a]	"very extensive"	108,000	38,500
as % of total	—	38%	38.5%

Sources: Kuo-fang-pu, *KJCS: Yü-chang hui-chan* (Taipei, 1967); idem, *KJCS: Kwei-Liu hui-chan* (Taipei, 1967); idem, *KJCS: Ch'ang-Heng hui-chan* (Taipei, 1967); Ho Yin-ch'in, *Wartime Military Report* (Taipei, 1962).
a. Total casualties for China in 1944 were 311,276 officers and soldiers.

eral Stilwell's command and consented to his plan to retake Burma. On the opposite side, the Japanese had eight divisions in Burma, including the famous Eighteenth Division, which was the veteran of the first Burma campaign and the conquest of Singapore and one of the best in the imperial army. The campaign began with an attack by the India-based Chinese troops in November, 1943, which was subsequently joined by other Chinese forces operating from Yünnan. The Chinese delivered one blow after another against the Japanese and by mid-July, 1944, when the Japanese were compelled into a general retreat, their casualties had reached 85 to 90 percent for many units, and the dead numbered 72,000 out of a total force of about 100,000 men.[173] By any standard, the Chinese had scored a stunning victory over the Japanese, and the ground was cleared for the accelerated flow of American lend-lease material into China in the spring of 1945.

Conclusion

In this chapter, we have traced the course of the war through the major campaigns. We have seen how Nationalist China lost a respectable fighting force at the very outset of the war, and how its efforts to recreate one produced repeated frustration. But the worst came only at the very end. Barely eight months before acknowledging defeat to the Allied powers, Japan delivered a mortal blow to the Nationalist Chinese army from which she never had time to recover, in spite of the Burma victory. The consequence was that, unlike other Allies who became stronger as they approached victory, Nationalist China was in a weaker military position on the eve of victory than at any previous point during the war.

As related earlier, the Chungking government's own effort at military training in 1942–44 produced negligible results. Insofar as the American role was concerned, although the thirty division objective was pursued by General Wedemeyer after he succeeded General Stilwell, precious time had been lost and the war was over much sooner than had been expected. All told, by September 1945, the United States had supplied thirty-nine Chinese divisions with enough ordnance to make them operable in combat with the principal exception of artillery pieces. Most of the supplies came rather hastily in the last months of the war.

But the most crucial aspect of American assistance—training—was far from completion. While the original plan called for two thirteen-week training cycles, the second cycle was never implemented. Consequently, during the four years of American assistance in China, only three divisions had been trained to American standards in India, eleven divisions had completed thirteen weeks of training in China, and twenty-two other divisions had an average of less than six weeks of training.[174] The succession of military disasters that culminated in Operation Ichigō resulted in the fact that the Chungking government was left with no significant military strength except for this American-trained force deployed in the Burma campaign.

Nationalist China's military defeats could not but have created profound repercussions on Chinese politics as well. The KMT had come to depend heavily upon its military might to safeguard its political existence. But as we will see in the following chapters, as the KMT's military strength was progressively whittled away, its relationships with other powerful political-military groups also deteriorated sharply. The KMT proved incapable of either replacing the central-regional antagonism with a new sense of patriotism and national unity in the context of a war of national survival, or overcoming this antagonism by creating a new popular base of political power. These failures would directly contribute to the collapse of the KMT regime.

Chapter 3

Relations among Military Groups

When we study the Chinese role in the war, it is necessary to keep in mind the fundamental differences between China and other allies. While America and England had a set of well-developed and highly integrated political institutions backed by a unity of national will in their war endeavor, China under the Nationalist regime was lacking in both. Therefore, both the standards we apply to judge China's war performance and the terms by which we try to analyze it must be different. Instead of viewing China as a modern nation-state at war, it would be far more appropriate to see her as a political-military coalition at war. As much as in the Nanking era, China during the war remained a loosely knit polity composed of the KMT, the CCP, and a host of regional groups. The amounts of power each group commanded, as well as the ratio of power between them, were not only affected by the course of military events, but in themselves constituted reliable determinants of what strategies and objectives each of them would pursue in the war. The realization of this fact is crucial if we wish to fully explore the motivations of the human actors in the war and the reverberations of the war.

This chapter represents an effort to explain, from the perspective of power relations between the central government and other groups, why the Chinese adopted certain strategies and what consequences they produced. For this purpose, the materials will be presented in two parts: the first part will look into the KMT's relations with the regional militarists, and the second part will examine the KMT's relations with the Communists.

Before proceeding with our substantive discussion, a brief comment on terminology is in order here. In the literature on the relationships of modern Chinese military units, it has been common to use the terms *ti-hsi* (branch, direct descent) and *tsa-p'ai* (miscellaneous units) to describe them.[1] Both terms carry connotations of personal ties. In the years after Chiang's emergence as the top military figure of the KMT, the distinction between *ti-hsi* and *tsa-p'ai* became more analogous to the distinction between "central" and "regional" forces. Basically, the central forces consisted of Chiang's associates or students from the Whampoa Military Academy. The regional forces were those commanded by generals not from Whampoa. These included not only units of direct warlord descent, but also some units that had originally joined forces with Chiang at the outset of the Northern Expedition but subsequently opposed him. Since, to some people, *ti-hsi* connotes legitimacy and *tsa-p'ai* connotes poor quality, the following discussion will employ the terms "central" and "regional" to sharpen the latent antagonism between two major trends in modern Chinese politics.

Relations between the KMT and Regionalists

1937–39

In studying the war, one is impressed by the constant need of the Chinese government to engage in complex and delicate political maneuvers before military assignments can be issued. Nor can one fail to realize that the question of whether a particular strategy could work or not depended as much on diplomacy among the military leaders as on the rationality of the strategy itself. The distribution of military-political power among the Chinese commanders themselves was at least as important a variable as enemy strength in deciding the outcome of any campaign.

In this respect, the Chinese military performance in north and east China from the outset of war provided sharp contrasts to illustrate this point. As was mentioned before, prior to the war, north China was under the exclusive control of northern generals who commanded over half a million men.[2]

Once the war in north China began, the immediate problem confronting the central government was how to set up a command system acceptable to all these generals. In August, the central government organized north China into three war zones; Chiang assumed direct command over the first war zone located in the northern section of the Peking-Hankow railway. Yen Hsi-shan was given command of the second war zone located in the Peking-Suiyüan railway, and Feng Yü-hsiang was invited out of retirement to command the sixth war zone along the northern section of the Peking-Pukow railway, because many of the units in this area used to be his own subordinates.

However, even this diplomatic arrangement failed to yield the intended results. Chiang had firm control over his own armies but had great difficulty with other regional units.[3] Thus even though some of Chiang's armies performed well, they were affected by the breakdown of command and suffered serious casualties.[4]

In Shansi, Yen Hsi-shan's troops conducted themselves poorly. Even as members of the same Shansi military structure, the commanders distrusted one another. There was little coordination and lower level commanders habitually ignored the orders from their senior officers. Some of Yen's generals showed no inclination to fight and gave up critical positions in quick succession, resulting in the loss of large quantities of irreplaceable equipment.[5] The utter disregard of national interest so outraged public opinion that Yen was obliged to execute one of his most trusted commanders, Li Fu-ying. This act had little effect, however, and the Japanese had no trouble seizing what they wanted, including the provincial capital, Taiyüan.

The worst conditions existed in the sixth war zone. Here the government had counted on Feng's relations with his former lieutenants to allow him to exercise effective control over the area, but the result was disappointing. By October, Feng himself had become highly critical of the armies under his command and reported that these regional units distrusted each other as much as they distrusted the central government. Such distrust sharpened each unit's self-preservation instinct and produced a reluctance to coordinate operations with other units for fear that they would be deserted at the critical moment.[6]

The dismal performance of many units in north China handicapped the government from the beginning in its effort to create a command structure to which all regional armies would respond favorably. When even Feng and Yen failed to persuade their commanders to put up stiff resistance in defense of their home ground, the government naturally became worried about the increased difficulties it might have to face in working with the regional forces if the war should drag on for long. Since armies from Shansi, Manchuria, as well as Feng Yü-hsiang's old northwestern armies had the reputation of being the better-trained and better-equipped of regional forces during the pre-Nationalist era, their poor performance at the very outset of the war inevitably gravely undermined the government's confidence in having to cooperate with the less reputable armies of the interior provinces later on.[7]

These thoughts probably played no small part in the government's subsequent decision to maximize the impact of the Shanghai campaign on the Japanese in order to shorten the war. For, in sharp contrast to the conduct of northern troops, Chiang's own command system in the Shanghai area was operating fairly effectively. Facing great odds, Chinese troops in this area showed great tenacity, resourcefulness, and courage that not only evoked immense national pride among the Chinese, but greatly impressed their adversaries and the international bystanders. But the cost of the campaign was also devastating.

Chiang and his supporters have since argued that while the Shanghai campaign was a military setback, it was a political victory because it solidified the foundation for a protracted war of national resistance. While there is some merit in this view, it completely evades the issue of the enormous political repercussions the Shanghai campaign had on China's domestic power relationship. Thus, after the Nationalists' Provisional Congress of 1938 elected Chiang the party's director-general, or *tsung-ts'ai,* most observers accepted at face value the view that Chiang had been made a virtual dictator of the country. Nothing could be further from the truth, for this mode of analysis only helps to divert our attention from the crucial issue of the power structure of wartime China, and the disparity between nominal and real power in the Chinese political universe. For while Chiang's personal prestige was enormously enhanced by the Shanghai campaign, those having intimate knowledge of the political game would have realized how much his real power had diminished. In this sense, Chiang's elevation to the *tsung-ts'ai* position may reflect his attempt to exploit newly created institutional power to compensate for, or conceal, the lack of military power. But since the KMT's prewar policies had made military power the primary currency in Chinese politics, the appearance of power could not long substitute for the substance of power, even in the midst of a national war.

As Chiang was soon to realize, the first six months of the war would be the last time in the war that he could realistically pursue a military solution. Henceforth, the task of managing a united front among the diverse political-military elements within the Chinese camp would often prove to be more exasperating than the task of fighting the enemy. As the evolution of events in the coming years was to show, Chiang's loss of military power during the initial stage of war disrupted the domestic military balance so drastically that it changed the complexion of the entire wartime political process and created a host of issues which in time would overtax the government and eventually lead to its collapse.

As China entered the second year of war, the central government was confronted with two major tasks: to rebuild a loyal army quickly, and to devise ways to enlist the continued support of the regional forces. Since the overwhelming majority of Chinese armies were now in the hands of regional commanders, the success of the army-rebuilding program hung on the cooperation of these commanders.

At the outset of the army training program, General Ch'en Ch'eng pointed out in December, 1938, "the most important part [of the training program] is to eliminate the concept of private interests, to convert all armies into genuine national armies, and to thoroughly eliminate the erroneous notion of self-preservation and self-protection."[8] Such demands diametrically opposed the logic of Chinese military politics and, as previously pointed out, had little prospect of being enforced unless the government had superior force or changed the terms of the political process. For the majority of regional commanders were just as determined to preserve their military power as ever, and the relationships between the government and regional commanders remained more diplomatic than administrative. The outbreak of war had caused a dramatic increase of the power of the military over the civilian. Yet only four to five of the ten war zones were commanded by men who had never rebelled against the government, and even in these cases, the commanders had little authority over the personnel or discipline over their subordinates in the regional units.[9]

The same problem with authority existed on a higher level as well. Not only was there little the government could do to war zone commanders like Yen Hsi-shan, it also faced stiff resistance in many provinces. The case of Szechwan is particularly illuminating, since it was the bastion of China's war efforts and where one would expect the central government to have the firmest control. This relationship had grave implications, because if the central government could not impose its authority in the province where China's wartime capital was located, the situation in more remote provinces would become far more untenable. In fact, Szechwan's conflicts with the central government had been continuous since the government had first moved to the province.

Although the death of Liu Hsiang in 1938 seemed to offer the government a golden opportunity to seize administrative control over the province, its attempt to appoint Chang Ch'ün the new governor had to be abandoned quickly; instead, the provincial military leader Wang Tsan-hsü was given the post. After considerable maneuvering, Chiang's own man, General Liu Chih, was appointed garrison commander of Chungking in February, 1939, and three months later, Chiang was able to name his own man to be mayor of Chungking. Finally, in September 1939, Chiang succeeded in sending Wang Tsan-hsü to the front when he himself assumed the post as Szechwan's acting governor. Only then did he gain full control of the provincial governmental apparatus in the city of Chungking, but Ch'engtu and the other cities as well as the vast countryside of the province remained firmly in the grip of the local militarists.[10]

Thus, if we examine the Sino-Japanese military conflict in conjunction with central-regional relations, we find that the central government had basically three alternatives. The first was to concentrate on internal housecleaning operations to solidify the national will of resistance. The second was to avoid the internal housecleaning by stepping up attacks against the Japanese in the hope that central forces could move back to their prewar power base before central-regional relationships deteriorated too far. The third was to avoid both issues and concentrate on using guerrilla warfare to erode Japanese occupation.

The first alternative would have run the risk of reviving regional suspicion against the central government, but would have been absolutely essential if the war was to be executed effectively in the long run. To defeat Japan, the Chinese certainly needed to create a well-trained, well-maintained army under unified national command and imbued with high combat spirit. To achieve this objective, recalcitrant regional commanders needed to be brought into line from time to time, but more importantly, the central government had to devise new programs, provide new leadership to tackle the defects in the Chinese army on a broad spectrum, and either to inspire regional military leaders to accept central leadership or to subvert their power by enlisting the support of their soldiers or the general populace directly. Yet because the government lacked a new approach, its leaders viewed the housecleaning exclusively as a function of the relative military strength between central and regional groups and concluded in 1939 that they simply could not survive another divisive struggle of this nature.

The third alternative pointed to an uncertain future. Not only did the government's military leaders lack the necessary expertise in the theory and practice of guerrilla warfare, but there were increasing signs that such a strategy would produce a head-on collision between the KMT and the CCP in the occupied areas. The utmost concern for Chiang's government became one of averting a central-regional confrontation while carrying on the war. Under these circumstances, the second alternative looked to the Chungking government as the most attractive. If the Japanese could be defeated by a Chinese offensive, then the Nationalists' return to the mid-Yangtze area would eventually lead to the retaking of their former power base in the lower Yangtze and would render the issue of central-regional conflict entirely academic. It was this Nationalist reluctance to face the painful issue of forging a new central-regional military relationship that led Chiang to continue to pursue a purely military solution. Hence, it was decided to launch the winter offensive of 1939.

The 1939 Winter Offensive

Contrary to the argument by some that the 1939 winter offensive was no more than grist for the central government's propaganda mills to win international sympathy and financial support,[11] the evidence suggests that it reflected a major Chinese strategic decision and a strong expectation that it would work. Since this strategy reflected the KMT's attempt to escape from the unpleasant political constraints that would have to be coped with if its regime were marooned in the interior provinces for a long time, the failure of the offensive should also be recognized as having had a profound impact on the KMT's subsequent thinking on the war and its own conduct of it.

Hindsight suggests that the government's sanguine expectation concerning the winter offensive ran into hard political-military realities. Brushing aside the caution of some lieutenants for a delay in launching the campaign or a curtailment of its scope,[12] Chiang believed that he could still inspire his generals into action and confidently ordered the offensive to proceed as scheduled.

But such beliefs were proven erroneous by the actual conduct of his generals during the offensive. Thus, for instance, prior to the offensive, Chiang had told the commander of the third war zone, General Ku Chu-t'ung, to give his field commanders broad powers as long as they were willing to attack the enemy aggressively. But once the campaign got underway, the commanders stubbornly refused to seize the initiative. All told, the third war zone mobilized fourteen divisions with artillery support to attack one single Japanese division, but the commanders gave up fighting after only three days. In the second war zone, Yen Hsi-shan's troops hardly made a move against the Japanese at all.[13] Typically, most commanders still valued their equipment more than the lives of their soldiers,

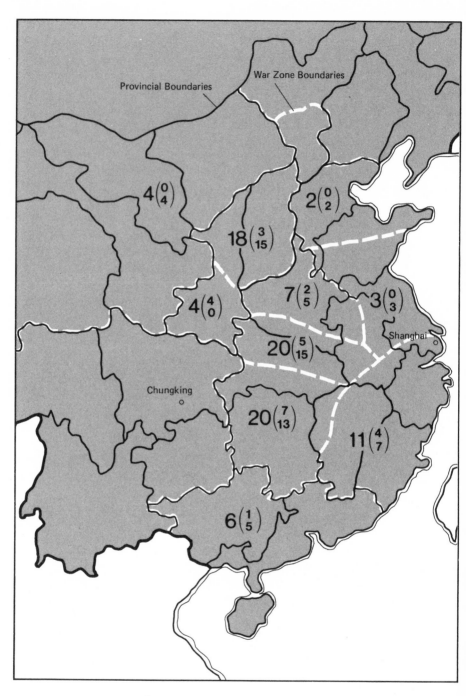

Map 2 Distribution of China's combat units (armies) in war zones during the 1939 winter offensive. Top number in parenthesis refers to Chiang's armies, bottom figure refers to regional armies. Total armies: Chiang 26, regional 69. (Data from *KJCS: erh-shih pa-nien tung-chi kung-shih.*)

or they continued to adhere to the ultraconservative tactic of concentrating a large force to attack a fixed enemy position in explicit violation of the instruction of the Chinese high command. Most troops were reluctant to move against the enemy unless they saw friendly units moving with them on both flanks.[14]

By committing himself to the winter offensive and expecting it to turn the tide against the enemy, Chiang made a supreme mistake in judging the reality of power in both political and military terms (map 2). In 1938–39, Chiang was much weaker militarily than in 1936–37, while many of his regional rivals had kept their power intact, which means that the latter had even less fear of reprisal from him. Even in those cases where the generals had been inspired by patriotism and chose to obey the central government, it would have taken a long time to change their lifelong habits of troop management and strategic and tactical predilections. Yet in his eagerness to reverse the trend of the war, Chiang overlooked these fundamental realities; with misjudgment and misconceptualization, combined with lack of preparation, the verdict of failure was inescapable.

The Aftermath of the Winter Offensive and a Summary of the 1937–40 Period

In the literature on Nationalist history, some have argued that once the primary purpose of the Shanghai campaign to invite immediate foreign intervention proved unrealizable, the Chinese adopted a holding pattern to wait for the eventual intervention by foreign powers. Such an interpretation does not take the 1939 winter offensive into sufficient account. For what we see is a Chiang Kai-shek whose definition of a long war was not really a very long one, and who was naive enough to think that he could bring about a military solution to the war on the basis of a temporary cooperation between his own loyal troops and those from regional backgrounds. Apparently Chiang still believed that it was possible to pursue a military solution to the war without undertaking any fundamental restructuring of the central-regional relationship.

Among the factors contributing to the failure of the winter offensive, the fact that Chinese generals would not and could not fight was to have a shattering impact on the central government's view of the future course of the war. It was made clear that after a year's preparation, and the presumed mobilization of some 50 percent of China's combat units, the offensive simply failed to materialize. Presiding over the Liuchow conference in late

February, 1940, to review the winter offensive, Chiang, after mentioning insufficient training and preparation as contributing factors, pinned the main blame on the confusion of command and the laxity of discipline perpetrated by the generals and called the offensive the "greatest blot of the National Revolutionary Army since the beginning of the war."[15]

More than was generally realized, the 1939 winter offensive was a watershed event in Chinese wartime history. The debacle led the government to conclude that since the armies in existence were incapable of mounting a massive offensive against the enemy, China would have to train a new army whose loyalty to the Chungking government would be absolutely insured. But after the debacle, such a policy of seeking military victory looked more and more impracticable from Chungking's perspective. For success, the creation of such a brand new and loyal army had to be preceded by the resolution of the proper relationship between the central government and the regional forces, as well as the extension of the central government's territorial and administrative control over the interior provinces. The Chungking leaders simply never found the formula to achieve these goals in the 1930s, nor did they know how to proceed after 1939. Their impotence in facing up to these challenges signalled the end of the phase of enthusiastic execution of the war.

The failure of the winter offensive also seemed to have the unfortunate effect of turning the government's underestimation of Japanese strength into overestimation. While the Chinese leaders in Chungking habitually emphasized the rapid deterioration of Japanese military strength with each passing month before 1939, the situation was reversed after that. It would become a recurrent theme for the Chinese to stress how much stronger the enemy had become in firepower and combat effectiveness, and how much more assistance the Chinese would need before they could ever mount another offensive against the enemy. As will be seen in greater detail later, in the years after 1940, domestic power calculations would again come to the fore in Chungking's conduct of the war.

More immediately, the greatest concern to the central government was probably the unfavorable balance of power between it and the regional leaders. Nominally, China had about four million men under arms at this time, organized in over 300 divisions, and Japanese military analysts credited the central government with controlling roughly one-third of these divisions as compared to two-thirds in the hands of regional commanders.[16] Yet of the troops identified as belonging to the central government, no more than about 30 divisions (500,000 men) could be considered loyal central troops, and the remainder as subsidiary or marginal units.[17] This unfavorable ratio of six to one assumed new significance when the government had to shelve its plan for a quick victory and to confront anew the issue of how to relate to the various political-military groups in the regions in a long war.

The Emergence of a New Relationship, 1941–45

When Japan attacked Pearl Harbor on December 7, 1941, China had been at war for 1,613 days. Finally, the United States became an ally of China, and the light at the end of a long tunnel seemed in sight. The central government promptly declared war against the Axis powers and sealed its destiny with the Western powers.

But the sense of euphoria was short-lived. The failure of the Soviet Union to join the Allied powers in declaring war against Japan was the first disappointment. In early January, 1942, Sino-British relations also soured temporarily when the British commandeered strategic materials stored at Rangoon that were earmarked for China's use. The Burma road, China's lifeline, was cut off by the Japanese on April 2.[18]

But most devastating to the government was the serious damage done in May, 1942, to its last elite troops, the Fifth and Sixth armies (the only two central elite units salvaged from the 1930s German training program) in Burma, from where they were driven into India and thus totally cut off from China. By July 7, 1942, when China commemorated the fifth anniversary of the war, it was in a gloomier mood than ever before.

Under these circumstances, the central government gradually realized that it had to tackle long-term problems like general mobilization, grain collection, and the stabilization of currency and price control, in order to survive many more years of fighting.[19] Since the attitudes of the militarists were crucial to China's continued resistance efforts, foremost among the government's concerns was keeping the regional military leaders in rein, to prevent them from interfering with the new programs without antagonizing them or upsetting the fragile anti-Japanese united front.

In the course of 1942–45, the Chungking government followed a two-pronged policy, both parts being essentially military in nature. First, the government tried to control the regionalists through two mechanisms that I shall call internal control and external control. Second, the government tried to introduce certain military reforms to upgrade the quality of Chungking's own army.

The Government's Control Policies

Internal Control—Political Work in the Army

It is well known that the very first attempt by the KMT to exercise internal control in the army was the political commissar system borrowed from the Soviet Red Army during the days when the KMT army was first created at Whampoa in 1924–25.[20] The original objective of introducing the political commissar system was to promote political education, to instill a national revolutionary spirit, raise fighting capacity, and solidify discipline.[21] Clearly, the primary responsibilities of the commissar were positive in nature: to transform the nature of the army, to rid it of the lifestyle and mentality of an armed, roving band under a warlord's personal management, and to turn it into a politicized instrument of revolutionary violence. To the extent that the issue of control arose, it was considered a secondary and passive goal, that is, to make sure that the revolutionary party, and not self-seeking warlords, would retain firm control of the guns.

Consequently, there would be a division of labor. The commander would be responsible for combat operational decisions; the commissar would be responsible for ideological rectitude and the physical and psychological well-being of the soldiers. They were to make sure that soldiers would be well-fed, well-clothed, properly trained and disciplined, well-treated by their officers, given medical treatment when wounded, and guaranteed a decent burial if killed in action. Finally, in the event of incapacitation or betrayal of the commander, the commissar would be empowered to exercise direct command over the troops. However, the function of control was clearly subordinate to the functions of management and ideological indoctrination, because if the latter were satisfactorily performed, then the need to perform the former presumably would not arise.

As more regional armies climbed on the KMT bandwagon during the Northern Expedition, their commanders were required to accept political commissars appointed by the party headquarters. In many cases, this requirement led to constant tension and clashes between the regional commanders and the commissars.[22] The fact that the Communists had gained a dominant position in the political departments alarmed not only traditional regionalists but also Chiang Kai-shek himself. Consequently, during the 1927 coup and purge of the Communists, Chiang moved to abolish the political department and the whole system of political work in his own army.

In the 1930s, in line with the KMT's new strategy of devoting 70 percent of their effort to political work and 30 percent to military work in the anti-Communist campaigns, political work in the army was revived under a political training department, organized by Ho Chung-han.[23] But beside the provinces officially designated as anti-Communist bandit-suppression areas, the KMT would only send political workers to those units whose commanders had granted the KMT permission to do so. However, by June, 1935, under Japanese pressure, all political workers were withdrawn along with the regular party organs from north China.[24]

Therefore, whatever political work there existed before 1937 was conducted very haphazardly and was dependent on the good will of regional commanders. At the outbreak of war, there were altogether only 368 political work teams with 3,421 workers for the entire army.[25] Even when a national political department (*cheng-chih pu*) was created in February, 1938, the initial purpose was to spread anti-Japanese feelings among officers and men rather than to use it as an instrument to integrate the armies, and regional and Communist workers were both allowed to participate in political work.[26]

It was not until March, 1939, that political work in the army was stepped up. But the party rather than the government was given a dominant role in political work, and the approach of the party was more formalistic than constructive. For instance, KMT organs were ordered revived down to the company level, officers and men were recruited into the party en masse, performance in KMT work became the major factor in determining the promotion of political workers, all cadets in military academies were required to join the party within one month of their enrollment, and non-KMT officers in the army were denied promotion.[27] To say the least, such policies aroused the intense fear among many commanders that the eventual beneficiary of political work would be Chiang's party and not they.

Soon, the deterioration of KMT-CCP relations led to the exclusion of pro-Communist elements from the political department, and political work in the army not only came under the sole control of the KMT, but took on an almost exclusive dimension—to guard against the potentially disloyal tendencies among the armies, particularly the regional armies. The collective security system was introduced into every squad. Soldiers were organized into a surveillance network in which one activist from every squad would spy on the rest of the squad.[28] This system was supplemented by Tai Li's Bureau of Military Statistics, whose agents permeated all military units. Official figures indicate that the organization of political work had become full grown by 1941 when the number of party committees on the company level exceeded 20,000, with many officers and men compelled to join the party.[29]

These growth figures on paper should not mislead us into thinking that political and party work in the army had improved their effectiveness. In fact, many factors existed to hamper the government's attempt to use political and party work to control armies.

Like other governmental functions, political work also suffered from a serious shortage of financial support. Most armies were underpaid, and political departments were no exception. Even in late 1943, each party committee on and above the divisional level or its equivalent received about C$80 per month to support its activities, an amount which was absolutely meaningless at the time. Below the regimental level, there was no independent budget.[30]

Personnel presented another problem. On December 1, 1938, General Ch'en Ch'eng indicated that the government planned to produce tens of thousands of political workers for the army before the end of 1941.[31] This objective was never realized. As late as 1944, only 15 percent of the 21,386 political workers above company levels engaged in full-time work,[32] and below the company level, there were no full-time workers. In July, 1945, General Chang Chih-chung, Minister of the Political Department, indicated that the entire political force in the Chinese army fell far short of the 40,000 workers stipulated in the table of organization. The mounting casualties, high priority assigned to combat duties, and disinterest in political work made understaffing of the political department a perennial problem.[33] Consequently, political workers were mostly drawn perfunctorily from among the existing officers and men within a unit. Included were men who had little or no special training, and whose ability to lift morale, to inspire loyalty, and to enforce discipline was entirely unreliable.

Since the political workers were planted primarily to put troops under surveillance, the strongest resistance to such work came, not unexpectedly, from the commanding officers who correctly recognized the threat posed by such a system. They resented having an in-house spy ring that reported their every move to the central government, and they genuinely feared that the political workers would sow dissension among the rank and file and undercut their power base from below. Therefore, whenever possible, they either tried to isolate the government-appointed workers in their units, or they would appoint their own men to serve as commissars in an exofficio capacity.[34]

Overall, the attempt to use the political commissar system to spy on regional commanders yielded some results, although of a negative and limited sort. Their presence among the armies served as an effective deterrent against acts of open disloyalty. After the establishment of Wang Ching-wei's government in Nanking, there were some significant defections to his side. One might surmise that, given the pessimism that prevailed in China after 1940, defections by regional commanders might have been more numerous had the central government not applied pressure through its military secret police and the commissars.

Such an internal control system could achieve few positive results. Given the highly fluid and ambiguous battlefield situation, commanders of military units still had a lot of autonomy, short of open rebellion against the central government. Many commanders achieved a tacit agreement with the Japanese not to attack each other, evaded hard fighting when pressed by the government into battle, and interfered with the process of civil government in their area almost at will. The internal control system was powerless to correct these deviations. The internal control also failed to improve the quality of the army. Political workers in the army made no visible contribution toward the betterment of the soldiers' livelihood. Wanton abuses of soldiers by their officers remained as prevalent as ever; discipline was generally poor, and even some of the best units suffered from serious lapses of discipline and aroused intense popular discontent. Very few armies ever attempted to do political work among the masses; both on the battlefields and in the rear, the armies remained isolated, alienated, and aloof from the general populace. In most cases, the Chinese people feared the Chinese armies just a shade less than they feared the Japanese.

It is apparent that the Chungking government engaged in a misguided effort in stressing the control and surveillance functions of the political workers to the exclusion of efforts aimed at the fundamental transformation of the Chinese army. The smooth functioning of political work must be predicated on a certain degree of cooperation between the combat officers and political workers. But the policy of the central government was openly discriminatory against non-KMT officers even when they were patriotic Chinese. The policy created an adversary relationship between the government and regionalists who either did everything possible to thwart political work or joined the party in name but retained autonomy in reality.

But in this acute confrontation between the government and the regional commanders, the soldiers were basically left out. Political work could have made a serious contribution in promoting the integration of the national army had its major emphasis been placed on arousing the combat spirit of the soldiers by informing them about what they were fighting for, protecting soldiers against physical abuse by their superiors, improving the livelihood of soldiers through better clothing, diet, medical attention, recreational activities, and insuring that affairs were conducted in conformity with the principles of honesty, fairness, efficiency, and discipline. If the central government had taken advantage of a national war to gain direct access to the soldiers in the various military units through its political workers and had performed these tasks, much progress might have been made in improving the political consciousness and the combat efficiency of the country's soldiers. Under these conditions, the warlord-type regional commanders would either have lost their followings or have been forcibly integrated into a national command structure.

External Control

Before the war, the government's repertoire of means of exercising external control over regional units on the whole was fairly limited. The government had little power over units that were protected by strong armies, difficult terrain, or remote location. What the government could do was to use either money or position to induce regional commanders to give their nominal allegiance to the central government, or to buy the defections of their subordinates. On rare occasions, the government could use actual force to punish disobedient commanders.

Once the war broke out, the relationship between the central government and the regional commanders underwent some subtle changes. The presence of a common enemy imposed strong inhibitions against either side starting a civil war. The regional commanders realized that the onus would be placed squarely on them if they openly defied the authority of the central government. On the other hand, it was no longer rational for the central government to undermine the combat strength of regional armies. By and large, during the first two to three years, the government was interested in enlisting regional forces to help it execute the war instead of subverting these forces. As a result, there were few outcries from regional forces alleging willful discrimination by the central government.

It was the central government's new perception of the seeming endlessness of the war after 1940, coupled with its frustration at the poor combat performance of some regional forces and the ineffectiveness of political work in these forces, that directed its attention to the issue of how to coexist with the regional forces in the interior. In power calculation, it became a major concern for the government to try tipping the balance in favor of the Whampoa group in relation to the regionalists. To achieve this objective, several means were employed. One was to give preferential treatment to the units led by Whampoa officers, i.e., when regional forces suffered casualties and lost equipment, they would not be adequately replenished. The central government would keep their designations and probably allow them to draw full pay for their paper strength, but in time they would simply wither out of existence. Another method was to break up existing regional units whenever an excuse existed and assign their components to other units. At times, the components would be absorbed into a loyal unit, while at other times, the components from several different regional forces would be put into a new unit so as to erase any regional identity. Finally, the central government could plant Whampoa graduates in regional armies and quickly promote them into command posts to seize control over regional forces.

But these methods were not always effective in eroding the loyalty structure in regional armies for several reasons. First, it was a standard wartime practice for the conscripts of one province to replenish that province's troops on a priority basis. Not infrequently, the central government machinery was entirely bypassed, and the regional commanders could reach an understanding with their own provincial conscription agencies for a direct supply of conscripts. Second, as armies had great power over civilian government, regional commanders short of arms did not have to rely on the central government but could obtain arms stockpiled by the people or from the black market.[35] Since the Peiyang period, there were always a lot of arms among the general public, and the fluid conditions of the war made any regional commander interested in buying arms able to do so. Third, during wartime, regional leaders competed to set up branch schools of the Central Army Officers' Academy in their respective provinces. These branch schools in fact became parts of the regional system and not outposts for the central government. Their graduates were assigned to their regional forces and could not be relied upon to promote the interests of the central government. In fact, graduates from the main campus and officers planted by the central government were often isolated and discriminated against if assigned to the regional forces.[36] The sheer mass of regional forces made the small number of graduates loyal to the central government an ineffective instrument of control.

As a result, unless the regionalists had the misfortune of being soundly defeated in a battle, they were relatively immune from the subtle forms of control by the central government. Over time, these tactics of the central government also became counterproductive because they taught the regional forces to evade orders and hard fighting against the enemy. Once subtlety failed, the central government found it necessary to resort to the threat of force to prevent regional forces from stepping out of line.

Nowhere was the central government's design to use implied force against potentially disloyal regional troops more apparent than in the pattern of troop deployment in the last four years of the war. As we discussed in the previous chapter, up to 1939–40, the overwhelming majority of central elite units were concentrated at the front facing the strongest enemies. After 1940, the government became more conservative in its use of force; it was content to hold the line and would only order limited offensives to change it. As it turned out, this coincided with the Japanese decision to scale down their attacks against the Chinese front. As later reflected in a document from Imperial Headquarters, ''Policy toward Chungking,'' dated May, 1942, the new Japanese policy after 1940–41 was made up of three components—planting a spy ring in Chungking to destabilize the Chinese central government, reassessing the peace terms to bring about China's capitulation, and promoting Japanese-Chinese racial harmony to drive Western influence out of Asia at the conclusion of the war.[37] Thus to the extent that offensives were launched at all, they were for the purpose of seizing or destroying the autumn harvest, disrupting transportation, or hampering the progress of the training program of the Chinese forces.

In time, the Chinese government recognized the new Japanese strategy and responded with a redeployment of its own forces. There were two components to its new approach. The first component, a plan which was not new, was to pry provincial forces from their home bases. The units from Szechwan, Kwangsi, and Kwangtung had been called up to participate in the campaigns in the lower Yangtze areas at the very outset of the war. This was logical as long as the battlefront was in the coastal provinces, but this practice gained a new dimension when the front was pushed back into the interior provinces. Instead of exploiting the strong regional sentiments of the provincial units to defend their own home, they were

permanently kept in distant provinces.[38] Meanwhile, the regional troops
from north China that had lost their home provinces (i.e., Feng Yü-hsiang
or Manchurian) were kept in other northern provinces and never allowed to
enter the southwest. By these measures, Chungking managed to keep potentially unreliable troops as far away from its site of power as possible.

The second component of the new approach was the creation of new
units and/or the redeployment of units loyal to the central government to fill
the vacuum left in the interior provinces. This, in turn, triggered a race
between the central government and the regional forces insofar as the
number of troops were concerned. In this context, it is relevant to note that
China had slightly less than 200 divisions in 1937, but had 300–350 divisions toward the end of the war. This numerical expansion became an
object of much criticism by both Chinese and Americans because China's
arsenals and other resources obviously could not keep them well supplied.
In fact, we might view the central government and regional groups as
engaged in a race to balance each other by either creating new units or
resuscitating old ones. The lack of central control over troop expansion is
attested to by the existence in any given year of an inordinately large
number of divisions bearing the designations ''new'' or ''temporary.''
These units weaved in and out of existence from year to year, or month to
month, and frequently even the names of their commanders remained
unknown to the central government. The net result was that the central
government and regional commanders were both victimized by the ''numbers illusion'' and created a force far too large for the nation's good.

Faced with this challenge, the central government, after 1940–41,
made sure that its own loyal units would be well-supported and assigned to
strategic areas for domestic political purposes. In this regard, government
policy was given a new sense of urgency by the establishment of Wang
Ching-wei's Nanking regime in March, 1940. In the following years,
Wang's regime provided a haven for regional commanders who felt pressure from either the Japanese, the Chinese Nationalists, or the Communists, but who were reluctant to collaborate directly with the Japanese
army. The defection rate was accelerated in 1942–43 as Japanese troops
turned their attention to pacification in the occupied area. By August,
1943, a total of 600,000 Chinese troops, almost all from regional backgrounds, had defected to Wang's government.[39] In the meantime, the
ambiguous relationship between some other regional forces and Japan was
quite worrisome. After the spring of 1940, Yen Hsi-shan in Shansi was

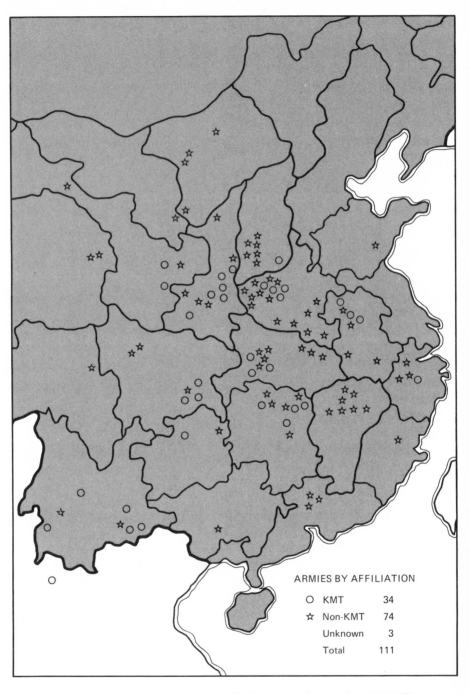

ARMIES BY AFFILIATION

○	KMT	34
☆	Non-KMT	74
	Unknown	3
	Total	111

Map 3 Distribution of Chinese army headquarters, September, 1943. (Data from *Ch'üan-kuo chün-tui tang-pu chu-ti-piao* [n.p., 1943.])

widely suspected of keeping a dialogue with his Japanese adversaries through civilian intermediaries.[40] If Shansi were lost, the Chinese position in north China would be greatly weakened.

This trend inevitably alarmed the Chungking government and further strengthened its decision to deploy loyal troops to check on regional troops as an insurance against future defections. By 1943, this pattern had become quite obvious (map 3). Although the Sino-Japanese front had changed little in these years, the location of the KMT's loyal units changed considerably. Specifically, we now find that (1) regional forces were spread out in all provinces; (2) troops from the same regional background were kept as far apart as possible; (3) wherever there were regional forces, there would be some central forces nearby; and (4) the deployment of both regional and central forces no longer have a close and distinct relationship to the intensity of the Japanese threat. In this respect, the Nationalist blockade of the CCP border regions was only a more flagrant case of the government's use of loyal troops for surveillance but by no means a unique one. The same Nationalist troops blockading the Communists were also there to keep a watchful eye on Moslem forces in Kansu, Tsinghai, and Ningsia, and Nationalist troops elsewhere certainly were watching the regional units in their respective areas. Inevitably, this new situation created serious ramifications for China's political and military options in the last years of the war.

One would imagine that, given the fact that central government units were ordinarily better equipped and better trained, it would make sense to deploy them in a concentrated form in the provinces of Honan, Hunan, and Hupei, as this was the area where the Japanese most logically would attack. If the central armies were exclusively assigned to guard these pathways, the Chinese would have greater strategic latitude. They could either defend their positions in depth, attack the approaching enemy from the flanks, or envelope the enemy from all sides. But when these units were strung out over long distances, the only way to use them was to demand that each of them defend its own assigned position without any expectation of reinforcements from neighboring units. For in fact, in the last two years of the war, the Chinese central government's armies were not only combat forces, but occupation forces. The incompatibility of these two tasks compelled the government to revert to the earlier strategy of positional warfare and once again to demand its generals to make a stand to the death every time they were attacked.

But this approach not only caused the Chinese to surrender the elements of mobility, surprise, and initiative in attack, it also enabled the enemy to choose the time and place to wipe out each individual Chinese defender with a modestly superior force. Furthermore, it created the danger of the collapse of an entire front if some Chinese units failed to stop the enemy at critical points. The rout of the Chinese army in Honan in 1944 was due in no small measure to this factor. The wide dispersion of better combat units also deprived China of the option of capitalizing on its numerical advantage and encouraged some war zones to develop into defacto semi-independent satrapies. The only seeming advantage from the government's point of view was that it also made it impossible for the Japanese to end the war with one single decisive blow, or for the regional generals to take advantage of a major crisis to seize control over the central government.

Another harmful consequence of this policy was that it further reinforced the conservative mentality of the commanders. Even conscientious commanders acquired, over time, the belief that their only responsibility was to hold off the enemy from their assigned territories and not to mount aggressive attacks to regain lost ones. The longer the army units stayed in a fixed territory, the more they got settled into a routine way of life. As Chinese troops had traditionally had to shift for themselves, soldiers tried their best to live off the localities in which they had been stationed. Commanders brought in their wives and began to raise families; they lived outside the barracks and lost touch with their soldiers. They were also constantly exposed to the temptation of exploiting their power and position for private gains. It became a common practice for officers to interfere with the civil administration in such matters as taxation, conscription, and personnel. In the worst cases, commanders profited directly from illicit trade with the occupied areas and thus developed a vested interest in a peaceful and undisturbed front. All these factors could not but be extremely detrimental to the offensive spirit of the troops involved.

Worse still, over the years even Chungking's own loyal troops entrusted with the assignment of checking on other unreliable troops were similarly corrupted in the process. Whereas in the early phase of the war, the central government usually could exercise tight control over its loyal units, that control was seriously eroded as the war went on. Even though these loyal troops remained loyal, their morale and discipline sagged and their combat effectiveness declined. In this sense, the government's policy actually backfired, for it reduced the overall military strength of its own troops.

Equally ominous was the emergence of factionalism that threatened to undermine the high degree of solidarity that once marked the Whampoa group. Before 1940, when members of this group were transferred frequently from one theater to another to fight the Japanese, they had little else to be concerned with. But after 1940, with the slowing down of the tempo of war and the tendency of their being assigned fixed territories for long periods of time, they came to acquire political and economic interests just like those of the regionalists. Ties developed under these new conditions among lesser leaders eventually formed the basis of factions inside the Whampoa group. While most senior members of the Whampoa group (e.g., Ch'ien Ta-chün, Liu Chih, and Chiang Ting-wen) steered clear of cultivating any personal following, there were at least three men who did cultivate such following.

The first informal faction evolved around Ch'en Ch'eng, whose power was built on the Fourteenth and Eighteenth armies he led during the 1930s. These units expanded during the war and were stationed in the ninth war zone when Ch'en Ch'eng was its commander. Well-known Nationalist generals who were identified as members of this faction included Lo Cho-ying, Fang T'ien, Ch'üeh Han-ch'ien, Li Chi-lan, and Hu Lien.

The second informal faction evolved around General T'ang En-po whose followers grew out of his Thirteenth Army. In time this expanded to eight armies and his main followers included Ch'en Ta-ch'ing, Shih Chüeh, Wang Chung-lien, and Chang Yao-ming. Until 1944, T'ang's base was in Honan.

The third faction was built from scratch by General Hu Tsung-nan after his First Army was decimated in the Shanghai campaign. During the 1940s, Sian became the center of Hu's power. At the height of his power, he controlled about twenty-seven divisions. Among his chief supporters were Li Wen, Li T'ieh-chün, Lo Lieh, Sheng Wen, and Yüan P'u. In addition, Hu also controlled a number of military schools and was generally believed to receive good supplies from the government.[41]

Although these generals constituted only a small numerical minority among the Whampoa graduates, they commanded the bulk of the government's military power, and their factional activities greatly compromised the cohesiveness of the group in the 1940s. While all of them remained loyal to the government, among themselves the relationships were often so strained as to call for Chiang's frequent personal intervention to maintain an equilibrium among these contending factions.

To sum up, in spite of the central government's attempt to employ methods of internal and external control over regional armies, the overall results were counterproductive. Indecisive efforts to reform the army and improve its combat effectiveness produced negligible results. The goals of undermining the regional character of many units and of increasing their combat effectiveness were often conflicting. When faced with such a contradiction, the central government seemed more interested in control than reform. Eventually, the central government's policy not only counted many regional units out of the Sino-Japanese military equation, but corrupted and paralyzed some of its own best troops.

The Government's Military Training Program

The preceding discussion of the failure of the central government to develop a sound political relationship with the regionalists also provides us with some insight into the failure of the government to implement military training, which in turn damaged the Sino-American alliance.

Although the United States began her alliance with China without any intention of influencing the latter's domestic politics, the disappointing performance of Chungking's army in the war eventually led the United States to adopt policies that perforce made domestic intervention a prerequisite of increased Chinese war participation. During the four years of this alliance, no other American policy had greater potential of upsetting the power distribution in Chinese domestic politics than America's suggestions on military reforms.

Once the objective of training the thirty divisions was set in early 1942, General Stilwell proceeded to make his specific recommendations to weed out incompetent officers, to bring all units up to strength, and to pool all available weapons to these divisions. At the time, Stilwell believed that a compact and effective army was so obviously in China's interest that Chiang, "with the U.S. on his side and back him" could not possibly fail to grasp this great opportunity.[42]

Yet, quite to the contrary, the Chungking government was apprehensive about these plans and used numerous pretexts to slow down or back out of its prior commitments. Thus although the Nationalists had agreed to create a force in preparation for the anticipated second Burma campaign (the Y-force), they were slow in naming the units for training or bringing them up to the promised strength. Whenever the Japanese mounted an attack, the Chinese would seize it as a pretext to divert the recruits away from the training program. In a letter to General George C. Marshall on

July 23, 1943, Stilwell diagnosed Chiang's lack of interest in army reform as stemming from his "fear of a challenge to his authority, as well as to his belief that air power is decisive and there is no use putting time on ground troops. Otherwise, he could not complacently take the terrible risk of leaving his army in its deplorable condition."[43]

While Stilwell might have been partially right, there was another angle that he did not take into sufficient account, namely, the power calculations of the central government with reference to its relationship with other regional groups. For within China's uninstitutionalized and fragmented political system, the army under Chungking's nominal control was but a loose coalition of semi-independent military forces held together by personal loyalties or regional sentiments, endowments, material rewards, or threats of reprisal. Many orders were not transmitted through the chain of command and expected to be obeyed; they were issued only after elaborate negotiation between the central government and the commanders or their representatives in Chungking.

Furthermore, from the Chungking government's perspective, the political and military realities in China had changed so much during the first four years of the war that the government was even less able to impose the suggested reforms on the generals through the regular bureaucratic channels than before. After 1942, the paramount interest of the Chungking government precisely concerned how it could exploit American assistance to build up its own military forces to reverse the unfavorable power relations with the regionalist leaders and reestablish a semblance of institutional authority over them.

But as Stilwell's recommendations were repeatedly ignored by the Chungking government, he finally concluded in November, 1943, that the only way to carry out the urgently needed reforms was for the United States to demand that Chiang surrender his full powers of command over the Chinese army.[44] Although Roosevelt originally resisted the suggestion, he was alarmed by the Chinese defeats during Operation Ichigō. The upshot was the transmittal of the famous letter to Chiang on July 6, 1944, in which the American president not only lectured the Chinese leader on how to handle the crisis at hand, but also presented his prescription by demanding Chiang to delegate full authority to General Stilwell.[45]

Of course the Chinese government was incapable of surrendering to the American general powers it hardly possessed. As Chiang's own political status within China vis-à-vis other military groups depended heavily upon his being treated by America as China's leader, he certainly had every interest in pretending that he indeed still had enormous power inside the country all during his dealings with the Americans. Yet when faced with an unequivocal American demand to deliver such power, even Chiang could not keep up his pretense. Finally, Chiang had to reveal his situation in a letter to Roosevelt dated July 8.

> While I fully agree with the principle of your suggestion that directly under me General Stilwell be given the command of all Chinese Army and American troops in this theater of war, I like to call your attention to the fact the Chinese troops and their internal political conditions are not as simple as those in other countries. Furthermore, they're not as easily directed as the limited number of Chinese troops who are now fighting in North Burma. Therefore, if this suggestion were carried out in haste it would not only fail to help the present war situation here but would also arouse misunderstanding and confusion which would be detrimental to Sino-American cooperation. This is the real fact of the situation and in expressing my views on your exacting and sincere suggestion, I have not tried to use any misleading or evasive language. Hence, I feel that there must be preparatory period in order to enable General Stilwell to have absolute command of the Chinese troops without any hindrance. In this way I shall not disappoint you in your expectation.
>
> I very much hope that you will be able to dispatch an influential personal representative who enjoys your complete confidence, is given with full power and has a far-sighted political vision and ability, to constantly collaborate with me and he may also adjust the relations between me and General Stilwell so as to enhance the cooperation between China and America. You will appreciate the fact that military cooperation in its absolute sense must be built on the foundation of political cooperation.[46]

This extremely revealing message marked the first time that Chiang ever committed to paper an admission to having problems with internal political groups. The message amounted to a frank admission that he was not on top of things in China—as frank an admission of his domestic weakness as probably any self-respecting national leader could be expected to make to an ally. Without naming the regional forces, Chiang indicated that he really did not have the power to tell his generals to obey Stilwell and pleaded for time to put things in order. Because he knew that the situation had become so desperate, Chiang begged the president to send a man in whom he would have complete confidence. Pointedly, Chiang preferred it to be a man with political vision and ability, and further observed that military cooperation must be built on the basis of political cooperation,

Chiang's greatest problem area. Chiang was really forced to make this highly humiliating confession of impotence only because the gravity of the Ichigō crisis and the Sino-American diplomatic impasse convinced him that nothing short of such a frank confession would assure him of continued American goodwill and assistance.

Soon afterward, Chiang also despatched H. H. K'ung to visit President Roosevelt to strike a bargain: that troops of questionable political reliability be excluded from Stilwell's command and therefore by implication be denied the American material assistance that would eventually flow from that command. To this, Roosevelt gave a firm no on August 21.[47]

While the Chinese were still vacillating, another letter from Roosevelt arrived on September 19. It repeated all the arguments that Stilwell had made to Chiang and warned that if China did not give all-out support to the Burma campaign, ''we will lose all chance of opening land communications with China and immediately jeopardize the air route over the Hump. For this you must yourself be prepared to accept the consequences and assume the personal responsibility.''[48]

In diplomatic usage, this amounted to an ultimatum. Four days later, Chiang formally requested the recall of Stilwell.

Our analysis suggests that in the Sino-American wartime alliance, the central government's political-military vulnerability was often the root of many other problems. In the very beginning of the thirty-division program, Stilwell used a simple logic—since there were enough arms within China for thirty divisions, all the government needed to do was to get rid of the ineffective units and repossess their arms.[49] As the government was in no position to enforce this recommendation, it showed no enthusiasm for the proposed army reform. Only gradually did the talk shift to American provision for the thirty divisions. By October, 1942, Stilwell was sufficiently impressed by the success of the American-sponsored program of training and equipping Chinese troops at Ramgarh, India, to propose American equipment and training for a second thirty divisions for 1943.[50] Yet during 1942–43 when the Americans pushed the Nationalists hard to commit themselves to the training programs, there emerged a classical standoff: the Americans wanted to bring the chosen Chinese units up to strength, weed out incompetent officers, train the soldiers and then issue new lend-lease equipment, but the Nationalists wanted to receive the equipment first and talk about reform later.[51]

As the Americans encountered enormous difficulties in delivering materials into China in 1942–43, the Chungking government also put off taking the risk to shake up its delicate relations with the regional forces. The Chungking government's resistance to reform reflected its apprehension that the delicate balance of military power that helped preserve the wartime coalition between the KMT and the various regional structures might be further disrupted to the detriment of its own interests unless the government's own troops were favored to receive American training and equipment. The American program presented the Chinese not only with a significant benefit, but also a dilemma. It would be obviously impossible to spread the favors equitably since only thirty divisions would be chosen. To have to designate these divisions would make the discrimination an open one, and factions excluded from this bonanza might even withdraw from the coalition. While the government would certainly have preferred to designate only central troops to receive training and equipment, such an act would have rekindled the suspicion and hostility that the regional leaders felt toward the KMT prior to the war and probably also lead to the disintegration of the coalition.

But the Americans' refusal to use precious lend-lease to back one Chinese internal faction against another, the loss of America's interest in the strategic value of the Chinese mainland, and the abrupt recall of Stilwell soon combined to diminish the American role in China's army training program. In the end, the most visible results of the American training and military assistance programs in China were the Y-force in Yünnan and the Ramgarh force in India. That the stumbling block to the Chinese government's acceptance of military reforms was more political than technical in nature was suggested by the success of these two programs.

The feasibility of the training of Chinese troops based in India for the Burma campaign depended on several favorable factors. First, America made a strong effort to support it with the necessary manpower and materials, which were in abundant store in India. Second, most Chinese regional armies were not interested in fighting in a foreign country, and therefore the Burma expeditionary force was composed only of units loyal to the central government. The physical isolation of Ramgarh from China proper made it possible for the training program to proceed without being subject to the crosscurrents of Chinese internal politics. The units in India were inspired only by nationalistic sentiments and not divided by regional loyalties. Finally, the various recommended reforms that were blocked within China were implemented here. Consequently, the welfare of the soldiers was given strong emphasis: pay was honestly delivered, living conditions were decent, and soldier-officer relations were greatly improved. Therefore, the Ramgarh success was due partly to American military assistance and partly to a combination of unique political and social factors not found inside China itself.

But success was much more qualified for the other component of the Chinese Expeditionary Force, the Y-force which was to cross the Salween River into Burma from Yünnan. In this case, the Chinese dragged their feet in naming the units, although eventually all the units chosen were loyal to the central government and training began in the spring of 1943 at Kunming. Furthermore, the local political situation in Yünnan seriously hindered the development of a sound command structure: independent commands had to be established to placate powerful military leaders in the province, and the expeditionary army had no control over its own rear.[52]

The Y-force program also proved less attractive from the government's point of view because the lend-lease contribution to the program would be modest and the Chinese were expected to furnish their own arms.[53] A simple calculation on the government's part cautioned it that the benefits of increasing the combat effectiveness of a few loyal units might be outweighed by the risks of antagonizing the local warlords, sowing dissension among its own loyal following about who would be chosen for the program, and of letting these loyal units slip from tight central control once American commanders were installed. But as long as some form of American assistance was forthcoming, the Chinese were still willing to cooperate, and the Y-force was eventually formed.

The rebuilding process in these forces continued uninterrupted by the transition of the American command from Stilwell to Wedemeyer in late 1944. If anything, several factors actually augured well for the Wedemeyer appointment from the beginning. First, unlike his unfamiliarity with Stilwell, Chiang had known Wedemeyer during the latter's service in the China-Burma-India theater and came to respect him as a professional soldier. Second, in appointing Wedemeyer, Roosevelt also finally decided to drop the long-standing demand that China surrender full command of the Chinese army to an American officer. Wedemeyer was to be strictly Chiang's chief of staff and nothing else, which greatly reduced the perceived threat that had colored Chiang's relationship with Stilwell. Finally, Wedemeyer's appointment was announced against the background of gradually increasing American lend-lease delivery in the midst of China's worst military crisis, both enabling Wedemeyer to speak with greater authority than his predecessor.

Soon after Wedemeyer assumed office in October, 1944, he began to deal with the reorganization of Chinese combat forces. The basic plan of training thirty divisions was inherited, now to be called the Alpha Plan. In late December, 1944, when Wedemeyer met with Chiang to work out the reform of the army, he made clear his position that "divisions which are loyal to the Generalissimo and soldiers who are willing to fight should receive priority in such a program," to which Chiang promptly gave his hearty endorsement. Thus in one stroke Wedemeyer removed Chiang's greatest anxiety since the military reform plan was first broached, and won him over as an ardent supporter of the new plan.[54]

In January, 1945, a Chinese command system was set up to carry out the plan. The initial purpose of training was to make each unit capable of fighting effectively three months after starting its training. Two thirteen-week training cycles were projected, the first one emphasizing weapon training and the second one, tactical training. Upon completion, it was expected that each Chinese division would have 10,000 men and a battalion of artillery to match a Japanese regiment.[55]

Equally encouraging was the fact that the Chinese government also dropped its guard and allowed the United States military to come into closer contact with other aspects of military life in China. For years, the Chinese had been reluctant to allow United States Army liaison teams to go out into the field, a policy that resulted in a shocking lack of information on the organization and operations of the Chinese army. In early 1945, the Chinese finally accepted American liaison teams down to the division level. In early 1945, the Chinese government also put an American general in charge of the Chinese military supply system, including improving the system of food rationing to the army, which in turn produced greater American participation in the process of the Chinese government than ever before attempted.[56]

Finally, even as the Alpha Plan was still on the drawing board, Wedemeyer rushed to draft the Beta Plan, which he presented to the Chinese government in February, 1945. According to the Beta Plan, Wedemeyer wanted the government to mount an offensive in southeast China leading to an attack against Canton and Hong Kong to reestablish sea communications with the Allies in early 1946. These moves then would constitute steps preliminary to the destruction of Japanese forces on the Asian continent. Wedemeyer's staff projected that a total of 208 Chinese divisions (with about 1,700,000 men) would be involved. On February 14, the Chinese again endorsed this plan without hesitation. As United States Army historians noted, "For the first time since China and the United

States became allies, the Generalissimo agreed to a major offensive effort within the historic provinces of China proper." [57]
But international events moved swiftly in the spring and summer of 1945, and the war against Japan was brought to an abrupt end in August. Therefore, as noted in the previous chapter, there was not enough time to fully implement the Alpha Plan, and the Beta Plan never got off the ground. On balance, therefore, the Chinese government's attempt to enlist American assistance to help rebuild the army yielded rather mixed results. The Americans were certainly exasperated by Chinese foot-dragging and became disillusioned with the value of the central government as a military ally. The regional commanders were angered by their exclusion from sharing the American lend-lease largess. The central government made some gains in American-trained and equipped troops, but such gains were counterbalanced by the severe losses it suffered within China itself, and by the loss of the goodwill of the regionalists.

Deterioration of Central-Regional Relationships, 1943–45

In the context of these American policies, the central-regional relationships only became progressively worse. The failure of the 1939–40 winter offensive and the 1942 Burma campaign produced a significant change in the perception of the regionalists toward the KMT. More than ever before, the regional militarists were prepared to challenge the authority of the central government. By May, 1943, there occurred several clashes between central and Szechwan forces. The friction was smoothed over only after the central government had sent Governor Chang Ch'ün and Finance Minister H. H. K'ung to confer with provincial general Liu Wen-hui at Chengtu.[58] Then in September, 1943, the three leading generals of Szechwan, Liu, P'an, and Teng, showed their nonsupport of the KMT's policy toward the Communists by declining to attend the party's eleventh session of the Central Executive Committee. In this significant gesture of defiance, they presumably had the support of Fu Tso-yi in Suiyüan and Ma Hung-Kuei in Ninghsia.[59]
Then in November, 1943, the so-called young generals plot was reported to have been foiled. While the details of this event remain shrouded in mystery, it allegedly was a plot designed to seize Chiang on his way back from the Cairo Conference and to force him to clean up his government. Significantly, it was reported to have been instigated by the

graduates of the *lu-chün ta-hsüeh* (staff college), a military institution rivaling the Whampoa Academy, and that several hundred officers, including some division commanders, might have been implicated. The plot was exposed by Tai Li's agents, and many leaders were executed or imprisoned.[60]

Menacing as this incident must have appeared to the central government, it was by no means an isolated one. At just about the same time, though possibly unrelated to the young officers' plot, another movement was being formed under the Kwangsi leader, General Li Chi-shen. Starting in early November, 1943, there were reports that Li was arranging for an understanding with commanders in south China for possible coordinated action in case of the collapse of the Chungking government. Li was reported to have reached informal agreements with Yü Han-mou, Chang Fa-k'uei, and Hsüeh Yüeh, commanders of the seventh, fourth, and ninth war zones, respectively, and wanted to invite the participation of Yünnan and Szechwan generals. At this point it was not yet a separatist movement, but one to insure unified and continued resistance if the central government should collapse.[61]

The government's first reaction was to invite Li, who was then chairman of the Kweilin office of the National Military Affairs Commission, to accept a new post at Chungking. When Li declined, Chungking went ahead to abolish the Kweilin office, but Li pressed on with his organizing activities.

But as the Chinese army suffered serious defeats in the early phase of Operation Ichigō in 1944, the Li Chi-shen movement also began to undergo subtle changes. Soon General Li accused the central government of implementing a deliberate plan "to sabotage and destroy the armies of those Southern leaders whose loyalty to the ruling clique is considered questionable."[62] By May, 1944, a tentative plan was drafted to join forces with all dissident groups and to schedule a meeting at Chengtu on October 10, 1944, for the establishment of a government of national defense that would continue the war, introduce democratic rule, release political prisoners, and abolish the secret police. The League of Democratic Parties had now become a prominent actor in the movement.[63] In another two months, the Chinese Communists were also brought in and the movement became clearly separatist in nature. In August, 1944, delegates from the league, the Communist party, and finally Li himself made repeated appeals to the Americans at Kweilin for political and military support for their new government that would replace Chiang Kai-shek. They informed the Americans that the movement also had the participation of political and military leaders from Kwangtung, Kwangsi, Hunan, Anhwei, Fukien, Szechwan, and Sikang.[64] When the Americans declined to become involved, and with the attitude of generals Li Tsung-jen and Pai Ch'ung-hsi in doubt, the separatist attempt was stalled.[65] This incident, however, made it amply clear to the Nationalist government that the latent anti-Chiang camp finally had escalated from rhetoric to political action and had broadened its base to include the politicians and the Communists, a fact that could not but cause Chungking a lot of anxiety. Equally unsettling to the Chungking government was the possibility that some among this group had also approached the Japanese for support, even though no concrete action came out of the rumored negotiations at this time.[66]

Concurrent with these developments was yet another antigovernment movement operated mainly out of Kunming (Yünnan). The central government never had a smooth relationship with Lung Yün, the governor of Yünnan, who had long been suspected of complicity in Wang Ching-wei's escape from China.[67] The central government had on several occasions contemplated replacing Lung Yün as governor only to decide against it for fear of provoking the 60,000 provincial troops under Lung's control.[68] Instead, in March, 1944, the government tried to ease the increasingly strained relationship between it and the Yünnan provincial government by dispatching a distinguished group of peacemakers including Madame Chiang Kai-shek, H. H. K'ung and his wife, and T. V. Soong.[69] But as the Japanese offensive moved closer to the southwest in mid-1944, Lung became more insistent on demanding that the central government supply him with American arms. When Lung's demands were ignored, his provincial press promptly launched open criticism against the central government.[70] It was rumored that Lung was in consultation with the regionalists to attempt a coordinated withdrawal of their troops from the front when the Japanese approached and let Chungking's loyal units be destroyed by the Japanese.[71] This scheme was coupled to a direct appeal to the Americans for arms and an offer that they would accept American command over their troops.[72] By December, Lung became more openly hostile to the central government and a Yünnan division under the command of his son actually clashed with the Fifth Army of the central government. Eventually, the government had to send emissaries to make peace.[73]

On the political front, Lung stepped up his promotion and protection of the cause of political dissidents in 1944. Kunming soon became a haven for university professors, liberals, and democratic elements critical of the central government. In December, 1944, these dissidents took a big step forward by forming the Democratic League. League leaders began actively negotiating with provincial militarists in January, 1945, to bring about the downfall of the Chungking government and install a coalition government. The league's representatives were active among provincial forces and had succeeded in enrolling many commanders as members.[74] The league also maintained close contact with militarists in other provinces. In Szechwan, the central government had become quite precarious with only about 40,000–50,000 men. On the other hand, General P'an Wen-hua had over 100,000 men in Szechwan, and Liu Wen-hui had two more divisions poised on the Szechwan-Sikang borders, which were described by an American military attaché as "the best armed soldiers I have seen in China."[75] At least since early fall, 1944, the Chengtu press had become highly critical of the Chungking government, and all three Szechwan generals predicted to Americans that a radical change of government would take place soon.[76] There was discussion that in the event of a Japanese invasion into the province, the local militarists would disarm the central government forces in the province that refused to go along with the replacement of Chiang Kai-shek by a coalition government. Although the threatened coup by the Szechwan generals never materialized, there was no doubt that the central government's position was shakier than ever as the war was brought to a sudden end.[77]

These developments graphically demonstrate the problems in the KMT's adherence to the policy of militarization either before or during the war. Even as China was fighting for its national survival, the KMT leaders continued to contemplate central-regional relations in *manipulative* rather than *integrative* terms. Thus, political work was corrupted and transformed into espionage against the regionalists, loyal central troops were deployed to put regional troops under surveillance, and discriminatory tactics were used against regional forces in the distribution of American military assistance. These divisive policies could not but increase the resentment of the regionalists. Consequently, the central-regional relationship remained an antagonistic one during the war. China, in fact, was a country under dual or multiple sovereignty during the war.

When we view the KMT's political-military history, we cannot help note the great changes the war had brought on it. Before the war, the KMT had firm control over the richest provinces in the lower Yangtze valley. After eight years of fighting, the KMT had not only failed to establish a

firm foothold in any of the interior provinces, but the last big blow to its
army raised serious doubts in the minds of its leaders about whether they
had sufficient military strength left to reoccupy their former power base
even after the Americans handed them the victory. In the wake of Operation Ichigō, which demolished the Chinese main forces in Honan, Hunan,
and Kwangsi, the small number of American-trained divisions of the
Y-force became by default the backbone of the central government's military might. The regional leaders were quick to realize this as well, and
were just as quick to translate their discontent with the Chungking government into conspiratorial acts or open defiance.

Relations between the Nationalists and the Communists

1937–40

As soon as the war broke out, the Communists quickly offered their support to the central government and accepted the incorporation of their own
forces into the national army. But the long history of mutual animosity was
not easily removed, and Nationalist criticisms of Communist independence
were voiced even during the early months of the war.[78]

The architect of the CCP's general strategy was of course Mao Tse-
tung. From the very beginning, Mao's position was that the CCP's role in
the united front was not to be one of a diffident junior partner, but rather
one of equality. The CCP would retain the options of either cooperation
with or struggling against the KMT as the specific occasion required and
would be guided by the overriding principle of maintaining independence
in ideology, in politics, and in organization.[79]

Although this view was briefly challenged by some party leaders who
believed that the CCP and the KMT should genuinely cooperate with each
other for the defeat of Japan,[80] by the party's Sixth Plenum in November,
1938, the party finally rejected Ch'en Shao-yü's recommendation of sub-
merging all Communist activities under the rubric of the united front and
rendering all-out assistance to the KMT against Japan, and adopted Mao's
proposal of maintaining the independence and integrity of the Communist
party.[81]

However, for quite some time afterward, the Communist conduct in
war was marked by elements of incongruence. On the one hand, the party

exerted full effort to expand its own military strength. The August, 1937, agreement between the KMT and the CCP limiting the latter's force to the Eighth Route Army and the New Fourth Army of 30,000 men was soon discarded. Also, within months, the Communists restored the political commissar system that had been abolished on orders of the central government, and they refused to permit the government to send anyone to work in the Red Army.[82] This was followed by the CCP's unilateral decision to send troops into Shantung and to step up its military recruitment campaign to expand their guerrilla and regional forces in occupied north China.[83]

On the other hand, the party encountered considerable difficulty in deciding what mode of warfare should be the main one. Some of the party's professional soldiers apparently concluded that guerrilla warfare alone could not defeat Japan, and believed that the Red Army was capable of making a greater contribution to the war by fighting a mobile or even positional war.[84] The joining of forces between the military professionals and party functionaries finally produced the so-called Hundred Regiments Campaign of August, 1940, which inflicted considerable damage on the Japanese forces in the Hopei-Shansi border area.[85]

But subsequent party documents revealed that the military commanders had acted without authorization, and the campaign had "fundamentally violated Chairman Mao's strategic deployment plan and tactical principles" and that this kind of hard fighting had caused the party great harm.[86] The high cost of the campaign actually strengthened Mao's hand in the subsequent direction of all major operations of the Red Army and silenced his opponents from among the ranks of the military professionals.

Thus, insofar as the conventional war was concerned, the KMT-CCP united front had reached a dead end by late 1940. Except for the P'inghsin-kuan and the Hundred Regiments campaigns, the Nationalists complained that they had received little assistance from their Communist allies.

But the single issue that caused KMT-CCP friction to escalate into an open military clash was their race to seize control over the occupied areas through the extension of guerrilla activities. For in the wake of the Chinese defeats in north and east China, a large number of soldiers had been left behind. In Hopei and Shantung, where the KMT military influence was totally absent, the remnants belonged primarily to the northwestern and Manchurian armies, while in east China they came mostly from central government forces and the southern regions. Confusing as the situation was behind the enemy lines, it also presented great opportunity for the Chinese, since of the 796 counties nominally lost to the Japanese by the end of 1938, the latter had complete control over only 59 of them.[87]

According to the Communists' own data, Shantung in the first two years of the war had developed a guerrilla force of over 100,000 men of which only a minority were under Communist influence.[88] The most powerful guerrilla force was commanded by Fan Tsu-hsien, who was a regionalist but also a member of the KMT's Shantung provincial committee, and who received arms and other supplies from the Chungking government.[89] On the basis of the strength of these progovernment units, the central government was able to restore the provincial government in March, 1938, and appointed Admiral Shen Hung-lieh as the new governor.[90] By late 1938, the Shantung provincial government had extended its influence into the eastern part of the province.[91]

In Hopei, the earliest organizers of guerrilla activities were also non-Communists. Of these, the most powerful was Chang Yin-wu, a Paoting Military Academy graduate and the former mayor of Peiping under regional militarists. His *min-chün,* or militia, was organized in December, 1937, and expanded into a force of 30,000 men in 1939.[92]

It was after the fall of Wuhan in the winter of 1938 that the government finally decided to systematize administrative control in the occupied areas, to mobilize the masses, and to promote guerrilla warfare there.[93] But this promptly produced high tension between the KMT and the CCP and soon led to open armed conflicts. In Hopei, repeated battles between the Communists and the militia in 1939–40 finally drove the latter to western Shantung and Honan provinces.[94] The Hopei provincial government was rendered untenable in the province under the attacks by the Communist forces.[95] In Shantung, Fan Tsu-hsien's death in November, 1938, caused his force to join hands with the Communists. Whereas the CCP was at first willing to work under the provincial government and eagerly sought government appointment of its agents as officials, in 1939 it began to openly challenge the provincial government, and by 1940 it appointed its own officials in defiance of that government.[96]

These developments indicate that even in 1939–40 the KMT had suffered setbacks in north China. Several causes are particularly important to the government's failure.

First, the KMT had lacked the political-military control in prewar years to lay a firm foundation in building guerrilla forces. Expedient personnel consideration persuaded the KMT to co-opt regional militarists like Lu Chung-lin, Shen Hung-lieh, and Yü Hsüeh-chung as representatives of the party and the government in the occupied areas. These generals had little appreciation of the intricacies of guerrilla warfare and little inclination to learn about them.

Second, the government failed to provide a corps of competent cadres to promote crucial basic-level work among the masses. After the hasty decision of 1938 to conduct a guerrilla war, only 4,000–5,000 people ever received any training in guerrilla work.[97] Nor was the KMT able to recruit local activists. Between 1938–40, the KMT only recruited about 25,000 members in Hopei.[98] Both numbers were too deficient to perform a meaningful task there.

Third, and most critical, the government lacked a comprehensive program to deal with the needs and aspirations of the people living in the occupied areas. In a secret memorandum to the KMT headquarters, Ch'en I-hsin, a leading member of the Hopei provincial party committee, accused the Chungking government of exercising remote control in ignorance. The Central Statistics Bureau (party secret police) did not even have a station in Hopei. Between 1938–40, Chungking never dispatched officials to investigate the situation in Hopei, loaned no financial support to Hopei, and generally preferred to stay out of the complicated personnel problems among the locals as long as they paid nominal allegiance to the central government. Consequently, the government was badly misinformed about the magnitude of the Communist efforts there, and was plainly surprised when the Communists finally kicked the KMT out in March, 1940.[99]

In general, the government's attitude toward the entire occupied area was still to appoint a few officials, reestablish nominal bureaucratic machinery, and give the appearance of conducting business as usual. When the government first pondered on the methods of extending work into the occupied areas in October, 1938, some leaders had suggested that there should be a separate and independent governing body for the occupied areas in order to free them from the problems of command structure confusion and personnel rivalry that were so disruptive in the free areas.[100] But the government was not prepared to challenge the reality of power governing the central-regional relationship. Therefore, even though the Chungking government set up a new organization called *chan-ti tang-cheng wei-yüan-hui* (Combat Area Party-Government Joint Commission) presumably to improve the effectiveness of its work at the front, this organization turned out to be just one more administrative agency above the provincial governments that could neither centralize all governmental powers for the guerrilla areas nor promote mobilization on the grassroots level. The style of governing remained little changed: there was total dependence on paper work, formal bureaucracy, local gentry, and local powerholders.

This stood in sharp contrast to the Communists, who not only brought in a large corps of dedicated, experienced guerrilla workers to organize and recruit local activists to become leaders, but also brought with them completely different political-social programs and style of government. Even KMT leaders in north China conceded that among the factors for the CCP's success were firm party control over the army and government, basic-level cadre initiatives in mobilization, clean and honest government, egalitarianism, and such attractive social programs as reduction of taxes and rents and redistribution of land.[101]

Here again, we find the legacy of the Northern Expedition continuing as a crushing burden on the KMT and that the seeds of the KMT's failure in north China had been planted long before the war by its inability to establish a meaningful political-military presence there. This failure prevented the government from preserving a semblance of order in the aftermath of the collapse of the regional forces. In fact, the KMT never had a force in north China either before the war, or in the two years after the outbreak of the war when the central government's total preoccupation was with waging a conventional war.

By 1939, when the central government decided to undertake guerrilla warfare, the field was already crowded with Communist and remnant regional forces. Chungking's attempt to reassert administrative control over guerrilla activities clashed with the Communist movement to create "one million soldiers" and "one million party members" in north China, and provoked the latter to step up its organizing activities there. By 1940–41, the leadership over guerrilla war had already passed into Communist hands, and only a few progovernment pockets of guerrilla activities survived to the end of the war.

As the government was in retreat in north China, its position in east China also became untenable under Communist pressure. Clashes between the CCP's New Fourth Army and the progovernment Eighty-ninth Army (a Kiangsu provincial army) in October, 1940, soon forced the evacuation of the Kiangsu provincial government into neighboring Anhwei.[102] Then in January, 1941, the famous New Fourth Army Incident occurred and signaled that both sides had lost their self-restraint and were willing to face the consequences of a civil war within the context of a war of national survival. Thereafter, KMT-CCP armed clashes escalated everywhere behind the enemy lines.

Thus, by early 1941, when the KMT took stock of the situation, it had to concede that its efforts to promote guerrilla war not only did not yield the intended results, but had produced Communist dominance in most occupied areas. Equally ominous, the Chungking government was informed by its secret service that the Communists were quietly conducting plans to infiltrate central military academies and loyal troops, to send Communist agents to serve as advisors to regional commanders, and to fraternize with the soldiers.[103] Thus, at a time when the government's military policy of aggressiveness toward the Japanese had just failed, its relationship with the Communists had also changed from lukewarm cooperation to an armed standoff. For all intents and purposes, the united front had completely collapsed.

The Transformation of the Red Army and Its Implications in KMT-CCP Relations, 1941–45

It is well known that Mao's military writings contained numerous suggestions that the secret of Communist military success rested on the concept of the people's war, that his army disdained traditional training, shunned conventional war, and instead emphasized local initiative, spontaneity, the resourcefulness, ingenuity and revolutionary élan of the individual combatants. The typical Communist fighter was depicted as a peasant who might be illiterate, but was patriotic and commanded enough native intelligence to outwit his enemy, and who was as equally versed in working with a hoe as with a rifle. As Mao put it, this army thrived on millet and rifles.

While there is much truth in this characterization of the Communist forces during the Sino-Japanese War, it would be wrong to assume that weapons and training were not important to the Communists or that they opposed conventional war, for upon closer examination we will find that not only was conventional training an important aspect of the CCP's army-building program, but that it had enormous impact on the subsequent relationship between the Communists and the Nationalists. In fact, it should be realized that Mao never adhered single-mindedly to the idea of people's war.

Instead, his views changed slowly over the years. In 1938, in his article, "On Protracted War," he was quite emphatic that "among the forms of warfare in the anti-Japanese war mobile warfare comes first and guerrilla warfare second," and that both the army and the people were the foundation of victory.[104] By late 1938, Mao was more explicit in his view on the importance of regular army and regular warfare. In "Problems of War and Strategy" (November, 1938), he asserted that there was a need to change the army's military strategy in the national war, and said,

> in the anti-Japanese war as a whole, regular warfare is primary and guerrilla warfare supplementary, for only regular warfare can decide the final outcome of the war. . . . Unless we understand this, *unless we recognize that regular warfare will decide the final outcome of the war, and unless we pay attention to building a regular army and to studying and directing regular warfare, we shall be unable to defeat Japan.* [Emphasis added][105]

While not giving up guerrilla warfare entirely, Mao went on to say, "It is also beyond doubt that in the long course of struggle the guerrilla units and guerrilla warfare will not remain as they are but will develop to a higher stage and evolve gradually into regular units and regular warfare."[106]

By the summer of 1940, the Communists already had half a million regular troops,[107] and the time seemed ripe for their military organization to depart from the amorphous guerrilla units which varied in size of manpower and types of equipment, generally disregarding rank stratification or rigid division of labor, and to evolve into a more rationalized and standardized force with new emphasis on the improvement of their equipment[108] and on military training.

With respect to the differentiation in the structures of the Red Army, the most important policy was the crystallization of the three-tier system. According to this system, on the lowest level were the self-defense teams (*tzu-wei-tui*), which enrolled all people between the ages of sixteen and fifty, and the militia (*min-ping*), which was composed of volunteers. Their primary responsibilities were to conduct guerrilla war against the Japanese and puppet forces, and to disrupt transportation and communication. The cadres of these two kinds of forces were drawn from local activists, and the weapons they used would be locally manufactured or seized from the enemies. Furthermore, members of these forces were expected to participate fully in the economic production process. On the intermediate level were a number of regional forces (*ti-fang pu-tui*) composed of semi-regular soldiers who operated in larger formations and over an area of several counties. They were better equipped and better trained than the local militia, and would be expected to participate in economic production, to resist Japanese mopping-up campaigns, to protect the harvest from enemy confiscation, or to fight against natural calamities. On the highest level were the main forces, which consisted of both the regulars and guerrilla units directly under the command of the central party headquarters or its regional bureaus.[109]

In the 1940s, the CCP's main interest was in promoting military forces of the higher types. The basic format used by the party was to graduate militia into regional regular forces, and to graduate regional regular forces into central main forces (*chu-li pu-tui*).[110] In time, there evolved a well-developed system of progressive advancement of lower forms of self-sufficient, independent guerrilla units toward a well-regimented, well-disciplined, and well-trained conventional army.

Most important to the process of regularization and professionalization was the emphasis on training in strategies and tactics. One measure of the CCP's commitment in this respect is the fairly large number of training manuals its military leaders compiled or translated from Soviet originals. The comprehensiveness of these manuals would be equal to or superior to the teaching materials used in any other contemporary Chinese military school, including the KMT's Central Army Officers' Academy.[111] After 1941, the party placed new emphasis on the quality rather than quantity of military training and stipulated that military subjects should constitute 50 percent of the time of instruction. Then the Politburo instructed in February, 1942, that "military cadres should study military science."[112]

In September, 1942, Mao enunciated that the policy of "better troops and simpler administration" was "a most important policy."[113] Specifically, the party introduced a systematic training schedule so that every regiment in the Red Army would devote six to eight months to training on a rotational basis.[114] In the winter of 1943, Mao and Chu Teh issued the call to conduct an "unprecedented, intense, and massive soldier-training movement" in the border regions with emphasis on individual combat skills. Upon its completion, Lin Piao concluded that the 1943 training had "yielded great results," and had "laid a broad-based foundation and brought these skills to unprecedented standards."[115]

In November, 1944, Lin Piao unveiled the party's 1944–45 plan for military training. In a series of lectures entitled "How We Are to Train the Army This Year," Lin announced that 40 percent of the time in the 1944–45 training season would be used to refine individual combat skills and 60 percent would be used to teach tactics for larger units. Lin stated in no uncertain terms that he wanted to "conduct conventional training and restore regular military life.''[116] Specifically, Lin said that the leadership would now pay more attention to such things as military etiquette, neatness in barracks, proper care of weapons, drills in formation, and so on, things that were the stock in trade of most conventional armies. He also asserted that these were very useful things to master.[117]

On the question of what kind of war the army should be trained to fight, Lin now stated emphatically that the army should fight big battles.

> Should the cadres learn to fight small guerrilla battles or big battles? Our answer to this question is that they should learn those subjects related to fighting big battles. Regiment and brigade level cadres should pay particular attention to learn how to direct big battles, to acquire knowledge in tactics, knowledge about new weapons, and knowledge in basic mathematics. . . . We should realize that in the future our fighting will transform into big battles and regular warfare involving large group-armies.[118]

In line with this new emphasis, the Communists also stressed the training of "special-skill soldiers" in artillery, engineering, communications, machine-gunnery, grenade-launching, etc.[119]

The results of the two successive years of massive and intensive military training were quite gratifying to the party. Partly this was due to the party's instruction to all branches of the party and government to render all-out support to the program. Partly it was due to the ingenuity of the Communists to take advantage of their safety in the border regions and the ample time on their hands to develop many highly original and thorough educational methods. These methods combined theory and practice, encouraged enlightenment instead of learning by rote, used model emulation, tournaments in martial arts, and other incentives to promote learning as well as a tireless effort to make every soldier and officer participate in every phase of the training from the drafting of schedules to the evaluation of achievements and shortcomings.[120]

Addressing the second session of the Second Border-Region People's Congress at the end of 1944, Lin Tsu-han said,

> As a preparatory step toward the counter-offensive against the Japanese, the Border-Region garrison forces in recent years have made many remarkable achievements in their own reconstruction work. In the military training, the tendency of disjunction between education and practice has been overcome and instead the popular line of "officers teach their men, soldiers teach each other, and men teach their officers" has been

adopted. Remarkable results have been achieved in the winter training. . . . The training of regulars and self-defense corps will be continued this year and, no doubt, their fighting strength will be further
raised.[121]

This success of training programs was undertaken in the context of a
continued vigorous Communist effort to accelerate the pace of promoting
lower types of military units into higher types, as well as to recruit more
soldiers directly into the regular forces. The years 1944–45 were particularly propitious to the Communists' effort to expand the military. The
CCP's expansion was rapid not only in the areas recently vacated by the
KMT during the Japanese attacks, but even in the Japanese occupied areas
in north China as a result of the diversion of crack Japanese combat units to
meet the mounting pressure in the Pacific.[122] Taking advantage of the devastating impact of Operation Ichigō upon the government forces, the Communists also obtained large quantities of weapons discarded by the government soldiers. By late 1944, General Yeh Chien-ying claimed that 62
percent of the Communist field forces and 50 percent of their local forces
were armed with rifles.[123] Such figures would mean that the proportion
of men in the Communist forces armed with rifles was actually much
higher than the majority of the KMT forces. When Mao wrote "On Coalition Government" in April, 1945, he was able to report that the Communist military had reached 910,000 regulars, and 2,200,000 militiamen
who remained on the production line.[124] To borrow a familiar Chinese
metaphor, the Communist party was no longer a dragon stranded in shal-
low waters: with the newly acquired size and equipment, the dragon was
ready to soar into the skies as the war approached its end.

The discussion of the rise of Communist military power cannot be
complete without a brief mention of America's proposal to use the Communist troops. Originally, the Americans had adopted a strictly neutral
attitude in KMT-CCP relations and avoided any official contact with the
Communists. The idea of using the Communist forces in the war first arose
only when the United States realized that it could not expect a speedy
revitalization of the central government forces to mount the second Burma
campaign. Further procrastination in the government's implementation of
reform in 1943 made the Communist troops appear to be an increasingly
viable alternative to government forces. Finally, at the end of August,
1943, General Stilwell made his first official recommendation for a joint

KMT-CCP military action in north China.[125] Not unexpectedly, the central government flatly rejected this proposal.

Either by coincidence or by design, the Communists stepped up their criticism of the central government visibly around this time. They began to assert that their troops made a far greater contribution to the war than government troops,[126] that central troops were not only unreliable and defected to the enemy, but that the government itself might have deliberately encouraged them to do so in a more sinister design to collaborate with the Japanese in a joint war against the Communists,[127] and that the government was investing a huge portion of its best forces in blockading the Communists rather than facing the enemy.[128]

As United States-KMT relations deteriorated, United States-CCP relations obviously improved. Under repeated American requests, the central government finally allowed the United States to send an observers' team to Yenan in the summer of 1944. Once in Yenan, members of the American team were warned by the Communist leaders that if the United States continued its policy of exclusive support for the KMT, its policy in China would fail. On the other hand, these leaders tried to reassure the American visitors that they shared America's interest in the speedy defeat of the Japanese and emphasized that they had been hindered from more aggressive action only because they had insufficient arms, promising that they would make good use of any arms supplied by the Americans to hasten the end of war. In fact, some Communist leaders showed a willingness to accept an American command over all Chinese troops, both KMT and CCP, and made suggestions on operational matters if American troops should plan to land in China.[129]

Needless to say, the KMT response to the developing ties between the CCP and the Americans was extremely hostile. That such a development should occur at a time when the government's own forces were being soundly beaten by the Japanese during Operation Ichigō was even more ominous to Nationalist leaders. In addition, they were alarmed by an escalation of the demands made by the Communist delegates in Chungking to the central government, and as the negotiation dragged on, the KMT and CCP positions on key issues remained as far apart as ever. Then at approximately the same time, the Soviet Union suddenly recalled its ambassador and all of its military advisors from China, which deepened the government's suspicion that the Communists were involved in a conspiracy against the government. Specifically, Chiang believed that the Communists were trying to discredit the government, to exploit the American government and public opinion to pressure the KMT to make concessions to the Communists, and possibly even to attempt to seize political power before the victorious end of the war.[130]

In the context of worsening relations between the government and the Communists, Operation Ichigō continued to expose the utter ineffectiveness of the government and regional forces. Convinced that only the use of Communist forces could reverse the tide of war, Stilwell made a categorical demand that the Communist Eighteenth Group Army be included under his yet-to-be-created command. Barely a week later, the Chinese government requested his recall.[131]

Conclusion

The history of the development of the Communist army suggests a pattern almost the exact opposite of that of the Nationalist army. Whereas the KMT lost the bulk of its best troops during the early months of the war, the initially modest Communist force escaped the brunt of Japanese attacks in north China. Between 1937 and 1939, when the KMT was still determined to use military means exclusively to end the war, the Communists were already laying the groundwork for revolutionary bases in occupied areas that were equipped to thrive under enemy pressures. By the spring of 1940, the KMT's policy of using a conventional army and strategies to overpower the Japanese was proven unrealistic by the failure of the government forces to mount a sustained offensive. In contrast, the key Communist bases in north and east China had been firmly established, from whence sustained guerrilla attacks could be launched against the Japanese.

But even more crucial changes in the military balance between the two sides took place after 1941. When the Communists first began to turn their attention toward the creation of a large military force, their goal was one million soldiers.[132] In November, 1943, Chinese Communists at Chungking told the Americans that the official figure of the Eighteenth Group Army and New Fourth Army totalled 500,000 regulars, while guerrillas counted for an additional two million.[133] The number of regulars was nearly doubled in the next fifteen months, until by the spring of 1945, the Red Army had already acquired a military strength of three million, of which about one million was regular force.

Equally crucial to the Communists was the quality of this force. Taking full advantage of the Japanese strategy of seeking out and annihilating the central government forces during these years, and the lack of further KMT attacks against the Shen-Kan-Ning border regions after 1942, the Communist leaders were able to develop a regular army of high quality out of an irregular force. In so doing, they successfully avoided some of the fatal mistakes committed by the Nationalists during and after the Northern Expedition. The Communists' policy was to refuse to make compromises to existing political-military groups. The party's corps of cadres readily became the backbone of the newly organized military force which recruited directly from the peasant masses, thereby establishing the principle of letting the party control the guns from the very outset. The three-tier system also enabled the party to weed out unfit elements and select the best candidates to be incorporated into the regular army. The party's ability to carry out a full-blown and prolonged ideological rectification campaign (*cheng-feng*) during 1942–44 was highly successful in stamping out whatever residual warlordism that remained in the army and turning it into a dedicated, well-indoctrinated, loyal, and disciplined instrument of the party. Finally, after 1942, the Communists had at least three uninterrupted years to implement successive waves of massive and intensive military training in the border regions. While these training programs still lacked the comprehensiveness and sophistication necessary to create a highly modernized army, they were solid, thorough, and covered all essential aspects of the strategies and tactics of conventional infantry warfare on a large scale. On the basis of available information, one has to conclude that the Communist regulars were far better grounded in the basics of war than any Chinese-trained government forces (American-trained government forces excepted).

It is recalled that when Mao first stressed the need to create such a regular army in his article, "Problems of War and Strategy," (November, 1938) he stated very clearly that the purpose of such an army was to fight the last phase of the war, "the phase of strategic offensive," on a massive conventional scale to annihilate the enemy. But by mid-1945, when the long process of his effort to tune his military machine reached completion, the enemy was unexpectedly defeated by two American atomic bombs. This left Mao in the most enviable position of possessing the force to achieve his long-range revolutionary goals domestically.

It is only natural that both Mao and Chiang were sensitive to this fundamental shift of the military balance to the Communists' favor. For

Mao, this sensitivity was reflected in both the tone and the content of his political statements during the war. Between 1937 and 1939, Mao was primarily concerned with laying down his theory of how best to fight against the Japanese. Thus the major topics he addressed himself to included analyses of current situations,[134] his theory on how to fight the war,[135] and his concern with the proper handling of the policy of the united front.[136]

After December, 1939, when the KMT offensive capabilities were shown to be nil, he switched his attention to the larger problem of the role of the Communist party in the process of revolution.[137] However, it was his article, "On New Democracy," that marked a watershed. Written in January, 1940, at a time when Communist military power began to match that of the central government, Mao now laid down the theoretical groundwork for the kind of Chinese political system he would like to see. This was his first explicit statement on internal politics since the war began.

As time went on, Mao became more openly critical of the central government and showed less and less restraint in accusing the latter of sabotaging the united front.[138] But most important, of course, was the article, "On Coalition Government." Written in April, 1945, when he had enough time to assess the damage of Operation Ichigō to Chungking's military position, Mao apparently concluded that the time was ripe to translate his theory on new democracy into concrete political demands. Now he openly attacked the KMT as not resisting the Japanese, but conspiring to plant the seeds for a renewed civil war against the Communists. In this document, Mao also presented a list of specific demands for the KMT, among which the most crucial were to terminate the KMT's one-party dictatorship and establish a coalition government incorporating all democratic elements, to give people more political rights, to nationalize the armies, and to institute long-delayed social and economic reforms. At the end of the long exposition, Mao warned darkly that armed with the experience of three earlier revolutions, the CCP could accomplish its great task and a new, democratic China would soon be born.

The implications of all these changes were not lost upon the KMT. After 1940, it must have become acutely aware that it was gradually losing the race against the Communists, even as it managed to force a stalemate upon the Japanese. For China, the war was never a simple military struggle—it was also a political war. Instead of just two sides, there were in fact five. A coalition of the Japanese and Wang Ching-wei was pitted against a united front of the KMT, the CCP, and the regionalists. In order to be successful, the united front had to be built with political means to win over the trust and cooperation of the three partners as well as the general populace. But these were precisely the skills the Nationalist leadership lacked.

A militaristic approach became clearly untenable once the war began. In spite of the KMT's excessive preoccupation with military might, its army actually became weaker in relation to both the regionalists and the Communists. The KMT's inability to transcend the threat or the application of naked violence in domestic politics led to its loss of the chance to mobilize nationalistic sentiments to bring the regionalists and the Communists into a full partnership. It even deprived itself of the opportunity to rearm and reform its own army with American assistance. Within the context of the KMT's inability to use political power to guide and constrain military power, the best possible outcome was a tenuous peaceful coexistence among the three mutually suspicious parties, and the worst possible one was armed conflict among them.

In the KMT-regional relationship, the KMT might have been able to neutralize the regionalists with methods of internal and external control, but in the KMT-CCP relationship both methods were ineffective. Internal control was impractical because the CCP's watertight organization was impervious to the KMT's attempt to infiltrate. External control was impossible because the CCP's military expansion occurred in places well beyond the reach of the Nationalist armies. Most important of all, whereas the KMT allowed the guns to control politics, the CCP never wavered from the principle of letting politics take command and the subordination of the guns to the party.[139]

Chapter 4

The Politics of Demoralization

Military disasters in China not only altered the balance of power between the central government and other domestic political-military groups, they also affected the quality of routine politics and the day-to-day discharge of public functions. Logically, we have to ask: What programs did the KMT government pursue? What constraints did it operate under? How successful were these programs? What consequences did the KMT's performance record have upon its political viability?

To answer these questions, this chapter will focus on the regime's futile efforts to introduce political reforms during the war, and to show that the KMT's failure to resolve the central-regional relationship very seriously hampered the government's ability to implement three crucial wartime policies—grain collection, conscription, and economic management. It will become clear that the mismanagement of government in these areas cost the Nationalists the support of the people and pushed it toward its demise four years after the conclusion of the war.

The New-*Hsien* Program

Even though many Nationalist leaders had anticipated a Sino-Japanese War, its actual occurrence caught them quite unprepared. The KMT's initial response was to try desperately to stem the tide of Japanese military advances. But after the Shanghai debacle, Chinese armies were on the retreat on all fronts, and it was not until 1939 that the government finally managed to stabilize a line of defense. It was only then that the KMT leaders faced the unpleasant reality of having to survive in parts of the country they had never penetrated before and to build these provinces up as bases to launch a counteroffensive. To consolidate the central government's position in these areas and to mobilize human and physical resources more effectively, the government's answer was the launching of the "new-*hsien* program."

The new-*hsien* program first took shape in June, 1939. The significance attached to this program was underlined by the objectives set for it. According to the Ministry of Interior, there were six major objectives to be achieved: (1) to strengthen the *hsien* government's position and functions; (2) to produce local cadres; (3) to encourage self-government; (4) to increase literacy; (5) to organize the populace; and (6) to improve the people's livelihood.[1] In other words, the *hsien* reorganization was seen both as the way to organize and mobilize the people to carry on the war, and to accelerate the process toward local self-government.[2] All these objectives were reported to be fulfilled in October, 1941.[3] By the spring of 1944, official statistics claimed that 1,103 out of 1,361 *hsiens* in seventeen provinces had gone through the reorganization (table 5). But a closer look will indicate that the accomplishments fell far short of the original expectations. In fact, what was billed as a major political reform designed to increase China's fighting capability and to accelerate the transition from political tutelage to constitutional politics ended in failure.[4] The intriguing questions inevitably are: What factors contributed to the failure? What was the magnitude of the failure? What implications did this failure have for the course of the war or the political future of the Nationalist regime?

Any inquiry into the causes of the failure of the new-*hsien* program must begin with the enormous difficulties created by the war. To mix a major political innovation with an all-out military effort would have been

TABLE 5
Official Claims of the Extent of *Hsien* Reorganization, February, 1944

Total number of *hsien* in China	1,361
Total number of *hsien* already reorganized	1,103
Number of *hsien* that had already undertaken the following activities:	
Census survey	729
Census registration	247
Land survey	160
Land sale tax collection	44
Hsien cooperatives	161
Police stations	484
Hsien health stations	828

Source: Wang Te-fu, *Hsin-hsien-chih chih chien-t'ao yü kai-chin* (Chungking, 1944), tables 1, 2.

extremely difficult under any circumstances. It was particularly difficult for China because of the disparities in technology and organization between her and the enemy.

However, the causes of the failure went deeper, and at least three of them should be discussed here: (1) poor institutional design; (2) lack of qualified personnel; and (3) the absence of the necessary political support.

Institutional Design

Although the implementation of the new-*hsien* program was preceded by long discussion and wide publicity, the drive toward institutional standardization and rationalization yielded few tangible results. Despite the emphasis on reducing the size of local government, making it more efficient, and clarifying the chain of command, by 1943 many *hsien* governments continued to have sprawling structures, confused functional specifications, and superfluous personnel.[5] Confusion over responsibilities and prerogatives produced constant friction among civil servants. As the chain of command within the *hsien* government broke down, serious morale and discipline problems emerged.[6] Consequently, the bureaucrats showed very poor attitudes toward the people, were passive toward their assignments, adhered to archaic methods in managing official business, and in general tried to do as little as possible. Their behavior was little different from that of the bureaucrats of the preceding thirty to forty years, and these shortcomings remained to the end of the war.[7]

The multitude of missions given to *hsien* government also far exceeded its capabilities. Under the pressing wartime demands to fulfill quotas on grain, conscription, bonds, labor service, and so on, *hsien* government was taxed beyond its limits, and neither the magistrate nor his staff could devote any attention to promoting the numerous other activities related to local self-government in the fields of public health, social welfare, education, or economic construction.[8]

The *hsien* government was also severely circumscribed by its financial resources. Under the 1939 law, the central government tried to make *hsien* and district governments dependent on national, not provincial, governments in order to undermine the provinces' fiscal autonomy. The most important methods used by the central government were: (1) to take over taxes formerly collected by the provinces (e.g., land taxes), and abolish the provinces' independent budgeting authority; (2) to centralize control over the collection of direct taxes on income, inheritance, business transaction, etc.; (3) to demand the remittance of all locally collected taxes to the national treasury; and (4) to allocate subsidies to provincial and local governments to meet their operating expenses.[9]

In reality, the central government was never able to unify or standardize the local tax collecting agencies. In many cases, when the local tax agents realized that they could not share certain taxes with the central government, they simply lost interest in collecting these taxes.[10]

The new-*hsien* program stipulated that the *hsien* income would consist of a portion of the land tax, about 30 percent of income tax, stamp tax, and inheritance tax, and several other minor taxes.[11] In comparison with the prewar period, the *hsien*'s legal tax base was drastically reduced after 1939, but its self-government functions were significantly broadened. As the national government's own fiscal policy ran into deep trouble, it was not in a position to increase its subsidies to the *hsien*. Consequently, in most cases, the *hsien*'s social-economic programs simply never had a chance to develop.[12] This problem was most graphically illustrated by the fiscal conditions in Hupei in 1941. According to official data, the regular revenues of all *hsien* and *hsiang* governments amounted to C$13 million. But in order to faithfully carry out all the activities stipulated under the new-*hsien* program, the expenditures for these governments would amount to C$75 million, resulting in a shortfall of C$62 million.[13] Similar conditions existed in all other provinces, and such lack of fiscal realism inevitably doomed the new-*hsien* program to fail.

Personnel

The success of any political reform is predicated on the existence of a corps of dedicated, disciplined, and competent cadres. The more sweeping and innovative the reforms and the greater the multitude of new tasks assigned to the reformed institutions, the more crucial the personnel would be. Therefore, the capability of the KMT government to provide the necessary manpower for the new-*hsien* organs became a key variable in determining the extent of its success.

When the new-*hsien* program was launched, the government estimated that the manpower requirement would be around 8.5 to 9 million people for the 1,300 *hsien* under the government's nominal control (table 6).

In 1941, the Ministry of Interior announced a set of guidelines for the

TABLE 6
Projected Manpower Requirement for New-*Hsien* Programs

Hsien magistrates	1,302
Key officials in *hsien* government	52,180
Hsiang chiefs	237,272
Pao-chia chiefs	6,559,817
Teachers, policemen, assemblymen, others	1,700,000–2,000,000
Total	8,600,000–8,900,000

Sources: Liu Chih-fan, "Hsin-hsien-chih chih shih-shih wen-t'i," in Kuang-tung sheng-cheng-fu, *Hsin-hsien-chih yen-chiu* (n. p., 1940), pp. 86–89; Wang Te-fu, *Hsin-hsien-chih chih chien-t'ao yü kai-chin* (Chungking, 1944), pp. 1–10.

appropriate educational and professional qualifications for the selection of *hsien*-level cadres. How the government proposed to meet these manpower requirements became an issue of first priority.

Basically, there were three channels through which the government could mobilize China's administrative talents: it could use the examination system to enlist talent from outside; it could promote talent from the existing bureaucratic manpower pool; or it could conduct its own training program to retool and to improve the caliber of its civil servants.

The Civil Service Examination System

The KMT government had conducted examinations from 1929 onward for the recruitment of civil servants of certain categories. However, the record of these examinations between 1930 and 1945 reveals that it was not an effective method of recruiting talent to support the new-*hsien* program for several reasons. First, the number of qualified candidates produced by national examinations was quite modest—some 3,000 in a fifteen-year period, of which only about 500 were ever assigned to local governments. An additional 46,000 went through the examinations held by various ministries or provincial governments, but the overall quality of these candidates was considerably lower than the national candidates and they were usually assigned to specialized agencies.[14]

Second, the geographical distribution of the candidates was quite uneven since some provinces never did hold examinations.[15] Thus many provinces (particularly the interior ones) had a few or almost no officials who had qualified through the examination channels.

All these facts bring us to the conclusion that the civil service system was grossly inadequate in meeting the demands for competent officials, and that the overwhelming majority of public servants gained their positions through other means that were less objective and impartial.[16]

The Civil Service Merit System

A different way of assuring the quality of civil servants was to select the right people for the right jobs from among the existing pool of civil servants. This was the merit (*cheng sheng*) system.

Although the basic laws of the merit system were passed in 1929, it was not until 1933 that they were actually implemented. During the years of 1930–45, some 64,000 civil servants were assigned ranks and posts in accordance with the merit method.[17] Of this number, no more than 35,000 served in the various governments on the *hsien* level and below.[18]

When combined with all other forms of screening, the total number of qualified bureaucrats for all positions in *hsien* and lower-level governments was less than 100,000 in 1944.[19]

Training Programs

The government's third method to satisfy its manpower requirement was to conduct massive training of existing cadres. Soon after the new-*hsien* program began, a host of general and special training programs was organized. On the national level, the Central Training Corps (*chung-yang hsün-lien t'uan*) offered *hsien* magistrates and chief functionaries a training course of one to three months. However, the total number of *hsien* cadres trained through the corps up to mid-1944 was less than 2,000.[20]

The provincial government and the special administrative districts were responsible for training *hsien* secretaries, section chiefs of police, public health, taxation, education, and the like, and the *hsien* governments were to provide training for the *hsiang, village*, and *pao-chia* cadres. While this three-tier system looked quite rational on paper, in reality the KMT achieved far from satisfactory results. Government data show that in the years after the new-*hsien* program was in operation, only 21 percent of cadres slated for training were ever trained. They also reveal significant provincial variations. The provinces that performed the best in training were those that either were removed from the main theaters of war (Fukien, Shantung), or were sparsely populated (Ninghsia, Kansu); the provinces that did most poorly were the most populous and strategically located ones where the success or failure of the new-*hsien* program would be crucial to the KMT regime.[21]

A second point to be noted is that only 40 percent of the trained personnel were *hsiang* and *pao-chia* cadres. The record shows great provincial disparity in training basic-level cadres. In the worst case, Yünnan had only 450 trained *hsiang-pao-chia* cadres by 1944.[22] Statistics released by the Ministry of Interior in 1943 showed that only 23 out of 177 special districts and 682 out of the 1,103 *hsien* ever conducted any training program at all. Most training attempts were handicapped by lack of funds and instructors,[23] and these can be assumed to be of very poor quality.

Undoubtedly the training program was a casualty of the war. To mobilize and equip manpower on a massive scale to meet the new responsibilities of the new-*hsien* program would require a substantial national financial investment over a number of years. The estimated cost of training the 8.5 million basic-level cadres was set at C$800 million, an amount that the war-torn government was in no position to spend.[24] Of course, the cost of training would have been greatly reduced had there been an available pool of educated people. But the educational progress in the decades preceding the war took place mostly in the coastal provinces where both the educational facilities and much of the trained manpower fell into Japanese hands. Improvements in education in the interior provinces only began after the outbreak of war and proceeded rather sluggishly.[25] A government survey in 1944 indicated that in the first few years of the war, the colleges produced fewer than 5,000 graduates each year, and middle schools produced fewer than 50,000.[26] Thus it became unrealistic for the government to expect to tap the pool of educated youth to meet its own manpower shortage.

The Quality of Local Cadres

The combined effect of the inability to implement a thorough and rational institutional change and the difficulty in finding qualified persons to assume positions of responsibility naturally resulted in a lack of improvement in the quality of government. Although we do not have comprehensive data for a national analysis of basic-level leadership, some preliminary conclusions can be drawn from provinces where data are available.

First, the cornerstone of the new-*hsien* program was the *hsien* magistrate, and his selection was a matter of critical importance. A 1929 law had stipulated that the candidate for *hsien* magistracy must either have passed national or provincial examinations for the post or have been certified by the Examination *Yüan* and appointed by the national government.[27]

However, since the national or the provincial governments failed to carry out the examinations regularly, during the years 1930–45, a mere 313 candidates qualified.[28] The merit system yielded equally poor results.[29] From 1930 up to mid-1944, the number of people qualified to be *hsien* magistrates through all modes of selection was about 1,000.[30] If we deduct natural attrition through retirement, death, and those who chose to work in provincial or national governments, there were an extremely inadequate number of qualified people to be magistrates.

This situation means that the overwhelming majority of *hsien* magistrates were appointed through irregular means. Often the provincial governor could appoint *hsien* magistrates without regard for national regulations. All the governor needed to do was to give a person a temporary appointment, which in fact could be extended indefinitely. As one high-ranking official in the Ministry of Interior testified in May, 1944, very few governors ever bothered to submit records of these temporary appointees to the central government for approval.[31]

It would be a mistake, however, to regard the provincial governors as having final authority in appointing or dismissing *hsien* personnel. More likely, they were vulnerable to pressure from local ruling elites or commanders of military units stationed nearby.[32] Governors of either central or regional background could be subject to similar types of pressure. Frequently, powerful generals would simply install their own protégés in *hsien* offices first and coerce the governor into acquiescence later.[33]

During the war years, the *hsien* government had great difficulty in attracting talent because of its weak financial situation.[34] The new *hsien* system not only dried up *hsien* governments' operating funds, but also made its pay scale fall far below that for provincial and national cadres.[35] Many *hsien* magistrates resigned or took unauthorized leave because they could not live on their salaries,[36] and even for those already in office, there was little job security as the turnover rate was exceedingly high.[37]

As qualified people declined to work on the basic levels, the kinds of people who actually served were often of questionable ability and morality. In addition to power considerations, appointments were swayed by family ties, friendship, graft, and the desire to build personal followings. Governor Wu Ting-ch'ang reported in 1943 that most *hsien* magistrates seemed to fall into two groups: those who had built a career in old-fashioned local government, or those who had held minor military posts as commanders of a company or battalion. He found both types to possess a passive mentality, arrogant bureaucratic style, and an inability to breathe new life into local politics or to serve as catalysts for reform.[38] When compounded with a lack of job security or the backing of their superiors, they soon discovered that the only way to survive in office or to get things done was to achieve accommodation or collusion with local leaders.[39]

Furthermore, as conscientious officials found it impossible to perform the many administrative, health, educational, welfare, and economic construction functions within the fiscal limits set by law, unscrupulous officials could usually exercise a great deal of latitude. Precisely because the central government had so little to offer to, or control over, the local government, local officials were usually at liberty to impose surcharges or new taxes upon the people, and they did so not to finance government projects but for self-enrichment. Consequently, there was a conspicuous multiplication of *hsien* and local taxes during the war, a situation reminiscent of the chaos once prevailing during the early warlord era.[40]

Again we can cite Szechwan as an illustration. In 1941, its 135 *hsien* imposed fifty-seven different rates of surcharge on contract tax alone, ranging from C$3 per C$100 to C$26 per C$100 of regular contract tax. The surcharge on land taxes also varied from one *hsien* to another.[41]

Even worse conditions prevailed on the *hsiang,* village, and *pao-chia* levels. A high-powered government investigation team dispatched to evaluate party and government work in all the provinces in 1941–42 found that exceedingly few *pao* or *chia* chiefs were qualified for their jobs.[42] The lack of prestige and authority and poor pay made these jobs unattractive.[43] As no administrative unit below the *hsiang* level had its own regular income, officials were forced to make ends meet through unlawful exactions from the people on a routine basis.[44] Not surprisingly, by 1944, the quality of *pao-chia* systems had deteriorated to such an extent that Sun Fo (then vice chairman of the Executive Yüan) was moved to state in public that "all these Chiefs are bad elements. Not even one out of ten is any good; all of them are local rascals and oppressive gentry and were formerly opponents of our revolution but are now holding most important positions in our government."[45]

How could this sorry state of affairs have come about? Why did the central government not do something to insure that only loyal and competent people were enlisted to manage local governments? Was the central government rendered helpless by forces beyond its control? These questions compel us to go beyond the institutional variables mentioned above and look at the political process itself.

Political Support

Central-Regional Tensions

No inquiry into the causes of the failure of the KMT's wartime reforms can be complete without a serious look at the political context within which the reforms were attempted. No political reform could ever be effective by administrative fiat. While institutional rationality and manpower sufficiency are important factors, the success of a reform must ultimately depend on a favorable political environment; on how receptive and cooperative the politically powerful elements are toward such a fundamental transformation of the nature and structure of the political game. Therefore, the failure of the new-*hsien* program can be understood in terms of the central government's inability to overcome the resistance of these elements to change. In China, it means that we must look again at the central-regional relationship.

One of the most crucial political trends of modern China was the progressive decline of central government power and the corresponding rise of regional power. Although this process first began in the second half of the nineteenth century, it was during the early Republican years that these regional power structures came into full maturity. Thus began modern regional power structures in Shansi, Hunan, Hupei, Szechwan, Yünnan, Kweichow, Kwangsi, and Kwangtung. Most of the southern militarists took advantage of the busy fighting among the powerful warlords in the north to consolidate their control in their respective spheres of influence, and remained immune from the central government between 1928 and 1936 when the KMT was fighting one challenger after another in central and north China. By the time the Sino-Japanese War forced the KMT to retreat to these provinces, it found the field already pre-empted by well-entrenched local regimes.[46]

Regionalism, defined as a collective consciousness displayed by the people of a given geographical area of their distinctiveness from their neighbors, was by no means a new phenomenon in twentieth-century China; it had been around for centuries. The foundations of regionalism were complex. Geographically, China was divided into numerous small communities often separated by natural barriers. In many such communities the people developed distinctive life-styles, folk arts, and different dialects, which generated a strong sense of distinct identity, particularly when reinforced by truncated patterns of commerce and communications. Ideologically, even as Confucianism served as an integrating force, it gave much latitude in the exercise of decision-making power to local groups under the nominal existence of a centralized bureaucratic empire. Bureaucratic practices like the quota system for civil service examinations or the patronage system further accentuated people's consciousness of their regional origins. Functionally, the central government was designed to play a very limited role, and there was a long tradition of local governments taking charge over a host of responsibilities in taxation, education, construction, law and security, social relief and welfare, and the like.[47]

While some measure of regional autonomy was always a part of the Chinese political reality, regionalism itself was raised to the level of political consciousness only during periods of political-military chaos. Regionalism became legitimate under these conditions because it offered the promise to "protect the land and pacify the people" (*pao-ching an-min*). It did not present itself as an alternative to the centralized bureaucratic system, but as a temporary solution until central authority was restored. In this sense, regionalism was never a competing ideology to centralism, but a justification for a transitional arrangement during the decline of central authority. The central government was willing to tolerate the reality of regional autonomy to a certain extent precisely because it seldom felt threatened by an ideology of regionalism as a new foundation of political legitimacy.

This relationship between the center and the regions began to change as modern nationalism replaced the imperial principle as the new ideological foundation of the Chinese state. Tension between regionalism and centralism mounted for two reasons. On the one hand, modern nationalism, being all-embracing in its claims, was far less tolerant with assertions of regional or subnational distinctiveness.[48] The inexorable expansion of the functional capabilities of the modern bureaucracy also enabled the nascent nationalist state to intrude into areas previously reserved for local leaders. On the other hand, the prolonged civil strife in the waning days of the imperial authority provided the opportunity for an increasing number of regional actors to make their appearance on the political stage.[49] Since the late nineteenth century, the rise of regionalism was probably facilitated by such factors as increasing economic differentiation, the organizations of new armies, reaction against Manchu autocratism, and the mounting interest of the provincial ruling class in their own affairs through the provincial assemblies and the constitutional movement.[50]

Although during the 1910s and 1920s, some regionalists briefly tried to advance regionalism in various forms (e.g., provincial constitutionalism, federalism, associations of autonomous provinces, etc.) as an ideological and institutional alternative to centralism, none ever attracted a significant following among the politically powerful strata.

Equally noteworthy was the fact that regionalism's claim to "protect the land and pacify the people" became increasingly disingenuous during the Peiyang era. The record of these years amply demonstrates that a political group's stand on regionalism or centralism tended to vary in proportion to its political-military fortune. In other words, the right of regional autonomy became the defense of the militarily weak to perpetuate their dictatorship within a province against those who were strong. But as soon as they themselves gained strength, they would easily convert to enthusiastic advocates of centralism. This was repeatedly demonstrated by the careers of big warlords like Chang Tso-lin and Yen Hsi-shan, or minor ones like Chao Heng-t'i and Lu Yung-hsiang.

In this context, one must also not fail to appreciate the true reality of regional rule. Among the numerous regimes that came into existence and vanished with rapid succession during the early twentieth century, very few were ever genuinely regional in character. Most were carpetbag regimes such as Lu Yung-hsiang in Chekiang and Ch'i Hsieh-yüan in Kiangsu in the 1920s, Kwangsi's control over Hunan, the Nineteenth Route Army-inspired "People's Government" in Fukien of the 1930s, or Hsüeh Yüeh's government in Hunan and Li Tsung-jen's government in Anhwei in the 1940s. The list could be extended much further. Even among regimes that were indigenous to a region, few ever satisfactorily performed the many socioeconomic-political functions that a government should perform.[51] Over time, most regimes in the province acquired a predominantly militaristic outlook. They subsisted upon the soldiers and guns they controlled and not on the support of the people.

Thus, during the war years, in the majority of cases, "regional" should more accurately mean the shared regional origin of the commanders and their soldiers, but not necessarily any affinity between their regimes and the people they ruled. For instance, a Szechwan army in Anhwei would still be labelled a regional army. Thus, regional entities were defined more by their "noncenter" or "anticentral" outlook than by their intrinsically regional qualities. This semantic confusion makes it somewhat harder to understand Nationalist politics properly, for in the language of Nationalist politics, a regional regime could move many times from one part of a province to another, or from one province to another province and still retain its "regional" label, as long as it resisted assimilation into the central system. As the general population was usually left out of the picture, regional and central powers struggled for political and military dominance. By the same token, the Chungking government's inability to resolve the central-regional tension inevitably had a most devastating impact on its capacity to execute the war.

In many ways, Szechwan offered an example of the most destructive relationship between the central government and a province during the war. A discussion of the Szechwan case may serve to illuminate the central-regional relationship in general.

With a territory of 1.2 million square kilometers and a population of over fifty million, Szechwan was the largest as well as the richest province in the country. It was also the most war-torn province. From 1911 to 1938, provincial warlords had fought over 470 civil wars of varying magnitudes. By 1930, Szechwan was reported to have 1.5 million men in arms either in the regular provincial armies, the militia, or banditry. The government was oppressive and the taxes were crushing. Education was neglected and the economy was in a shambles. In a word, it was the worst-governed province, although in a typical warlord style.[52]

Even during the 1930s, Szechwan militarists continued as masters of their defense zones. Civil wars served as the final arbiter of territorial and power relationships among the warlords. The role of the central government was to confirm what the wars had settled. The first time the central government directed its attention to Szechwan affairs was in 1934 when the Communists were driven through the province on their Long March. Chiang had originally wanted to dispatch some central troops into Szechwan to pursue the fleeing Communists, but had to abandon the plan when Liu Hsiang objected. Instead, a compromise was worked out to allow Chiang to dispatch a staff corps headed by Ho Kuo-kuang, a man acceptable to Liu. Soon the staff corps was expanded into the Chungking headquarters of the Generalissimo of the Supreme Military Council (wei-yüan-chang hsin-ying) and given nominal jurisdiction over Szechwan, Yünnan, Kweichow, and Sikang. In reality, however, political, economic, and military powers remained firmly in the hands of the provincial warlords.[53]

The Japanese invasion and the subsequent military defeats of the central government forced the local leaders to confront the new realities of the war. The physical relocation of the central government to Chungking increased the contradictions between the KMT and the provincial power structures. As related in previous chapters on the war, the preoccupation of

Chiang's armies with the fighting in the east created an impasse between the KMT and Szechwan forces, and neither was able to impose its will upon the other. Hence it was not until November, 1940, that the central government's appointment of Chang Ch'ün as governor was accepted by the provincial militarists, but the latter continued to preserve their own territorial regimes. Thus, in the 1940s, the city of Chengtu, which was only 250 miles from Chungking, became the bastion of antigovernment elements under the protection of Teng Hsi-hou and Liu Wen-hui. The political scene in Chengtu was vividly described in an American Office of Strategic Service (OSS) memo in February, 1945.

> These people are backward warlords and disappointed politicians. Their purpose is to oppose the government regardless of whether or not the government is a satisfactory one. The object of their opposition is to force the government to compromise with them, to protect the unscrupulous, and to place disappointed politicians in high government positions. Their opposition toward the government is a form of blackmail. On the one hand, Ch'engtu warlords deal in opium and disturb commodity prices by hoarding food, and on the other, they call for democracy. Some of the less-important persons there stirred trouble only to get themselves appointed to high positions.[54]

Just as in Chengtu, many other areas in Szechwan were in the hands of local gentry, chambers of commerce, secret societies, local bullies, and warlords who completely paralyzed the party and government.[55] When Chang Ch'ün first became governor in 1941, he openly lamented the vestiges of the feudal system of independent spheres of influence as interfering with national laws and institutions.[56] Four years later, when he summed up wartime politics in the province, he again said that the internal division of the province by warlords, particularly in the western section, seriously retarded all attempts toward economic reconstruction and exacerbated social erosion as manifested by the widespread opium addiction, gambling, the pervasive influence of secret societies, and the constant harrassment by bandits.[57] None of these things would have been possible without the protection of local militarists in defiance of the central government.

Politically, the disintegration manifested itself in the local leaders' strong resistance against any central government effort to penetrate into their private domains. The local leaders showed no interest in cooperating with the central government in promoting political reforms which they knew would eventually undercut their own power. Consequently, while they could not prevent the central government from initiating reforms, they were perfectly able to sabotage them. Furthermore, their concern with building up their own positions often compelled local politicians to seek the support of the vested interest groups in the traditional socio-political order, such as landlords, militia leaders, secret societies, and local bullies. During the war, local politicians often embroiled officials in factional feuds, obstructed the judicial process, blocked the collection of taxes, forced the government to appoint their cronies to official positions, and in general made life miserable for the government.[58]

As the war dragged on, the central government's inability to establish firm control over Szechwan came to have even graver implications. Szechwan, with its 139 *hsien,* constituted 30 percent of the number of administrative units in nonoccupied China. Furthermore, its population exceeded the combined total of the provinces of Yünnan, Kweichow, Kwangsi, and Shensi, the only important provinces that remained entirely free from Japanese armies at the time.[59]

Indeed, the central government-Szechwan relationship mirrored the relationship between the central government and many other provinces. Yünnan under Lung Yün, Kwangsi under Huang Hsü-ch'u, Kwangtung under Li Han-hun, Sikang under Liu Wen-hui, and Shansi under Yen Hsi-shan were all beyond the control of the central government.

But in order to fully understand the strength of local resistance, we must go beyond the provincial entities and look at the structures of power at the very basic levels. For just as Chungking's power failed to penetrate the provinces, the power of many provincial governments also could not reach the counties and villages. Even under nominally regional regimes, there usually existed subprovincial military-political power structures that remained out of the effective reach of the provincial government.[60] This consideration compels us to take a close look at local power structures.

Local Power Structures

The Chinese countryside had long been governed by a duopoly of both the formal local government and the informal government composed of the local elite. From the imperial past, there existed a division of labor with the local elite performing certain functions that the local government was unable or poorly equipped to perform.[61] Even after the collapse of the imperial order, the local elite continued to play a key role in local politics. Writing about the basic power structure in rural China of the 1940s, the noted sociologist Fei Hsiao-tung observed:

Public affairs included problems of irrigation, self-defense, mediation in personal disputes, mutual aid, recreation, and religious activities. In China, such things are community affairs. . . . They are not an affair of government but are managed by the local community under the leadership of the better-educated and wealthier family heads.[62]

In his report of a village in Szechwan just before the Communist takeover, A. Doak Barnett wrote,

Practically speaking, in a rural area such as Hsiehmahsiang, many local affairs are out of the realm of government, and are regulated by tradition and by non-governmental groups such as families, clans, and secret societies.[63]

The problem of resistance to central policies of course extended all the way to the local society where the entrenched social and economic forces constituted the last wall of resistance against centrally directed bureaucratic penetration. In most cases, the power on the county and village levels was firmly lodged in the hands of the local ruling families. Each village was usually controlled by a few dominant families. They maintained a virtual monopoly of power by consulting each other and acting in concert. They acted as the custodians of tradition, the guardians of morality, the promoters of education and religious faith. But they also ran the village government either directly or through their proxies to collect taxes, issue licenses, and allocate labor service. Finally, they monopolized the physical power on the village level and exercised the power to interpret, implement, or even make their own laws. They not only financed, equipped, and commanded the militia, but often entered into league with gangster-type secret societies to oppress the people at will. In many cases, these families literally held the power of life and death over the peasants.[64] Frequently, these powerful families' influence could extend far beyond their own small areas. They could enter into pacts of mutual assistance with powerful families from other localities to have a decisive voice in county or even provincial politics. They could exploit the court system to engage in protracted law suits against officials who caused them trouble. When their interests were seriously jeopardized, many would not hesitate to pick up arms in open defiance against the government.

While there was a continuity of the linkage between the local formal government and the local ruling class from the imperial past to the war years, the rural situation did not remain static. At least three significant changes had occurred to affect the quality of rural life. First, there was a considerable exodus of traditional elite from the villages to the urban centers to become commercial entrepreneurs or professionals, thereby weakening their organic links with the villages. Insofar as they kept their properties back home, their interests would be placed under the care of hired managers, an arrangement that usually increased the economic burden of the peasants.[65]

Second, there was a significant breakdown of the relatively homogeneous composition of the ruling elite. In his study of the late Ch'ing period, Tung-tsu Ch'u still believed that "the privileged status of the Chinese gentry did not derive from wealth or the ownership of landed property."[66] Rather, "membership was based upon the attainment of bureaucratic status or of the qualifications of such status."[67] In other words, they were degree-holders imbued with Confucian ethics.

In the four decades following the abolition of the civil service examination in 1905, there was probably an increasing trend for elite status to be equated with economic power per se. In the midst of the collapsing social and moral order of the early twentieth century, there emerged a group of nouveaux riches who gained wealth through gambling, smuggling, hoarding, opium trade, and other illicit activities. Their ascendance in rural areas might have further scared the traditional gentry away from the home villages. As these people made their fortunes in nonagricultural activities and often outside their own localities, they would feel little constrained by traditional values such as hard work, frugality, or compassion for the less fortunate villagers.[68] This probably produced a sharpening class conflict between the ruling elite and the masses along economic lines.

Third, in the twentieth century, the army definitely became a vehicle for rapid upward social mobility. A great number of soldiers brought their fortunes back to their native villages, purchased land, and became powerful local figures. The war itself might have enhanced their power in their respective localities. As our earlier discussion on the distribution of military units suggested, a large number of regular provincial troops were sent from the interior to the front to assume combat duty. Meanwhile, the few central government units dispatched to the interior were usually stationed in base areas around big cities like Chungking or Kunming to keep watch over the regional armies left behind. Between them there existed a stalemate. Consequently, a military power vacuum was created in the vast countryside, facilitating its occupation by numerous locally organized armed individuals or groups, including secret societies and bandits. These men of violence created an atmosphere in the countryside in which the threat of violence became the most effective arbiter of local affairs.

A most vivid portrait of the power of a minor militarist in his locality was offered by Fei Hsiao-tung. He told us of how a regiment commander in the Yünnan army had amassed several thousand *taels* of silver during his military exploits, wielded enormous influence over the appointment and dismissal of the *hsien* magistrates, had become a big landlord, and been picked by the government to represent his county in the National Assembly. Meanwhile, his relatives began to commit "many wicked deeds, such as beating the common people and blackmailing them." Finally, when they directly threatened the established gentry and rich merchant families, the latter decided to appease them by offering them plum positions in the county government so that they could enrich themselves through bribery and embezzlement.[69]

Another sign of the rise of violence in village life was the influence of secret societies, which usually allied with the landed classes and indulged in several typical activities: they coerced businessmen to submit "protection fees," collected commissions from gambling houses, ran opium dens, engaged in illegal sales of arms and contrabands, and conspired with bandits.[70]

Therefore, our conception of rural power structures and the relationship between the elite and masses must incorporate the very significant changes occurring in the decades preceding the war. In the case of Szechwan, the most populous province in the war, the changes were brought about by a number of factors—the decline of old-style landlords and the sale of their land, the concentration of land into the hands of militarists and newly rising bureaucrats, the transfer of land from peasants in debt to their creditors (money lenders), and the seizure of land by armed local bullies and tyrants.[71]

In the 1920s and 1930s, this new rural elite had already devised numerous ways to shield itself from the exactions of warlords. Even though civil wars in Szechwan were numerous and warlords' main revenues came from land taxes, the heavy burdens were invariably placed on the shoulders of the poor, ignorant, and helpless peasants, while the landlords either escaped unscathed or perhaps even profited as the warlords' local agents.[72] Therefore, long before the arrival of the Nationalists, the rural power structures had developed certain styles of operations in dealing with the peasant populations and certain defense mechanisms against pressures from outside (table 7).

TABLE 7
Transformation of the Composition of Landlords in Szechwan, mid-1930s

	Type of landlord		Amount of Land Owned	
Area	New Landlords[a]	Old-style Landlords[b]	New Landlords[a]	Old-style Landlords[b]
East	46%	51.2%	88%	10%
South	42.6	52.6	86.8	10.8
West	71	27	87	11
North	73	26	87	3

a. "New landlords" here means militarists, new bureaucrats, militia leaders, money lenders, and local bullies.
b. "Old landlords" here means prosperous farmers, traditional gentry families.
Sources: Chang Hsiao-mei, *Ssu-ch'uan ching-chi ts'an-k'ao tzu-liao* (Shanghai, 1939), section A, pp. 23–24.

Given this reality of power at the local level, it is not surprising that the records of regional or provincial politicians during the war were replete with complaints about their inability to cope with "local tyrants and bad gentry" (*t'u-hao lieh-shen*). Not only did Chungking-appointed officials encounter enormous resistance, but even some powerful provincial and regional leaders had trouble extending their control into the localities. Governor Wu Ting-ch'ang of Kweichow, a KMT man, complained that personnel problems created by local gentry caused him much greater pain than administrative issues and warned that the control of society could easily slip into the hands of secret societies completely.[73] Governor Li Han-hun of Kwangtung, a powerful regional militarist in his own right, repeatedly expressed his frustration at his inability to exercise control over local governments under his jurisdiction.[74] No less a figure than Ch'en Kuo-fu once confessed that he was powerless to protect a *hsien* magistrate from the vendettas of local potentates after the magistrate had already been driven from office.[75] Finally, Li Tsung-huang, who replaced Lung Yün as the governor of Yünnan in 1945, described the Yünnan countryside scene as follows:

> The bad gentry and local tyrants conspired with each other in schemes of corruption. The clerks and other low-ranking agents of local government competed with each other in extortions and oppression. . . . They embezzled public funds; they sucked the juice and blood of the people. Such endless exploitation produced enormous turmoil among the people. [Author's translation][76]

It should be noted that even in a rigidly controlled province like Kwangsi, the government ran into stiff opposition from the local elites when it tried to implement some reforms in the 1930s. Despite the superior military power in the government's hands, the power struggle ended inconclusively when the Sino-Japanese War broke out,[77] and the provincial government never quite succeeded in exercising tight control over the countryside during the war itself.

It is clear from the preceding discussion that if the KMT had wished to execute the war by mobilizing the nationalistic sentiments of the masses and the meager resources of the country, it would have had to arouse the masses from political apathy, give them a personal stake in winning the war, and convince them that the sacrifices were being shared fairly and equitably. Indeed, one oft-used wartime slogan was "Let those who have money contribute money, and let those who have labor contribute labor" (yu-ch'ien ch'u-ch'ien, yu-li ch'u-li). In a sense, this should have been the paramount goal of the new-*hsien* system. Yet the realization of this goal might have necessitated not only a material mobilization with everyone contributing more for national survival, but a social mobilization to shift the greater share of the sacrifices onto the class that was most capable of absorbing it, the local elites. Like so many other well-intended institutional reforms before it, the new-*hsien* system only played into the hands of the local ruling elites determined to protect their own interests. The Chungking government never resolved the contradiction between the mobilization goals of the new-*hsien* system and Chungking's own dependence on the defenders of rural status quo and stagnation to implement the system.

Therefore, as long as Chungking had to appease the regional and local powerholders, the prospects of any meaningful reforms were doomed. The political cost for the KMT was an extremely high one. In the three areas that most affected the people's livelihood and the execution of the war—land-grain tax collection, the conscription system, and general economic policy—we will find that the Chungking government's inability to discharge its functions properly eventually would cause such widespread alienation and demoralization of the people as to endanger the KMT's very survival.

But before we enter into a substantive discussion of these three specific wartime policies, one question still remains: in light of the political realities depicted earlier, why were the KMT leaders oblivious of them? How could they design and promulgate a new-*hsien* system in 1939 that was so unrealistic as, for instance, to call for a task force of trained and paid cadres by the millions?

While it would be difficult to document the process of intellectual fermentation of the program, several plausible explanations may be tentatively offered here.

First and foremost is Chiang's preoccupation with the military-diplomatic aspects of the war, to the neglect of domestic political and social issues. Two implications flowed from this factor. Chiang seemed to believe that he only needed the military to survive the war and the Americans to win the war. As Chiang was known to be a person who concentrated all powers into his own hands by wearing different hats in all offices, his attention span was severely overloaded, leaving little room for long-term problems that did not flash signals of imminent danger. His subordinates were known to deliberately hide the unpleasant truths of local politics from him, which might have led him to make gross miscalculations concerning the effort it might require to implement the new-*hsien* system.

On the other hand, Chiang's behavior during the Nanking period has already provided us with some clues to his basic political approach. His didactic, moralizing tendencies reflected an authoritarian view of society and state marked by strict hierarchy and order. From this mentality easily flowed the assumption that the bulk of the nation's political problems could be solved by more governmental directives and instructions. In conducting political activities, we find KMT officials to have changed little over the years. These KMT officials remained remote from the people, regarded the people as inferior and ignorant, and expected them to be the passive recipients of government policy, but never the participants of the political process. Even under the mounting crisis atmosphere of the war, they still labored to preserve the dignity of officialdom through observance of traditional ritualism and pious rhetoric.

The persistent use of the highly stylized classical language rather than the more popular vernacular in official communications was but one indication of the KMT's bureaucratic approach. Such a policy automatically excluded the bulk of the poorly educated masses from the arena of political communications. This kind of formalism inevitably exacerbated the disjunction between political discourse and political reality. Yet many KMT leaders seemed to genuinely believe that they had accomplished something by indulging in linguistic exercises and expected their rhetoric to have real impact on the public. Even as the enemy was closing in from all directions, KMT officials still preferred the security offered by their offices. From there, they could continue to churn out reams of paperwork on fancy projects and utopian objectives, rather than rolling up their sleeves and mingling with the crowd to engage in serious investigation and socioeconomic reconstruction with dedication and perseverance.

The new-*hsien* program also provided a glaring illustration of the intellectual lethargy and organizational ineptitude of the KMT leadership. The concept of a new system was accepted by Chiang in April, 1939, when he became aware of the unwieldiness of the old system for collecting taxes and conscripts. Within a month, a special commission was set up to draft a comprehensive revamping of *hsien* government. However, the commission was only given a staff of eighteen people and a monthly budget of C$8,100.[78] Under the stewardship of Li Tsung-huang, the KMT's expert on local government, the basic plan was finalized within two months (after eight hastily held meetings of some bureaucrats and scholars in Chungking) and promulgated with Chiang's personal blessings to the whole country for immediate implementation. The government further set the target date for the completion of this gigantic institutional revamping at three years. Even Li himself acknowledged later that this timetable was impossible to meet.[79] But Chiang declared himself satisfied with the plan on paper and warned that any official who questioned its feasibility would be regarded as cowardly and unrevolutionary.[80]

In all, during a span of only twenty-eight months, the commission rammed through forty-six sets of major laws, released over eighty publications, and reviewed the organizational charters of numerous *hsiens* from the seventeen provinces.[81] The Chungking government's cavalier pursuit of neatness and rationality on paper had indeed reached a new height. But the paperwork had no relevance to political reality, and for the KMT leaders to expect otherwise was only an act of self-delusion on a grand scale.

Major Policy Failures of the Kuomintang Government

Land Tax Collection

Land tax had been under provincial control since the beginning of the Republic, while the central government relied on the customs, salt, and consolidated taxes, which constituted over 75 percent of the latter's revenues up to 1937.[82] Geographically, the main sources of these revenues were in the coastal areas where the KMT government had a firm control before the war. Through a legislative maneuver, the KMT government attempted in the 1930s to assign a greater portion of the land tax to the *hsien* governments (as a part of the political reform package) and leave a smaller portion to the provincial government. However, the inability of the central government to extend its power into the interior provinces meant that most provinces were free to preserve their own semi-independent tax structures in those years.[83]

When the war broke out, the central government's immediate concern was to encourage production, stockpiling, and efficient distribution of grain to meet emergency needs.[84] But the government was losing territory at an alarming rate, and the major communications arteries were paralyzed by Japanese air raids. Soon there emerged a serious disparity in grain prices, which in turn threatened grain supply to the army and the government employees.[85] In early 1940, a major grain crisis was at hand.[86] The government was also rudely awakened to the fact that its regular revenue bases had been seriously eroded by inflation while the land tax rates remained unchanged.[87] As grain prices skyrocketed, the situation obviously required a fundamental revamping of the collection machinery from top to bottom.[88]

Finally in July, 1941, the government created a Ministry of Grain Management (*liang shih pu*) to assure adequate supplies to the army and government employees, as well as to make grain available to the general public at equitable prices. Since the central government's traditional revenue sources had basically been lost to the enemy, under the new system the National Government reclaimed the right from the provinces to collect land tax, now to be paid in grain instead of cash. In order to assure control over surplus grain and to combat inflation, the government also declared in 1942 that it would purchase surplus grain from the producers at fixed prices and sell it to the general public on a license basis.[89]

Equally noteworthy was the government's hope to tighten its fiscal control over the local government, to cut off the revenue base of provincial governments and make provincial and *hsien* governments dependent on subsidies from the national government. It had also hoped that the new land tax system would expedite the process of land registration and survey, abolish unauthorized exactions by local governments, but still obtain a fourfold increase in real revenues as a result of reform. It believed that this increase would enable both the central and local governments to spend more on economic construction and social services.[90]

Hence, four years of war had elapsed before the government was able to develop a coherent policy on the grain issue, a policy that signified a central government attempt to extend its power directly into China's countryside and to exercise direct control over its people's productive activities on a scale unprecedented in modern Chinese history. But it soon became apparent that some of the prerequisites for the successful implementation of the grain policy were absent. The very first obstacle confronting the government was how to determine the tax scale. Prolonged political disorder in preceding generations had brought great confusion to landholding records in all the provinces. Under the warlords, there was deliberate falsification of records, ever-rising tax rates, and widespread corruption by the collecting agents.[91] According to Professor John Lossing Buck, in 1937 about one-third of the land possessed by large and small holders was not even on the tax rolls.[92] Up to December, 1940, only 234 *hsien* had completed the land registration process,[93] but even fewer *hsien* had ever verified the registration with actual land survey.[94]

In almost all provinces in the 1940s, the old records were still in the custody of the traditional local clerks (*she shu*) who alone could understand and interpret them. This fact compelled the central government to rely almost exclusively on the existing basic-level personnel to collect taxes in much the same way as they had for generations, even though the new system presupposed a greater degree of control from the central government.

This situation created the opportunity for all kinds of illegal acts. Landlords and other powerful local elements either refused to register their landholdings or broke up their holdings into smaller parcels to evade tax payments. Embezzlement by tax collectors, the use of militia or soldiers to compel collections, the arbitrary assessment of quotas, the use of enclosure or the imposition of heavy fines for late payments, and the levying of unauthorized additional taxes were all common practices that the *pao-chia* chiefs and other local power holders played a major role in perpetrating.[95]

The government's policy of compulsory purchase of grain from producers at a fixed price fared no better. Every province took the liberty of setting its own quota and price for such purchases.[96] In the absence of land survey and registration and a reliable census, as well as some reliable measurement of local output and consumption figures, the central government had to permit the provincial governments to impose their own quota upon the *hsien* governments, which in turn would apportion it to the *hsiang* and village governments. The whole system in fact was controlled by local power holders and worked very much like the arbitrary *t'an-k'uan* system (emergency assessment) of the 1920s.[97]

The poor implementation of the grain policy was due in no small measure to the shortage of qualified cadres. In 1941, the central government had less than 200 qualified people in the entire country to put the policy in motion.[98] Training of grain tax specialists began hastily in 1942, but by 1943, when the total manpower employed in the grain tax branches on all levels had reached 175,000, only some 9,000 of them had undergone any training at all, mostly short term.[99] This means that the same people who collected land taxes for the warlords now were relied upon to implement the new grain policy.

Beyond the government's manpower shortage, the complexities of the grain collection procedures also created ample potential for injustices. Prior to 1941, people paid land taxes in cash to collectors who visited the villages. After 1941, people had to transport the bulky grain at their own expense to collecting stations in each *hsien*. Typically, this meant that people had to carry sacks of grain on their own backs or by draft animals and spend several days making delivery. At the collecting stations, the taxpayers were vulnerable to various forms of harrassment by the collectors who might reject grain for alleged inferior quality, or use illegal scales to weigh it.[100]

Once collected, the grain needed to be concentrated in places where storage facilities were available. Again, the *hsien* government would press people into work gangs to transport it, often at grossly inadequate wages.

By 1941, the government simply did not have the support of a modern infrastructure to mobilize the country's physical resources equal to the task of fighting a well-equipped and highly mobile enemy force at a sustained pace. The interior provinces were particularly hard hit because of their difficult mountainous terrain and lack of modern transportation. On the average, some two-thirds of the grain (about forty million *shih*) would have to be retransported annually over long distances to the troops. Yet in 1942, only 100 trucks were assigned for grain transportation. In 1943–44, the government organized a fleet of 440 wooden carts and 900 wooden boats for transportation, but these efforts were too meager to satisfy the overall needs. No wonder the Minister of Grain Management identified transportation as his most difficult problem during the war.[101]

Grain storage presented a further challenge. Not only had the traditional government never been called upon to handle a storage problem of such magnitude, but the traditional granary system had been widely damaged during the preceding half century. Between 1941 and 1944, the government was able to increase storage capacity by twenty-six million *shih*, but the actual capacity was less than half of what was required.[102] As a result, the government resorted to seizure of civilian residences, schools, and other buildings and converted them into temporary storage. The severe lack of facilities not only produced waste and damage to the grain, but created numerous opportunities for local bureaucrats to indulge in corruption and oppression.[103]

The final step of the new grain policy was its allocation and actual distribution to the military units. But the confusion of the military command system and the general tendency of the military to take precedence over the civilian government greatly exacerbated the difficulties in grain distribution. In violation of the law, troops often took grain out of storage without authorization, or seized whatever grain they could lay their hands on directly from the villages. In some areas, the *hsien* magistrates actually encouraged the troops to collect their own grain so that the *hsien* government did not have to worry about collection, transportation, and storage.[104]

In administering the compulsory purchase policy, the government routinely paid prices far below the market prices, only a small fraction of which would be paid in cash, while the balance would be paid in government bonds that soon lost their value due to inflation.[105]

The provinces enjoyed great latitude in deciding not only how much grain was to be purchased each year, but how the payment would be made. After 1943, nine provinces converted compulsory ''purchase'' to compulsory ''loan'' of grain and stopped making payments to farmers. One province, Anhwei, even converted it to compulsory ''donation.'' By 1944, in fact, all provinces had converted to compulsory loan to various degrees. Thus by an expedient change of the law, the farmers' burden was significantly increased.[106]

While in the interior provinces it was the *hsien* government that took charge of the compulsory purchase or loan, along the front it was the troops that had the responsibility to round up any surplus grain before the Japanese and puppet forces could reach it. Frequently, purchase amounted to outright confiscation.

While the new grain policy was originally designed to meet the demands of the army, government employees, and the civilian population simultaneously, the results lagged far behind these ambitious goals. During the 1940s, the grain from land tax alone was insufficient to meet the military needs, and had to be supplemented by compulsory purchase. As for government employees, only those of the central government in Chungking were placed on a ration system. Central government employees elsewhere as well as most provincial employees were given stipends that were invariably inadequate to keep up with the rising price of grain everywhere.[107] In addition, the new grain policy cut deeply into the provincial and *hsien* government budgets. For instance, in Chekiang, the authorized provincial government budget of 1941 was only one-thirtieth of its 1937 budget, while the *hsien* budget was only one-sixth of its prewar level.[108] But with the central government being as weak as it was, there was nothing to prevent the local governments from levying additional grain tax from the people to meet their own needs. Therefore, for instance, in 1942, some twenty million *shih* of grain had been levied by local governments independent of the national levy; this amounted to nearly one-quarter of the national combined total of both tax and purchase.[109]

As for the general consumers, their needs were so huge that the government was never able to control a sufficient amount of grain from the villages to enforce a comprehensive price control system during the war. Consequently, most urban residents were at the mercy of grain hoarders and runaway inflation.[110]

It would be difficult to appreciate the magnitude of the challenge that the KMT government faced in its wartime grain policy without putting the grain issue in its proper historical perspective.The supply of grain in the market before the war was a function of the size of grain output and population. As government figures on prewar grain output show, the provinces of Kiangsu, Honan, Hupei, Kwangtung, and Szechwan were the top producers in the country, but the provinces that regularly reported surplus grain for export were Kiangsu, Hunan, and Anhwei. Szechwan and Chekiang were occasional exporters, but the other provinces were either deficient in grain or managed to be self-sufficient.[111]

The war forced an entirely different situation upon the government. By 1941, only the provinces of Szechwan, Yünnan, Kweichow, Hunan, Kwangsi, Honan, and Shensi were free from enemy forces. In this vast area, only Szechwan and Hunan were regular surplus provinces.

It should be recalled that at the height of militarism in modern China in the 1920s, the whole country supported a military force of 2.5 to 3 million soldiers. But in the 1940s, the unoccupied provinces, whose total grain output was less than 50 percent of China's prewar total, had to support a military force of much larger size[112] and also sustain a level of military activity far above any ever experienced by the country before.

Consequently, the burden on the people in these provinces was exceptionally heavy.

But the burden was particularly heavy for the southwestern provinces of Szechwan, Kwangsi, Yünnan, and Kweichow. Before the war, the combined grain output of these provinces constituted about 22 percent of the national total. By 1941, they contributed 31.5 percent of the combined national total in taxes and purchased grain.[113] The dependency of the government on this region was to increase with years. If we look at the years 1941–45, Szechwan alone contributed 31.6 percent of the national total.[114]

Although at the official rate, tax in kind and compulsory purchase should constitute about 5 to 6 percent of grain output in Nationalist China,[115] the real burden must have been considerably higher, possibly over 10 percent, when all illegal exactions were included (table 8).[116] In view of the subsistence level of living most Chinese farmers led, this already constituted a serious drain of their resources. But even worse was the fact that the burden of war was quite unevenly and unjustly distributed. The poor peasants were deprived of their livelihood, while the rich peasants and landlords not only evaded the taxes but often became hoarders of grain and made huge profits. Not surprisingly, peasant uprisings began to threaten the government in the interior provinces soon after the implementation of the new land tax policy. These disturbances occurred in Kweichow, Tsinghai, Ninghsia, Kansu, and even Szechwan itself in 1942–43, sometimes involving 50,000 armed peasants or more in protest of the corruption and inefficiency of the government's tax collection system.[117] At times even provincial or local garrison troops would desert and join their ranks. The situation obviously got worse with time, and there was

TABLE 8
Grain Obtained by the Central Government through Tax and Purchase, 1941–45

Year	Total Amount (in *shih*)
1941	43,120,684
1942	65,966,400
1943	64,476,404
1944	56,958,745
1945	29,591,826

Source: Hsü K'an, *Hsü K'o-t' ing hsien-sheng wen-ts'un,* (Taipei, 1970) pp. 187–90.

Note: The above annual totals are composed of 52.5% in current tax, 23% in advance payment of tax, and 24.5% in purchase. Illegal local levies or military seizures are not included.

a noticeable increase in banditry in these provinces when peasants joined with existing bandit groups.[118]

Finally, the grain policy was entirely dependent on the course of the war. Had the war gone well for China, her grain supply base would have been broadened. But in fact, the territorial control of the government declined. The grain-producing provinces of Hunan, Honan, Kiangsi, and Chekiang were partially occupied at all times. In addition, after 1940, when the general war reached an impasse, the Japanese developed the strategy of making forays into government-held territories at harvest seasons for the specific purpose of seizing or destroying grain. Deprived of their regular supplies, the government troops resorted to wholesale confiscation of grain from the people. This was precisely what happened in Honan in 1942–43. When the armies of T'ang En-po were driven by the Japanese into western Honan, they imposed grain taxes on the people that sometimes reached 30 to 50 percent of the crop.[119]

The peasants were forced to pay or face arrest or execution. Many had to sell land or even members of family to meet these obligations. As conditions in Honan had already been deteriorating for several years, a serious famine situation was created and some twenty to thirty million people were driven to the brink of death by starvation. But these troops continued to press their demands on the people and the central government offered no relief.[120]

By far the most severe blow to the government's grain policy came in 1944 with Operation Ichigō. The Japanese forces seized Honan in its entirety, as well as large areas in Hunan, Kwangsi, and Kiangsi. In these areas, the harvest of 1944 was entirely lost to the enemy and enormous pressure was placed on Szechwan to support the huge numbers of defeated troops congested in the southwestern corner of the country. With the war drawing to its conclusion, the grain tax burden of the people in the interior provinces also reached its peak. The combined effects of large numbers of refugees, accelerating grain price rise, the breakdown of the administrative machinery, and the military's taking things into their own hands created a situation of lawlessness and exploitation that bordered on anarchy and plunged the government into a situation of unprecedented gloom and despair. By any standard, the utterly ineffective and oppressive methods the government employed to implement its grain policy must be regarded as a key reason why the government lost the support of the rural population in the waning years of the war.

Conscription Policy

When the warlords needed soldiers in the early twentieth century, they relied either on voluntary enlistment or impressment. The first attempt to introduce a conscription system was made in 1933. But strenuous Japanese pressure forced the government to limit its geographical application to the Nanking area alone.[121] When the war broke out, this system was hastily extended to all parts of the country. But by 1941, this system was proven to be totally ineffective. As a result, a new system was adopted whereby the whole country was organized into fifteen "army-control areas" corresponding to the provinces, and 109 "division-control areas" corresponding to the administrative special districts. With minor revisions, this sytem lasted the entire duration of the war.

The primary purpose of the 1941 reorganization was to strengthen the cooperation between the army and the civilian government. The system assigned to all military units specific geographical areas from which they were to draw conscripts. Generally, each division-control area was responsible for supplying manpower to an army: a high-ranking officer from the army would serve as the ex officio commander of the division-control area. In 1943, the government decided to combine conscription with an army retraining program. According to this program, every army was to send one of its three divisions to its designated division-control area for regrouping and training while keeping the other two divisions in combat position. This regrouping and training program was to be conducted on a rotational basis so that theoretically all three divisions would have been strengthened within a certain period of time.[122]

Just as with the grain policy, the linchpin of the conscription policy was the cadres on the *hsien* level and lower, and therefore both policies shared similar difficulties. Not surprisingly, qualified cadres were in woefully short supply. Between 1936 and 1946, a total of only 3,048 *hsien*-level cadres had received a one- to two-month training on the management of conscription affairs.[123] Consequently, the same people who mismanaged other governmental policies also mismanaged conscription. Underage children and sole sons of families were routinely drafted even though they were specifically exempted by law, while sons of landlords, wealthy merchants, and secret society leaders were either illegally exempted or could pay others to answer the call. As no reliable census was ever taken, local officials resorted to large-scale manufacturing or falsification of existing records to show favoritism or to sell exemptions at a price. Equally prevalent was the practice by these local officials of pocketing government stipends intended for family support of the draftees.[124]

The men who were eventually drafted usually came from the poorest one-third or one-half of the families in the village who could not buy their way out and who could least afford to leave their families behind. Sometimes when local draftees were insufficient, village heads or *pao-chia* chiefs would send out police and militiamen to round up hapless passersby in the vicinity.[125] In some localities, there was even a black market where professional deserters would answer draft calls for anyone able to pay the right price. Also organized racketeers would kidnap tourists and sell them to village heads to meet the quota.[126]

Because there was a general lack of health clinics or medical examiners, sick men were drafted while healthy ones went free.[127] Once conscripts were collected, they faced further abuses on their way to the training camps. For many of them, their health had been ruined before they reached their destination. Thus, it was not surprising that Governor Chang Ch'un reported that only 28.9 percent of Szechwan's 1942 draftees met the Chinese health standards.[128]

Given such miserable treatment, morale and desertion of draftees became major problems. Frequently, only half of the draftees would ever reach base camp.[129] In the course of the war, government records show that some fourteen million people had been conscripted, although the actual figure should have been considerably higher.[130] In any event, this represented a large segment of the rural population in the interior provinces whose lives were traumatized or destroyed by the conscription system. Since there was no regularized discharge system for soldiers, and since China's total battlefield casualties were roughly three million, it leaves the whereabouts of about eleven million, or 80 percent, of the conscripts unaccounted for. We can only reasonably conclude that they either deserted or perished as the victims of a brutalized life in the army.

In no small measure, institutional confusion added to the difficulties of the conscription system.[131] It was not until the winter of 1943 that the government made an effort to integrate all aspects of conscription under a new ministry, the Ministry of Conscription (*ping-yi pu*). By this late date, however, the reorganization yielded few results.[132]

The upshot was that the conscription system during wartime remained a highly fragmented and localized system. The central government in Chungking decided how many men it needed each year and assigned a quota to each province. Once the quota was assigned, Chungking had little control over how it was to be met. Typically, each province would subdivide the quota to the *hsien* and the villages, and the manner of implementation hinged on the honesty, morality, and efficiency of local cadres. Often, even the provincial governors were powerless to intervene in the process.

Almost all provinces faced their own problems in implementing this system. In 1942, Governor Chang of Szechwan candidly acknowledged that conscription in the province was a mess and showed every sign of inefficiency and corruption.[133] More surprising is the fact that even a province like Kwangsi encountered mounting troubles in carrying out its conscription policy. Before the war, Kwangsi was governed by a fairly popular regime. It was also one of the very few provinces to have adopted a highly successful conscription program on a regular basis. During the war, Kwangsi continued to be beyond the reach of the central government, but by the 1940s its conscription program ran into serious resistance and the desertion rate began to climb.[134] In most other provinces, where the quality of government was far inferior to that of Kwangsi, the conscription policy inflicted indescribable suffering and injustice upon the people and turned them against the government in increasing numbers.

In connection with conscription were various forms of forced labor to perform military-related works. While the vast agrarian population provided the easiest solution to China's manpower needs, the implementation of the policy was frequently arbitrary, reckless, and downright inhuman. Even during harvest season, men, women, and children would be rounded up to serve as military porters or to work at construction sites. No provisions were made by the government to find substitute labor to attend to their farms during their absence. Government demands for civilian labor increased dramatically in the last years of the war. The most publicized case was the building of the Chengtu airbase to accommodate American B-29s. Without the aid of modern machines, about 400,000 Chinese laborers toiled for three months and completed the project literally with their bare hands.[135]

Just as with the grain tax, the temptation for the army to intervene directly in conscription was too great to resist. The pressure of war and the confused command system allowed military commanders to subvert the distinctions between military and civilian functions at will. Many commanders, resorting to warlord-type tactics, not only issued orders to *hsien* magistrates directly, but sometimes subjected them to humiliation and physical abuse. In addition, they assumed the authority to appoint or dismiss *hsiang* or *pao-chia* chiefs, or to lend their weight to local factional struggles. In many places, a veritable military dictatorship existed.[136] Every time a major campaign took place, the demands for conscripts surged dramatically, forcing the local government to resort to high-handed tactics to fill the badly depleted ranks of the armies. On several occasions after 1939, massive civil disturbances broke out in Szechwan in protest against the accelerated pace of conscription programs.[137]

Like other governmental activities, conscription reflected the fundamental shift of the balance of military and political power from the coastal provinces to the interior provinces. From July, 1937, to February, 1940, manpower for China's armies was fairly evenly distributed geographically. Szechwan only contributed 14.8 percent of the total supply of conscripts while the combined total of the southwestern provinces was 27.1 percent of the national total, 7,898,139.[138] The situation began to change after 1940 when Chinese armies were forced to retreat further into the interior provinces. The contribution of Szechwan increased to 20 percent in 1941 and 30.2 percent in 1945. Meanwhile, the combined contribution of the southwest was 31.3 percent in 1941, and 42.9 percent in 1945.[139] Clearly, by the second half of the war, the southwestern provinces had become the main suppliers of both human and physical resources to keep China in the war.[140] And this dependence gave the local leaders tremendous power to interfere with the government's policy.

Furthermore, up to 1940, the government policy was to supply regular armies with soldiers from the various existing provincial garrison troops on a priority basis. But by 1940, this source had been exhausted. Thereafter, the general practice was to supply troops with strong provincial loyalty with conscripts from their respective provinces, and to supply other nonprovincial troops with conscripts from nearby areas.[141] Although this supply policy was dictated by logistics, it unwittingly strengthened the regional loyalty structures of many provincial armies. In comparison, units considered loyal to the central government would be assigned to supply areas on a more random basis. The long-range effect was to shift the military balance of power among the major military groups from the rough prewar geographical equilibrium to a situation in which the soldiers and the commanders from southwestern provinces retained or even enhanced their local loyalty and solidarity, while the units from the central government command became a collection of men from diverse geographical backgrounds.

Economic Policy

While the mismanagement of land and conscription policies hit the country's agrarian population particularly hard, the urban dwellers, the salaried classes, and industrial labor were also the victims of poor government. In order to appreciate their plight and resentment against the government, one needs to examine the policy of fiscal irresponsibility of the Chungking government and its profound ramifications.

As noted previously, in the Nanking period the central government's major sources of revenues were customs, salt taxes, and taxes from monopolies and factory production. In particular, customs collection usually constituted well over half the total revenue from taxes. Shortly after the beginning of the war, much of these traditional sources had fallen into enemy hands. By 1939, these sources of taxes constituted only 5 percent of Chungking's revenues in cash.[142]

On the other hand, during the prewar decade, about 40 to 45 percent of the government's general cash budgetary expenditures was devoted to military purposes, about 30 percent for debt service, and the remaining for all other civilian programs.[143] Once the war began, the military costs outstripped all other expenses by a wide margin and continued to mount in absolute terms each year. Therefore, the central government's most pressing concern was how to bridge the gap between the shrinking revenue base and the ever-expanding military expenditures. Even as the policy of taxes in kind and compulsory purchase of grain inflicted enormous hardship on the rural population, their total cash value was small in relation to the total expenditures of the government. In the four years of the policy's implementation in 1942–45, these taxes constituted between 18 to 28 percent of the government's total receipts. Combined with all categories of direct and indirect taxes and public borrowing, they constituted from as little as 20 percent (1941) to no more than 50 percent (1943) of the government's total receipts.[144] This means that the government had to find ways to make up the difference. Under these conditions, the government resorted to the easiest way out, borrowing from the banks.[145] In order to meet the government's needs, the banks turned on their printing presses. While the annual rate of increase of the bank's total note issue was already considerable between 1937 and 1941, it grew ominously after mid-1942, when the government's military defeats seemed irreversible for a long time to come and when the government itself was totally isolated in the interior provinces where it could only conduct business in cash. It reached 124 percent in 1942, 114 percent in 1943, 152 percent in 1944, and 194 percent in 1945 up to V-J Day.[146] While the bank note issue outstanding was C$2 billion in 1937, it reached C$1,031 billion in 1945.[147]

It is obvious from the above description of the imbalance between revenues and expenditures that something was seriously wrong. What then were the causes of the problem?

Declining Sources of Revenues

On the revenue side, the most obvious reason for the difficulties was the military setbacks suffered by the government. After the fall of Canton and Wuhan in the autumn of 1938, yield from salt, customs, and the consolidated taxes on industrial products was reduced to a minimum due to the loss of the major cities in east China. Among traditional taxes, the land tax, business tax, and contract tax were the three major sources of income for provincial governments. But many of the provinces that remained under Chungking (e.g., Shensi, Kweichow, Kwangsi, and the Moslem provinces) were among the lowest revenue-producing provinces in China. Consequently, even when the central government took over these taxes from the provinces in 1940, the net income was insignificant.[148]

Chungking's financial difficulties were in no small measure compounded by the shrinking industrial base under its control. The modernized sectors of the Chinese economy had been concentrated in the Peking-Tientsin and Shanghai areas. The interior provinces were extremely underdeveloped.[149]

During the first weeks of war, the Peking-Tientsin area was quickly lost. During the siege of Shanghai, frantic efforts by the central government succeeded in salvaging some 600 factories, 120,000 tons of industrial equipment, and about 10,000 industrial workers. This subsequently became the backbone of China's wartime industry.[150] Between 1937 and 1945, the central government made gigantic efforts to expand industrial output. While the nominal number of industrial plants in the interior increased to 4,400 in 1945,[151] the overwhelming majority of them were very small, had insufficient capital, obsolete machines, and their output was both crude and insignificant.

Up to the spring of 1942, the Burma road was moving about 15,000 tons of materials into Kunming each month.[152] But when the road was lost, China's imports of machinery and industrial raw materials came to a complete halt. In spite of domestic efforts to increase production, the results were extremely disappointing. Thus, by 1944, the entire government-controlled area produced annually only 40,134 tons (metric) of iron, 13,361 tons of steel, 40,655 barrels of cement, 4,677 lathes, and 14,487 horsepower of motors. The output of some minerals including tungsten and tin actually declined drastically.[153] Meanwhile, the capacity of China's arsenals was reduced to 50 percent of its prewar level. There was little coordination among government agencies or between government and private firms on production of war materials and essential supplies, no working arrangement to set priorities on production, on transportation, allocation, or requisition and stockpiling of materials and facilities. In fact, it was not until late 1944 that Donald Nelson of the American War Production Board persuaded the Chinese government to organize a Chinese War Production Board to attempt to exercise some control over production.[154] But it was also in 1944 that China's productivity suffered the greatest damage due to Operation Ichigō. Hardest hit were the factories located in Honan, Hunan, and Kwangsi, where over 90 percent of the capacity in some industries was destroyed.[155] Under these adverse circumstances, the government not only could not draw revenues from the industries, but could not even rely on them to meet the basic military and civilian needs.

In the context of a declining traditional revenue base, the government failed to open up new sources of revenue and to develop a structure on direct taxes such as income, excess profit, business, and so on, until 1936. But government efforts to collect these taxes were not only hampered by war, but also by poor laws and improper management. The system depended on self-assessment, but Chinese business never developed modern accounting practices and therefore the problems of concealment and falsification of records of personal and business incomes were even more serious than in the collection of land taxes. On top of these evasive measures by businessmen was of course the corruption and inexperience of the tax administration that the central government found already in existence in the interior provinces. The consequences were that direct taxes constituted only 12 percent of the government's cash budgetary receipts in 1943, and barely 5 percent in 1944.[156] This inevitably raises the very disturbing question of socioeconomic justice, as the business community shared an inordinately small part of the burden of China's war effort.

The government also failed to tap the business and financial communities' resources through the issuance of domestic public loans. Shortly after the fighting began, a very successful campaign was mounted to offer the so-called Liberty Loan of C$500 million to finance war costs. But subsequent government high-handedness, rising inflation, and accelerating military defeats caused public enthusiasm to decline. Beginning in 1942, the government began to force bonds upon wealthy individuals and commercial enterprises, even to the point of assigning quotas to provinces. But the will or the administrative machinery to enforce this measure was lacking and as a result, public issues played a very minor part in the finances throughout the war. From 1937 to 1944, public borrowing amounted to only C$15,522 million.[157] In fact, the majority of these bonds and issues was absorbed by banks and government-managed enterprises, which in no way eased the government's own financial situation.[158]

Unlike previous Chinese governments in modern times, which could usually turn to foreign governments for assistance during financial stress, the KMT government was forced to rely primarily on the country's domestic resources to deal with the economic problem. Before the Pacific war, total foreign credits authorized to China amounted to about $500 million, with half of it coming from the USSR, mostly in military supplies and services. It was not until November, 1940, that the United States extended for the first time a credit of $50 million to China for monetary protection and management. American lend-lease to China up to 1941 was only $26 million compared to the $1.5 billion sent to her European allies.[159] Before the Pacific war, American-authorized credits amounted to $170 million, and Great Britain's amounted to $78 million. Of the $500 million, however, only about $350 million were utilized.[160] This sum was far from adequate for meeting China's needs for monetary support, industrialization projects, or shoring up the government's fiscal position.

By 1942, Soviet aid had dried up. In that year, however, $500 million of credits were extended by the United States, which became the only important source of foreign aid during the rest of the war.

In March, 1942, the Chinese government issued two kinds of securities, the United States Dollar Saving Certificates ($100 million) and the Allied Victory United States Dollar Loan ($100 million). Since the common people had little capital to subscribe, the success of these programs depended primarily on the government's ability to persuade or coerce the wealthy and powerful elements of the society to subscribe. If these programs had been successful, the government would have obtained a sizable amount of surplus resources from the privileged classes, shifted the burden of war to those better equipped to bear it, freed hoarded commodities to the markets, and significantly retarded the momentum of inflation. But the government simply did not have the means or the resolve to put pressure on the privileged classes, and the securities were so poorly handled as to have negligible effect on the general economy.[161]

After it became clear that the sale of dollar-backed securities would not bring in much revenue, the government began in 1942 to plan to offer the sale of gold to strengthen the currency, on the assumption that wealthy people would hoard gold and release goods to the market. By July, 1943, the Chinese government obtained the consent of the United States government to utilize $200 million of the $500 million credit for the purchase of gold to be shipped to China.[162] Yet differences between the White House and the United States Treasury Department seriously hampered this policy, and during the most critical months of 1943–44, only $23 million worth of gold was delivered to China.[163] All told, the Chinese government had utilized $580 million of nonmilitary credits from all foreign sources during the entire 1937–45 period (Soviet military aid and Western lend-lease aid not included.)[164] Not only was this amount insufficient to remedy the situation, but the news that China's gold stocks had been exhausted and that future American support was uncertain actually caused the government's fiscal position to worsen after the second half of 1944.

Weakening Budgetary Control

Insofar as the government's expenditures were concerned, the primary responsibility for the national budget-making policy must rest squarely on the shoulders of the Nationalist leaders, particularly Chiang Kai-shek and his finance minister, H. H. K'ung. It was they who decided to make promiscuous use of the printing press to solve the problems of mounting war costs. The government never developed a sound budgetary procedure: budget requests were haphazardly prepared by lower agencies; no system of priorities existed; the screening process was faulty or nonexistent; allocations were frequently made on personal and factional grounds in total disregard for the merit of the projects involved; and there was a very ineffective and often corrupt system of accounting to check on performance. Consequently, considerable amounts could have been saved if the central government had imposed more control and discipline on its own budgeting and accounting agencies.

However, the problem went deeper, and in order to appreciate the constraints upon the central government, references must be made again to central-regional relations in wartime China.

Obviously, the single most important reason why war expenditures soared was the compulsive desire of China's leaders to maintain a huge army, an army that was kept for the purpose of preserving the delicate domestic balance of power among the contending political groups, but which did not contribute to national defense. If China's 300-odd divisions had been reduced to 100 divisions as Stilwell had recommended, its military burden might have been reduced by more than half, and it would have been an improved military instrument. But in fact, the number of armed personnel of all descriptions on the payroll reached about five million in 1945, as compared with about two million in 1937.[165]

Another major fiscal drain of the government was the need to support a huge bureaucracy of several million men. Even in the midst of a national crisis, the KMT leaders remained rigidly addicted to the bureaucratic model. Instead of using propaganda and organization to mobilize the people into voluntary participation in various war-related activities, the KMT tried to handle every new activity by creating a new bureaucratic organ. Typically, most agencies were overstaffed but underutilized, and the bureaucrats were divorced from the productive process and leading a parasitic existence. This was exactly what had happened to the new-*hsien* system, whose many new agencies placed far greater burden on the people's resources than their putative benefits to the people could justify. In this connection, it is important to point out that during the crucial tenth plenum of the KMT's Central Executive Committee (CEC) in November-December, 1942, strong emphasis was placed by the leadership itself on budgetary retrenchment, equalization and simplification of taxes, reforms of local government, and even a radical reduction in the size of the army.[166] Had the central government been able to implement these policies, enormous relief to the government's financial difficulties would have been obtained. But in the end, the leadership conceded that immense "practical difficulties"[167] were involved, and never devised a way to persuade the regional leaders to accept the merits of "better soldiers and simpler administration" (*ching-ping chien-cheng*).

The government's inability to carry out overall fiscal planning was compounded by its inability to attain a degree of administrative organization and efficiency permitting national mobilization and controls required of an economy on a war footing. The government failed to extend effective control over the heads of the provincial and local governments to reach the masses directly. Not only were provincial and local governments and sometimes military leaders at liberty to collect unauthorized taxes, some of them even continued to circulate their own currencies. Provincial banks in almost every province continued to circulate or issue their own notes, a situation very reminiscent of the warlord era.[168] Yünnan offered one of the more graphic illustrations. As late as 1944, there were still about $500 million in New Yünnan currency in circulation in the countryside. These notes were used to acquire national currency with which the Yünnan authorities bought foreign exchange and gold smuggled in from India.[169]

Much more threatening to the government's position was the growth of illegal trade between KMT-held and Japanese-occupied territories. Despite the Chungking government's official ban, a substantial trade went on all the time. It usually involved the shipment of raw materials including such strategic items as tungsten, tung oil, iron, and tin from interior provinces in exchange for manufactured articles from the occupied areas. As mentioned earlier, this flourishing trade was itself a by-product of the military stalemate and of Chungking's policy to assign Chinese combat units to fixed-point garrison duties for long periods of time. Inevitably, such trade, in order to be safe and prosperous, must come under the protection of powerful military figures. Interested local militarists not only sent soldiers to escort the transit of goods or to provide means of transportation, they also provided complex credit and financing arrangements. In almost every sector of the front, whether in north, central, or southwestern China, large amounts of trade with the enemy were conducted along well-established routes every month.[170] It was sometimes reported that the Japanese offered either counterfeit or bona fide Chinese currency they seized to buy Chinese goods at deliberately inflated prices to wage economic warfare against the Chungking government.[171] Not only did such trade have a demoralizing effect on the Chinese soldiers, it also interfered seriously with Chungking's attempt to impose some order and discipline on China's economic life.

A further manifestation of the central government's feeble fiscal position vis-à-vis the provinces was the size of their revenues. Presumably, the budgets of provincial and local governments should be covered primarily by subsidies from the central government; in fact, such subsidies were insignificant.[172] The provinces and local governments collected their own revenues quite independent of the central government. A comparison between the provincial/local budgets and the central government's income from all direct taxes, indirect taxes, and other nonborrowed incomes reveals that before 1940, the former was about 85 percent of the latter, but after 1940 the figures were 288 percent in 1941, 120 percent in 1942, 89 percent in 1943, 108 percent in 1944, and 230 percent in 1945.[173] This means that the provincial and local governments had been able to defy the central government and exercise better control over the sources of revenue than the central government, and that the only alternative the latter had was to print more money.

The Inflationary Spiral

Any agrarian country engaged in fighting a prolonged war against a modern enemy like Japan would probably have gotten into serious economic trouble. In China, the difficulties were exacerbated by a disruption of trade and transportation, destruction of productive capacity, damage to the skilled labor force, the creation of a huge refugee problem, periodic natural disasters, and famine.[174] The severity of the problems facing the central government in China, however, was due to its own feeble internal political and military position. The KMT's incompetence in controlling the army and the local administration, its inability to introduce a more equitable scheme of distributing the financial burdens of the war, its failure to broaden the tax base or to enlist public enthusiasm in support of its internal bond issues through appeals to patriotism combined to force the government to look to the banks as the source of financial rescue. Although note issue was already substantial in the first four years of the war, after 1941 until 1945, it had become astronomical in proportion. This, in turn, created some very damaging effects on the quality of government and the livelihood of the people.

On a general level, the preoccupation with military activities and the uncontrollability of the army further minimized the nonmilitary functions of government. Throughout the war, the annual national outlay for economic development and reconstruction, water conservancy, agriculture, forestry, communications, cultural and educational activities, health, welfare, relief, etc., constituted 9 to 12 percent of the national expenditures between 1937 and 1945.[175] Possibly much of this figure represented administrative expenses and not project costs. In other words, the crucial functions associated with political tutelage and economic construction were nearly completely suspended for eight years and the politics of militarization reached a new height.

More specifically, the government's irresponsible currency policy inevitably triggered spiraling inflation. In the beginning, the annual inflation was kept within tolerable limits. Thus, if the average retail price index equaled one in early 1937, it went up to sixteen by December, 1941.[176] The closing of the Burma road in the spring of 1942 came as a shattering blow to the Chinese economy as imports of consumer goods, industrial machinery, and raw materials were totally suspended. In the following three years, the lend-lease consisted exclusively of military supplies. Despite China's repeated requests to import some consumer items, such as textiles for civilian use to counter the inflation, it was not until May, 1945, that the United States government endorsed the idea, but too late to have any counterinflationary effect.[177] Meanwhile, the existing productive capacity in the southwest was repeatedly damaged by enemy aerial bombing and ground attacks. As a result, the average retail index in free China increased to 66 by December, 1942, to 228 by December, 1943, 755 by December, 1944, and finally to over 2,600 by V-J Day in 1945.[178] It became quite apparent in the last four years of the war that the more the government resorted to the printing press to obtain temporary fiscal relief, the more it exacerbated the inflationary process, the consequence being that the cost of living outdistanced the volume of note issue by an increasingly wide margin each year. The rate of turnover of money was so accelerated by inflation by the spring of 1944 that banks in big cities like Chungking, Kunming, or Kweiyang occasionally ran out of cash and were forced to suspend business temporarily to wait for fresh supplies to arrive.[179] Chinese defeats during Operation Ichigō had a further devastating impact on the economy as the price rise quickened in the second half of 1944 and continued to soar until the very end of the war.

One immediate result of runaway inflation was that it depressed the production process because plant owners were never sure if the money they made in selling their manufactured goods would be enough to purchase raw materials in the future. More widespread, however, was the natural reaction of both producers and merchants to engage in hoarding and speculation. They helped push up prices even faster, and some made windfall profits in the process. Typically, these hoarders and speculators were entirely out of the range of the central government's control and under the protection of regional power structures. Beginning in November, 1938, the central government had issued numerous laws and experimented with various mechanisms to take charge of production and distribution of certain commodities through monopoly, fixed "fair prices," imposed ceilings on wholesale and retail profits, or limited the quantity of stocks held by merchants. In 1939–41, new laws were made to extend the list of commodities under price control. In December, 1942, the government issued a comprehensive set of price control regulations, which gave itself power to fix not only prices, but transportation costs and wages, and to try violators of these regulations under martial law.[180]

Yet the government was never in command of the situation. It operated upon inadequate information and faulty statistics and had to cope with vastly diversified local market conditions over a huge geographical area. Its failure to devise a clearly defined, coherent, and comprehensive plan often aggravated market confusion. In addition to defective planning and preparation, the central government also lacked trustworthy machinery for implementation. Almost invariably, the central government had to rely on the *hsien* governments, the chambers of commerce, or the guilds or unions of individual localities to determine the price ceilings and stock limitations.[181] In so doing, the Chungking government surrendered to the local power holders and hoarders and speculators the nominal government authority to combat the very same economic crimes the latter were themselves engaged in.[182]

Consequently, only in Chungking and very few other places could the central government enforce price controls through regular administrative channels, and this was reflected in the more moderate inflation rates in Chungking than in other cities like Chengtu, Kweiyang, or Kunming.[183] However, when in 1943 Chiang took a personal interest in cracking down on speculators in commodities and controlling prices in Chungking, many merchants responded by offering only goods of inferior quality for sale, or they tampered with their weights and measures. But worst of all, many speculators simply went to Chengtu and other places remote from KMT power to carry on their activities.[184]

Elsewhere in the provinces, the central government's need to regulate the flow of commodities, to ban trade with the enemy, to prevent hoarding and speculation, and to obtain more taxes could only be enforced by setting up numerous checkpoints along highways, railways, and waterways. In many cases, the government had to rely heavily on special economic agents or secret police to enforce these policies, precisely because Chungking exerted so little control over the regular administrative organs that remained in the hands of the regional and local leaders. This system was bound to be self-defeating, for it only obstructed trade without necessarily increasing the government's revenues. The cost of collecting revenues was enormous, the potential for abuses and corruption was great; the general public and the independent producers and merchants suffered great inconvenience and economic losses, but the hoarders and speculators backed by powerful organizations and influential friends in the army and government were little affected by this system. In a way, it amounted to a reincarnation of the much-hated *likin* system of the 1920s under a new guise.

The history of the war clearly suggests a pattern of mutual reinforcement between inflation and budget increase. The political and military weakness of the Chungking government, as well as the lack of foresight of the Nationalist financial managers, led to the original decision to print more currency as the easy way out of mounting financial obligations incurred under the war; this in turn triggered the inflation spiral. As prices went up, the size of the budget had to be increased every year, which could only be met by printing more money. To borrow a Chinese proverb, the solution was like "drinking poison to kill thirst." It diverted the government's attention away from seeking a fundamental solution for strengthening the tax system through a restructuring of the central-regional political-military relationship, and the cost of evasion was a rapid deterioration in the quality of government.

The government's irresponsible fiscal policy and the resultant inflation drastically altered the distribution of wealth and financial burden of the war among the different segments of the population. Unlike the land-tax policy, which badly hurt the rural population, the fiscal policy and inflation had the most devastating impact in the cities and towns. While the trading classes were able to ride on the crest of inflation, and some even made themselves rich by hoarding and speculation, the overwhelming majority of salaried classes were impoverished. Worst hit were of course the soldiers. In the face of inflation at a monthly rate of 10 to 20 percent, their pay lagged hopelessly behind. Next came the government employees, teachers, and college professors. According to Nankai University's Statistical Service, by the end of 1943, incomes of salaried workers had increased only 31 times over the 1937 level, but the cost of living had increased 183 times.[185] Many capable and conscientious people simply refused to enter into public service because they could not make ends meet with their official salaries, thus causing a serious shortage of competent and dedicated cadres to run many of the crucial government programs. Some who stayed in public service had to hold several jobs at the same time in order to draw several salaries concurrently, or to pursue sideline businesses to supplement their official incomes. Either way, the quality of their official performance suffered seriously. Finally, a large number of public servants simply threw their scruples to the winds and indulged in reckless corruption.

The last groups to suffer severely from inflationary finance were the wage laborers and small retailers in the urban areas. Caught between ever-rising farm prices and exploitation by civil servants, they were constantly threatened with financial disaster and even starvation. Their dependence on the money economy made them highly vulnerable to the inflationary process. They had to shift from day to day, to make quick adjustments to the whimsical economic winds, in order to avert potentially instant financial ruin.

To sum up, the longer the KMT government stayed in the war, the more devastating the impact of its economic policies. The deterioration seemed to accelerate after 1943 until the very end of the war. Plagued by low pay, malnutrition, and nonexistent medical attention, the combat spirit among China's soldiers declined precipitously. Inflation destroyed the morality of public officials and caused a corresponding decline in public trust and support in the government. Intellectuals were alienated by witnessing the emergence of a class of nouveaux riches through illegality and the impoverishment of honest and hardworking laborers and small businessmen. By 1944–45, as inflation gained even greater momentum, the nonagrarian population had also become so thoroughly demoralized that the damage to the legitimacy of the KMT government had very possibly reached a point beyond repair.

Conclusion

Nothing posed a greater threat to the survival of the Nationalist regime than the Sino-Japanese War. The Japanese invaders were not only better armed, better trained, and better provisioned than any of the KMT's erstwhile challengers, they also entirely changed the sociopolitical, economic, and military milieu for the Nationalists. As our earlier military analysis showed, although the KMT government lost its power base in the first six months of the war, the first four years of fighting produced relatively few strains in the relationship between the KMT and the regional forces, because Chiang had preoccupied himself with the search for a military solution. While some provinces contributed troops to the war, the main fighting was done in east China away from the regional hotbeds, and supported by resources directly mobilized by the Nanking government.

Relations between the KMT and the regionalists deteriorated after 1940–41 when the central army was grievously crippled, when the government was pushed deep into the interior, and when it had exhausted its independent resources. The central government remained in a militarily weak position throughout the remaining years of the war. Its forces were employed to resist the Japanese, blockade the Communists, and put Chinese troops of questionable loyalty under surveillance, but performed none of these tasks satisfactorily. As the central government remained stranded in the interior, it had to turn to the local resources to sustain what now appeared to be a long struggle. In order to utilize these resources, the KMT needed to gain control over the local governments. It was then that the presence of the central government collided head-on with the vested interests of local political-military power holders.

The fatal flaw in the government's policy was that it recoiled from seeking a fundamental resolution to the central-regional dilemma. It never succeeded in winning over the unreserved support of the regionalists by nationalistic appeals. Nor did it develop any competence in mass mobilization to challenge the regionalists' power base from below. Instead, the KMT tried to continue the policy of the prewar era and chose to compromise with the power holders whenever necessary in order to maintain the sociopolitical status quo. Under these conditions, the scope of the government's programs had to be severely circumscribed, and only those tolerated or approved by the local ruling classes could be implemented. Worse still, the Nationalist regime continued to adhere to a strictly bureaucratic approach that precluded mass participation in the political process. Due to the government's own manpower shortage and lack of organizational finesse, it had to rely on existing members of the local governments and rendered its policies vulnerable to all the evils that had distinguished provincial politics in the interior for decades.

The inauguration of the government's new policies gave observers the impression that it was determined to make them work. At the Third National Finance Conference of June, 1941, the government put strong emphasis on the need to maintain economic stability, and asserted that the winning of the war would henceforth consist of 30 percent military work, but 70 percent economic work.[186] In June, 1941, Chiang personally stated, "the current policy on grain is the key to our survival or destruction in our effort to execute the war and reconstruct our nation."[187] One year later, Chiang identified grain collection and conscription as the two most critical functions of the government and instructed that henceforth the *hsien* magistrates must exert their utmost effort to carry out these two assignments.[188] But such repeated exhortations had little effect on the political realities in the provinces where the *hsien* magistrates, the *hsiang* chiefs, and *pao-chia* chiefs were either local power holders or their surrogates.[189] The corruption and incompetence of these local officials became a serious liability to the central government, which was unable to check or replace them. The inability of the government to impose discipline was evidenced by the fact that in the last five years of the war only thirty-five cadres in the entire nation were severely punished for mishandling the grain policy, while in fact cadre misconduct had been of monumental proportions.[190]

As wartime difficulties increased, there was mounting criticism of the unequal distribution of the grain tax burden which discriminated against the poor. In 1941–42, there arose a strong demand, even within the party and the national government, to revamp the tax system and increase the tax rate for the rich. But after much debate, the government concluded in June, 1942, that it was powerless to change the situation because it did not have the local-level cadres to supervise the faithful implementation of a more just system.[191] When in September, 1944, the devastation of the war finally compelled the government to request the big landlords to contribute more grain, most provinces simply refused to respond.[192]

The national economic policies also created utter chaos. Because of poor institutional design and lack of organizational strength, the central government's attempt to break up the provincial strongholds by centralizing more revenue power into the hands of the Chungking government was a total failure. Chungking's attempt to extend direct control by setting up its own specialized agencies in the provinces only exacerbated the problems of cancerous bureaucratic growth, confused the chain of command, increased waste and inefficiency, and generated new hostility between national and local bureaucrats. In fact, Chungking's policy probably succeeded in undercutting the effectiveness of those provincial and local administrators who operated by its rules, but hardly had any impact on those who were determined to protect their own interests.[193]

Soon many provincial and local governments developed several countermeasures. They would overwhelm the central government with demands for more subsidies than the central government was capable of granting, or take a cut of the revenue reserved only for the central government, or impose unauthorized surcharges and new taxes; or they would borrow from the banks, float their own bonds, or even circulate their own currencies.[194] While in some cases the central government's policies might cause some inconveniences, in most cases the provincial and local governments would get what they wanted. By and large, the KMT's attempt to control the purse strings never broke the back of the local power structures, and again the central government decided to compromise with these power structures. Predictably, the people developed extremely negative attitudes toward politics as time passed and learned to regard the government as a symbol of exaction and oppression marked by too many laws, too many agencies, and too many officials.[195] Thus, widespread popular alienation became an inescapable outcome.

But the information presented in this chapter may force us to rethink the conventional view that the KMT was either the creature of reactionary rural elites, or that it allied with them and actively promoted their class interests. During the war, the Chungking government had remained foreign to the people in the southwest, and the rural elites there were very hostile to the Nationalist intruders. The government never planted deep organizational roots among the people, and it failed to receive the cooperation of the rural elites because the government's programs ran counter to their interests. As a result, instead of allying with the rural elites, the KMT had to resort to a combination of threats and concessions to implement such programs. But as the war went on, the KMT's threats lost considerable credibility, so the government's primary strategy was to pursue a policy of dependence through concessions and accommodations to the rural elites. This policy only further damaged the KMT's standing in the eyes of the masses.

As China moved toward the end of war, its domestic economy and politics had reached worse conditions than ever. More land and people were lost by Chungking in late 1944 and early 1945 than any previous year since 1938. There had been huge destruction of property and loss of capital. Japan's invasion had devastated the country's remaining economic infrastructure. Average prices had escalated to over 2,600 times the 1937 level, and the exchange rate shot up from the C$3 per American dollar in 1937 to C$2,750 per dollar in 1945. Inflation had drained working capital and diverted businessmen from honest trade into hoarding and speculation. It also dealt severe blows to the livelihood of the urban classes, the soldiers, wage laborers, intellectuals, and public servants.

On the other hand, the land-tax collection and conscription policies not only seriously undermined agricultural productivity, but imposed the heaviest portion of the economic burden of the war upon the poorest and most hardworking elements of the rural masses. Many of them also suffered humiliation, physical brutality, sickness, or even death as a result of conscription. Meanwhile, the rich and powerful in the countryside and in the cities not only were exempted from these burdens, but made fortunes out of national calamities.

In 1937, the Nationalist government entered the war as the champion of nationalism. But the cumulative effect of the war only magnified the corruption and ineptitude of the regime. The long years of the central government's own administrative abuses and its dependence on regional and local power structures made the government appear in the people's eyes as a symbol of oppression and exploitation, and provoked widespread disillusionment and alienation among the people.

Addressing himself to the question of the cause of the KMT's collapse on the mainland, the highly respected leader of China's Third Force, Carsun Chang, once offered this observation:

> My own answer can be summarized in one little word—"tutelage"; it is as simple as that. Tutelage meant in practice the desire of the KMT's followers to perpetuate the conditions which placed political power in their own hands. They merely gave lip-service to constitutionalism as a sop to Dr. Sun's followers and to show that his teaching was not forgotten. Since there was no constitution, no parliament, and no responsible cabinet, all questions . . . were decided by the party. The people had no right to question the party.[196]

In fact, however, it may be argued that the cause of the KMT's failure was not too much tutelage, but too little of it. Basically China's most critical problems during the war existed on the local and mass levels. Without sufficient mass support and participation, parliamentary democracy would have had little meaning. It was also a fact that, other than the Communists, none of the political parties in wartime China succeeded in cultivating, or were even interested in, a mass following. On the other hand, Sun's theory of political tutelage itself imposed an ideological obligation upon the government to grant the common people more rights in local self-government.

In the original conception of the new-*hsien* system, Sun's revolutionary rhetoric was still accepted as the guideline. Thus, under the new-*hsien* system, popularly elected assemblies would run the county's affairs; education would be extended to the mass level; cooperatives would be organized; the interests of tenants were to be protected; fiscal rationality was to be achieved. In addition, the *hsien* government would be responsible for promoting industry, agriculture, irrigation, transportation, communications, public health, protection of women's rights, and social welfare and relief work.[197] All these looked very similar to the experimental *hsien* program of the Nanking years. Again, one may speculate that, had even some of these tasks been promoted vigorously, mass participation and mobilization could have fundamentally resolved the central government's dilemma in dealing with the regional power holders. It could have brought higher ethical standards to bureaucratic conduct on the local level and greatly improved the image of the government among the masses. However, our earlier discussion on the Nanking period offered no reason for optimism.

In the final analysis, the Chungking government never made efficient use of the eight years of war to devise ways to extend its normative or coercive powers into the social fabric of interior China. It failed to establish an organic linkage between Chungking and the thousands of small communities in rural China. The latter remained firmly in the grips of power holders who kept the substance of their rule intact, even as they adapted themselves to the new nomenclatures and offices under the new-*hsien* system. It would be safe to say that the existence of the KMT government totally failed to affect the people's livelihood in any positive way from the *hsien* level downward; if anything, it only exacerbated it.[198]

The materials presented in this chapter inevitably generate the question: What role did the Nationalist party play during the war? A strong party could have prevented political stagnation and decay, and forged the diverse human elements into a genuinely national community and a centralized political system. In the following chapter, we will examine the structures and distribution of power within the party to see why it, too, failed to provide the leadership necessary to fulfill such a mission.

Chapter 5

The Nature of the Kuomintang

Given the Kuomintang's deteriorating military situation and the decline of the equality of its government, it seems that the only way Nationalist leaders might have averted total disaster was to invigorate the party to become an effective political instrument. If armed with a corps of competent and dedicated cadres, the KMT leaders could have conceivably shifted China's internal political process from a militaristic orientation to one emphasizing ideology and organization. Through mobilization and propaganda, the party might have proceeded to isolate the holders of traditional military power and eventually to make military power irrelevant in the domestic political process. That the KMT failed to follow this approach has been conclusively demonstrated by history, but the reasons for its failure still warrant a full exploration.

The main purpose of the present chapter is to trace the profound structural and behavioral transformation of the party from the Nanking era through the war years on two separate levels: that of the rank and file and that of the leadership. The general characteristics of party life on each level before the war will be briefly discussed only to bring into sharp relief the change that occurred during the war. An attempt will be made to explain why these changes occurred and what impact they had on the party.

The Rank and File before the War

For practical purposes, the KMT did not become a modern political party until its 1924 decision to recruit a broad-based rank and file. Between 1924 and 1927, some 175,000 members were recruited into the party.[1] The cost of this rapid recruitment was the infiltration of Communist members into the party as well as the uneven expansion of the party, which caused many basic-level organs to fall into the hands of local interests.[2] As the party moved into the lower Yangtze area, it also brought the same recruitment policy of emphasizing quantity at the expense of quality.[3]

However, from a sociological point of view, the party acquired a new identity after the purge of Communists in 1927. By the beginning of the Nanking era, the party was becoming an urban-based political movement, primarily entrenched in the eastern and southern coastal provinces, drawing mostly from the modern classes (government, business, or student) with much higher educational achievements than the rest of the population.[4] The party retained these characteristics in the 1930s.[5]

The most intriguing aspect of party development in the prewar years is that its membership never exceeded 600,000 in the civilian sectors.[6] In fact, civilian membership always lagged behind membership in the military, sometimes by a very wide margin.

When all categories of membership were computed, the KMT constituted about 1/300 of the country's total population.[7] This indicates that the KMT was more militarized than civilianized and never achieved the momentum of growth that marked some other modern political parties in the West. This phenomenon severely undercut the role assigned to the party by Sun Yat-sen to implement his program of political tutelage. The size alone shows that the KMT was actually an elite-oriented and not a mass-oriented political organization. Why did the party not expand as vigorously as its contemporary authoritarian or totalitarian counterparts like the Soviet Communist party or the Italian Fascist party?

The answers are admittedly complex, but the following factors seem to have played an important role.

First, the party leadership encountered considerable difficulty in transforming a formerly Kwangtung-based party into a Yangtze-based party. The arrangement of collective leadership did not work out after Sun's death, and a continuing feud among Hu Han-min, Wang Ching-wei, and Chiang Kai-shek robbed the party of a clear sense of direction for many years.[8] Even after the anti-Communist purge, the party's organization and activities remained in disarray,[9] and the party never quite developed a centralized and coherent recruitment policy in the 1930s.

Second, both Chiang's need to wage civil wars against his rivals and the uncertainties of territorial control led him to give clear preference to building the party within the army at the expense of the civilian sectors. The shifting military situation undoubtedly hampered the party's efforts to exercise effective control over regional or local party organs, and caused basic-level structures to be miserably neglected. More fundamentally, the internal split within the party seriously undermined the party's prestige among the people. After the 1927 anti-CCP purge and the concommitent eclipse of the KMT's own left wing, both events in which the local elites played an active role, the local elites' influence expanded considerably. Thereafter, the party had to bargain and compromise with the local elites, but was never quite able to control them.[10] This caused a significant decline of interest among the people to join the KMT as a vehicle to achieve revolutionary goals. In many areas beyond Nanking's military reach, the party actually suffered severe reductions. Thus, for instance, Kwangsi had 128,394 members in 1926, but only 5,671 in 1934, and party branches existed only in twenty-nine of Kwangsi's ninety-four counties.[11]

Third, Chiang seemed to have developed serious reservations about the party during his early career within the KMT that prejudiced his policy even after he gained control over the party itself. Possibly because Chiang's early responsibilities were confined exclusively to the military while other KMT leaders controlled the party's organizational work, he voiced his reservations about the party as early as 1926. At this time he said that the principle of party control over the government should not entitle all party members to special political or administrative status, and he complained bitterly about party members taking an opposition posture against the government. While conceding in principle that the government must be under the party's leadership, Chiang nevertheless maintained that the rank and file of the party must obey and cooperate with government officials.[12]

Even as Chiang later gained ascendancy within the KMT, he continued to adhere to the position that party control over the state did not mean that party members should control the state. To him, it only meant that party ideology should be used to guide the state, and he sternly criticized as self-seeking and nonrevolutionary those party members who believed that they were entitled to active roles in the administration.[13]

In contrast to his frank admiration for the military organization and the many putative martial virtues, Chiang's intermittent attention to party affairs throughout the Nanking era was accented by harsh criticism. Over the years, several "defects" of the party members seemed to have particularly irked Chiang. First, the party members were accused of lacking discipline, being unwilling to endure hardship, being guilty of corruption and nepotism, wanting to become officials, showing irresponsibility and insubordination, and interfering recklessly with the work of the regular army and government.[14] Second, Chiang identified the party's fundamental weakness as a lack of unity of will among the members which caused constant squabbling.[15] Chiang was unhappy both with party members clinging to backward thoughts and with others who had been misled by the radical view that the KMT should ally only with the working classes.[16] To Chiang, the only solution was to achieve unity and solidarity among party members through comradeship and sincerity.[17] Finally, Chiang accused most party members of only "carrying the party label (*chao-p'ai*) but not doing real work."[18]

The upshot was that during the years when Chiang's power was on the climb, he preferred a party-state relationship on the local level that actually aimed to shield the bureaucratic apparatus from party interference, to reduce the role of the rank and file of the party to "propagandizing" (emitting empty words) among the people, and to use their own personal conduct to persuade the people to obey government directives. While Hu Han-min had wanted to insist on the principle of placing the party above the government and the army in conformity with the dictate of Sun's notion of tutelage, such views were effectively silenced when Hu himself was placed under house arrest in April, 1931. Thereafter, the political trend under Chiang was toward the absorption of a large number of Peiyang-styled bureaucratic careerists into key positions of the Nanking government, a separation of party from the state, a downgrading of the importance of the party, and the ascendancy of military authority over both the party and the government on the local level.[19]

To the extent that party activities were pursued at all during the Nanking era, they often suffered from a high degree of formalism and bureaucratism. Even early in 1928, Ch'en Kung-po had already warned that the twin evils threatening the party life were, first, a decaying process (*fu hua*) as evidenced by the breakdown of discipline on the basic level and the alienation of the party from both the government and the people, and second, a tendency toward reaction, toward reliance on commandism and coercion instead of leadership and education.[20]

In the 1930s, the party had become a huge bureaucracy, and party members had become bureaucratized by occupying themselves with paperwork and dissociating themselves from the real concerns of the people. Once the Communists had been purged, the KMT practically suspended all efforts toward mass movements, particularly among workers and peasants.[21] The main reason for this decision was that KMT members simply could not compete effectively against CCP members in organizing, controlling, and mobilizing the various peasant or workers' associations. Under the CCP influence, these mass organizations assumed broad administrative powers in many localities and directly threatened the formal government. Under rising protests by warlords, conservative KMT leaders, and the upper classes in the lower Yangtze area, the KMT finally decided to do away with this kind of "lawlessness" altogether.[22]

Instead, there was a conspicuous trend toward the bureaucratization of party branches, and the party itself degenerated into a secretive, vengeful, petty, and counterproductive political force. By abandoning its mass base, and by failing to find a constructive role for the party, the rank and file also failed to serve as the link to bridge the communications gap between the national leaders and grassroots sentiments and grievances. Without sufficient inspiration and guidance from above, the KMT membership failed to serve as the catalyst to bring about either a liberal constitutional regime, or a revolutionary, egalitarian, populist movement based on the support of either urban or rural masses.[23] Instead, the KMT grew increasingly in favor of a conservative, authoritarian, etatist approach, and relied more and more on civil and military bureaucrats to achieve the party's conventional goals of wealth and power.[24]

Therefore, to sum up, in the decade before the war, the KMT slowly assumed the qualities of an elitist political party rather than of a party oriented toward, or based upon support from, the masses. The shift of its power base from Kwangtung to the Yangtze delta was accompanied by some tentative gains in the southwest and in the north, but actually the party existence in these areas was only tolerated but never enthusiastically supported by local authorities. The party also did not use its time efficiently to evolve a close working relationship with the people and in most cases did not live up to the tasks associated with political tutelage.

Emerging from the above description is, therefore, a KMT rank and file that was neglected by its leaders, never steeled in the fire of revolution, and demonstrated serious organizational and behavioral vulnerability. As long as the KMT military firmly controlled the lower Yangtze valley, the party center could count on the loyalty of the party membership and use it to help promote the government's policies in some limited ways. But the party rank and file had never acquired the experience of standing at the forefront of an intense ideological or organizational struggle to spread socioeconomic revolution. In other words, even under the extremely favorable circumstances of the Nanking era, the party rank and file never gained any meaningful experience in conducting political tutelage. Its credentials as a revolutionary vanguard were extremely suspect, if not wholly nonexistent.

The Rank and File during the War

The most devastating effect of the war on the party was that it robbed the party of its lower Yangtze power base and produced such structural and personnel changes as to stretch the coping skills of the already defective prewar party machine beyond the breaking point.

During the first two years of the war, the military debacle caused nearly total disruption of the organization of the party in the lower Yangtze area and heavy depletion of its ranks. When the party recovered enough to take its first wartime census in 1939, it registered less than one-third of its prewar strength.[25] The recruitment tempo picked up after 1939 and by December 31, 1944, the party climbed to a total civilian membership of 2,555,279 persons.[26] Behind these impressive figures, however, were concealed a number of crucial alterations in the demographic composition of its membership.

For one thing, the prewar pattern of geographical distribution of the membership was disrupted.[27] As the war progressed, this trend became more clearly confirmed (table 9). In 1929, members from Kiangsu constituted 10.25 percent of the total national membership; members from Kwangtung accounted for 27.43 percent.[28] By 1945, Kiangsu had fallen behind eighteen other provinces (including the sparsely populated Sinkiang) to a paltry 0.77 percent of the national total. Kwangtung's share also dropped to 8.23 percent. In contrast, Szechwan in 1929 only accounted for 0.31 percent of the national total, but by 1945 Szechwan had climbed to the top with 10.13 percent. Of the provinces over which the KMT exercised firm control in the prewar years, only Kiangsi remained within the fold while others had slipped out of control.[29]

The shift of the party's center of geographical gravity was accompanied by changes in its social characteristics. Table 10, on the attributes of new recruits of 1942–44, suggests several interesting things.

First, government employees constituted 25 to 30 percent of annual intake of the party.[30] Among other factors, the expansion of membership in the interior was owed greatly to the party's decision to require most members of the civil government to join the party. Thus, instead of sending qualified party members to occupy governmental positions, the party took the reverse step of co-opting all existing bureaucrats in provincial and local governments throughout the country into the party with little or no screening. Rather than the party serving as the leading nucleus in government organs, the old-fashioned bureaucrats not only retained their control over the local bureaucracy, but made inroads into and corrupted the party. The particular timing of this new policy (adopted on the eve of the war), coupled with the demolition of the party and governmental structure in the east, served to create overnight and by default a huge bureaucratic wing of the party weighing decisively in favor of the existing power structures in the interior and the southwestern provinces.

Second, the category of agriculture had become the second most numerous category. This is curious because the party never launched any

TABLE 9
Provincial Origins of Party Members, 1941–45

Province	1941	1945
Kiangsu	1.23%	0.77%
Chekiang	10.56	9.54
Anhwei	7.11	7.28
Kiangsi	5.75	4.60
Hupei	6.06	9.26
Hunan	9.92	7.08
Szechwan	10.58	10.13
Sikang	0.41	0.73
Hopei	1.21	0.67
Shantung	0.56	0.94
Shansi	2.23	2.20
Honan	5.65	4.58
Shensi	5.35	5.24
Kansu	1.86	2.97
Ninhsia	0.24	0.52
Chinghai	0.58	1.00
Fukien	6.27	8.88
Kwangtung	10.54	8.23
Kwangsi	5.85	5.93
Yünnan	1.67	2.53
Kweichow	5.30	4.30
Suiyüan, Jehol, Chahar	0.43	0.54
Manchuria	—	1.11
Sinkiang	—	0.97
Total	100.00	100.00

Sources: KMT, Bureau of Statistics, *Chung-kuo Kuo-min-tang tang-wu t'ung-chi chi-yao, 1941* (Chungking, 1941), p. 6; idem, *Chung-kuo Kuo-min-tang tang-wu t'ung-chi chi-yao, 1945* (Chungking, 1945), tables 1, 2, pp. 1–2.

Note: The total numbers of party members were 1,037,525 for 1941 and 2,957,687 for 1945, excluding members in the army and overseas.

TABLE 10
Profile of Party Recruits, 1942–44

Age Distribution	1942	1943	1944
Below 20	6.6%	5.2%	5.7%
20–29	48.5	49.2	42.9
30–39	30.4	30.9	31.3
40–49	11.4	11.3	14.7
50–59	2.4	2.7	4.3
60–69	0.3	0.4	0.6
Over 70	0.02	0.02	0.04
Unknown			0.5

Educational Qualifications	1942	1943	1944
College	2.7%	4.3%	3.3%
Military school	0.8	1.0	0.9
Special (gov't) training	7.0	7.9	3.3
Middle school	26.8	33.3	24.4
Primary school	30.0	28.4	30.2
Family tutoring	21.6	16.3	24.2
Uneducated	0.7	0.5	1.6
Others	10.4	8.3	12.0

Professional Background	1942	1943	1944
Agriculture	29.1%	22.2%	39.3%
Industries	6.4	8.7	7.6
Business	10.9	9.7	9.8
Party affairs	0.3	0.4	0.2
Government service	29.0	30.8	20.5
Liberal professions	11.5	14.9	10.9
Social service	1.1	1.6	0.8
No profession (students)	9.5	8.7	7.2
Unemployed	0.5	0.5	0.9
Unknown	1.7	1.5	2.6
Total number	257,622	268,639	633,825

Sources: For educational qualifications: KMT, Bureau of Statistics, *Chung-kuo Kuo-min-tang tang-wu t'ung chi chi-yao, 1944* (Chungking, 1944), tables 7–8, pp. 7–8; idem, *Chung-kuo Kuo-min-tang tang-wu t'ung chi chi-yao, 1945* (Chungking, 1945), tables 7–9, pp. 7–9. For professional background: Idem, *Chung-kuo Kuo-min-tang tang-wu t'ung chi chi-yao, 1944* (Chungkin, 1944), table 9, p. 9; idem, *Chung-kuo Kuo-min-tang tang-wu t'ung chi chi-yao, 1945* (Chungking, 1945), tables 7–9, pp. 7–9.

Note: "Liberal professions" in Chinese parlance means lawyers, journalists, doctors, academics, artists, etc.

meaningful drive to recruit peasants. A check of the members' educational profiles shows them to be far too well educated to be peasants. It can be safely assumed that people claiming agricultural profession were actually rural elites (landowners and landlords) and not peasants.

Third, although "workers" and "businessmen" remained roughly the same proportion in the KMT as in prewar years, we must take into account the very different economic context of the interior provinces. Whereas the workers in the coastal provinces tended to work in modern and relatively large-scale industries (often financed by, and doing business with, foreign capital), the workers of the interior tended to work in traditional cottage industries (the only type existing there). Likewise, whereas the prewar businessmen of the coast tended to be engaged in banking and finance or industries (again, often associated with foreign capital), the businessmen of the interior tended to be small retailers associated with native small-scale capital and handling domestic products or agricultural produce. Thus the complexion of economic life of these two different periods compels us to interpret different sociological implications into the figures.

Fourth, the number of people engaged in party work had become extremely small, around 1 percent. This reflects the decline in the quality and scope of wartime party activities because there were only 25,000 party workers in 1944, as compared with 36,000 in 1936.

Fifth, although there was little difference in the members' age distribution since 1937, there was a significant change in their educational qualifications. Strangely, more members in the 1940s had received traditional family tutoring than was the case ten years earlier in 1933. This can only mean that the party members of the 1940s were more tradition-bound and more closely tied to the old order than their predecessors. Furthermore, whereas the percentage of middle-school-educated members remained roughly similar (around 30 percent), there was a higher percentage than before of members who had received only primary school education, and a sharp decline in the percentage of uneducated in the 1940s. On the other hand, there was an equally sharp drop in the number of college educated members and nearly no members with a foreign education.

Hence, what we know about the qualities of the recruits of the 1940s stood in sharp contrast to the qualities of the party's leadership at the same time. For while the prewar rank and file was lost to the Japanese, the party's leadership successfully retreated to the hinterland and managed to hold on to their functional preserves in the central party hierarchy. In 1934,

75 percent of those in the party's national headquarters having some degree of decision-making power (here defined as those above the rank of *tsung-kan-shih* or chief clerks in functional sections and departments) came from six provinces of which Kiangsu and Chekiang combined for a total of 42 percent. Six years after the war started, the same six provinces still produced nearly 70 percent of the key functionaries of the party center, while the party members of these same provinces constituted only 35 percent of the national total. The combined total of Kiangsu and Chekiang men was still 34 percent of the leadership.[31]

In addition to the geographical differences, a quick survey of the educational qualifications of the personnel in the national headquarters for the year 1941 shows that 64.1 percent had a college degree, 25.3 percent had a high school education, 4.5 percent had studied in military academies, 3.6 percent had other types of education, and 2.5 percent had unknown educational backgrounds.[32] During the Nanking decade, at least a certain measure of empathy and identification existed between the leaders and the rank and file because they came from the same geographical regions, had been exposed to similar intellectual and psychological currents, and generally lived in the same socioeconomic milieu.

This profile was discordant with that of the rank and file of the war years because, as the section of table 10 on educational qualifications shows, there was an appreciable lowering of the educational qualifications of the members recruited since the start of the war. In the 1930s, the KMT members' educational profile resembled a spindle with a bulging middle segment of middle-school-educated members, and smaller and yet still substantial minorities of highly and poorly educated people on both ends. In the 1940s, both ends of the spindle had been flattened and the profile more closely resembled the shape of a disc with the overwhelming majority having primary to middle school education (or the equivalent) and little else.[33] The decline of educational qualifications of the membership during the war only lengthened the intellectual distance between it and the leaders.

Furthermore, the consequence of the wholesale co-optation policy of the KMT was that many members from the interior had already been in the employ of the old regional regimes dating back from the warlord era, or they had been the backbone of the traditional socioeconomic-political order backed by local military power when the KMT arrived on the scene in the late 1930s. By and large, the interior had been little affected by the social, economic, political, and intellectual forces that had convulsed the eastern provinces. Thus, wartime recruits came primarily from smaller cities and towns where the traditional influence remained strong. As they had already participated in the prevailing sociopolitical order for some time, their only reason for joining the party was to preserve their careers and vested interests, rather than having been inspired by the party's ideology or programs. The rather limited development of modern educational institutions in the interior produced few among them who were interested in intellectual or ideological issues that concerned the easterners.

Consequently, when one talks about the KMT during wartime, one must keep in mind the very sharp differences in the social and geographical backgrounds, educational qualifications, intellectual orientations, and personal temperaments between these two distinct groups. In fact, we may view the party as having two rather incongruent components: a more cosmopolitan, well-educated leadership and a more earthbound parochial rank and file preoccupied with the preservation of the sociopolitical status quo and basically uninterested in the outside world. Wartime stresses only aggravated this incongruence and created serious organizational problems within the party. When such a leadership was thrust upon a population that harbored strong misgivings about outsiders, and when such a leadership was constantly harrassed by Japanese advances, it tended to lose touch with the sentiments and aspirations of the rank and file and to develop no rapport with the general public. As communications between these two groups became increasingly difficult, the isolation of the leadership from the rank and file could only lead to the development of a "siege mentality" among the leaders and widespread apathy among members.

Since the party's own statistics identified the overwhelming majority of members as participating in basic-level organs or work units, generally meaning *hsien* levels or lower, the best indicators of the party's organizational weaknesses are to be found in party activities on the levels of *hsien* and below as well.

In 1938, Chiang had identified the three major tasks of the party work to be: first, to provide for the organization, training, and discipline of party members; second, to supervise and assist the government in implementing national policies; and third, to lead, assist, and enlighten the masses through propaganda and mobilization.[34] Chiang further instructed that the top priority of party work must be placed on the *hsien* level and "the *hsien* party committee must be the organ to provide political leadership and social cohesion for the entire *hsien*. Everything should be tied together by the party committee, and everything should be initiated by the party committee."[35]

Among these tasks, there is no doubt that party-government relationship was the most important. Yet it was precisely at the lower level that the party-government linkage was the most fragile. In a comprehensive reform proposal submitted by the chief party secretary of Chungking in 1940, Ch'en Fang-hsien pointed out that the most serious crisis facing the party was the nonexistence of party leadership over the government. According to Ch'en, part of the problem stemmed from the understaffing of the party organs on the municipal and *hsien* levels and below so that they could not provide constant supervision over the government in discharging its various functions. But more fundamentally, the problem was the outright resentment and resistance of government officials against party leadership. Whether in personnel or policy issues, the *hsien* government usually did not bother to solicit the advice of the party committee. As Ch'en observed,

> Even if the party committee made the slightest criticism, the *hsien* government would regard it as interference. If the party committee offered suggestions, they would be ignored by the *hsien* government. If the *hsien* party committee pursued the matter by submitting reports to the National Party Headquarters, the latter often either avoided making judgments, or dismissed them as petty quarrels between party and government officials, or even accused the party committee of creating unnecessary troubles. The most usual disposition by the National Party Headquarters was to disregard such reports. This was the primary reason that led to widespread demoralization among the party rank and file and to an emptiness in party work.[36]

Similar complaints about the impotence of the party in *hsien* politics were echoed by other well-known party leaders.[37]

The inability of the leadership to send its own trusted followers to man the vast governmental structure in the interior produced one of two consequences. In some cases, the KMT loyalists dispatched to local works found themselves isolated and resented by the local political structures. In most cases, however, the tactic of wholesale co-optation of local ruling elites into the party resulted in the party's own identity and structures being submerged under the local structures and personalities. In either case, the party became a shell with no substance. Local leaders either totally ignored the party or reduced it to a puppet to serve their traditional interests.[38]

Not surprisingly, the party also could not penetrate down to the mass level to provide leadership or show a greater presence in popular organizations. Since there were substantial linguistic and cultural barriers to penetrate the subsoil of the social structures in the interior by outside cadres, only the indigenous cadres could have bridged the gap between the national leaders and the local people. In late 1940, the Ministry of Social Affairs was created and was promptly controlled by the C.C. faction through one of its leaders, Ku Cheng-kang. The ministry was generally viewed as an attempt to extend party influence and organization into every phase of social life.[39] But as the party's own statistics show, the KMT's efforts to establish a presence in the voluntary associations of Chinese society amounted to a dismal failure.[40] By 1941, the party had established party organs in less than 6 percent of the nation's private secondary associations. In crucial interior provinces such as Szechwan, Yünnan, and Kweichow, the party had barely scratched the surface of the social fabric.

In the case of Szechwan, it was evident that the local secret society (*ko-lao-hui*) had far greater and far more pervasive influence than the Nationalist party. Not only were Szechwan political, military, and business leaders members of the *ko-lao-hui*, but that half of the population of Chengtu was reported to be associated with it in some fashion. In fact, many *ko-lao-hui* agents had penetrated the party's own secret police, and frequently party or government activities could be undertaken only after being approved by local *ko-lao-hui* leaders.[41] Such a situation lasted to the end of the war.

The KMT's Inability to Revitalize Itself

At least by 1942, if not sooner, Chiang himself recognized the seriousness of the problem and sought to upgrade the quality of party workers on the *hsien* level as a way of strengthening party power. In his address to the tenth plenum of the Party Congress on November 23, 1942, Chiang attributed the decline of party power to the inferior caliber of the party secretaries and the insufficiency of operating funds for party activities. Thereafter, the selection of more qualified party members to take charge of *hsien* committees was to be given top priority. Chiang further introduced the new rule of appointing *hsien* party secretaries to concurrently serve as *hsien* magistrates in order to increase the party's leadership over the government.[42] But this solution was to prove impractical because it confused the symptoms with the cause. Neither the central party nor the central government succeeded in appointing many party secretaries to be *hsien* magistrates for the simple reason that the appointive power was wielded mostly by local and regional political-military leaders.

The Nationalist party's attempt to strengthen itself failed in several other ways. As an attempt to bolster its basic-level organizations, the party had wanted to establish committees in all administrative districts, *hsiang,* and *cheng,* and cells (*hsiao-tsu*) in all *pao.*[43] But by 1944, only 60,953 of the 230,000 *hsiang* and *cheng* under the government's nominal control had established committees.[44] The most basic of all organs, the cell, posed the greatest problem. Even when we accept party claims at face value, only 167,314 of the over half a million *pao* in the countryside reported the existence of a cell in 1944.[45]

The main reason for the party's inability to expand organizations was that, despite the party's policy to co-opt members into the party indiscriminately, it in fact faced considerable difficulties in attracting respondents at all times. Even in 1940–41 when the party mounted a massive recruitment campaign in coordination with the newly installed new-*hsien* program, the actual number of recruits was less than 30 percent of the target figure.[46] The failure to arouse spontaneous enthusiasm for the party often resulted in abuses in recruitment bordering on impressment, which inevitably turned more people against the party and caused its prestige to decline.[47]

People declined to join the party not merely because it provided no prospects for upward mobility (since all the power holders had already joined the party and were unmovable from their bureaucratic strongholds), but also because the party could do little else with its feeble financial support. During the 1930s, the party drew about 2 to 5 percent of the central government's budget to finance its own activities.[48] During the war, money became scarce,[49] and the little that did become available invariably went to high party organs at the expense of lower organs. More seriously, on the *hsiang* and *cheng* levels and below, all personnel were unpaid and all party activities were supported by the dues of its members, amounting to twenty cents per month in 1940, an absolutely ridiculous sum to support any party activities.[50] This lack of funds frequently forced *hsien-* and lower-level party organs to completely suspend work for long periods of time.[51] In view of the general poverty inflicted by the war, this lack of funds created strong disincentive for people to get involved in basic-level party work, and those already assigned to such work were anxious to get out.[52]

The shortage of competent cadres had been another serious problem for the party for a long time. After the anti-Communist purge, the suspension of party works among the masses and in schools produced a serious hiatus in the supply of fresh young cadres for more than a decade. During the Nanking era, the great expansion of activities in economic affairs, government, army, and communications siphoned off more talent from the party.[53] Thus, for example, the Central Party Academy was originally established explicitly to train high-caliber party cadres. In reality, however, it became a college of public administration and more graduates sought bureaucratic assignments than party posts.[54]

After the war broke out, the KMT hastily organized a number of training programs on national, provincial, and local levels. But under wartime conditions, the training of party cadres was decisively eclipsed by other more urgent needs. Thus between 1937 and 1941, cadres engaged in party work only accounted for 6.5 percent of trainees in national training programs and 2.1 percent of the trainees in local training programs.[55] Meager as they were, these figures again reveal the low priority given to local party work in comparison with high-level party work. The neglect of training for party workers continued to the end of the war.[56]

The combined weight of the previously mentioned factors inevitably produced serious morale and discipline problems among the rank and file. Historically, the KMT had never been a party noted for strict discipline, except when the offenders had been Communists or Communist sympathizers. The party did much to undermine its own credibility in disciplinary matters in the 1930s when waves of anti-Chiang leaders were "permanently expelled" from the party, only to be reinstated shortly after their differences had been patched up. This situation made a mockery of the justice and fairness of the party's disciplinary policies and machinery, and accentuated the fact that discipline was the verdict of Chiang's personal machine.

Discipline continued to be lax during the first four years of the war. Between 1937 and 1941, despite massive demonstrations by members of incompetence, cowardice, corruption, and even treason, only 1,827 cases of alleged violations of party discipline were ever brought to the attention of the Central Control Committee (*chung-yang chien-ch'a wei-yüan-hui*) and less than one-third of these cases resulted in permanent expulsion, while others brought mild warnings or temporary suspension of membership rights.[57]

Clearly the Central Control Committee was totally ineffective.[58] In an attempt to tighten up discipline, the KMT established a "surveillance network for party members" (*tang-yüan chien-ch'a-wang*). This concept was a radical departure from the relaxed attitude of the party in the past and clearly reflected its growing concern over the worsening problem.[59] Introduced in October, 1940, the surveillance system was meant to formalize and to complement the activities that had long been carried out undercover by the party's Central Bureau of Statistics. Yet in spite of the fanfare it created, the effectiveness of the surveillance system is very much in doubt. In any event, it is revealing that a sprawling system of over 44,000 surveillance agents in 1944 only brought 541 aberrant members to serious punishment.[60] Such a record conclusively demonstrates that a party member during the war years could reasonably expect to get away with any crime, as long as he did not openly defect to the Japanese or the Chinese Communist side. Discipline within the party during the war was but a fiction.

From the above description, it is clear that public contempt for the KMT was well-deserved. Even those who remained faithful to the party's political ideals despised the way party committees conducted themselves on the local level.[61] The party's secretary-general, Wu T'ieh-ch'eng, acknowledged in 1944 that the party was obviously unable to arouse any enthusiasm among its basic level members, even to participate in cell activities. He was greatly disturbed by such apathy, but professed his inability to improve the situation.[62]

In short, the party machine whose growth had been stunted by the trend of militarization of the Nanking years, but which at least managed to perform limited governing functions, now became totally unwieldy shortly after the war started under the combined new strains of the geographical, structural, and demographic changes discussed above. Chiang's own criticism against the party became increasingly frequent and harsh after the Provisional Congress of March, 1938. In his wartime speeches on party affairs, Chiang repeated an inventory of party shortcomings that included lax discipline, low morale, organizational ineptitude, bureaucratization of party organs, and the corruption of party officials, all of which had given the party a bad name.[63] His indictment was echoed by his party secretary-general and chief of organization who said in late 1942 that morale and style of work in many *hsien* party committees were so embarrassingly poor that he "could not bear to visit their offices."[64]

By May, 1944, public anger against the party had reached such a high pitch that members of the otherwise docile CEC found themselves venting their frustration against the Organization Department and party leaders in a very acrimonious session.[65] While these criticisms indicated that some party leaders were not unaware of the problems, the telling point was that they were never able to conduct a *cheng-feng* (rectification) campaign as the Communists did. The most distinguished organizational mark of the party is that it had been truncated into two parts. The rank and file who swelled the party drew their power and support from the local structures outside the party, and they in turn gave their primary allegiance to these local structures. The national party leaders transplanted from the east coast continued in their nominal roles, but failed to develop new organizational means to assert control over the rank and file. The party had simply gotten out of hand. In retrospect, the KMT did not engage in any meaningful party-building programs during the eight long years of war for two reasons. The most immediate reason was that the party had acquired dead weight in such haste that the party itself was rendered organizationally paralyzed as well as spiritually impoverished.

     But a more fundamental reason might be Chiang's perception of the nature of the Chinese revolution and the role of the party in it. Given Chiang's prewar disposition against the party in favor of the state and the army, it might have been difficult for him to design new ways to strengthen the party even if he now wanted to do so. It was equally plausible that he was not terribly disturbed by the decline of party power, even as he became quite openly contemptuous of the party's failings. For Chiang's view of the Chinese revolution seemed to have remained rigid despite the momentous pressures brought about by the war. The evidence is to be found in his book, *Chung-kuo chih ming-yün* (*China's Destiny*). Released in 1943, this book contained the most authoritative statement of Chiang's unchanging view of the KMT's revolutionary objectives. The bulk of this work was devoted to an emotional account of China's humiliation suffered at the hands of foreign imperialists, and a rededication of national will to over-throw the unequal treaties as the paramount goal of the national revolution. Believing that China's internal problem of feudalism as manifested by warlordism had been eliminated, Chiang saw little need to extend the internal revolution into the socioeconomic realm. Rather, he asserted that the country's revolutionary zeal must now be directed exclusively to the unfinished business of abrogating the unequal treaties, and appealed to the people to help fulfill "China's destiny" by their demonstration of "unity," "solidarity," "public-spiritedness," and "law-abidingness." [66]

     Since, according to Chiang, the need for internal socioeconomic revolution was nonexistent, the enfeeblement of the party would not seem to have any particularly grave implications as long as the KMT leaders actually controlled the apparatus of the Chungking government. In the meantime, the elimination of the unequal treaties was believed to be realizable primarily by military means combined with diplomatic skill.

Given such a view of the KMT leadership, it is not surprising that it could afford to allow the rank and file not only to fail to be the agents of political tutelage, but to become part and parcel of the system of corruption and oppression.

Factional Activities before the War—Some Methodological Problems

In his study of early Republican politics, Professor Andrew Nathan defines a faction as a structure "mobilized on the basis of clientist ties to engage in politics and consisting of a few rather than a great many layers of personnel."[67] He further argues,

> What all these configurations (factions) share in common is the one-to-one, rather than corporate, pattern of relationships between leaders (or sub-leaders) and followers. Structurally, the faction is articulated through one or more nodes, and it is recruited and coordinated on the basis of the personal exchange relationships I have called clientist ties.[68]

Probably one of the most often made criticisms against the Kuomintang was its reckless attitude toward factional infighting among its leaders. To some commentators, the KMT means little more than the aggregate of its factions. Yet despite the existence of known factions and a high degree of factional activities within the party, the study of factionalism has advanced very little in the last three decades. Two factors have contributed to this situation.

First of all, under the KMT, the term "faction" had assumed ideologically pejorative connotations.[69] It is well known that the Ch'en brothers steadfastly scoffed at the suggestion that they were the leaders of the C.C. faction, and insisted that the C.C. never existed.[70] The reticence of the leaders was reinforced by the reluctance of the followers to own up to their factional affiliation. Unlike their Peiyang predecessors who unabashedly acknowledged their factional loyalties, Nationalist politicians were discreet enough not to reveal their own factional identities, although they were never reluctant to accuse others of having factional ties.

Second, factions in the 1930s tended to become more complex, encompassing members of diverse geographical, social, educational and professional backgrounds. Also, the factions became more complex in the sense that the number of people mobilized into factional activities had increased sharply as factional politics now pervaded all aspects of public life. During the Peiyang period, factional politics were visible within the army, the cabinet, and the parliament. Under the Nationalists, factional politics extended into the schools, the business world, the lower levels of government, various social activities, banking, and industries. These factors rendered it difficult to construct a refined model of factional politics for the Nationalist era. Such an endeavor must wait until we can gather a mass of biographical data on large numbers of political actors on the national, provincial, and local levels. What is attempted here is to provide a preliminary examination of certain aspects of KMT politics in a factional perspective. A crude approximation to reality is all that can be hoped for at this time.

In discussing Nationalist politics, a distinction should be made between two types of factions. One type of faction refers to territorially based political-military groups such as Feng Yü-hsiang, Yen Hsi-shan, or Lung Yün, and many others whose activities were discussed in chapters 1–4. Although these people were nominally party leaders, they had little patience with party work. Whenever they challenged Chiang, they did so outside the party framework. We choose to exclude them from the category ''party factions.''

What we will include is a second type of faction that engaged primarily in intraparty activities. These drew support from party members, operated in areas recognized as the party's domain, and competed for control over party organizations and resources. Of this type, the most famous are the C.C., the Action Society, the Political Science Faction, the Western Hill Faction, and the Reorganization Faction. In the Nanking era, these factions played rather different roles. As our main interest is in factional politics of the 1940s, our discussion of the 1930s will do no more than just sketch the factional lineup.

The Action Society

The accurate official title for the Action Society formed in April 1932 was *san-min-chu-i li-hsing-she* (Society for the Practice of the Three People's Principles), while popularly it was better known as the *lan-i-she* (blueshirts). Most of its original organizers were Whampoa graduates handpicked by Chiang.[71] On the popular level, the better known *Fu-hsing-she* (Restoration Society) was established in July, 1934. In fact, the Restoration Society was a front organization with no independent structure or personnel. From the national level down to the local level, the activities nominally attributed to the Restoration Society were in fact performed by cadres from either the Action Society or the Association of Revolutionary Youth.

Basically, there were three areas in which the Action Society was most influential. Political indoctrination in the armed forces was under the direction of Ho Chung-han; the Special Forces (*pieh-tung-tui*) were led by K'ang Tse; and the military secret police (Bureau of Military Statistics, or *chün-t'ung*) was headed by Tai Li. Of these three, the secret police was the least developed in terms of organizational sophistication, size of manpower, and functional specificity. The political indoctrination was concerned with winning over the allegiance of regional military units either through indoctrination or infiltration and surveillance, and the function of the Special Forces was to use paramilitary means to engage in popular agitation and mobilization in areas immediately adjacent to the Communist bases.

Although the predominantly military cast of the Action Society would have made it logical to confine its activities to strictly military-related areas, success soon encouraged it to expand into new directions. By late 1933, it had invaded the world of arts and literature and established its presence in some educational institutions through the introduction of military training into regular school curriculum.

The high secrecy surrounding the activities of the Action Society has made it difficult to gauge its prewar strength, but one confidential Japanese government report gave its total manpower at 14,000 at the end of 1935.[72]

The C.C.

It was generally assumed that the C.C. was formed in the summer of 1927 when Chiang needed more loyal followers to replace the Communists in responsible party and government positions. Ch'en Kuo-fu's control over the Central Organization Department in 1928 gave him wide discretionary powers over the implementation of the general registration program designed to weed out hidden Communists and their sympathizers, and led to the rapid rise of his followers in many provincial committees. It also led to the formation of the party secret police, the Central Bureau of Statistics, or *chung-t'ung*.

Within a short time, the C.C. preempted the field of party cadre training and made inroads into public education, publishing, finance, business, and industry.[73] One measure of its growth was its increased representation in the Central Executive Committee. By 1935, 50 out of 180 (or 27 percent) of CEC members were reported to have C.C. affiliation. It was also estimated that the peak strength of the faction's membership in the prewar years probably reached 10,000 persons. Territorially, the C.C. was most active in Kiangsu, Chekiang, Anhwei, Fukien, and Kiangsi.[74]

The Reorganization Faction

Although Wang Ching-wei had differed with Chiang on many issues both before and during the Northern Expedition, the impetus that drove him to organize a formal faction of his own was the rapid rise of Chiang's power after the anti-Communist purge. The creation of the *chung-kuo kuo-min-tang kai-tsu t'ung-chih-hui* (Association for the Reorganization of the Kuomintang) in Shanghai in the spring of 1928 marked the beginning of a Wang Ching-wei political machine.

Before long, the faction was reported to have a force of ten thousand strong.[75] A cursory review of its leadership roster reveals that it was not a geographically based group since the leaders were often drawn from all over the country. Nor was it a strictly functionally based group, because many of them had senior status in the party, but had performed few concrete assignments for the party. The reasons for the rapid expansion of the faction were that it offered all the dissidents within the party a ready organizational outlet to manifest their displeasure against Chiang Kai-shek under the leadership of a widely respected man, Wang himself.

But within the faction, fundamental differences existed and inevitably hindered its solidarity.[76] In 1929, Wang finally conceded the need to engage in armed confrontation with Chiang and collaborated with Feng Yü-hsiang, Yen Hsi-shan, and Li Tsung-jen to convene the so-called Expanded Congress. But military reverses suffered by Wang's military allies quickly forced him to abandon their scheme. Wang and Chiang patched up their differences after the Manchurian Incident of 1931, and cooperated closely in the national government. However, Wang's injury in an assassination plot in 1935 forced him into prolonged absence from national politics. Finally, the sudden death of Hu Han-min in May, 1936, removed a powerful incentive for Chiang to continue his cooperation with Wang. Thus as China moved closer to a path of war in 1936–37, the leaderless Reorganizationists also began to lose strength in Chinese politics.

The Political Science Faction and the Western Hill Faction

The Political Science faction had been an amorphous group long before the KMT assumed power.[77] This group established connection with Chiang in 1926 when the latter needed experienced bureaucrats to fill governmental positions. Its members included intellectuals, military officers, bankers, and financiers, concentrated primarily in the bureaucracy, with particular emphasis on economic affairs. Consequently, their activities centered in the big urban areas where administrative and industrial powers were concentrated. Throughout the Nanking era, this group was content to carve out a small area in the administrative hierarchy as its preserve. Its reputed leaders, such as Chang Ch'ün, Yang Yung-t'ai, and Huang Fu were basically strategists and politicians retained by Chiang as advisors on an individual basis.[78] Huang Fu was not even a member of the KMT. These leaders showed no inclination to create their own formal organization either along functional or territorial lines. Consequently, the Political Science faction should be regarded as one of the triumvirate of Chiang's personal power machine.

Of all the factions, the Western Hill faction had the smallest size and the most fragile political structure. Although some of its leaders, such as Lin Sen, Shao Yüan-ch'ung, and Yeh Ch'u-ts'ang, later occupied lofty posts in the government, their strength was predicated on their anti-Communist credentials, personal reputation, and seniority in the party. They never developed any formal organization, nor did they evolve any distinct platform outside of their uncompromising anti-CCP stance. Hence, although they continued to be referred to as the Western Hillers, they hardly posed any threat to Chiang, which explains why they were given high ceremonial positions in the party and government in the 1930s. They usually stayed out of intraparty embroilments, once the party had accepted their ideological line.

Broadly speaking, the most intense struggles within the party in the 1930s occurred between the pro-Chiang and anti-Chiang factions. In the pattern of competition, the anti-Chiang forces repeatedly demonstrated that they lacked organizational finesse and military prowess. In fact, even in the 1930s, it was already quite clear that the military was the final arbiter of intraparty struggles. As Chiang scored one military victory after another over his opponents, his supporters in the party obtained more opportunities to expand both territorially and functionally. In general, the victories on the battlefield enabled the Whampoa-dominated Action Society to expand operations into newly conquered territories. But the Action Society did not have the manpower to handle all the issues confronting the conquerors. In time, the C.C. was brought in to organize the regular party activities and, to a lesser degree, the Political Science faction was given a share in the civil administration. Chiang's strength lay precisely in the fact that his personal machine was the most integral one consisting of these three functionally distinct elements. Even though frictions occasionally existed among these elements (e.g., the C.C. faction's opposition to Yang Yung-t'ai), Chiang usually was able to contain them and to prevent any one of them from achieving supremacy. Although in some bandit-suppression areas the Whampoa group clearly enjoyed an edge,[79] overall there existed a state of equilibrium among the factions, and only Chiang was in command of all three factions.

In contrast, Chiang's rivals were either traditional militarists who retained most of the characteristics of the warlord era or political factions having a narrow base exclusively within the party. As the latter lacked military muscle, the former lacked organizational sophistication. Only a joining of forces of these two categories of factions could have posed a genuine threat to Chiang. But between 1928 and 1937, these two categories of factions either chose to challenge Chiang in their separate ways, or were so poorly orchestrated in the very few cases of cooperation that they never succeeded in threatening the pro-Chiang factions.

However, this pattern of struggle also had debilitating effects on the pro-Chiang factions. Basically, these factions grew excessively dependent on a pattern in which the Whampoa army defeated the enemy first, and then the party moved into an already pacified area to set up headquarters and carry party work into the bureaucracy, the schools, and the business world. Military security became an absolutely necessary prerequisite for conducting party activities. In contradistinction to Sun's original concept of using the party to spearhead a revolutionary movement, the KMT actually displayed no inclination to venture into hostile territories to wage ideological and organizational battles long before the arrival of its own soldiers.

Over time, the party developed a mentality of complete dependence on the KMT's military superiority to overcome all obstacles. Instead of maintaining close contact with the masses or inspiring them with ideology and programs, Nationalist leaders became accustomed to conducting their work only in a highly bureaucratic, formalistic, and commandistic style. As a result, this mentality created a serious impediment to the party's work during the war, when it no longer was afforded the luxury of military protection either in the enemy-held areas or even in the territories under nominal government jurisdiction.

Equally noteworthy was the very existence of factions within the Chiang camp. With few exceptions, the factions were formed by particularistic interpersonal ties. None of the pro-Chiang factions could be really identified with a political platform or socioeconomic program. Factions were formed as collective security pacts to protect and promote leaders' private interests. That these factions were used by Chiang to indulge in power struggles against his own rivals should not obscure the fact that factional life was intrinsically corrupting. For those KMT leaders who eagerly participated in this game, they acquired the disposition to view politics not in terms of policy options but in terms of power gains. Their extreme sensitivity to the nuances of power shifts and their preoccupation with "winning" or "losing" threatened to turn power into the ultimate aim of the political process. Over time, they tended to lose sight of the larger moral and philosophical issues from which a revolutionary party must continuously derive its meaning and dynamism. Therefore, even though the pro-Chiang factions avoided fratricide before the war, their very existence had without doubt seriously eroded the moral strength and revolutionary commitment of the party. The long-term danger to the party was to become clear only during the war. For once power, defined in terms of territorial aggrandizement or bureaucratic expansion, was no longer easily obtainable, the factions would become so disoriented as to become thoroughly demoralized and paralyzed in the political process.

Intensification of Factional Struggle during the War

Many students of KMT politics subscribe to the view that the worst aspect of its wartime regime was the ascendancy of unprincipled factional strife and that the reason for it was Chiang's realization after 1941 that he could let the United States win a sure victory for him, and therefore he could use China's resources to build up his own fascist regime. It is further believed that in order to remain supreme in the game, Chiang deliberately encouraged the expansion of factions and manipulated one against the other. Finally, it is believed that the factions were the culprits that perpetrated the incompetence, corruption, and cynicism evidenced in wartime politics, and that Chiang was a masterful juggler of political groups and exploited them to increase his own dictatorial powers.[80]

While the harmful effects of wanton factional struggles on the morale and quality of wartime government were so obvious as to need no further elaboration, the reasons for the surge of factionalism and its long-term ramifications deserve to be closely examined. Whether Chiang deliberately encouraged factionalism will remain unclear for as long as his personal files are closed to scholarly perusal. The facts presented in this chapter may offer us some clues to a different but equally plausible interpretation of the factional phenomenon. Basically, my argument is that the surge of factional activities was not the result of a willful design either by Chiang to aggrandize his dictatorial powers or by the very factions themselves to aggressively expand their own power. On the contrary, if we take a structural perspective, the surge of factionalism signifies a reaction of the party leaders against the deterioration of their own political-military power vis-à-vis the regional leaders; it was an expression of their frustration with their impotence in extending regular organizational control over the rank and file, the lack of prospects for normal party growth, and their attempt to grab the largest possible portion of a shrinking political pie.

No sooner had the war started than the national leaders found themselves increasingly excluded from the lower levels of party and government. The power holders of the interior provinces showed no inclination to share power with the party's center, not to mention accepting the latter's guidance. Typically, the regional leaders either appointed their own party committeemen or accepted a few appointees from the national party headquarters and proceeded to isolate them. These regionalists acquired their party membership as a simple matter of political expedience; in the meantime, they set up tight defenses around their territorial and functional domains against the intrusion of the party center. In effect, the local governments and society were declared off limits to national organizing efforts, and trespassing by national leaders often met with violent reaction. This was a markedly different experience for the national leaders, who had always been assured of easy access to the government and society in the eastern provinces before the war. Having never developed the expertise for mass mobilization to subvert the established sociopolitical order from below, and disheartened by the lack of military progress along the front, the national leaders drifted toward an even greater degree of conservatism and seized whatever outlets possible to spend their organizational energy.

Hence, as the power base was severely contracted, the arena for waging political combat was contracted accordingly. Thus, their activities now were mainly confined to the national level and a few functional areas on the provincial and local levels not yet preempted by the established local power holders. Political struggles waged in such a situation became more vitriolic precisely because there were so few resources available and everybody wanted to get them. Cynicism crept into factional politics with the realization by the participants that, with the war's outcome well beyond their control, their best strategy was to maneuver themselves into a position to reap the fruits of victory when victory did come. From the perspective of the war years, these fruits would include control over the People's Political Council, the Sixth Party Congress, the election of the members to the National Assembly, the Legislative Yüan, the Control Yüan, and finally a constitutionally elected presidency.

It soon became apparent that both the identity of factions as well as the pattern of their interrelations departed quite visibly from the prewar years. Capitalizing on the war, Chiang assumed the position of *tsung-ts'ai* or director-general of the party in April, 1938. The immediate impact of this development was the further erosion of the political stock of the Reorganizationists. Now, with Chiang installed as the supreme leader of the party, Wang Ching-wei was condemned to a junior position, which he found hard to swallow. Finally, when Wang bolted the party and defected to the Japanese side, he also wrote the death warrant for the Reorganizationists. After 1939, the Reorganization faction simply ceased to be a factor in party politics.

The fate of the Political Science faction was slightly better. However, during the war this faction proved totally unable to make any headway organizationally, remained isolated from the general public, and became entirely parasitic in the national bureaucracy. By 1943, it had become quite difficult to define the strength of the faction with any degree of accuracy. After the death of Huang Fu and Yang Yung-t'ai, Chang Ch'ün became the faction's leader.[81] These people's influence was largely personal and their official positions largely the favors of Chiang. They commanded neither a constituency among the masses nor a military following: they managed to maintain a low profile in the arena of political struggle and therefore seldom made a target for other factions.[82]

The Kwangtung-based party seniors had lost their territorial control by mid-1938 with the sudden loss of Canton. In subsequent years, although Kwangtung leaders continued to occupy high party and government positions, they became generals without soldiers. Likewise, the Western Hill faction had been further enfeebled as its members advanced in age and became isolated in exalted but powerless positions.

These developments set the stage for the pro-Chiang factions to confront each other, and the story of wartime factional politics, in contradistinction to the Nanking era, was largely the story of the rivalry of factions that all grew out of Chiang's personal machine.

Division within Chiang's Camp

Reports of hostility among these factions began to circulate almost as soon as the war began.[83] Once the factional struggle began, it threatened to be uncontrollable. The party's secretary-general and its chairman of the Organization Department between 1938 and 1944, Chu Chia-hua, lamented that the "biggest problem within the party" since the war was "personnel," because leaders cultivated their own followings.[84] The very first instruction on how to improve party work that Chiang issued after he became *tsung-ts'ai* included an injunction against factional activities.[85] Yet as the years went by, the situation only got worse.

By and large, the C.C. encountered considerable difficulties in holding on to its influence in the party during the war. Since the national party could neither organize nor propagandize effectively, the departments of Organization and Propaganda, the traditional strongholds of the C.C. before the war, were no longer as powerful as they once were. For most of the war years even the posts of chairman of the Organization Department and the secretary-general of the party went to non-C.C. men.[86]

However, Ch'en Kuo-fu was the head of the Central Broadcasting Administration, which gave him some control over the mass media. A more important position held by him was Chief of the Personnel Section of the Generalissimo's Secretariat, which made him privy to state secrets as well as powers of appointment, dismissal, promotion, and demotion over some central government officials. Ch'en Li-fu was the minister of education, which gave him considerable control over the colleges and universities. During any given year, three to five other C.C. leaders would hold ministerial or vice-ministerial positions in the Chungking government and some twenty-three to twenty-five would be members of the party's Central Executive Committee.[87]

The one area in which the C.C. gained some strength during the war was its covert operations. Precisely because the party was not able to strike roots in the basic levels of the society and government through regular open channels, it found it necessary to resort to such extraordinary covert means as intimidation, pecuniary inducements, and outright brutality to get what it wanted. As so often was the case, where normative power failed, coercive means would be resorted to. During the war, the Central Bureau of Statistics was dramatically expanded. The bureau was responsible for official intelligence and the compilation of dossiers on all governmental employees. An office of investigation (*tiao-ch'a-shih*) was attached to most party and government organs and routinely reported on the private lives, official activities, thoughts, associations, loyalty, and performance of officials, high and low. Such information gave the C.C. considerable tactical advantage in waging political combat with their rivals. The bureau also exercised surveillance over the activities of all other political parties and semi-official groups, religious sects, trade unions, guilds, chambers of commerce, and the like.[88] When the universities in the southwest became the bastions of China's liberal-democratic parties, C.C. agents' presence on the campuses also became conspicuous. They penetrated school administrations, spied on student activities, and intimidated outspoken professors. It was reliably reported that the party secret police ran its own thought-correction camps in at least nine provinces, and suspects and dissidents were routinely subject to interrogation, torture, and forced labor.[89]

In time, covert activities became the backbone to sustain the political power of the C.C. faction. Although the harshness and arbitrariness of such activities aroused bitter resentment from both the general public and other political activists, and rightly so, they themselves bore testimony to the fact that the C.C. was so reduced from its prewar power that it found the only feasible way to stay alive was to resort to coercion. Yet even in the much confined area of activities the C.C. now carved out for itself, it did not enjoy an uncontested authority. For although the Central Bureau of Statistics was responsible for civilian and governmental security (including anti-Communist and anti-Wang activities), while the Bureau of Military Statistics was responsible for military intelligence (on both friendly and enemy armies), the scheme did not work out neatly.

The position of the C.C. suffered a serious setback with the establishment of the Combat Area Party-Government Joint Commission (*chan-ti tang-cheng wei-yüan-hui*). In each war zone, this organ was superimposed on all existing regular party and government agencies, and the highest *military* officer in the area would have the full authority to control and coordinate army, party, and governmental affairs.[90] As almost all military commanders (both regional and Whampoa) were wary of party influence (particularly C.C. activities), they now could easily neglect or thwart its activities.[91]

However, the one area that generated the keenest competition and most intense hostility between the C.C. and the *Fu-hsing-she* (now commonly used as a synonym for the Action Society) was in the youth organizations after the Party Congress passed the resolution in March, 1938, to create the *San-min-chu-i ch'ing-nien-t'uan* (Youth Corps of the Three People's Principles). The original idea for a youth corps was to use it to spearhead an anti-Communist offensive and to forge a broad united front with all other political parties.[92] There is no doubt that the *Fu-hsing-she* lobbied hard for the creation of the Youth Corps, and the resolution represented a resounding victory for this faction. Most key leaders of the Youth Corps were long-standing members of the former Action Society and they adopted a highly aggressive expansionist policy from the very beginning. They deliberately broadcast the rumor that Chiang had become totally disillusioned with the corruption and inefficiency of the regular party and intended eventually to replace it with the Youth Corps. In many places, the Youth Corps adopted confrontation tactics against the party by augmenting its ranks with nonyouths, local bullies, and bad gentry members to overpower regular local party organs.[93] Even in the first two years, the organizational work of the Youth Corps already indicated that its directors had no intention of staying within the bounds of youth work alone.

Organizationally, the Youth Corps duplicated the regular party and set up branches both in the schools and in the *hsien*.[94] It ran its own training programs for cadres, school youths, social youths, and conducted a host of activities usually reserved for the regular party organs.[95] The professional backgrounds of its 1941 membership showed that students constituted only 44 percent, but those who were already in the army, party, and government constituted 50 percent of the total.[96] As most people working for the army, party, or government had already joined the party, the Youth Corps' attempt to enroll them was correctly interpreted by many as a clear sign to wean these people from the party into a separate faction. In fact, the Youth Corps had become so aggressive in its recruitment and so contemptuous of the regular party organs and leaders that many party secretaries bitterly complained to the national party headquarters. However, the party's secretary-general could do no more than try to calm them.[97]

Despite repeated injunctions by the standing committee of the CEC or Chiang himself against mutual recrimination and unprincipled sabotage of each other,[98] the corps went its own way, and its relations with the C.C. stayed poisoned to the very end of the war. As one report from the Central Bureau of Statistics complained in 1945, in some localities the corps was so aggressive as to cause the party to be completely paralyzed.[99] In the course of the confrontation, the Youth Corps increased its strength: by July, 1944, it had set up branches in over seven hundred *hsien* with a membership of 647,763.[100]

As we discussed earlier, the Action Society's functions before the war covered three areas—political indoctrination, military intelligence, and anti-Communist activities and Special Forces. After the New Fourth Army Incident, anti-Communist activities became fully integrated with regular military activities and the responsibilities of military commanders. In order to insure the reliability of the military commanders, the Bureau of Military Statistics (or *chün-t'ung*) developed into an extensive bureaucracy. *Chün-t'ung* agents were assigned to the headquarters of war zones and those of divisions. The same was true with respect to provincial garrison commands, the police stations in large cities and towns, as well as numerous checkpoints along the major thoroughfares. Finally, *chün-t'ung* agents were also empowered to check subversive economic activities among the people such as hoarding, speculation, and black marketeering.[101] By virtue of such broad responsibilities, *chün-t'ung* and Tai Li himself became far more indispensible than the Ch'en brothers to Chiang. *Chün-t'ung* operations were generously funded, and its agents soon permeated all aspects of wartime life. By mid-1944, Tai Li's agents in the regular military secret police and special forces numbered over 300,000 with stations located in virtually all major governmental and private institutions.[102]

The political stock of the *Fu-hsing-she,* and particularly that of the Youth Corps, was raised considerably in its pitched battle against the C.C. when it joined forces with Chiang's eldest son, Chiang Ching-kuo, in the winter of 1943. Summoned from his office as a commissioner of a special administrative district in southern Kiangsi, the young Chiang was given control over the Youth Army, the Central Cadre School, and eventually the Youth Corps itself. With his easy access to his father, his presence added a new dimension to the power struggle and placed the C.C. at a severe disadvantage.

Summary of Factionalism during the War

The preceding analysis of wartime factional struggles shows that, within the party, the decimation or eclipse of some prewar factions set the stage for a confrontation between the C.C. and the *Fu-hsing-she*. Instead of peaceful coexistence, they now regarded each other as mortal enemies, precisely because they realized that their isolation from the masses would compel them to draw sustenance from the upper reaches of the society and government. As the spoils were limited, the factions only fought harder to get them. Hence the intensification of factional struggle on higher levels and the impotence of the party on the basic levels were really two sides of the same coin. Instead of trying to explore revolutionary methods to mobilize the masses ideologically and organizationally, the Nationalist leaders devoted all their energy and resources to achieving a dominant position in the high echelons of the KMT hierarchy. Factional leaders probably realized that whereas the local leaders of the interior could block them from striking roots there as long as the war lasted, these local leaders could not compete with them when the rich eastern provinces were repossessed at the war's end. The end of war would bring an entirely new ball game. The inevitable rush back to the coast to reclaim the lost land and resources would benefit only the faction that had already achieved a decidedly dominant position before the rush began. It is probably this calculation that led the factions to view the struggles as more than necessary to ride out the difficult war years; they were actually warm-up rounds for the big postwar showdown.

In their eagerness to obtain a larger share of the available resources, the KMT factions not only tried to reduce the share of competing factions, but together they resolutely denied China's other minority political parties any meaningful role in the governing process. In 1942, the government bowed to public pressure and reconstituted the Third People's Political Council (PPC) in an attempt to unify all the political groups to wage a common resistance struggle. Even though the PPC was only a consultative, and not a legislative, body, the KMT factions exerted great effort to insure that they would dominate both the general membership and the key committees. By 1943, most of the minority parties had become so resentful of the KMT's exclusivistic approach that many of their leaders refused to participate in the PPC.[103]

As China's military and economic crises worsened in 1944–45, the abuses of the factions became even more blatant and repugnant. Not only were corruption and cynicism more pronounced, but the party relied more and more on intimidation and violence to suppress popular discontent. Such policies were bound to be counterproductive, for the repressive measures of the KMT generated so much hostility that the political opposition was finally driven to the conclusion that they had to work for the overthrow of the party-government even if they had to conspire with the provincial warlords. The dramatically stepped-up antigovernment activities of the Democratic League in 1944-45 must be viewed as an act of desperation against the monopolistic policies of the KMT factions.

Finally, an appreciation of the KMT factions' anxiety over shrinking resources can help us understand why these factions plundered the people of the Japanese-occupied areas with such reckless abandon when they returned. At the end of the war, the vast, newly liberated areas became a free-for-all in which factional members in the army, party, and government laid claims on residences, factories, banks, warehouses, schools, vessels, vehicles, publishing houses, newspapers, and a thousand other valuable items with total disregard to law, political principles, or human decency. The collapse of discipline was complete and competing claims were often settled by armed confrontation. It is then that we see the full impact of the devastation befalling party life during the war years. Behaving like men long suffering from undernourishment, these factions now tried to gobble up everything within reach with total disregard for their own good or that of their party. Instead of being liberators, they considered themselves the conquerors, in many ways worse than the Japanese. Undoubtedly the harsh conditions of the party life during the war had taken its toll and precipitated such an outcome, and in the process of acting out their long-repressed frustrations, the factions also sealed the fate of their party.

Some Reflections on the
Various Interpretations of the Kuomintang

The discussion of the vicissitudes of the KMT through the trying war years may provide us with some insight into a number of theoretical issues that have interested scholars for many years. At least four approaches are popular in the literature on the KMT. While it is impossible for us to critique these approaches in detail here, it is only appropriate that we should try to highlight these approaches and compare our findings with them.

The KMT as an Elitist Party

There is a generally accepted assumption that the study of the top leaders of the Nationalist party will yield much insight into the nature of the Nationalist regime. Of all scholarly attempts, none has surpassed in scope and depth the pioneer work by North and Pool originally published in 1952, and its findings are still basically accepted by students of Chinese politics.[104]

As is well known, the North-Pool study identified the Central Executive Committee as the locus of party power and its members as constituting the members of the KMT elite. While the data presently available can allow us to add little to the excellent sociological profile of the KMT's CEC presented in this work, we have to be cautious about what implications we can legitimately draw from a study of such a nature. Basically two problems are involved. The first: To what extent is it accurate to view CEC members as the elite of the KMT? The second: Does a study of a narrow segment of the KMT elite provide us with an accurate appreciation of the power structure of the Chinese under Nationalist rule? To put it differently, was the KMT power structure coterminous with Nationalist China's power structure, or were they sufficiently different to warrant separate investigations? Both are conceptual issues of no small consequence.

The question with respect to whether the CEC constituted the KMT elite evolves around the concept of "elite" as well as the choice of locating that elite in the KMT organizational framework.

Conceptually speaking, individuals identified as members of a power elite must not only occupy (or have occupied) nominally high offices in the established order, they must also have influence over important decisions.[105] A more stringent test of an elite would require it to meet the following criteria: (1) Its members must be clearly identifiable; (2) It must engage in making important decisions; and (3) These decisions must prevail over the wishes of the rank and file in most instances.[106] These observations are relevant to the KMT study.

From a formalistic, structural point of view, there are sound reasons to regard the CEC as the KMT elite. According to the party constitution, the supreme organ of the party was the National Congress. But when the Congress was not in session, the CEC was empowered to deliberate and decide on major policies in its name, and to exercise exclusive control over the central administrative machinery of the party. During the period of political tutelage (1931–48), the CEC enjoyed the additional authority of electing and appointing the president of the republic, state councillors, and presidents and vice-presidents of the five *yüan* of the national government.[107]

These stipulations give the impression that the CEC enjoyed a great deal of power within the party. While this was formalistically correct, the operational reality was quite different. For in fact, the CEC's role had undergone tremendous changes over the years, and any disregard of these changes could produce serious conceptual and methodological difficulties. For one thing, the membership of the CEC grew from 24 in 1924 to 119 in 1935, and to 223 in 1945. As both the National Congress and the CEC grew in size, decision-making powers were first exercised by the standing committee of the CEC and later by the Political Council (*cheng-chih hui-i*), which by July, 1936, had become an official party body.[108] After 1939, the membership of the council was expanded to include the chairman and vice-chairman of the CEC, the president of the national government, the presidents and vice-presidents of the five *yüan* and the Military Commission, and the members of the standing committee of the CEC as ex officio members. This meant that those responsible for governmental functions were made members of a party organ designed to oversee such functions.[109] Since the mid-1930s, and particularly since the institution of the *tsung-ts'ai* system in 1938, most crucial party decisions were made either by Chiang alone, in consultation with his close advisors, or in negotiation with his political rivals. That most CEC members hardly ever tasted power, not to mention making decisions, was attested by the account presented by Lai Lien, a member of the fifth and sixth CEC and one who was widely regarded as a prominent party "leader."

> For a long time after my election to the CEC, I had no concrete job. Other than attending the Monday morning sermons at the Central Party Headquarters and a few other inconsequential meetings, I had no way of getting involved in the government's domestic or foreign policies. My only source of the important political development was the daily reading of newspapers. Although some CEC members were highly influential, many others were as jobless as I was. . . . I soon realized that if a person did not cultivate special liaisons, all gates to politics would be closed to him. He would be standing at the fringe of the political arena, not knowing what was going on, and unable even to find a suitable employment.[110]

This was hardly a self-portrait of a member of an elite, but was obviously a true account of a predicament shared by many others in the CEC.

Furthermore, the selection of CEC membership contained many irregularities, as the history of the 1930s demonstrated. For example, during 1931–32, both the Nanking government and Kwangtung held their own Fourth National Congress. When the Wang Ching-wei faction realized that it had nothing to gain from either, it held its own Congress. Eventually, all three factions compromised and agreed on a ratio of representation within the amalgamated CEC.[111] Party elder statesmen and splinter groups like the Western Hill faction customarily were assigned a quota of membership in the CEC to placate them, but were given no access to the decision-making machinery. On the other hand, military groups often had their civilian subordinates appointed as members. This then raises the question of the reliability of a sociological profile of CEC members who were only the surrogates, and not the true holders of power. A significant degree of distortion inevitably results from such factors.

But the most important factor in CEC membership selection was the question of who controlled the party's Organization Department and who had access to Chiang. After being made *tsung-ts'ai* in 1938, it became a frequent practice for Chiang to handpick many members and to veto others. Yet as Chinese politics became dichotomized into two separate layers (national politics and local politics), the local potentates were powerless to manipulate the composition of the CEC because they had no access to central organizational machinery, and consequently, their representation in this national body was almost nil. But on the other hand, they did not have to be bothered with the CEC either because they ran their own semi-independent local kingdoms.

Thus, at any time, the national groups out of favor with Chiang and most local groups having no access to, or interest in, national party affairs would not be represented in the CEC. But this does not mean that they were without power—military, political, and economic—in their respective regions. Even before the war, the narrow territorial base of the KMT already cast doubt on the utility of equating the KMT elite with Nationalist China's power elite. At the end of their study, North and Pool concluded,

> The picture which emerges from this statistical analysis of the leadership of the two leading Chinese parties of the past quarter century has been summarized earlier in one word, "polarization." The Kuomintang, however, permitted itself to come increasingly under the control of backward-looking elements oriented toward securing personal economic advantage in *business activities*. Those factions and individuals with other orientations were gradually squeezed out. At the same time the

Communist party managed to transform itself from an intellectually oriented organization into a rural mass-oriented one. . . . In view of this polarization in the composition and orientation of the two major parties in China, and in view of the disorganization of Chinese society, it is not surprising that the struggle between parties eventually became civil war, nor is it surprising that the Communists won. [Emphasis added][112]

This suggestion of the transformation of the KMT is at variance with the documentation presented in the preceding pages on the dynamics of factional growth. (The issue of whether the business influence within the party grew or declined will be discussed presently.) The dichotomy presented by North and Pool is debatable for two reasons. First, they misinterpreted the developmental trend within the KMT because they erroneously treated the CEC as if it really had decision-making powers. In fact, it was little more than a rubber stamp. Second, by incorporating all six National Congresses, their study purports to be a comprehensive study of the KMT elite during the entire 1924-49 era. Yet ten crucial years elapsed between the Fifth Congress of 1935 and the Sixth Congress of 1945, and it was during this ten years that the KMT itself underwent the most profound transformation in terms of its human composition, territorial control, organizational strength, internal distribution of power, and general political orientation. The party was simply not the same before 1937 and after. As such changes were not recorded or reflected in the CEC membership of the Fifth and Sixth Congresses, a great deal of the most crucial things that one would like to learn about the party were glossed over. Thus it was within the peculiar wartime context that it becomes relevant to ask the question: How much power was the KMT exercising upon the country? If, as was argued before, the party could neither penetrate nor lead the local party organs, then the CEC was a hollow organ and did not constitute an elite within the KMT. In fact, the KMT itself was not much of an elite in Nationalist China either.

The KMT as a Probusiness Party

Closely related to the study of party leadership is the somewhat less well-documented but probably more often offered thesis that the KMT was a party serving the interests of monied classes of the eastern seaboard. There are several parts to this argument. From the viewpoint of social background, some point to the long-standing connections between Chiang, H. H. K'ung, and T. V. Soong, and stock market or banking interests in

Shanghai. Others argue that the KMT's alliance with the business world was consummated in 1927 when Chiang was looking for allies after his break with the Soviet advisors, and the Shanghai businessmen were looking for a moderating force to check the threat posed by the CCP-controlled trade and labor unions. In subsequent years, the need to finance the civil wars further wedded the political and military power of the party to the commercial power of the Shanghai-based capitalists.[113]

Even though most advocates of this thesis seldom bother to back their assertions with hard data, there is some circumstantial evidence to suggest that the relationship between the KMT and the business world might have gone beyond a mere collusion of interests to a point where business actually made decisions on behalf of the party. Thus, for example, one could identify a group of Kiangsu and Chekiang leaders who served as responsible officers in a number of banks and/or industrial enterprises.[114] By 1937, this same group had produced four ministers and three vice-ministers for the Nanking government, eleven members of the National Economic Commission (*ch'üan-kuo ching-chi wei-yüan-hui*), seventeen members of the Ministry of Finance's Financial Affairs Consultative Commission, and five commissioners of financial affairs in the provinces.[115]

However, in spite of such facts, the thesis of the KMT's probusiness orientation, even insofar as the Nanking era was concerned, must be questioned for several reasons.

First, while the business world undoubtedly made significant financial contributions to many KMT projects (including military campaigns), it is worth remembering that business had never been able to stand entirely above political involvement from the early days of the Republic. The emergence of the capitalists in modern form was as much tied to politics as to economics long before the establishment of the Nationalist regime. The Peking government of the 1910s and 1920s had no hesitation in turning to the domestic capital market to bail itself out of financial straits through floating bonds, borrowing loans, or even imposing assessment from the select number of modern-styled banks or other industrial enterprises which sprang up in the major cities. On the other hand, these banks and enterprises also regarded the bonds and loans from the government as an investment from which they could make huge profits. Consequently, they also tried to cultivate good working relations with political factions within the Peking government. During the 1916–28 period, Peking politics had already become inextricably woven with the presidents or directors of some of China's leading banks and industrial enterprises.[116]

This historical backdrop suggests that there was nothing novel about the KMT's trying to involve the capitalists and financiers in the political arena. Both the survival instinct and good business sense of the capitalists would persuade them to collaborate with whichever government happened to be in power. What was new was that the site of political and military power had shifted from north China to the lower Yangtze delta after 1928, where the capitalists' interests were now given greater roles to play than was previously the case.

Second, the thesis is encumbered by a broader theoretical problem. Terms like "capitalists," "bourgeoisie," and "businessmen" have been used interchangeably in most works and have been given such imprecise definitions that there is a general tendency to forget that there was a variety of interests in the business world and that there existed as much potential for conflict as for convergence of interests among its different sectors. Glossed over were the profound differences between traders, bankers, and industrialists of all sizes and descriptions. Thus, for example, many advocates of the KMT-business ties made the assumption that labor-capital contradiction was of central concern to business, and that the KMT's suppression of the labor movement in 1927 was a unifying factor in the KMT-business relationship. In reality, labor-management conflict was a central issue for textile factory owners and local officials that hardly concerned the bankers because the latter had not invested enough in textile mills to be worried about it. The same divergence of interests existed in other areas of the KMT-business relationship. In taxation matters, for example, the success of one sector of business in avoiding taxes usually meant increased burden for another sector. Furthermore, bankers would buy new government bonds only if the bonds were secured on tax revenues which often meant new taxes for other business groups.[117] These examples show that many conflicts occurred between business sectors or even within the same sector and raises serious doubt about the propriety, both conceptually and methodologically, of treating Shanghai businessmen as a social group or class capable of acting for itself as a unified political force.

Third, while a high degree of interaction between the KMT and business certainly occurred as a consequence of the enormous financial resources concentrated in the Shanghai area, the real question is still whether the KMT served the interests of Shanghai business.

Recent scholarship suggests that the putative KMT-Shanghai capitalist alliance was short-lived. In his struggle against the Wuhan radicals in 1927, Chiang was already resorting to arrest, kidnapping, blackmail, and outright confiscation to extort contributions from reluctant capitalists in Shanghai. Between 1929 and 1930, Chiang maneuvered to cut down the influence of the Shanghai capitalists by reorganizing and gaining a domination over the Shanghai Chamber of Commerce.[118] These facts led Parks M. Coble, Jr., to argue,

> Generalizations on the class basis of the Kuomintang which suggest that it was allied with the urban capitalist class must be regarded as false. Such a generalization implies that Nanking represented the interests of the capitalists and that the latter gained substantial benefits from their ties to the government. This was not the case. As the Third Party Congress made clear, the dominant leadership of the Kuomintang was anti-capitalist in its policies.[119]

Substantively, the thesis of KMT-capitalist alliance also failed to explain convincingly what interests of these capitalists would be served by their giving support to the numerous and costly civil wars the KMT fought against foes in the north, west, and south China, which were quite remote from the capitalists' concerns. Presumably from the point of view of ideology and self-interests, the only foes the Shanghai group would be interested in exterminating would be the Communists in their vicinity. Yet Chiang obviously expended more energy on his non-Communist enemies between 1928 and 1932 than on the Communists, thereby causing three successive failures to his anti-Communist campaigns. Li Tsung-jen informed us that the Shanghai capitalists were in fact even reluctant to help the KMT fight the Communists. According to Li, Chiang summoned about two dozen leading Shanghai financiers and industrialists in 1928 to raise a huge loan to fight the CCP. When the Shanghai leaders resisted, Chiang informed them that they would not be allowed to go home unless the funds were raised. Subsequently, the funds were raised but no troops were dispatched to Kiangsi to fight the Communists.[120]

We must realize that while the KMT did not allow business to dictate policies, business was by no means subservient to the KMT either, whenever its sectoral interests were jeopardized. Partly, this was possible because the KMT was preoccupied with its own security in the face of constant challenges from domestic and foreign foes and only wanted to extract as much money from the business as possible, but otherwise tolerated the socioeconomic and political status quo. The KMT simply was too busy and had too little energy to deal with the business world on a sustained basis. Equally important was the fact that business not only could pool its own resources to resist or sabotage KMT policies, but sometimes would ally with foreign governments and companies to force the KMT to back down. Consequently, the KMT-business relationship was marked by intermittent conflicts or cooperation over relatively few issues. By and large, many sectors of Shanghai business were able to preserve substantial independence vis-à-vis the KMT.[121] In this sense, it may be more appropriate to view the relationship not as one side dictating policy to the other, but as an intense bargaining process in which either side might win or lose depending on their relative strengths regarding a particular issue at a particular time.

Finally, we must remember that even inside the KMT, those identified as the ringleaders of the capitalists' faction (K'ung and Soong) were in a minority in its factional lineup and their power was never territorial, and even within the national government their power was restricted to the ministries of Finance and Foreign Affairs. Their relations with the C.C. were tense from the very beginning and their relationship with the Whampoa group was nearly nonexistent. Not surprisingly, therefore, key sectors of Shanghai business were totally unconsulted in Chiang's deliberation over where to fight the Japanese in 1937, and his final choice to fight in Shanghai made the industries there the biggest losers among China's civilian population. Hence, to depict the KMT leadership as beholden to the interests of the capitalists is to take too narrow a view insofar as the Nanking decade was concerned.

The really crucial point of our present study of the party is that, whatever the relationship between the KMT and the capitalists might have been before the war, it was decidedly not the same after the war broke out. The immediate result was of course the severance of physical contact between the two. In 1935, Shanghai had 6,123 factories registered with the Chinese government. By 1938, only 342 (or 5.6 percent) had evacuated with the government to the interior.[122] Like their depositors, most banks stayed behind. Between 1937 and 1941, the Shanghai capitalists continued to maintain surreptitious liaison with the KMT by taking refuge behind the city's international settlements, although what they did were mostly symbolic patriotic gestures which had no impact on government finances. After 1941, the Japanese seizure of the international settlements, coupled with more stringent economic control policies, stopped the physical flow of capital completely. In the meantime, the Wang Ching-wei regime also had offered the Shanghai capitalists enough assurances of order and prosperity to win over a significant portion of them.

In contrast, in the interior, the KMT government's inability to lick inflation and its appeasement of the traditional forces of society (landlords, militarists, and secret society leaders) alienated the industrialists and merchants more and more.[123] While the so-called K'ung-Soong group continued to manage wartime finances, its role was more akin to that of an administrator than a power broker.

The extent to which capitalist influence had waned within the party during the war was fully revealed only at the war's end. As soon as the advance parties of the KMT government reached the port cities, they immediately embarked on a confiscation spree that completely devastated the economic structure there. First, the exchange ratio between the currencies of free China and puppet regime was put at 1:200, which overnight wiped out the lifelong savings of the urban middle classes. Second, the new masters proceeded to confiscate or lay claim to commercial and industrial assets of all descriptions on grounds that they were enemy properties or their owners had collaborated with the enemies, which included practically everybody. While the ministries of Economic Affairs and Finances (organs controlled by K'ung and Soong) should have jurisdiction over the disposition of such properties, it was in fact the C.C. and the Fu-hsing-she (particularly the Bureau of Military Statistics) that played the key roles. Their goal was neither rejuvenation of the war-torn economy of the liberated areas nor the restoration of the power of the capitalists to their prewar status. They were simply interested in self-enrichment and factional aggrandizement. Here again we see the debilitating effect of the war on the party. Eight years after it left east China, the KMT had returned as much an enemy of the monied class as to the general public. No wonder that during the civil war of 1945-49 the monied class in east China refused to cooperate with the government either in its effort to curb the runaway inflation or in its new currency policy (the gold *yüan*), and even the harshest reprisals of Chiang Ching-kuo against it could not save the situation.

The KMT as a Fascist Party

The third approach tries to ascribe to the KMT certain structural or behavioral characteristics that are commonly associated with a fascist regime.[124]

There is certainly much in the theory and practice of the KMT to lend support to characterizing it as a fascist regime. First, the original conception of the *lan-i-she* was widely attributed to the pamphlet that Liu Chien-ch'ün wrote in 1931, "Some Suggestions on Restructuring Our Party," which was obviously inspired by fascist ideas.[125] Second, various statements made by Chiang and his lieutenants contained strong suggestions of the glorification of the supreme leader ("one doctrine, one leader, one nation") and demand for blind obedience and loyalty to this leader.[126] Third, some structural features within the KMT had their fascist counterparts. The development of the two secret police services can be conveniently likened to the SS and the Gestapo. The creation of the Youth Corps has been compared with the fascist idea of training youth to develop a superior corps of men and women to take over the government. Furthermore, Chiang's own work, *China's Destiny,* provided references to ultranationalistic appeals that under wartime atmosphere could easily be interpreted as reflecting his grandiose visions of resurrecting past Chinese glories and reaffirming Chinese ethnocentrism over her neighbors, which might lead logically to a Chinese variation of a putschist policy in Asia.[127]

The thesis that the KMT was a fascist party was given strong emphasis by Professor Eastman in his book, *The Abortive Revolution.* He identified a group of Chinese officers and party workers as embracing the fascist ideology under the influence of German military advisors in China. Soon Chiang Kai-shek himself became "an enthusiastic admirer of fascism." Furthermore, by the mid-1930s, the " 'fascistization' of the Blue Shirts was an accomplished fact," and Chiang and his cohorts were possibly involved in a plot to abandon Sun's Three People's Principles in favor of fascism.[128]

However, there are other factors that might mitigate the uncritical acceptance of the full implications of such a categorization. First, people like Liu Chien-ch'ün seemed to have a simplistic understanding of fascism and accepted it not so much as a new political gospel as the latest and most effective protest against Western domination. It is relevant to note that at the time when the fascist movement produced voluminous discussion in the West, both favorable and hostile, there was relatively little discussion or translation of such literature in the Chinese press. One gets the strong impression that what attracted the KMT leaders to this foreign doctrine was the supposed iron discipline and efficiency that such a regime produced, both characteristics that the Chinese leaders found lacking in their own country.[129] Liu's appreciation of fascism was at best superficial, since he had neither been to Europe to witness fascism at work nor did he read European languages. Among the people handpicked by Chiang to create the Action Society, only Kwei Yung-ch'ing had ever studied in Germany as a naval cadet. Most others, including Teng Wen-i and Ho Chung-han, the leading ideologues, had been to Japan or the Soviet Union.[130] Their views might have been just as strongly influenced by prewar Japanese militarism and authoritarianism or Soviet totalitarianism. Not surprisingly, therefore, these people in later years accomplished little in the way of presenting a comprehensive blueprint or programs for the complete transformation of Chinese society, economy, or politics. Their strongest interest was to devise an efficient way to tighten discipline within the party through unquestioned loyalty to the leader so that domestic and international opposition could be removed from the path of revolution. These facts put the KMT's fascist credentials under a cloud. Were the KMT leaders influenced more by Germany and Italy, or did they borrow an adulterated fascist model secondhand from Japan?[131] To what extent were the Chinese equating fascism with Soviet totalitarianism or Japanese militarism? Further research would help clarify this issue.

On the other hand, from the mid-nineteenth century on, the search for wealth and power was the burning desire of all Chinese leaders. The question was, how? Sun Yat-sen was the one who stressed that China's weakness stemmed basically from the lack of discipline and unity of will among her people ("a sheet of sand") and advocated the need to impose a high degree of regimentation. Sun wanted to mold a new nationalist man, to awaken the spirit of collective identity, to revive China's pride in its traditional culture (*ku-yu wen-hua*), and also to create a virtuous and efficient government to supervise state-sponsored and state-directed programs of economic development under single-party auspices.

To achieve these objectives, Sun asserted that students, soldiers, and civil servants should be subject to a special code of conduct, and should not have political freedom; instead, they should give unswerving loyalty to the party. Thus, some two decades before the rise of modern fascism, it was in fact Sun who insisted that his revolutionary followers pledge their loyalty to him personally. With the involvement of Soviet advisors in the party's reorganization in 1923–24, the principle of democratic centralism was also confirmed within the party. Chiang was merely following Sun's footsteps in asserting absolute powers of *tsung-ts'ai* during the war. Hence, the intellectual genesis of the KMT's authoritarianism had relatively little to do with fascism.[132]

In practice, however, the "führer principle" was also more apparent than real in Nationalist China, despite the tireless efforts of Chiang and his lieutenants to build him up as the national hero and savior. The discussion in the preceding part of this chapter suggests that Chiang was far from exercising dictatorial powers either in the party or in the government. In the party, the rampant development of factional struggle was simply beyond Chiang's power to arrest; the best he could do was to play one against another to keep himself on top of the situation. In the government, his powers were severely circumscribed by the resistance of other powerful groups that had long been entrenched in various regions. Unlike Hitler, who used his iron-tight control over the bureaucracy to monopolize the youth organizations, the trade unions, the church, and every other aspect of the people's economic and social life, and used the Gestapo to deal with occasional political dissidents, Chiang's regime during the war was reduced to almost total reliance on his secret service, because he could exert little organizational control over the society and the government.

In the final analysis, Chiang's propensity to allow his secret service to employ ruthless tactics to suppress his opponents and to make himself deeply resented by the people was not so much a sign of a megalomaniac with an insatiable appetite for power,[133] but was in itself testimony to his exasperation and frustration over the constraining political environment. Lacking the support of regional powerholders and unable to mobilize lower-level cadres, the only way the KMT knew to provide some semblance of governing was through the irregular system of the secret service. If this formulation is accurate, then some of the neofascist tactics that the KMT employed really concealed a regime of impotence.

The KMT as a Mass-Movement Regime

By the same token, the characterization of the decline and fall of the KMT as a case of the extinction of a revolutionary movement also needs some rethinking. Even in his study of the prewar KMT, Professor Tien had already concluded that all the pro-Chiang factions were basically conservative in terms of their membership, ideological outlook, and political goals, that their domination led the party to shift from a revolutionary party to one committed to the status quo.[134] This view was echoed by Professor Eastman in his more recent work, *The Abortive Revolution*.[135] But the theory itself was best developed by Professor Tucker in his discussion of "the revolutionary mass-movement regime under single-party auspices."[136]

There is little doubt that the KMT regime was born in a revolutionary struggle aimed at establishing the dominance of a single party. There is a greater problem regarding whether it could be viewed as the mass-movement regime, which in turn raises the question of the causes and the process of its becoming extinct. According to Tucker, "In the typical case, the mass movement is organized during the revolutionary struggle for power and as a means of waging this struggle. Once the regime is in being, the mass movement is enlarged and given new tasks of various kinds in the continuing revolution of national renewal."[137] Furthermore, the mass movement is closely guided by a party, with its cellular structure or "cells" penetrating the old society.[138]

The history of the KMT tells us that its brief flirtation with mass movements occurred during its first united front with the Communists and that these movements fell largely under Communist control. After 1927, the KMT foreswore mass movements as a general rule, although in certain bandit-suppression areas limited attempts at propagandizing and organizing the masses were continued. Consequently, the KMT was never a mass-based party before the war, with a total membership of slightly more than half a million people.

What really matters is that once the war started, even this ambivalent attitude toward mass movements was met by strong local traditional resistance. Our data show that the KMT was totally ineffective in extending the organizational weapon, the cell, into the old society in the interior provinces. Nor was it able to establish new footholds in the functional and professional areas. Not only were there few people who ever were drawn into public life due to the party's work, but even those who nominally joined and worked for the party on the basic levels were themselves drawn into such tracks for nonparty reasons, i.e., merely to wear the party badge to cling to their old jobs. The effect of the conduct of such people, if anything, was to discredit the party in the public mind. This fact casts further doubt on the validity of viewing the KMT as a bona fide fascist party. As a totalitarian party, a fascist party is supposed to possess the ability to demolish the traditional psychological defenses of the people (particularly secondary associational ties), to atomize them, and thereby expose them to the direct manipulative influence of the state and its auxiliary organs.[139] Yet in China, the KMT was actually further insulated and removed from the people during the war than ever before.

This understanding is also related to the second issue raised in Tucker's theory, that of extinction of the movement-regime. Again, according to Tucker, in the case of a "nationalist movement-regime," there are usually two revolutionary goals involved. First, the creation of a sovereign nation-state, and second, the modernization of the state. Or, to put it differently, there are two stages of a revolution. First, the stage of political revolution, and second, the stage of social revolution. It often happens that purely nationalist revolutionary movement-regimes spend their force after the completion of the first goal and never embark on the second revolution, thus becoming extinct. In Tucker's analysis, the Kuomintang was specifically used to illustrate how a movement-regime became extinct.[140]

Again, the issue here is how to interpret the stages of the KMT revolution and how to identify the sociopolitical forces that shaped the development of the party. The weight of the present study suggests that, in fact, the KMT never achieved the goal of creating an integrated nation-state. The KMT during the Nanking era seemed to be divided on how much energy to allocate to accomplishing political-military unification as compared with economic construction. It ended up giving clear preference to achieving political unification through military means, and never developed a mobilization model that could have generated momentum for sweeping socioeconomic reforms on a self-sustaining basis. Since the KMT was always confined to the superstructure of the state and never struck roots in the subsoil of the Chinese polity, it was not the process of deradicalization that caused the party to become extinct. If anything, the KMT became extinct during the war because the party machine molded in the Nanking decade was so defective that it simply could not cope with the stresses of the war.

Conclusion

Having critiqued the various interpretations of the KMT, it is incumbent upon the author to integrate the major findings documented in the present study into a coherent statement. Two related issues will be addressed here as a way of concluding this research. They are, first, what kind of regime existed in Nationalist China? Second, how should the history of the Nationalist regime be interpreted?

The Nature of the Regime in Nationalist China

The basic assumption underlying this study is that the Nationalist regime was a highly militarized organization. Although this regime had its formal party apparatus and bureaucratic structure, it was basically a coalition of military principals juxtaposed along the central-regional axis. Even in the 1930s, it was military power calculations that determined the regime's political programs and strategies, out of which a peculiar model of compromise politics emerged.[141]

After the outbreak of the war, and particularly 1940, the decentralized system of defense pushed the regional military even further to the political forefront as many commanders became direct managers of local politics and economy. Therefore, if there ever were a ruling elite in wartime China, it was not the Central Executive Committee of the KMT, nor the Council of Ministers of the central government, but the powerful generals who actually controlled armies, territories, population, markets, productive capabilities, as well as formal governmental organs on many different levels.

The most comprehensive and authoritative primary source that I have been able to find on Chinese generals during the war is the 1944 edition of *Records on General Officers* compiled by the Chinese government.[142] This voluminous document contains the current positions, past careers, origins of birth, ages, and educational backgrounds of 4,188 officers above the rank of major general on active duty in the army. On the basis of this document, we are able to draw a crude profile of this group of political actors (table 11).

Since educational affiliation was the most reliable test of political loyalty under the Nationalist regime, the data show that the Whampoa group was in a clear minority among the top military power holders. Not only were the provincial and local military schools the bastions of regional

TABLE 11
Educational Profile of Chinese Generals, 1944

	Total		Full Generals		Lt. Generals		Major Generals	
Whampoa academy	1,177	28%	9[a]	11%	153	16%	1,024	32%
Paoting academy	1,015	24	28	35	371	40	616	19
Foreign academy[b]	427	10	17	21	117	12	293	9
Local academy and from ranks	1,569	38	26	33	303	32	1,222	40
Total	4,188	100%	80	100%	944	100%	3,164	100%

Source: Kuo-fang-pu, *Lu-chün chün-kuan-tso tzu-chi-pu, 1944* (Chungking, 1944), vol. 1, *chiang-chün chien.*
a. Including those whose careers were closely associated with Whampoa, e.g., Chiang Kai-shek.
b. Including all foreign military academies and civilian schools. Those few (9) who had attended either Whampoa or Paoting before receiving foreign education were discounted.

power, but the composition of the Paoting and foreign schools, as well as the assignments of their graduates, was such that during their existence they were actually the training grounds for regional armies rather than the central armies. Therefore, the composition of the entire corps of general officers was marked by a preponderance of those whose primary political and professional orientations were regional, over those who were unquestionably loyal to the central government by a margin of three to one.

It is apparent, however, that not every general had equal power. Given the size of the country's land and army, and the complexities of its government and society, it is natural that some were more powerful than others, despite ranks and official titles. I believe that two categories of generals were primarily responsible for shaping the power structure in China.

The first category includes combat unit commanders. Except for brief periods of time, the division (*shih*) was the basic strategic unit because it had the capability to operate independently. Organizationally, three divisions made up an army (*chün*), and several armies (usually two to five) constituted a group-army (*chi-t' uan chün*). Strictly speaking, all the military units should have been exclusively concerned with fighting. In practice, however, the commanders all acquired intense interests in local administration if only to insure the survival of their units. The supply of conscripts, grain, housing, fuel, bearers, and emergency funds were all issues that prompted most commanders to interfere with the normal process of local government. The more enterprising ones, of course, would go further into such areas as protecting business, gambling, profiteering through the black market or smuggling, and promoting one local faction against another.

Above the military units were the commanders of the war zones. Although their primary responsibility was to direct troops, these war zone commanders were concurrently the ranking party functionaries as well as the superior of the provincial governors in their zones. Consequently, war zone commanders enjoyed broad legal powers over the appointment and dismissal, promotion and demotion of personnel in all branches of the party and government. They also had great latitude in setting up or dismantling administrative agencies, and they had the authority to promulgate regulations valid exclusively in their own zones. Together, these commanders were the men who controlled the guns.

The second category includes the so-called administrative generals. By definition of law, these generals were entrusted with specified functions within the civilian government that were of a military nature. Specifically, the following types of agencies were involved:

1. Conscription-district administration (*chün-kuan-ch'ü*);
2. Provincial Enlistment and Recruitment Bureau (*chao-mu-chü*);
3. Military training departments;
4. Provincial Garrison Command (*ching-pei tsung-pu*), Provincial Security Command (*pao-an ssu-ling-pu*), and District Garrison Command (*shou-pei-ch'ü*).

Generals who fit these criteria are taken out of the total list and studied as a group. The data are presented in table 12. On the basis of this table, we can extrapolate some preliminary observations.

First, insofar as educational background was concerned, Whampoa graduates were in a clear minority in all cases. Among both combat and administrative generals, they constituted 36 percent. While there was no clear pattern of the concentration of Whampoa graduates among the different levels of administrative generals, there was a decreasing number of Whampoa graduates among the combat generals as one moves up the military hierarchy. The situation for Paoting graduates was the reverse; they were most numerous among the top level and decreased in the lower level of combat generals, for the obvious reason that the school had ceased

TABLE 12
Profile of China's Most Powerful Generals, 1944

	Rank				
Education	CO, Deputies, War Zone	CO, Deputies, Group Army	CO, Army	CO, Division	Administrative COs
Whampoa	1	31	40	132	99
Paoting	18	36			76
			37	48	
Foreign	4	5			15
Provincial school or					
ranks	13	23	34	101	85
Total	36	95	111	314	275
				(33 unknown)	
Average age	52	47.4	46.6	41.6	45

Source: Kuo-fang-pu, *Lu-chün chun-kuan-tso tzu-chi-pu, 1944,* (Chungking, 1944), vol. 1, *chiang-chün chien.*

to exist a long time ago. Among the administrative generals who were usually lower-grade generals, Paoting graduates constituted only 28 percent. Generals who had studied in a foreign country constituted a very small segment in all cases, but generals who had graduated only from provincial military schools or had risen from the ranks constituted nearly one-third in all cases. Combined, they confirmed our earlier conclusion that about two-thirds of China's most powerful generals had strong regional attachments and poor professional training.

Second, if we look at the issue of political loyalty at the very top, the picture is rather disconcerting from the government's point of view. Among a total of thirty-six commanders or deputy commanders of war zones, fourteen (39 percent) had rebelled against Nanking before 1937. Eleven (30.5 percent) were considered absolutely loyal to the government, but the loyalty of eleven others remained ambiguous. Furthermore, the geographical distribution of these commanders and deputy commanders was such that only five of the fourteen war zones and their equivalents were in the hands of the KMT's loyalists.

Third, if we look at the actual control of combat troops, we find that although Whampoa graduates nominally commanded 132, 42 percent, of China's 314 divisions, their actual power was considerably less. Our understanding of military politics during the war suggests that when the central government firmly controlled a division, it would fill all its top positions with loyal persons. In other words, the hallmark of a loyal division was that its commander, deputy commander, and/or political commissar were all Whampoa graduates. When we apply this test to the divisions, we find that only 74 (23.5 percent) division fit this description. These divisions can be regarded as the core of the Whampoa strength. On the other hand, we also find that there were 66 divisions that had no Whampoa graduates in any of the top positions. These divisions can be regarded as the core of the regional strength.

The remaining 174 divisions, then, became the target of a tug of war between the central government and regional forces. Since only graduates from the early Whampoa classes had gained enough seniority to qualify for top positions, and since such persons were few and well known to the central government, we may assume that whenever the government record failed to list the occupants of these positions for any division, such occupants were not Whampoa graduates. If this hypothesis is sound, then the best possible interpretation of the data in the KMT's favor would identify 58 of the 174 divisions as under partial KMT control, but would identify the remaining 116 divisions as primarily regional divisions in which the KMT made varying degrees of infiltration short of control. When compared with 1937, it is clear that the central government had scored some success by 1944 in either creating new divisions under Whampoa commands or infiltrating existing regional divisions with Whampoa graduates. But the central government remained a minority in the Chinese army. Beyond these figures, there might have been a more serious but hidden problem; the prewar KMT crack units were recruited from the lower Yangtze provinces. But these units had been destroyed. In the eight years of war, even units under the nominal control of Whampoa graduates had to be recruited from the interior provinces. Given the popular antipathy of the people in the interior against easterners and the conventional command styles of the Whampoa graduates, could they really win the loyalty of the soldiers? The probability would be low indeed.

Finally, although the record does not give information on family backgrounds, their average age indicates that most of them began their military careers in the 1910s and 1920s. Together with the information about their professional training, they allow us to make certain tentative deductions from what we know about that historic period. It seems safe to assume that, except for those who attended the very few good modern military schools (including Whampoa and the Japanese schools), the military men as a group were not likely to have come from the prosperous rural or urban classes. In the early twentieth century, and particularly during the Peiyang period when the misconduct of numerous warlords caused widespread popular disgust and contempt, very few gentry or merchant families would have sent their sons to a military career as their first choice. Besides, by this time, many from the traditional gentry had already become urbanized and had developed extensive political and economic interests in the urban areas.[143] Our understanding about the early Peiyang period informs us that only families too poor to afford a western-style education would send their sons to military schools or directly to the barracks, and that the majority of Chinese military schools offered a poor education.[144]

Therefore, the old-style military men who joined the armies under the Peiyang years were neither steeped in Confucian ethics nor in western ideologies or technical training. Their political vision was archaic and their political style ranged from conservative to outright reactionary. But as they moved up the ladder of military success, they became the new governors of their localities. They also bought land and engaged in commerce; but they almost never ventured into banking, industries, academic pursuits, or foreign commerce. Yet it would be erroneous to regard them as nothing more than the defenders of the landowning or business interests, as the history of the 1920s and 1930s abounds with instances of oppression and exactions of the landlords and businessmen by warlords. The militarists depended on military power, and they defended the status quo only because they or their relatives and friends were the direct beneficiaries of such a system. They were the creators of a special kind of political system in which power was predicated on the possession of guns, but landowning and commercial pursuits were but the mere trappings of their power. Anybody who stood in their way of obtaining and preserving such power would be their enemy.

To sum up, then, the bulk of the country's elites consisted of militarists more oriented to parochial than to nationalistic interests. Many had local power structures to defend, but few had any concern for national or international issues. Their intellectual training and material interests fueled their anti-integrationist sentiments. It was an elite with diverse loyalties and no unifying purpose. The KMT regime was built on a marriage of political expediency among the newly emerged military wing of Chiang Kai-shek's party from east China, the remnants of the defunct Peiyang order in north China, and the military tyrants and local bad gentry and bullies of the interior provinces.

An Alternative Interpretation of Nationalist China

At the very outset of this study, the history of the first ten years of the KMT regime was reviewed to suggest the thesis that the KMT sacrificed its ideological commitment and organizational integrity in order to achieve an easy military victory, and that the strategy of the Northern Expedition was a major mistake. Between 1927 and 1937, the KMT made little progress in achieving military integration, but its persistent fixation with the efficacy of military power distracted the party leaders from any serious attempt to develop tactics to wage revolutionary struggles against its opponents in the realms of ideology and organization. Instead, the party became an appendage to the army, acquired the habit of functioning in a highly bureaucratic manner, only after the army had demolished all opposition. The party leaders adopted an etatist orientation by concentrating on the development of the superstructure of a modern state in the urban areas in the lower Yangtze valley. Consequently, the party itself never acquired the necessary skills for combating entrenched local and regional power structures through political mobilization and socioeconomic reforms.

Such a party was woefully unprepared to assume the myriad of new responsibilities thrust upon it by the Sino-Japanese War. Given the enormous human and physical resources the resistance movement would require, the KMT should have adopted a policy of total mobilization. Ironically, it was the KMT's nemesis, Mao Tse-tung, who first recognized the need for such a policy. In August, 1937, Mao offered a ten-point action program, which included mobilization of the military strength of the people of the whole country, reform of the government apparatus, adoption of wartime financial and economic policies, and improvement of the people's livelihood. He concluded with a prophetic warning, "It is imperative to discard the policy of resistance by the Government alone and to enforce the policy of total resistance by the whole nation."[145]

Then in his famous article, "On Protracted War," of May, 1938, Mao again considered political mobilization and argued,

> What does political mobilization mean? First, it means telling the army and the people about the political aim of the war. It is necessary for every soldier and civilian to see why the war must be fought and how it concerns him. . . . Secondly, it is not enough merely to explain the aim to them; the steps and policies for its attainment must also be given, that is, there must be a political program. . . . Without a clear-cut, concrete political program it is impossible to mobilize all the armed forces and the whole people to carry the war against Japan through to the end. Thirdly, how should we mobilize them? By word of mouth, by leaflets and films, through schools, through the mass organizations and through our cadres. What has been done so far in the Kuomintang areas is only a drop in the ocean, and moreover it has been done in a manner ill-suited to the people's tastes and in a spirit uncongenial to them; this must be drastically changed. Fourthly, to mobilize once is not enough; political mobilization for the War of Resistance must be continuous. Our job is not to recite our political program to the people, for nobody will listen to such recitations; we must link the political mobilization for the war with developments in the war and with the life of the soldiers and people, and make it a continuous movement. This is a matter of immense importance on which our victory in the war primarily depends.[146]

Hindsight suggests that Mao's position was eminently sensible and his criticism of the KMT equally well-taken. But why did the KMT fail to carry out a policy of mass mobilization? The present work shows that up to 1939–40, Chiang and other Nationalist leaders believed that it was not necessary to mobilize the masses. They believed the war could be concluded by strictly military means. Their conviction in the primacy of military power in turn prompted them to shun the strenuous efforts that national programs of mass mobilization would have required. The fundamental cause of the problem was Chiang's conceptualization of the issue. In September, 1935, Chiang had delivered a major speech on the theme of national, general mobilization to a gathering of high-ranking generals and officials at the Omei Training Corps and concluded with these words:

> The most important pre-condition of general mobilization is "organization."... The purpose of organization is to impose control.... The methods of control are similar to those adopted in military organization. When we say "control," we mean the militarization of the whole country.... No organization in a modern society is more rationally managed than the army. The army is organized according to the most rational principles, and everything is placed under the tight organization and strict discipline. Thus, once an order is given, an army of thousands, or even millions, could be mobilized within hours. What we require now is that the whole population of our nation can be as swiftly mobilized as the army. If we possess such a strict, huge, and healthy organization, then we will have achieved complete militarization, and will be able to institute a national general mobilization.[147]

Equally revealing is Chiang's perception of control as exercised in a strictly hierarchical context. Since the whole nation should operate like an army, therefore, mobilization should involve a situation wherein the commanders gave orders and the men obeyed them. Finally, Chiang specified four mobilization goals to be pursued—a militaristic education (*chün-kuo-min ti chiao-yü*), a militaristic economy (*chün-kuo-min ti ching-chi*), a militaristic society (*chün-kuo-min ti she-hui*), and militaristic politics (*chün-kuo-min ti cheng-chih*).[148] This conceptualization left little room for any constructive roles to be played by the party. No wonder, then, that as the politics of the 1930s became more militarized, the party also became highly fossilized. The enormous losses the party suffered during the early stages of the war and its separation from its prewar power base in east China were further blows. Once the party was pushed into the interior provinces and deprived of a superior military power to back it up, it was soon swamped by local opportunists who had been absorbed indiscriminately and en masse into the party.

The truth is that, during the war, party work was nonexistent on the mass level, and the party organs, wherever existing, were controlled and exploited by local leaders to advance their own vested interests. In an attempt to maintain the facade of a united front in national resistance, the KMT gave up any attempt to wage revolutionary struggles and chose to defer to the local power holders to do whatever they wish. The national party became an empty shell and its leaders were reduced to soldierless generals. Consequently, factional intrigues thrived during this period as everyone jockeyed for position in preparation for the expected big rush back to the coastal provinces. Instead of being a purifying and energizing agent in the muddy waters of wartime politics, the party leaders themselves became passive, unimaginative, petty, corrupt, and indulged in constant bickering and back-stabbing. Thus the KMT suffered an almost total loss of vitality during the war.

Our analysis of the nature of the KMT inevitably leads to a question of larger theoretical import: How do we account for the demise of the Nationalist regime in the revolutionary process of the 1940s?

Over the years, this inquiry has generated considerable disagreement. One school of thought has identified the Sino-Japanese War as the sole factor explaining the KMT's demise. It has been variously suggested that the KMT regime might have thrived had there been no war or had the war occurred much later. Many supporters of the KMT have speculated that, if given a few more years, Chiang might have exterminated the Communists, subdued the regionalists, and reunified the country.

The materials presented in this work strongly suggest, however, that the root causes of the KMT's failure were in existence long before the outbreak of the war, and were primarily endogenous and not exogenous. The militarization of politics, the pursuit of etatist objectives, the exceedingly narrow definition of revolution as the elimination of domestic and foreign political-military rivals had all been firmly established as features of the KMT's programs of the Nanking decade. These features in turn produced serious structural and operational deficiencies in the party-government that would have led to an uncertain future regardless of the KMT's international difficulties.

After 1937, admittedly, with China's meager resources, any government would have had trouble executing the war against Japan. But the pressures of war were particularly devastating to the KMT regime, precisely because of these endogenous features. For while the party's military power had been a major medium of the Nationalist political process of 1927–37, it was crippled shortly after fighting began. Consequently, it was no later than 1939–40 that the relationship between Chungking and other regional groups began to undergo a significant change. Not only were the militarists aware of their improved position vis-à-vis Chungking in strictly military power terms, but they also realized that the second half of the war would bring increasing intrusion of their power bases in the interior by the central government, and therefore heavier demands and interferences upon them—a prospect that was unpleasant to the regionalists and one that could get worse as the years proceeded. Hence, resistance and obstructionism by the regionalists against Chungking mounted correspondingly.

It may be argued that even during the war, regional resistance by the power holders need not have become an insurmountable obstacle. As Selden's study suggests, the Communists in north China also had to face suspicious local residents, strange customs, different dialects, and entrenched power structures whenever they moved into a new region to set up a revolutionary base. But the Communists basically overcame these obstacles through imaginative organizational means and appealing socioeconomic programs. The KMT's fault was that it closed off its own options by pursuing only militaristic solutions.

In order to execute the war, the KMT had to gain access to the human and physical resources in the interior; but once it lost its military leverage over the regionalists, it had to depend completely on them. To the extent that the regionalists granted the Chungking government access to local resources, the latter had to use the existing power structures and local elites to carry out its policies. The central government became beholden to the local power holders and studiously avoided upsetting the local status quo.

Such an arrangement could not be expected to adequately cope with the war-related problems. In fact, as chapter 4 shows, people's confidence in the government declined precipitously as they suffered progressive disadvantages under the government's mismanagement of critical programs. For not only did the government's many policies do violence to the people's sense of justice and decency on a priori grounds, but they caused greater suffering and material losses than any previous regime had ever inflicted.

Our examination of specific government policies indicates that the marriage of convenience between Chungking and the regional power structures brought about results that generated widespread discontent among the peasants and urbanites alike. During the period of 1942–45, one can detect the KMT response to the deteriorating situation as regressing from "business as usual" to "elite intransigence," and to "siege mentality."

This discussion, however, does not warrant the inference that the KMT collapse was caused by a revolutionary groundswell in the interior provinces. Popular apathy and disillusionment were but one aspect of the crisis confronted by the Chungking government. Even as the peasants obviously suffered much deprivation during the war, this would not necessarily lend support to the thesis that the peasants in the interior played a pivotal role in the ensuing revolutionary situation, or that they responded readily to the CCP's revolutionary call. Even under the crushing burden of the 1940s, most peasants in the interior continued to demonstrate a surprising capacity to absorb hardship and pain. Accounts by A. Doak Barnett of the southwest on the eve of the Communist takeover offered strong indications that the peasants there still endured the status quo as stoically as they could, and showed few signs of being radicalized by their wartime experience. Peasant discontent definitely increased their passive resistance to the various extractive operations of the government, which in turn damaged the government's ability to survive. It might even have caused more widespread desertion of rural boys from the army.

Yet even the riots and rebellions by peasants were localized and were triggered by specific issues of personalities, and not a generalized protest against the overall system. This traditional outlook and poor organization explained why they at no time posed a mortal threat to the Chungking government. Barnett's accounts suggested that the peasants basically adhered to their traditional way of life, accepted the prevailing socio-economic-political order meekly, and showed little inclination for being agitated by anything resembling a land revolution.[149]

By the same token, it would be inaccurate to attribute a class basis to the KMT. Many have suggested that the KMT was allied to the landlords in the interior. The alleged result of this alliance was that the KMT pursued a conservative, antiliberal, and anti-CCP policy and suppressed the more liberal, progressive elements within the party. Our discussion of the preceding pages showed that the KMT never really had an alliance with the landlords, although it showed great dependence upon them. It would be more appropriate to view the KMT as a civil-military bureaucracy suspended only on the national level without a class foundation. With the people of the interior incarcerated behind the high walls of numerous semi-independent local power structures, the Chungking government had an army, a party, and a national bureaucracy, but never a mass following. By far the most devastating effect of the war upon the Chungking leaders was their utter inability to establish direct and meaningful contact with the people.

The cumulative effect of this prolonged isolation was that the KMT leaders gradually lost their raison d'être, moral strength, and either the willpower or the capacity to really govern. They became painfully aware that they belonged only to a formal structure that had become increasingly impotent to affect either the course of the war or the people outside Chungking. Under these circumstances, the decaying process set in. While a few principled officials in the government became totally frustrated and paralyzed, the ranks of the opportunists multiplied and seized every chance to indulge in corruption, embezzlement, and other forms of debauchery and decadence. The fight over the shrinking pie of resources discussed earlier in this chapter became ever more vicious and provided an unmistakable sign of the moral and spiritual bankruptcy of the Kuomintang.

In this general context, the events of 1944 were simply overwhelming. As analyzed in detail in chapter 3, the Japanese attack, Operation Ichigō, coming in the seventh year of the war, stretched Chungking's last economic and political capabilities beyond the point of exhaustion. Crops and industries were destroyed, inflation skyrocketed, huge numbers of people became refugees, and government oppression became worse than ever. Equally important was the decimation of the central government's remaining military stock (manpower and weapons) within China proper. The concurrence of both conditions not only destroyed the legitimacy of the government in the eyes of the people, but more importantly, plunged the KMT leaders into a greater depth of gloom and despair from which they never recovered.

By late 1944, the Chungking government was already in no position to threaten reprisals against its regional opponents. Although the poorly coordinated regionalists' separatist movement was temporarily stifled, the incident signaled the final collapse of Chungking's strategy of surviving through the war by eschewing social and economic reforms in exchange for the forebearance and collaboration of the regionalists. The regionalists' lackadaisical participation in the war was brought about only by their fear of the KMT's military retaliation. Once the KMT lost its capability to make that threat, the KMT-sponsored united front from above also lost its appeal to the regionalists and local power holders. The defeats of 1944 were so extensive that the Chungking government would probably have had difficulty maintaining itself in power had the war lasted a little longer. For by this time, the KMT's moral decay and spiritual defeat had become nearly complete and irreversible.

Hindsight suggests that the KMT paid an exceedingly high price for adhering to its strategy of compromise with the regional and local power structures. The pursuit of this illusory strategy caused the KMT to forfeit an opportunity to assume the role of the champion of socioeconomic justice and to deny itself the option of forging a broader united front from below with the masses. As the Sino-Japanese War drew to a close, the desertion of the regionalists, the alienation of the Democratic League and other progressive political groups, and the moral degeneration of the Kuomintang's own leadership had reached such a massive scale that the KMT's political fate was probably sealed even before the civil war erupted.

Abbreviations

Bōeichō	Bōeichō Bōei Kenkūjo Senshishitsu
CJCC	Wu Hsiang-hsiang. *Ti-erh-tz'u Chung Jih chan-cheng shih*. 2 vols. Taipei, 1973.
CKS	Chiang Kai-shek
The German Advisors Group	Kuo-fang-pu. *Te-kuo chu Hua chün-shih ku-wen-t'uan kung-tso chi-yao*. Taipei, 1969.
KJCS: (subtitle)	Kuo-fang-pu. *K'ang Jih chan-shih:* (*individual subtitle for campaign*[*s*]). 100 vols. Taipei, 1967.
KMT	Kuomintang
MKTS	Liu Shao-t'ang. *Min-kuo ta-shih jih-chih*. 2 vols. Taipei, 1973–.
Wartime Military Report	Ho Ying-ch'in. *Ho shang-chiang k'ang-chan ch'i-chien chün-shih pao-kao*. 2 vols. Taipei, 1962.

241

Notes

Introduction

1. Ch'ien Tuan-sheng, *The Government and Politics of China* (Cambridge, Mass., 1950); Harold D. Lasswell, ed., *World Revolutionary Elites* (Cambridge, Mass., 1965).
2. Tien Hung-mao, *Government and Politics in Kuomintang China, 1927–1937* (Stanford, Calif., 1972); Lloyd E. Eastman, *The Abortive Revolution: China Under Nationalist Rule, 1927–1937* (Cambridge, Mass., 1974).
3. John Israel, *Student Nationalism in China, 1927–1937* (Stanford, Calif., 1966); James C. Thompson, Jr., *While China Faced West: American Reformers in Nationalist China, 1928–1937* (Cambridge, Mass., 1969); Sih, Paul K. T., ed., *The Strenuous Decade: China's Nation-Building Efforts, 1927–1937* (New York, 1970); Arthur N. Young, *China and the Helping Hand, 1937–1945* (Cambridge, Mass., 1963); idem, *China's Nation-Building Effort, 1927–1937: The Financial and Economic Record* (Stanford, Calif., 1971).
4. David Easton, *A Systems Analysis of Political Life* (New York, 1965), pp. 267–77.

Chapter 1

1. Sun's works can be found in *Kuo-fu ch'üan-chi*, 6 vols. (Taipei, 1961).
2. "Chien-kuo ta-kang," in *Kuo-fu ch'üan-chi*, vol. 1, pp. 1–15; "Ti-fang tzu-chih k'ai-shih shih-shih fa," in *Kuo-fu ch'üan-chi*, vol. 6, pp. 160–65. For recent works that deal with various aspects of Sun's revolutionary theories, see Harold Z. Schiffrin, *Sun Yat-sen and the Origin of the Chinese Revolution* (Berkeley, Calif., 1968); C. Martin Wilbur, *Sun Yat-sen: Frustrated Patriot* (New York, 1976); and Robert E. Bedeski, "The Tutelary State and National Revolution in Kuomintang Ideology, 1928-1931," *China Quarterly*, no. 46 (April-June, 1971):309–17.
3. For a more detailed discussion, see Donald A. Jordan, *Northern Expedition: China's National Revolution of 1926–1928* (Honolulu, 1976), pp. 3–65.

243

4. Patrick Cavendish, "The 'New China' of the Kuomintang," in *Modern China's Search for a Political Form,* ed. Jack Gray, (London, 1969), pp. 141–44.

5. As quoted in Cavendish, "'New China,'" pp. 147, 172.

6. Chiang Kai-shek's speech to the Peking press on July 13, 1928, in *Kuo-wen chou-pao,* July 22, 1928; Kuo-fang-pu, *Te-kuo chu Hua chün-shih ku-wen-t'uan kung-tso chi-yao* (hereafter *The German Advisors Group*) (Taipei, 1969), pp. 28–29.

7. H. G. W. Woodhead, ed., *The China Year Book, 1929–30* (Shanghai, 1930), pp. 1181–83.

8. Liu Shao-t'ang, *Min-kuo ta-shih jih-chih* (hereafter *MKTS*) (Taipei, 1973–), vol. 1, p. 375.

9. T'ao Chü-yin, *Chiang Pai-li hsien sheng chuan* (Shanghai, 1948), pp. 100–101; Hsü Kao-yang, *Kuo-fang nien-chien* (Hong Kong, 1969), pt. 2, pp. 165–70; *The China Year Book, 1929–30,* pp. 740–44; Diana Lary, *Region and Nation: The Kwangsi Clique in Chinese Politics, 1925–1937* (Cambridge, Mass., 1974), pp. 115–28.

10. CKS, *Chiang tsung-t'ung chi* (Taipei, 1960), vol. 1, pp. 536–37.

11. Fu Pao-cheng, "Tsai Hua te-kuo chün-shih ku-wen shih chuan," *Chuan-chi wen-hsüeh* 23, no. 3 (September, 1973):5–10; Kuo-fang-pu, *The German Advisors Group,* pp. 4–5; Hu Sung-p'ing, *Chu Chia-hua hsien-sheng nien-p'u* (Taipei, 1969), pp. 18–19; F. F. Liu, *A Military History of Modern China, 1924–1949* (Princeton, N.J., 1956), pp. 61–63.

12. Fu Pao-cheng, "Tsai Hua te-kuo," *Chuan-chi wen-hsüeh* 24, no. 1 (January, 1974):90–98; also 25, no. 1 (July, 1974):90–98.

13. His works included *Gedanken eines Soldaten* (1929), *Landes Verteidigung* (1930), and *Die Reicheswehr* (1932).

14. Sai-k'e-t'e (von Seeckt), *I-ke chün-jen chih ssu-hsiang* (Nanking, 1937), p. 69.

15. Ibid., pp. 70–72.

16. Hsin Ta-mu, "Fa-erh-keng-hao-sheng chiang-chün hui-i ti Chiang wei-yüan-chang yü Chung-kuo, 1934–1938," *Chuan-chi wen-hsüeh* 19, no. 5 (November, 1971):46–52.

17. Ibid.

18. Ibid.; Hung Sung-p'ing, *Chu Chia-hua,* pp. 30–31.

19. Hua-mei ch'u-pan kung-ssu, ed., *Chung-kuo ch'üan-mien k'ang-chan ta-shih-chi,* vol. 1 (Shanghai, 1938), entry of May 23, 1938.

20. Wu Hsiang-hsiang, *Ti-erh-tz'u Chung Jih chan-cheng shih* (hereafter *CJCC*) (Taipei, 1973), vol. 1, pp. 294–98.

21. Liu, *A Military History,* p. 102.

22. For a list of these schools, see ibid., pp. 84–85.

23. Ibid., pp. 87–88.

24. Fu Pao-cheng, "Tsai Hua te-kuo," *Chuan-chi wen-hsüeh* 25, no. 3 (September, 1974):94–98; Kuo-fang-pu, *Fa-kuo chu Hua chün-shih ku-wen-t'uan kung-tso chi-yao* (Taipei, 1968).

25. Liu, *A Military History,* pp. 61–63; Fu Pao-cheng, "Tsai Hua te-kuo,"

Chuan-chi wen-hsüeh 25, no. 1 (July, 1974): 90–98; Hsin Ta-mu, "Fa-erh-keng-hao-sheng," *Chuan-chi wen-hsüeh* 19, no. 5 (November, 1971):46–52.

26. Fu Pao-cheng, "Tsai Hua te-kuo," *Chuan-chi wen-hsüeh* 25, no. 3 (September, 1974):99–102.

27. Frank Dorn, *The Sino-Japanese War, 1937–41: From Marco Polo Bridge to Pearl Harbor* (New York, 1974), pp. 189–90, 200–201; Fu Pao-cheng, "Tsai Hua te-kuo," *Chuan-chi wen-hsüeh* 25, no. 1 (July, 1974):90–98.

28. Wu Hsiang-hsiang, *CJCC*, vol. 1, p. 325.

29. Hsin Ta-mu. "Fa-erh-keng-hao-sheng," *Chuan-chi wen-hsüeh* 21, no. 1 (July, 1972):67.

30. The whole embassy had a staff of ten and operated on a monthly budget of only U.S.$1,430. It was run very chaotically and maintained only intermittent communication with Nanking. See Ch'eng T'ien-fang, *Ch'eng T'ien-fang tsao-nien hui-i-lu* (Taipei, 1968), pp. 104–11, 122–31, for a detailed description of the quality of work of the Chinese embassy in Berlin.

31. Hu Sung-p'ing, *Chu Chia-hua*, pp. 18–19, 22–23, 28–35.

32. Ch'eng T'ien-fang, *Hui-i-lu*, pp. 104–8.

33. Ch'eng T'ien-ku, *Ch'eng T'ien-ku hui-i-lu* (Hong Kong, 1978), pp. 281–82.

34. Lary, *Region and Nation*, pp. 138–45.

35. Ibid.; Huang Hsü-ch'u, "Kwang-hsi yü chung-yang nien-yü-nien lai pei-huan li-ho i-shu," *Ch'un ch'iu*, no. 117 (May 16, 1962):5–7, 12.

36. Lary, *Region and Nation*, pp. 163–93; Huang Hsü-ch'u, "Pai Ch'ung-hsi k'ou-chung ti 'san-tzu cheng-ts'e'," *Ch'un ch'iu*, no. 294 (October 1, 1969):10–14.

37. Lary, *Region and Nation*, pp. 194–99; Huang Hsü-ch'u, "Kwang-hsi yü chung-yang," *Ch'un ch'iu*, no. 127 (October 16, 1962):16–9, 23.

38. Huang Shao-hung, *Wu-shih hui-i* (Hangchow, 1945), pp. 310–11; Liu Shao-t'ang, *MKTS*, vol. 1, pp. 543–47.

39. *North China Herald*, April 20, 1929; reports by J. V. A. MacMurray to the Secretary of State, March 29, 1929, 983.00/10358, and April 16, 1929, 982.00/10389 of *State Department Records;* Li Tsung-jen, *The Memoirs of Li Tsung-jen* (Boulder, Colo., 1978), p. 261.

40. *North China Herald*, May 25, 1929.

41. *China Weekly Review*, June 8, 1929, p. 52.

42. James Sheridan, *Chinese Warlord: The Career of Feng Yü-hsiang* (Stanford, Calif., 1966), pp. 265–67.

43. Liu Shao-t'ang, *MKTS*, vol. 1, pp. 468–70, 489–92.

44. Shen I-yün, *I-yün hui-i* (Taipei, 1968), pp. 501–10.

45. Ch'in Te-shun, *Ch'in Te-shun hui-i-lu* (Taipei, 1967), pp. 31–32.

46. Liu Chien-ch'ün, *Yin-ho i-wang* (Taipei, 1966), pp. 94–96.

47. Ch'in Te-shun, *Hui-i-lu*, pp. 167–68; for a more thorough exploration of Japanese strategic thinking, see Mark R. Peattie, *Ishiwara Kanji and Japan's Confrontation with the West* (Princeton, N.J., 1975), chaps. 2–4; for a detailed description of Japanese overtures to Chinese leaders, see B. Winston, Kahn, *Doihara Kenji and the North China Autonomy Movement, 1935–36* (Temple, Ariz., 1973).

48. For a recent treatment of the event, see Wu Tien-wei, *The Sian Incident: A Pivotal Point in Modern Chinese History* (Ann Arbor, Mich., 1976).
49. For a discussion of Szechwan military factions, see Chou K'ai-ch'ing, *Min-kuo Ssu-ch'uan shih-shih* (Taipei, 1969), pp. 99–106; a more general treatment of Szechwan's confusing military conditions can be found in Robert Kapp, *Szechwan and the Chinese Republic: Provincial Militarism and Central Power, 1911–1938* (New Haven, Conn., 1973).
50. Liu Shao-t'ang, *MKTS*, vol. 1, pp. 385–552; Hsü Chien-nung, *Tsui chin Ssu-ch'uan ts'ai-cheng lun* (Chungking, 1940), pp. 9–12, 111, 158–59.
51. Ho Kuo-kuang, *Pa-shih tzu-shu* (Taipei, 1964), pp. 18–25, 36.
52. Liu Shao-t'ang, *MKTS*, vol. 1, pp. 531–33.
53. Ch'en Pu-lei, *Ch'en Pu-lei hui-i-lu* (Hong Kong, 1962), p. 79.
54. Liu Shao-t'ang, *MKTS*, vol. 1, p. 523; Ho Kuo-kuang, *Pa-shih tzu-shu*, p. 36.
55. Liu Shao-t'ang, *MKTS*, vol. 1, p. 555; Ch'en Tao, "Wo ho Ch'en Kuo-fu, Tai Chi-t'ao ti chiu chiao-tao," *Ch'un ch'iu*, no. 250 (December 1, 1967):17–18; Lei Hsiao-ch'in, "Liu Hsiang yü Wang Ling-chi," *Chung-wai tsa-chih* 5, no. 4 (April, 1969):22–23; also see Kapp, *Szechwan and the Chinese Republic*.
56. Liu Shao-t'ang, *MKTS*, vol. 1, pp. 559–60.
57. For more detailed discussions on military operations, see Kuo-fang-pu, *Chiao-fei chan shih* (Taipei, 1962), vol. 2.
58. Ibid.
59. Ibid.
60. Liu Shao-t'ang, *MKTS*, vol. 1, p. 485.
61. Kuo-fang-pu, *Chiao-fei chan shih*, vol. 3.
62. The force deployment during the various anti-Communist campaigns is summarized as follows:

Sequence of Campaigns	Government Troops	Regional/*Chiang* Ratio (in divisions)	Communist Troops
1	44,000	11/1	42,000
2	113,000	10/1	66,000
3	130,000	8/6	53,000
4	153,000	7/5	64,000
5	300,000(?)	21/17	100,000(?)

Source of data: Kuo-fang-pu, *Chiao-fei chan-shih*, vols. 2–5.

63. Thus the agents planted in the Nineteenth Route Army caused many defections even before fighting began, which led to the abrupt collapse of the Fukien rebellion in December, 1933; see Li Tsung-jen; *Memoirs*, pp. 300–302. For the subversive activities of KMT agents in Kwangsi, see Huang Hsü-ch'u, "Yeh Ch'i to ma shih-shih ti chen-hsiang," *Ch'un ch'iu*, no. 193 (July 16, 1965):17–19.
64. For a description of the role of bribery in the Kwangsi revolt of 1929, see Chang Jen-min, "Wo ts'ung Hsiang-kang mao-hsien hui Wu-chou ti ching-

kuo,'' *Ch'un ch'iu*, no. 309 (May 16, 1970):12–15; for bribery in the 1930 Central Plains War, see Carsun Chang, *The Third Force in China* (New York, 1952), p. 92; Li Tsung-jen, *Memoirs*, pp. 267–74, 308; and Donald G. Gillin, *Warlord: Yen Hsi-shan in Shansi Province, 1911–1949* (Princeton, N.J., 1967), p. 115.

65. A recent example is by Pichon P. Y. Loh, *The Early Chiang Kai-shek: A Study of His Personality and Politics: 1887–1924* (New York, 1971), particularly pp. 12–13, 51–52.

66. For a recent book that covers familiar ground of Chiang's life story, see Li Tung-fang, *Chiang kung Chieh-shih hsü-chuan* (Taipei, 1976).

67. CKS, "Chün-sheng tsa-chih fa-k'an-tz'u," in *Tzu-fan lu* pt. 1 (n.p., 1931), pp. 413–17.

68. Ibid., pp. 319–76.

69. Thus, for example, of the sixty-eight major speeches he delivered during 1924–28, about fifty dealt with exclusively military subjects, and the other eighteen carried heavy military connotations, CKS, *Chiang tsung-t'ung chi*, vol. 1, pp. 391–560.

70. CKS speech, December 10, 1928, *Chiang tsung-t'ung chi*, vol. 1, p. 518.

71. CKS speech, "The Path of China's Reconstruction," July 18, 1928, *Chiang tsung-t'ung chi*, vol. 1, p. 516.

72. CKS speech, April 25, 1929, *Chiang tsung-t'ung chi*, vol. 1, p. 541.

73. Ibid., p. 516.

74. CKS speech, December 14, 1932, *Chiang tsung-t'ung chi*, vol. 1, p. 608.

75. CKS speech, "Key Points in Current Hsien Politics," November 30, 1928, *Chiang tsung-t'ung chi*, vol. 1, p. 517.

76. CKS speech, "Education, Livelihood, and Defense," February 12, 1934, *Chiang tsung-t'ung chi*, vol. 1, pp. 729–32.

77. CKS speech, "The Vitality of a Modern State," September 18, 1935, *Chiang tsung-t'ung chi*, vol. 1, pp. 906–11.

78. CKS speech, September 17, 1935, *Chiang tsung-t'ung chi*, vol. 1, p. 905.

79. Sih, *The Strenuous Decade;* Young, *China's Nation-Building Effort.*

80. CKS speech, November 25, 1930, *Chiang tsung-t'ung chi*, vol. 1, p. 561; CKS speech, December 14, 1932, *Chiang tsung-t'ung chi*, vol. 1, p. 608.

81. CKS speeches in *Chiang tsung-t'ung chi:* "Hsien Magistrate is the Basic Power in Politics," July 12, 1932, vol. 1, pp. 595–601; "Education, Livelihood, and Defense," February 12, 1934, vol. 1, pp. 729–33; "The Promotion of Hsien Politics and Political Reconstruction," March 13, 1936, vol. 1, pp. 927–34.

82. Li Tsung-huang, *Li Tsung-huang hui-i-lu* (Taipei, 1972), pp. 262–66; Ch'en Kuo-fu, *Ch'en Kuo-fu hsien-sheng ch'üan-chi* (Taipei, 1952), vol. 5, pp. 117–37.

83. Li Tsung-huang, *Hui-i-lu*, pp. 276–80.

84. Ch'en Kuo-fu, *Ch'üan-chi*, vol. 5, pp. 117–18, 149; for socioeconomic statistics on Chiang-ning, see Feng Ho-fa, ed., *Chung-kuo nung-ts'un ching-chi tzu-liao* (reprint, ed., Taipei, 1978), pp. 168, 434–65.

85. Ch'en Kuo-fu, *Ch'üan-chi*, vol. 5, pp. 118–37; also see Guy Alitto, "Rural

Reconstruction—Experimental Hsien and Credit Cooperatives: A General Survey,'' paper delivered at a seminar on local and provincial politics in Nationalist China, Boulder, Colorado, October, 1974.

86. CKS speech, "Future Path of Political Reform," March 18, 1934, *Chiang tsung-t'ung chi,* vol. 1, pp. 744–48.

87. CKS speech, "The Promotion of Hsien Politics and Political Reconstruction," March 13, 1936, *Chiang tsung-t'ung chi,* vol. 1, pp. 927–34.

88. Tien Hung-mao, *Kuomintang China,* pp. 27, 180–81.

89. Li Tsung-jen, *Memoirs,* p. 263.

90. CKS speech, December 14, 1932, *Chiang tsung-t'ung chi,* vol. 1, p. 608.

91. Tien Hung-mao, *Kuomintang China,* pp. 107–8, 110–13.

92. Ch'en Kuo-fu, *Ch'üan-chi,* vol. 5, p. 114.

93. William Wei, "The KMT in Kiangsi: The Suppression of the Communist Bases, 1930–1934" (Ph.D. diss., University of Michigan, 1978).

√ 94. Arif Dirlik, "The Ideological Foundation of the New Life Movement: A Study in Counterrevolution," *Journal of Asian Studies* 34, no. 4 (August, 1975):945–80.

95. For discussion of the movement, see Tien Hung-mao, *Kuomintang China,* pp. 70, 98, 100.

96. Cavendish, "The 'New China' of the Kuomintang," p. 165.

97. Quoted in F. F. Liu, *A Military History,* p. 93; for a discussion of the influence of von Seeckt on Chiang, see Hu Sung-p'ing, *Chu Chia-hua hsien-sheng nien-p'u,* pp. 30–31, 33–35.

98. Kuo-fang-pu, *The German Advisors Group,* pp. 41–42.

99. Cavendish, "The 'New China' of the Kuomintang," pp. 165, 178.

100. CKS speech, "The Necessary Qualifications of Citizens of a Modern State," September 21, 1935, *Chiang tsung-t'ung chi,* vol. 1, pp. 915–17.

Chapter 2

1. Kuo-fang-pu, *K'ang Jih chan-shih: ch'i-ch'i shih-pien yü P'ing-Chin tso-chan* (hereafter *KJCS:subtitle*) (Taipei, 1967), pp. 2–7, 42.

2. James B. Crowley, *Japan's Quest for Autonomy, National Security and Foreign Policy, 1930–1938* (Princeton, N.J., 1966), p. 345; for a detailed Japanese account of the unfolding of the crisis and Tokyo's policies, see Teradaira Tadasuke, *Rokōkyō jihen* (Tokyo, 1970), particularly pp. 54–281, 289–313; the Japanese army's operational records of this incident can be found in Bōeichō, *Shina jihen Rikugun sakusen* (Tokyo, 1976), vol. 1, pp. 138–77; Uemura Shinichi, *Nikka jihen,* pp. 57–110, in *Nihon gaikō shi* ed. Kajima Institute of International Peace, vol. 20 (Tokyo, 1971–); for a personal account of the incident by the commander of the Japanese force in north China, see Tsunoda Jun, ed., *Nitchū sensō,* vol. 4, pp. 529–43, 561–74, in *Gendaishi shiryō* (Tokyo, 1962–).

3. CKS speech, July 17, 1937, in *Chiang tsung-t'ung chi,* vol. 1, pp. 962–63.

4. Kuo-fang-pu, *KJCS: Chin-P'u t'ieh-lu pei-tuan yüan-hsien chih tso-chan,* p. 9.
5. Kuo-fang-pu, *KJCS: Sung-Hu hui-chan,* pp. 5–6.
6. *Foreign Relations of the United States, Diplomatic Papers, 1937* (Washington, D.C., 1954), vol. 3, pp. 363–66, 385–86; Uemura Shinichi, *Nikka jihen,* pp. 111–14, 119, 125, 146, 153; also see Bōeichō, *Shina jihen Rikugun sakusen,* vol. 1, pp. 257–62; Tsunoda Jun, *Nitchū sensō* vol. 4, pp. 364–70, 385–87; Shigemitsu Mamoru, *Shōwa no dōran* (Tokyo, 1952), vol. 1, pp. 171–75.
7. Kuo-fang-pu, *KJCS: Sung-Hu hui-chan,* pp. 6–7; T'ang Chung, *K'ang-chan pi-chi* (n.p., n.d.).
8. T'ang Chung, *ibid.;* Li Tsung-jen, "Li Tsung-jen hui-i-lu," *Ming pao* 12, no. 7 (July, 1977):29; Kuo-fang-pu, *KJCS: Sung-Hu hui-chan,* pp. 9–14.
9. Kuo-fang-pu, *KJCS: Sung-Hu hui-chan,* pp. 65–66, 186–87, chart 5.
10. Frank Dorn, *The Sino-Japanese War, 1937–41: From Marco Polo Bridge to Pearl Harbor* (New York, 1974), p. 74; Tsunoda Jun, *Nitchū sensō,* vol. 4, pp. 371–82, 387–93.
11. Kuo-fang-pu, *KJCS: Sung-Hu hui-chan,* pp. 295–300; Bōeichō, *Shina jihen Rikugun sakusen,* vol. 1, p. 275–82; Nippon Kokusai Seiji Gakukai, ed., *Taiheiyō sensō e no Michi* (Tokyo, 1963), vol. 4, pp. 17–40.
12. Pai Ch'ung-hsi's speech of January 4, 1938, "Ti-i-ch'i k'ang-chan ti chiao-hsün," in Feng Chü-p'ei, *K'ang-chan chung ti ti-wu-lu-chün* (Hankow, 1938), p. 119; for other estimates, see Frank Dorn, *Sino-Japanese War,* pp. 78–79; F. F. Liu, *A Military History of Modern China, 1924–1949* (Princeton, N.J., 1956), pp. 197–211; Ho Ying-ch'in, *Ho shang-chiang k'ang-chan ch'i-chien chün-shih pao-kao* (Taipei, 1962) (hereafter *Wartime Military Report*), vol. 2, table 4; and Hu Tsung-nan, *Tsung-nan wen-ts'un* (Taipei, 1963), pp. 117, 137.
13. *Chung-kuo ch'üan-mien k'ang-chan ta-shih-chi,* vol. 1, entry of December 31, 1937; Kuo-fang-pu, *KJCS: Sung-Hu hui-chan,* pp. 191, 247–48; Chao Tseng-ch'ou, et al., *K'ang-chan chi-shih* (Taipei, 1961), vol. 1, p. 88; Wu Hsiang-hsiang, *CJCC,* pp. 399–402.
14. Chang Kan-p'ing, *K'ang Jih ming-chiang Kuan Lin-chen* (Hong Kong, 1969), pp. 102–3; Kuo Chi-t'ang, *Chung-kuo lu-chün ti-san-fang-mien-chün k'ang-chan chi-shih* (Taipei, 1962), p. 45.
15. Liu, *A Military History,* p. 145; Nozawa Yutaka, ed. *Nitchū sensō* pt. 2, pp. 18–28, in *Taiheiyō sensō shi,* vol. 3, ed. Rekishigaku Kenkyukai (Toyko, 1976). Ch'en Ch'eng, *Pa-nien k'ang-chan ching-kuo kai-yao* (Nanking, 1946), table 9; Ho Ying-ch'in, *Wartime Military Report,* vol. 2, table 40.
16. Barbara W. Tuchman, *Stilwell and the American Experience in China, 1911–1945* (New York, 1970), pp. 213–14; Dorn, *Sino-Japanese War,* p. 128.
17. John Hunter Boyle, *China and Japan at War, 1937–1945: The Politics of Collaboration* (Stanford, Calif., 1972), pp. 108–10; for a critical review of the contradictory policies of Shidehara Kijūro and Tanaka Giïchi toward

China, see Nobuya Bamba, *Japanese Diplomacy in A Dilemma: New Light on Japan's China Policy, 1924–1929* (Vancouver, B.C., 1972), pp. 283–382.

18. *Foreign Relations of the United States, Diplomatic Papers, 1937,* vol. 3, pp. 256–58; Lincoln Li, *The Japanese Army in North China: 1937–1941: Problems of Political and Economic Control* (Tokyo, 1975), pp. 19–36, 41–45; for an incisive interpretation of Japan's diplomatic moves before and after the July 7 incident, see Crowley, *Japan's Quest for Autonomy,* pp. 301–10, 326–27, 350–60, 376–77.

19. For example, both Li Tsung-jen and Pai Ch'ung-hsi strongly urged Chiang to make a nominal stand at Shanghai and withdraw inland to fight the long war. See Huang Hsü-ch'u, "Wo yü Pai Ch'ung-hsi tsui-hou ti kuan-hsi," *Ch'un ch'iu,* no. 313 (July 16, 1970):6–7.

20. Kan Chieh-hou, *K'ang-chan chung chün-shih wai-chiao ti chuan-pien* (n.p., 1938), pp. 30–32.

21. Ho Ying-ch'in, *Wartime Military Report,* vol. 1, pp. 7–14.

22. Kuo-fang-pu, *The German Advisors Group,* pp. 45, 49.

23. Ibid., pp. 56–60.

24. Chang Chüeh-wu, *Sung-Hu k'ang Jih K'ang-chan so te chih ching-nien yü chiao-hsün* (Nanking, 1932), pp. 247–53.

25. Ibid., preface, pp. 1–2, 198–201.

26. CKS, *Chiang tsung-t'ung chi,* vol. 1, pp. 799–805.

27. Ibid., vol. 1, p. 798.

28. Ch'en Ch'eng, *Ti-i wai-wu yü fu-hsing min-tsu* (Nanking, 1936), p. 66.

29. CKS, *Chiang tsung-t'ung chi,* vol. 1, p. 798.

30. Kuo-fang-pu, *The German Advisors Group,* p. 60.

31. Ibid., p. 65.

32. CKS, *Chiang tsung-t'ung chi,* vol. 1, p. 798; Ch'en Ch'eng, *Pa-nien k'ang-chan ching-kuo kai-yao* (Nanking, 1946), p. 2.

33. Ch'en Ch'eng, *Pa-nien k'ang-chan ching-kuo kai-yao,* p. 2; Ho Ying-ch'in, *Wartime Military Report,* vol. 1, p. 2.

34. According to Tuchman, Joseph W. Stilwell estimated that the central government had 1,300,000 men in 1936 while the provincials had 360,000. See Barbara W. Tuchman, *Stilwell and the American Experience in China, 1911–1945* (New York, 1970), p. 135.

35. Ch'en Ch'eng, *Pa-nien k'ang-chan ching-kuo kai-yao,* table 2; Dorn, *Sino-Japanese War,* pp. 7–9.

36. CKS speech, September 9, 1925, in *Chiang tsung-t'ung chi,* vol. 1, p. 462.

37. Wu Hsiang-hsiang, *CJCC,* vol. 1, pp. 435–36.

38. Bōeichō, *Shina jihen Rikugun sakusen,* vol. 2, pp. 24–42; Tuchman, *Stilwell,* pp. 231–37.

39. Dorn, *Sino-Japanese War,* pp. 156–58.

40. Kuo-fang-pu, *KJCS: Hsü-chou hui-chan,* p. 261.

41. Dorn, *Sino-Japanese War,* pp. 156–58.

42. Chao Tseng-ch'ou, et al., *K'ang-chan chi-shih,* vol. 1, p. 118; Wu Hsiang-hsiang, *CJCC,* vol. 1, pp. 446–47.

43. Bōeichō, *Shina jihen Rikugun sakusen,* vol. 2, pp. 136–218; Nippon Kokusai

Seiji Gakukai, ed., *Taiheiyō sensō e no Michi,* vol. 4, pp. 43–53; Tsunoda Jun, *Nitchū sensō,* vol. 2, pp. 269–72, 286–301.

44. Dorn, *Sino-Japanese War,* pp. 180–81.

45. Kuo-fang-pu, *KJCS: Wu-han hui-chan,* pp. 899–900.

46. Kuo-fang-pu, *Chung Jih chan-cheng shih-lüeh* (Taipei, 1962), pp. 221–28.

47. Nippon Kokusai Seiji Gakukai, ed., *Taiheiyō sensō e no Michi,* vol. 6, pp. 53–54; Tsunoda Jun, *Nitchū sensō,* vol. 2, pp. 273–80; *Hua-nan lun-hsien-ch'ü t'e-chi* (n.p., n.d.), pp. 1–4.

48. Wu Hsiang-hsiang, *CJCC,* vol. 1, pp. 456, 463–64.

49. *Ho-p'ing fan-kung chien-kuo wen-hsien* (Nanking, 1944), vol. 1, "Japan," pp. 1–2.

50. Nozawa Yutaka, ed., *Nitchū sensō,* pt. 2, pp. 162–69; Wu Hsiang-hsiang, *CJCC,* vol. 1, p. 573.

51. Chang Ch'i-yün, *K'ang Jih chan-shih* (Taipei, 1966), pp. 57–58.

52. CKS, *Chiang tsung-t'ung chi,* vol. 1, p. 1064.

53. Ch'en Ch'eng, *Ti-erh-ch'i k'ang-chan kuan-yü cheng-hsün kung-tso chih chih-shih* (n.p., 1938), pp. 151–61; CKS, *Chiang tsung-t'ung chi,* vol. 1, pp. 980–81; Ch'en Ch'eng, *Ti-i wai-wu yü fu-hsing min-tsu,* pp. 150–52.

54. Chiang Chün-chang, *Chung-hua min-kuo chien-kuo shih* (Taipei, 1957), pp. 228–29.

55. Kuo-fang-pu, *KJCS: erh-shih-pa-nien tung-chi kung-shih,* p. 497.

56. Liu Shao-t'ang, *MKTS,* vol. 1, pp. 584–87.

57. CKS, *Chiang tsung-t'ung chi,* vol. 1, p. 798.

58. Ibid., vol. 1, pp. 1012–13.

59. CKS, *Nan-yü chün-shih hui-i k'ai-hui hsün-tz'u* (n.p., 1938).

60. Kuo-fang-pu, *KJCS: Nan-ch'ang hui-chan,* p. 1.

61. Ch'en Ch'eng speech of October 15, 1938, "The New Developments in the War and Our Understanding and Determination," in Ch'en Ch'eng, *Ti-erh-ch'i k'ang-chan kuan-yü cheng-hsün kung-tso chih chih-shih* (n.p., 1938), pp. 2–3.

62. Sai-k'e-t'e (von Seeckt), *I ke chün-jen chih ssu-hsiang* (Nanking, 1937), p. 96.

63. Huang Hsü-ch'u, "Pai Ch'ung-hsi liang-tu jen fu-ts'an-mou-chang chih i," *Ch'un ch'iu,* no. 233 (March 16, 1967):3–5.

64. Huang Hsü-ch'u, "Kwang-hsi yü chung-yang nien-yü-nien lai pei-huan li-ho i-shu," *Ch'un ch'iu,* no. 131 (December 16, 1962):11; Huang Shao-hung, *Wu-shih hui-i,* vol. 2 (Hangchow, 1945), pp. 414–15.

65. Wang Ch'eng-sheng, "Liu-shih-nien-lai ti Chung-kuo," *Chung-wai tsa-chih* 8 (November, 1970):77–90.

66. Traveling through Hunan and Kiangsi in the spring of 1938, Stilwell witnessed much evidence of the existence of training in guerrilla warfare, see Tuchman, *Stillwell,* pp. 231–37; Ho Ying-ch'in reported to the KMT CEC plenums that of the 17,681 engagements of all magnitude the Chinese made against the Japanese during January, 1939, and February, 1941, about 56 percent were termed "small scale" conventional ones, and 44 percent were "guerrilla" ones. See Wang Ch'eng-sheng, ibid.

67. For two accounts of personal involvement in China's response to the German offer of mediation, see Hsü Yung-p'ing, *Ch'en Pu-lei hsien-sheng chuan* (Taipei, 1977), pp. 162–63; Ch'en T'ien-ku, *Ch'en T'ien-ku hui-i-lu* (Hong Kong, 1978), pp. 321–23; also Shigemitsu Mamoru, *Shōwa no dōran*, vol. 1, pp. 175–81; Uemura Shinichi, *Nikka jihen*, pp. 176–229.

68. CKS, *Chiang tsung-t'ung chi*, vol. 1, p. 982.

69. CKS speech of November 25, 1938, in *Nan-yü chün-shih hui-i k'ai-hui hsün-tz'u*.

70. Chang Ch'i-yün, *Tang-shih kai-yao* (Taipei, 1960), vol. 3, p. 136.

71. Liu Shao-t'ang, *MKTS*, vol. 1, p. 620.

72. Sun Fo's speech in Chung-hua pien-i-kuan, ed., *Wei-ta-ti hsin Chung-kuo* (Chungking, 1939), p. 239; Hsieh Chiao-min, *China: Ageless Land and Countless People* (Princeton, N.J., 1967), p. 56.

73. Liu Shao-t'ang, *MKTS*, vol. 1, p. 609; Dorn, *Sino-Japanese War*, pp. 269, 283.

74. Kuo-fang-pu, *KJCS: erh-shih-pa-nien tung-chi kung-shih*, pp. 13, 30–31.

75. Liu Shao-t'ang, *MKTS*, vol. 1, p. 612.

76. Kuo-fang-pu, *KJCS: erh-shih-pa-nien tung-chi kung-shih*, p. 7, table 10.

77. Dorn, *Sino-Japanese War*, pp. 249, 304–5.

78. Liu Shao-t'ang, *MKTS*, vol. 1, p. 597.

79. Ibid., p. 656.

80. Ibid., pp. 605–8.

81. CKS, *Chiang tsung-t'ung chi*, vol. 1, pp. 1183–84.

82. Kuo-fang-pu, *KJCS: erh-shih-pa-nien tung-chi kung-shih*, pp. 20–21.

83. Ibid., pp. 29–30.

84. Ibid., p. 32.

85. Tetsuya Kataoka, *Resistance and Revolution in China: The Communists and the Second United Front* (Berkeley, Calif., 1974), p. 171; Bōeichō, *Daihonkan Rikusōbu* (Tokyo, 1973), vol. 1, pp. 619–22.

86. Kuo-fang-pu, *Chung Jih chan-cheng shih-lüeh*, vol. 3, pp. 298–311; Tsunoda Jun, *Nitchū sensō*, vol. 2, pp. 424–25, 436–51.

87. Liu Shao-t'ang, *MKTS*, vol. 1, pp. 610–15.

88. Kuo-fang-pu, *KJCS: Kuei-nan hui-chan*, p. 64, table 7; Huang Hsü-ch'u, "Pa-nien k'ang-chan hui-i-lu," *Ch'un ch'iu*, no. 81 (November 16, 1960):2–4; an official Japanese army account of the winter offensive can be found in Bōeichō, *Shina jihen Rijugun sakusen*, vol. 3, pp. 93–111.

89. Wu Hsiang-hsiang, *CJCC*, vol. 1, p. 454.

90. Arthur Young, *China and the Helping Hand, 1937–1945* (Cambridge, Mass., 1963), pp. 22, 125; Radio Moscow broadcast of April 6, 1967, in *Fei O tseng-chih yüan-shih tzu-liao hui-pien*, ed. Kuo-chi kuan-hsi yen-chiu-so, vol. 9, pp. 141–42 (Taipei, 1960–).

91. Liu, *A Military History*, pp. 169–70; Arthur Young suggested that the 1937–39 Soviet aid included one thousand planes, two thousand volunteer pilots in rotation, five hundred military advisors, and arms sufficient to equip ten reorganized Chinese divisions. See his *China and the Helping Hand*, p. 125.

92. Ho Ying-ch'in, *Wartime Military Report*, vol. 1, p. 279; Kuo-fang-pu, *KJCS: erh-shih-pa-nien tung-chi kung-shih*, p. 17.

93. Liu, *A Military History*, p. 205.

94. Kuo-fang-pu, *KJCS: erh-shih-pa-nien tung-chi kung-shih*, p. 505.

95. Ibid., pp. 501–2.

96. Kuo-fang-pu, *KJCS: Kuei-nan hui-chan*, pp. 269–72.

97. Kuo-fang-pu, *Lu-chün chün-kuan hsüeh-hsiao hsiao-shih* (Taipei, 1969), pt. 3, pp. 131–35.

98. Liu, *A Military History*, pp. 147–48.

99. Li Tsung-jen, *The Memoirs of Li Tsung-jen* (Boulder, Colo., 1978), p. 324.

100. Ibid., pp. 326, 425–26.

101. Liu Shao-t'ang, *MKTS*, vol. 1, pp. 618–19.

102. Kataoka, *Resistance and Revolution in China*, pp. 199–200.

103. Bōeichō, *Hokushi no chiansen* (Tokyo, 1971), vol. 1, supplement, chart 5; Bōeichō, *Daihonkan Rikusōbu*, vol. 2, supplement, chart 3.

104. Kuo-fang-pu, *KJCS: Tsao-i hui-chan*, chart 7; Kuo-fang-pu, *KJCS: Yün-nan hui-chan*, chart 18; Kuo-fang-pu, *KJCS: Chin-nan hui-chan*, chart 16.

105. Chün-shih wei-yüan-hui, *Ti-erh-ch'i k'ang-chan ti-i-chieh-tuan kuo-chün tso-chan chih ching-nien chiao-hsün* (Chungking, 1942), pp. 9–11; Kuo-fang-pu, *KJCS: Tsao-I hui-chan*, pp. 174–83; Kuo-fang-pu, *KJCS: ti-erh-tz'u Ch'ang-sha hui-chan*, pp. 295–96.

106. CKS, *Chiang tsung-t'ung chi*, vol. 2, pp. 1376–77.

107. Bōeichō, *Daihonkan Rikusōbu*, vol. 2, p. 202.

108. Pai Ch'ung-hsi, *K'ang-chan pa-nien chün-shih kai-k'uang* (n.p., 1946), pp. 8–9.

109. Chang Ch'i-yün, *K'ang Jih chan-shih*, pp. 325–28.

110. Charles F. Romanus and Riley Sunderland, *Stilwell's Mission to China* (Washington, D.C., 1953), p. 167; Tuchman, *Stilwell*, p. 395.

111. Charles F. Romanus and Riley Sunderland, *Stilwell's Command Problems* (Washington, D.C., 1956), p. 472.

112. Roland G. Ruppenthal, *Logistical Support of the Armies*, (Washington, D.C., 1955), vol. 2, pp. 306–7.

113. Charles F. Romanus and Riley Sunderland, *Time Runs Out in CBI* (Washington, D.C., 1958), pp. 19, 341–42.

114. Major General Patrick J. Hurley to President Roosevelt, CFB 24103, October 10, 1944, *Foreign Relations of the United States, Diplomatic Papers: 1944, China*, vol. 4, pp. 168–69.

115. Leslie Anders, *The Ledo Road: General Joseph W. Stilwell's Highway to China* (Norman, Okla., 1965), pp. 233–40; Romanus and Sunderland, *Time Runs Out in CBI*, pp. 317–18, tables 4, 5.

116. Young, *China and the Helping Hand*, App. 2, p. 441.

117. Ibid., p. 340.

118. Ibid., p. 350.

119. Romanus and Sunderland, *Stilwell's Command Problems*, p. 4.

120. Feng Yü-hsiang reported that a Yünnan unit had to use 35 percent of its men to transport rice, 25 percent to fetch firewood, and 10 percent to do barrack

duties, so that only 30 percent was left for combat duty; see his *Wo so jen-shih ti Chiang Chieh-shih* (Hong Kong, 1949), p. 143.

121. Kuo-fang-pu, *KJCS: Yü-chung hui-chan*, pp. 315–17; Kou Chi-t'ang, *Chung-kuo lu-chün ti-san-fang-mien-chün k'ang-chan chi-shih*, pp. 219, 238–40.

122. Ho Ying-ch'in, *Wartime Military Report*, vol. 1, pp. 149–50; Kuo-fang-pu, *Lu-chün chün-kuan hsüeh-hsiao hsiao-shih*, pt. 3, pp. 93–94.

123. Kuo-fang-pu, *Lu-chün chün-kuan hsüeh-hsiao hsiao-shih*, pt. 3, pp. 91, 138, 233–40, 431–580.

124. Pai Ch'ung-hsi, *K'ang-chan pa-nien chün-shih kai-k'uang*, p. 11; Ho Ying-ch'in, *Wartime Military Report*, vol. 2, p. 660.

125. Hsü Kao-yang, *Kuo-fang nien-chien*, pt. 2, pp. 66–70; Ho Ying-ch'in, *Wartime Military Report*, vol. 2, p. 660.

126. Ho Ying-ch'in, *Wartime Military Report*, vol. 2, p. 562.

127. Liu, *A Military History*, p. 149.

128. Kuo-fang-pu, *Lu-chün chün-kuan-tso tzu-chi-pu, 1944* (Chungking, 1944), vol. 1, "Chiang-kuan, chien."

129. Wan Yao-huang, "Chu ch'ih lu-chün ta-hsüeh shih-ch'i ti hui-i," *Chuan-chi wen-hsüeh*, vol. 24, no. 1 (January, 1974):81–82; *ibid.*, vol. 24, no. 2 (February, 1974):75–78; Liu, *A Military History*, pp. 106–7.

130. Hsü Kao-yang, *Kuo-fang nien-chien* (Hong Kong, 1969), pt. 2, "Military Affairs," pp. 68–69.

131. Albert C. Wedemeyer, *Wedemeyer Reports!* (New York, 1958), p. 325.

132. Kuo-fang-pu, *KJCS: Ch'ang-te hui-chan*, pp. 219–24.

133. Memorandum of conversation, by the Second Secretary of Embassy in China, Davies, to General Stilwell, March 15, 1943, 740.0011 Pacific War/3206, *Foreign Relations of the United States, Diplomatic Papers: 1943, China*, pp. 33–36; Romanus and Sunderland, *Time Runs Out in CBI*, pp. 66–67.

134. Tuchman, *Stilwell*, p. 339.

135. The Ambassador in China, Gauss, to the Secretary of State, No. 1780, November 5, 1943, 740.0011 Pacific War/3559, *Foreign Relations, 1943, China*, pp. 158–60.

136. CKS, *Chiang tsung-t'ung chi*, vol. 2, pp. 1430–34, 1444.

137. Romanus and Sunderland, *Stilwell's Mission to China*, pp. 25–27.

138. Theodore H. White, ed., *The Stilwell Papers* (New York, 1962), p. 132; Tuchman, *Stilwell*, pp. 390–94.

139. Romanus and Sunderland, *Stilwell's Command Problems*, p. 427.

140. Shigemitsu Mamoru, *Shōwa no dōran*, vol. 2, pp. 158–74; Bōeichō, *Shōwa jūshichi-hachinen no Shina Hakengun* (Tokyo, 1972), pp. 306–15; Bōeichō, *Daihonkan Rikusōbu*, vol. 3, pp. 526–27, 598–600.

141. Bōeichō, *Daihonkan Rikusōbu*, vol. 3, pp. 526–27, 598–600.

142. Ibid., vol. 4, pp. 195–96.

143. Ibid., vol. 4, p. 369.

144. Ibid., vol. 4, pp. 370–620; Aoi Shinichi, ed., *Taiheiyō sensō*, pt. 2, pp. 66–67, in *Taiheiyō sensō shi*, vol. 5, ed. Rekishigaku Kenkyukai (Tokyo, 1976); Bōeichō, *Shōwa jūshichi-hachinen no Shina Hakengun*, pp. 9–96.

145. Bōeichō, *Daihonkan Rikusōbu*, vol. 6, p. 297.

146. Ibid., vol. 7, pp. 191, 215; Sanematsu Yuzuru, ed., *Taiheiyō senso*, vol. 5, pp. 426, 825–26, in *Gendaishi shiryō* (Tokyo, 1962–).

147. Bōeichō, *Daihonkan Rikusōbu*, vol. 6, p. 222; for an account of Japan's declining ability to secure its sea lanes, see Bōeichō, *Kaijō goei sen* (Tokyo, 1971).

148. Bōeichō, *Daihonkan Rikusōbu*, vol. 7, p. 224; Sanematsu Yuzuru, *Taiheiyō senso*, vol. 5, pp. 558–68.

149. Bōeichō, *Daihonkan Rikusōbu*, vol. 7, pp. 229–31.

150. Ibid., vol. 7, pp. 229–31, 233; for a detailed discussion of Japan's shipping losses and their impact on logistics, see also Aoi Shinichi, *Taiheiyō senso*, vol. 2, pp. 43–48.

151. Aoi Shinichi, *Taiheiyō senso*, pt. 2, pp. 85–90; by the end of 1944, total petroleum import and production was only 14 percent of the 1940 level, and total inventory was only 28 percent of the 1940 level. Extensive statistics on the damage inflicted by the United States attacks on Japan's shipping and logistic capacity, on her production of airplanes, naval vessels, etc. can be found in Sanematsu Yuzuru, *Taiheiyō senso*, vol. 5, pp. 69–557. A thorough discussion of Japan's wartime mobilization policies, production targets, and shortages can be found in Nakamura Takafusa, ed., *Kodda sōdōin* (Tokyo, 1970), vol. 1.

152. Bōeichō, *Daihonkan Rikusōbu*, vol. 7, pp. 548–53.

153. Bōeichō, *Ichigō Sakusen (1) Konan no kaisen* (Tokyo, 1967), p. 3.

154. Bōeichō, *Daihonkan Rikusōbu*, vol. 7, pp. 187–90.

155. Bōeichō, *Ichigō Sakusen (1) Konan no kaisen*, pp. 1–2; Sanematsu Yuzuru, *Taiheiyō senso*, vol. 4, pp. 138–40, 143–44.

156. Wu Hsiang-hsiang, *CJCC*, vol. 2, p. 991.

157. Kou Chi-t'ang, *Chung-kuo lu-chün ti-san-fang-mien-chün k'ang-chan chi-shih*, pp. 226–27, 231.

158. Bōeichō, *Ichigō Sakusen (1) Konan no kaisen*, pp. 231–74, 287, 288–318, 319–41, 357, 362, 373–75, 485, 514–15, 524; the Japanese claims are corroborated by the Chinese own war records. The Chinese acknowledged very heavy casualties but gave no grand total, which itself was a departure from their standard practice in other campaigns. My tabulations of some main Chinese units came up with a total of 50,000 dead. See Kuo-fang-pu, *KJCS: Yü-chung hui-chan*, all 6 vols.

159. Kuo-fang-pu, *KJCS: Yü-chung hui-chan*, vol. 6, p. 325.

160. Ibid., vol. 1, pp. 74–76.

161. Bōeichō, *Ichigō Sakusen (1) Konan no kaisen*, pp. 231–74, 287, 288–318.

162. Bōeichō, *Ichigō Sakusen (2) Konan no kaisen* (Tokyo, 1967), pp. 341–42; Wu Hsiang-hsiang, *CJCC*, vol. 2, p. 1002; Kuo-fang-pu, *KJCS: Ch'ang-Heng hui-chan*, pp. 151–59.

163. Bōeichō, *Ichigō Sakusen (2) Konan no kaisen*, pp. 330–31, 556; an official army account of the operation to seize the railway in Kwangtung is given in Bōeichō, *Shōwa nijūnen no Shina Hakengun* (Tokyo, 1973), vol. 1, pp. 1–178.

164. Wu Hsiang-hsiang, *CJCC*, vol. 2, p. 1021; for a detailed Japanese official account of this operation, see Bōeichō, *Kaigun Shōgō sakusen* (Tokyo, 1972), 2 vols.

165. Bōeichō, *Ichigō Sakusen (3) Keisei no kaisen* (Tokyo, 1969), pp. 333–34.

166. Yang Sheng, "Sha-ch'ang erh-shih-nien," *Chung-wai tsa-chih,* vol. 8, no. 5 (November, 1970):11–15; Huang Hsü-ch'u, "Pa-nien k'ang-chan hui-i-lu," *Ch'un ch'iu,* no. 89 (March 16, 1961):2–4.

167. Bōeichō, *Ichigō Sakusen (3) Keisei no kaisen,* p. 681.

168. Romanus and Sunderland, *Time Runs Out in CBI,* pp. 55–56.

169. Bōeichō, *Ichigō Sakusen (1) Kōnan no kaisen,* pp. 7–8, 50–51, 83.

170. Ibid., passim.

171. Because Hu had sent some of his units to support the Honan defense, it is difficult to know how badly they had suffered. It is my estimate that some twelve to fifteen of Hu's divisions had not seen any fighting at all. See Kuo-fang-pu, *KJCS: Yü-chung hui-chan,* passim.

172. Bōeichō, *Ichigō Sakusen (1) Kōnan no kaisen,* p. 600; Bōeichō, *Ichigō Sakusen (2) Kōnan no kaisen,* p. 175; Bōeichō, *Ichigō Sakusen (3) Keisei no kaisen,* pp. 685–86.

173. Aoi shinichi, *Taiheiyō sensō,* part 2, pp. 249–52; Tuchman, *Stilwell,* pp. 533–80.

174. Romanus and Sunderland, *Time Runs Out in CBI,* p. 368 and p. 372, table 6.

Chapter 3

1. Donald Gillin, "Problems of Centralization in Republican China: The Case of Ch'en Ch'eng and the Kuomintang," *Journal of Asian Studies* 24, no. 4 (August, 1970):835–50; Hsi-sheng Ch'i, *Warlord Politics in China, 1916–1928* (Stanford, Calif., 1976), pp. 66–68.

2. Yu-chün, "Sui-yüan yu yu nien ssu nien," *Ch'un ch'iu,* no. 58 (December 1, 1959):5–7; Li T'ien-lin, "Ts'ung hang-wu chiang-chün Wan Fu-lin shuo ch'i," *Chuan-chi wen-hsüeh* 21, no. 5 (November, 1972):58–59.

3. As Chiang's deputy, General Liu Chih, recalled, "The troops I found under my command in this campaign were very complicated, with different histories, and diverse equipment. . . . as this was the first time they participated in anti-Japanese war, the old grudges remained, which created difficulties in insuring the obedience to commands or even efforts at coordination." See Liu Chih, *Wo ti hui-i* (Taipei, 1966), p. 148.

4. Chang Kan-p'ing, *K'ang Jih ming-chiang Kuan Lin-cheng* (Hong Kong, 1969), pp. 102–3.

5. Donald G. Gillin, *Warlord: Yen Hsi-shan in Shansi Province, 1911–1949* (Princeton, N.J., 1967), pp. 258–59.

6. Feng Yü-hsiang's report, dated October 13, 1937, in Kuo-fang-pu, *KJCS: Chin-P'u t'ieh-lu pei-tuan yüan-hsien chih tso-chan,* pp. 15–19, 87–88, 97–99.

7. Shortly after the outbreak of the war, Liu Hsiang of Szechwan and Lung Yün

of Yünnan both sought to dissuade Kwangsi leaders from joining the Nanking government's rank. They feared that Chiang might use the war as a pretext to seize Kwangsi and thereby endanger their own provinces. See Li Tsung-jen, *The Memoirs of Li Tsung-jen* (Boulder, Colo., 1978), p. 321.

8. Ch'en Ch'eng, *Ti-erh-ch'i k'ang-chan kuan-yü cheng-hsün kung-tso chih chih-shih* (n.p., 1938), p. 117.

9. Ibid., pp. 53–62, Ch'en Ch'eng's speech of November 29, 1938.

√ 10. For sequence of events, see Liu Shao-t'ang, *MKTS*, vol. 1, pp. 581–608.

11. Frank Dorn, *The Sino-Japanese War, 1937–41: From Marco Polo Bridge to Pearl Harbor* (New York, 1974), p. 321.

12. Kuo-fang-pu, *KJCS: erh-shih-pa-nien tung-chi kung-shih*, pp. 25–26.

13. Ibid., pp. 581–86; CKS, *Chiang tsung-t'ung chi*, vol. 1, p. 1228.

14. CKS, *Chiang tsung-t'ung chi*, vol. 1, p. 1228.

15. Kuo-fang-pu, *KJCS: erh-shih-pa-nien tung-chi kung-shih*, pp. 581–86.

16. Bōeichō, *Hokushi no chiansen*, vol. 1, supplement, chart 7.

17. Charles F. Romanus and Riley Sunderland, *Stilwell's Mission to China* (Washington, D.C., 1953), p. 35; F. F. Liu, *A Military History of Modern China, 1924–1949* (Princeton, N.J., 1956), p. 134.

18. Kao Yin-tsu, *Chung-hua min-kuo ta-shih-chi* (Taipei, 1957), pp. 483, 484–85, 487.

19. Ibid., pp. 488–96.

20. C. Martin Wilbur and Julie Lien-ying How, eds., *Documents on Communism, Nationalism, and Soviet Advisers in China, 1918–1927* (New York, 1956), pp. 200–202.

21. Ibid., p. 200.

22. Huang Shao-hung, *Wu shih hui i* (Hangchow, 1945), vol. 1, pp. 123–26.

23. Wu Hsiang-hsiang, *Min-kuo pai-jen chuan* (Taipei, 1971), vol. 4, pp. 257–68.

24. William L. Tung, *Revolutionary China: A Personal Account, 1926–1949* (New York, 1973), p. 172.

25. Chün-shih wei-yüan-hui, *Chün-tui cheng-chih kung-tso chiang-i kang-yao* (Chungking, 1940), pp. 1–4.

26. Wu Hsiang-hsiang, *Min-kuo pai-jen chuan*, vol. 4, pp. 257–68; ibid.

√ 27. Chung-kuo Kuo-ming-tang (hereafter KMT), Department of Organization, *Pa-nien lai chih chün-tui tang-wu* (Nanking, 1946), pp. 1–2, 9–13.

28. Ibid., pp. 18–20, 33–35.

29. Ibid., p. 8.

30. KMT, Central Executive Committee, *Chung-yang hsün-lien-t'uan tang-cheng hsün-lien-pan kung-tso t'ao-lun tzu-liao hsüan-lu tseng-pien* (Chungking, 1943), p. 36.

31. Ch'en Ch'eng, *Ti-erh-ch'i k'ang-chan kuan-yü cheng hsün kung-tso chih chih-shih*, pp. 7–17; Chang Chih-chung, *Chün-shih-wei-yüan-hui cheng-chih-pu kung-tso kai-k'uang* (Chungking, 1945), pp. 1–2.

32. KMT, Department of Organization, *Pa-nien lai chih chün-tui tang-wu*, pp. 122–23.

33. Chang Chih-chung, *Cheng-chih-pu kung-tso*, pp. 1–2.

34. For illustrations, see Lu-chün hsin-pien ti-san-shih-chinn-shih, *Lu-chün hsin-pien ti-san-shih-chiu-shih kai-k'uang* (n.p., 1943).
35. *The Amerasia Papers: A Clue to the Catastrophe of China* (Washington, D.C., 1970), vol. 1, no. 111, pp. 654–55; Li Tsung-jen, *Memoirs,* p. 322.
36. Conversation with General P. Y. Hu, June 17, 1976, at Taipei, Taiwan.
37. Bōeichō, *Daihonkan Rikusōbu,* vol. 4, pp. 195–96.
38. For examples, see *Ch'üan-kuo chün-tui tang-pu chu-ti-piao* (n.p., 1943).
39. The Chargé in China, Atcheson, to the Secretary of State, no. 1528, August 31, 1943, 740.0011 Pacific War/3450: Telegram, *Foreign Relations of the United States, Diplomatic Papers: 1943, China,* (Washington, D.C., 1957), pp. 108–9.
40. Gillin, *Yen Hsi-shan in Shansi,* pp. 279–82.
41. Kuo-fang-pu, *Lu-chün chün-kuan hsüeh-hsiao hsiao-shih,* pt. 3, pp. 431–580.
42. Theodore H. White, ed., *The Stilwell Papers* (New York, 1962), p. 132; Barbara W. Tuchman, *Stilwell and the American Experience in China, 1911–1945* (New York, 1970), pp. 390–94.
43. White, *The Stilwell Papers,* p. 180.
44. Charles F. Romanus and Riley Sunderland, *Stilwell's Command Problems* (Washington, D.C., 1956), pp. 63–4.
45. Tuchman, *Stilwell,* p. 601.
46. Generalissimo Chiang Kai-shek to President Roosevelt, July 8, 1944, *Foreign Relations of the United States, Diplomatic Papers: 1944, China* (Washington, D.C., 1967), vol. 4, pp. 120–21.
47. President Roosevelt to Generalissimo Chiang Kai-shek, August 21, 1944, ibid., p. 149.
48. President Roosevelt to Generalissimo Chiang Kai-shek, September 16, 1944, ibid., p. 157.
49. Romanus and Sunderland, *Stilwell's Mission to China,* pp. 234–35.
50. Ibid., p. 225.
51. Romanus and Sunderland, *Stilwell's Command Problems,* p. 26.
52. Romanus and Sunderland, *Stilwell's Mission to China,* p. 296.
53. Ibid., p. 301.
54. Charles F. Romanus and Riley Sunderland, *Time Runs Out in CBI* (New York, 1958), p. 63, 68, 232.
55. Ibid., p. 233.
56. Ibid., p. 235, 242–47.
57. Ibid., pp. 333–6.
58. The Chargé in China, Atcheson, to the Secretary of State, no. 1194, May 18, 1943, 893.105/94, *Foreign Relations, 1943, China,* pp. 236–37.
59. The Chargé in China, Atcheson, to the Secretary of State, no. 1741, September 17, 1943, 893.00/15124: Telegram, *Foreign Relations, 1943, China,* p. 340; The Ambassador in China, Gauss, to the Secretary of State, no. 2030, January 15, 1944, 893.00/15254, *Foreign Relations, 1944, China,* pp. 305–7.
60. The Ambassador in China, Gauss, to the Secretary of State: no. 2118, Feb-

ruary 3, 1944, 893.00/15273; no. 2030, January 15, 1944, 893.00/15254; no. 151, January 24, 1944, 893.00/15241: Telegram; no. 2161, February 15, 1944, 893.00/19279, all in *Foreign Relations, 1944, China*, pp. 305-7, 312-13, 319-26, 334-45.

61. The Ambassador in China, Gauss, to the Secretary of State, no. 1829, November 18, 1943, 893.00/15197, *Foreign Relations, 1943, China*, pp. 380-82.

62. Ringwalt memo to Ambassador Gauss, July 6, 1944, 893.00/7-644, enclosure, *Foreign Relations, 1944, China*, pp. 466-68.

63. The consul at Kweilin, Ringwalt, to the Ambassador in China, Gauss, no. 112, May 8, 1944, 893.00/15420, *Foreign Relations, 1944, China*, pp. 414-15.

64. The Ambassador in China, Gauss, to the Secretary of State: no. 1385, August 10, 1944, 893.00/8-1044: Telegram; no. 1416, August 16, 1944, 893.00/8-1644: Telegram; no. 2900, August 23, 1944, 893.00/8-2344, *Foreign Relations, 1944, China*, pp. 505-6, 509-10, 512-15.

65. Romanus and Sunderland, *Stilwell's Command Problems*, p. 411; *Amerasia Papers*, vol. 1, no. 137, pp. 778-86.

66. Romanus and Sunderland, *Stilwell's Command Problems*, p. 410; In a 1952 interview, Marshal Hata and General Okamura, both commanders-in-chief of the China Expeditionary Army, confirmed this report, see Romanus and Sunderland, *Time Runs Out in CBI*, pp. 8-9.

67. *Amerasia Papers*, vol. 2, no. 226, p. 1244.

68. Ibid., vol. 1, no. 66, pp. 426-27.

69. The consul at Kunming, Ringwalt, to the Secretary of State, A-10, March 9, 1944, 893.5151/990: Airgram, *Foreign Relations, 1944, China*, pp. 374-75.

70. Langdon to State Department, October 19, 1944, no. 94, 740.0011 Pacific War/10-1944, *Foreign Relations, 1944, China*, pp. 175-76.

71. Richard M. Service to Hurley, January 20, 1945, 740.0011 P.W./1-2045, *Foreign Relations, 1945, China*, pp. 178-80.

72. Ibid.; The Consul General at Kunming, Langdon, to the Secretary of State, no. 94, October 19, 1944, 740.0011 P.W./10-1944, *Foreign Relations, 1944, China*, pp. 175-76.

73. The Consul General at Kunming, Langdon, to the Ambassador in China, Gauss, no. 35, August 18, 1944, 740.0011 P.W./8-1844, *Foreign Relations, 1944, China*, pp. 144-45.

74. *Amerasia Papers*, vol. 2, no. 233, pp. 1261-63.

75. Ibid., vol. 1, no. 111, pp. 654-55.

76. The Second Secretary of Embassy in China, Penfield, to the Secretary of State, no. 53, October 28, 1944, 893.00/10-2844, *Foreign Relations, 1944, China*, pp. 660-61.

77. Paul Frillman and Graham Peck, *China, the Remembered Life* (Boston, 1968), p. 224; *Amerasia Papers*, vols. 1, 2, nos. 112, 233, pp. 656-62, 1261-63.

78. Huang Shao-hung, *Wu-shih hui-i*, vol. 2, pp. 338-39, 345-47; Tetsuya Kataoka, *Resistance and Revolution in China: The Communists and the*

Second United Front (Berkeley, Calif., 1974), p. 63; Hu Hua, *Chung-kuo hsin-min-chu chu-i ke-ming shih ts'an-k'ao tzu-liao,* as quoted in Wang Chien-min, *Chung-kuo Kung-ch'an-tang shih-kao* (Taipei, 1965), vol. 3, pp. 180–83; According to accusations made by Red Guards during the Cultural Revolution, P'eng Te-huai said in December, 1937, that the victory of P'inghsinkuan should belong to both the Communists and Chungking troops and that it was unfair to place too much blame on the government troops. See Ting Wang, ed., *P'eng Te-huai wen-t'i ch'üan-chi* (Hong kong, 1969), pp. 384–86.

79. *Mao Tse-tung hsüan-chi* (Peking, 1964), pp. 512–20, 527–28; Hsü Kuan-san, "Liu Shao-ch'i yü Mao Tse-tung," *Ming pao,* 1, no. 8 (August, 1966):65.

80. Wang Chien-min, *Chung-kuo Kung-ch'an-tang shih-kao* (Taipei, 1965), vol. 3, pp. 119–20.

81. Ibid., vol. 3, pp. 131–32.

82. Ibid., vol. 3, p. 131.

83. *Mao Tse-tung hsüan-chi,* pp. 525–28; Kataoka, *Resistance and Revolution in China,* pp. 136–37.

84. According to Red Guards accusation in 1967, P'eng Te-huai had defied Mao's policy of relying on the masses to establish revolutionary bases and wage guerrilla warfare by suggesting that mobile warfare conducted by regulars would make more sense. See Yu-lien ch'u-pan-she, *P'eng Te-huai* (Hong kong, 1969), pp. 123–24; Kataoka, *Resistance and Revolution in China,* pp. 70–71.

85. *Hsin-hua jih-pao,* Chungking edition, September 9, 1940, as quoted in Wang Chien-min, *Chung-kuo Kung-ch'an-tang shih-kao,* vol. 3, pp. 183–87.

86. Accusations made by the Ching-kang-shan Regiment of Ch'ing-hua University Red Guards in November, 1967, as quoted in Ting Wang, *P'eng Te-huai wen-t'i ch'üan-chi,* pp. 384–86; P'eng Te-huai's own admission can be found in ibid., p. 10; *Mao Tse-tung ssu-hsiang wan-sui,* (n.p., n.d.), p. 478; Kataoka, *Resistance and Revolution in China,* pp. 219–20.

87. Chung-hua pien-i-kuan, ed., *Wei-ta ti hsin Chung-kuo* (Chungking, 1939), p. 253.

88. Sheng-huo shu-tien, *Pao-wei Hua-pei ti yu-chi-chan* (Yenan, 1938), pp. 11–16.

89. Chiang K'e-fu, *K'ang Jih keng-chü-ti Lu-hsi-pei ch'ü* (n.p., 1939), pp. 11, 18–19, 25–28.

90. Ibid., pp. 13–17.

91. *Shan-tung sheng ti-shih-san-ch'ü k'ang-chan chi-shih* (n.p., 1940), no pagination.

92. Wang Wei-wen, *K'u-ts'eng en-kan ti Ho-pei min-chün* (Chungking, 1939), pp. 1–10; *Erh-nien lai chih Ho-pei tang-wu* (n.p., 1939), various pagination.

93. Pai Ch'ung-hsi's speech in *Wei-ta ti hsin Chung-kuo,* pp. 205–19.

94. Ch'iao Ming-li, *Ho-pei min-chün li-shih kai-yao* (n.p., 1941), no pagination.

95. Ch'en I-hsin, *Chung-kung tsai Ho-pei chih mien-mien kuan* (Lin-hsien,

Honan, 1940), pp. 6–26, 33–45, 58–562; Ho-pei min-chün tsung-chih-hui-pu, *Hsien-ke kuan-hsin Ho-pei wen-t'i ti p'eng-yu* (n.p., 1939), pp. 24–27.

96. Shen Hung-lieh, *Shan-tung tang-cheng-chün chiao-shou ta-kang* (n.p., 1941), pp. 59–63.

97. Ho Ying-ch'in, *Wartime Military Report,* vol. 1, pp. 242–43.

98. *Erh-nien lai chih Ho-pei tang-wu.*

99. Ch'en I-hsin, *Kai-chin Ho-pei sheng tang-wu i-chien-shu* (n.p., 1940).

100. Huang Shao-hung, *Wu-shih hui-i,* vol. 2, pp. 523–24; Huang Hsü-ch'u, "Chi Huang Shao-hung yü Chiang hsien-sheng kuan-hsi shih-mo," *Ch'un ch'iu,* no. 306 (April 1, 1970):23–26; Kuo Chi-t'ang, *Chung-kuo lu-chün ti-san-fang-mien-chün k'ang-chan chi-shih* (Taipei, 1962), p. 243; For a personal account of the problem of governing an occupied area, see Len Hsin, "Ts'ung ts'an-chia k'ang-chan tao mu-tu Jih-chün t'ou-hsiang," *Chuan-chi wen-hsüeh* 5, no. 1 (July, 1964):42.

101. Ch'en I-hsin, *Kai-chin Ho-pei sheng tang-wu i-chien shu.*

102. Liu Shao-t'ang, *MKTS,* vol. 1, p. 623.

103. Kung-lun ch'u-pan-she, *Chung-kung chih mi-mi chün-shih kung-tso* (n.p., 1941), pp. 3–9, 13–38.

104. *Mao Tse-tung hsüan-chi,* pp. 488–502.

105. Ibid., p. 540.

106. Ibid., p. 541.

107. Ibid., p. 946.

108. KMT, Bureau of Statistics, *Chung-kuo Kung-ch'an-tang wu-li t'ung-chi* (Chungking, 1940), pp. 1–8; idem, *Chung-kung chih chün-tui tsu-chih yü yün-yung* (Chungking, 1940), pu-6.

109. Chang Yüan-shou, *Min-ping kung-tso hsüan-chi* (CCP Central China Bureau, 1942), pp. 1–3; *Amerasia Papers,* vol. 2, no. 246, pp. 1329–36, report by Raymond P. Ludden, dated February 12, 1945; Chu Te, "Lun chieh-fang ch'ü chan-ch'ang," in Li Chin, *Chan-tou chung ti chieh-fang-ch'ü min-ping* (n.p., n.d.), pp. 23–24.

110. Li Chin, *Chan-tou chung ti chieh-fang-ch'ü min-ping,* pp. 3–4, 91–92.

111. Numerous titles are in the holdings of the Bureau of Investigation, Ministry of Justice, at Hsin-tien, Taiwan.

112. *Amerasia Papers,* vol. 1, no. 11, pp. 166–73.

113. *Mao Tse-tung hsüan-chi,* pp. 881–84.

114. Ho Lung, *Ho Lung tsai pien-ch'ü kao-kan-hui pao-kao* (n.p., 1944), pp. 6–13; Liu Yen-te, *Cheng-tun san-feng ts'an-k'ao ts'ai-liao* (Yenan, n.d.), pp. 19–31.

115. Lin Piao, *Chin-nien tseng-yang lien-ping* (T'ai-hang Military District, 1944), pp. 1–3.

116. Ibid., pp. 5–6.

117. Ibid., pp. 5–6, 8–10.

118. Ibid., pp. 17–78.

119. Ibid., p. 20.

120. Ibid., pp. 24–25, 27–31.

121. *Amerasia Papers,* vol. 2, no. 218, pp. 1204-10.
122. Ibid., vol. 2, no. 250, pp. 1342-45.
123. Ibid., vol. 1, no. 140, pp. 800-806.
124. *Mao Tse-tung hsüan-chi,* p. 1039.
125. Romanus and Sunderland, *Stilwell's Mission to China,* p. 368; Tuchman, *Stilwell,* p. 495.
126. *Kuo Kung liang-tang k'ang-chan ch'eng-chi ti pi-chiao* (Yenan, 1943), pp. 1-30; Sheng-huo shu-tien, ed., *Chung-kuo ti-hou k'ang Jih min-chu keng-chü-ti kai-k'uang* (Yenan, 1944), passim; The Ambassador in China, Gauss, to the Secretary of State, no. 2814, July 29, 1944, 740.0011 Pacific War/7-2944, *Foreign Relations, 1944, China,* pp. 489-90; *Amerasia papers,* vols. 1, 2, nos. 43, 141, 186, pp. 320-30, 806-17, 1069-79.
127. Joseph W. Esherick, *Lost Chance in China: The World War II Dispatches of John S. Service* (New York, 1974), pp. 49-56.
128. In a talk with Hurley at Yenan on November 8, 1944, Mao claimed that out of the KMT's 1,950,000 troops, 779,000 were used to blockade the CCP, while all CCP troops were deployed against the Japanese. See "Memorandum of Conversation, Yenan," November 8, 1944, 893.00/1-1049, *Foreign Relations, 1944, China,* p. 682; *Amerasia Papers,* vol. 2, no. 186, pp. 1069-79.
129. *Amerasia Papers,* vol. 1, no. 122(d), pp. 706-8.
130. Chiang Ching-kuo, *Wo ti fu-ch'ing* (Taipei, 1959), pp. 34-35.
131. Tuchman, *Stilwell,* p. 619.
132. Kataoka, *Resistance and Revolution in China,* p. 144.
133. The Ambassador in China, Gauss, to the Secretary of State, no. 1764, November 2, 1943, 893.00/15181, *Foreign Relations, 1943, China,* pp. 372-73.
134. Mao Tse-tung, *Mao Tse-tung hsüan-chi,* ed. Chung-kung chung-yang Mao Tse-tung hsüan-chi ch'u-pan wei-yüan-hui, "Interview with the British Journalist James Betram," pp. 363-76; ibid., "The Situation and Tasks in the Anti-Japanese War after the Fall of Shanghai and T'aiyüan," pp. 377-90.
135. Ibid., "Problems of Strategy in Guerilla War Against Japan," pp. 395-428; ibid., "On Protracted War," pp. 429-506; ibid., "The Role of the Chinese Communist Party in the National War," pp. 507-24; ibid., "Problems of War and Strategy," pp. 529-44.
136. Ibid., "The Question of Independence and Initiative within the United Front," pp. 525-28; ibid., "Oppose Capitulationist Activity," pp. 559-63.
137. Ibid., "The Chinese Revolution and the Chinese Communist Party," pp. 615-50.
138. Ibid., "Freely Expand the Anti-Japanese Forces and Resist the Onslaught of the Anti-Communist Die-hards," pp. 749-54; ibid., "Order and Statement on the Southern Anhwei Incident," pp. 769-76; ibid., "Some Pointed Questions for the Kuomintang," pp. 905-12.
139. For a recent analysis of the Chinese Communist mode of government during the war, see Mark Selden, *The Yenan Way in Revolutionary China* (Cambridge, Mass., 1971).

Chapter 4

1. Nei-cheng-pu, *Ko sheng shih-shih hsien ko-chi tsu-chih kang-yao ch'eng-chi tsung-pao-kao t'i-yao,* (Chungking, 1943), pp. 1–11.
2. For a detailed discussion of all the functions assigned to the *hsien*, see Li Tsung-huang, *Hsin-hsien-chih chiang-yen-chi* (Chungking, 1939), pp. 11–19.
3. Chang Wei-han, *Ko sheng shih-shih hsin-hsien-chih chih chien-t'ao* (Chungking, 1944), pp. 1–3; Li Tsung-huang, *Li Tsung-huang hui-i-lu,* (Taipei, 1972), vol. 1, pp. 144–45.
4. Nei-cheng-pu, *Ko sheng shih-shih hsien ko-chi tsu-chih kang-yao ch'eng-chi tsung-pao-kao t'i-yao,* passim.
5. Ibid., p. 1–11; Huang Shao-hung, *Wu-shih hui-i,* (Hangchow, 1945), vol. 20, pp. 441–44; Nei-cheng-pu, *Ti-san-tz'u ch'üan-kuo nei-cheng hui-i pao-kao-shu* (Chungking, 1942), pp. 97–116.
6. Chang Ch'ün, speech of July 26, 1941, in his *Chang Yüeh-chün hsien-sheng tsai Ch'uan yen-lun hsüan-chi* (Taipei, 1968), pp. 51–60.
7. Ibid., pp. 371–77.
8. Chang Wei-han, *Ko-sheng shih-shih hsin-hsien-chih chih chien-t'ao,* pp. 1–10; Nei-cheng-pu, *Ko-sheng shih-shih hsien ko-chi tsu-chih kang-yao ch'eng-chi tsung-pao-kao t'i-yao,* pp. 1–11.
9. Ts'ai-cheng-pu, *Ti-san-tz'u ch'üan-kuo ts'ai-cheng hui-i hui-pien* (reprint ed., Taipei, 1972), pt. 1, pp. 3–4.
10. Ibid., pt. 1, p. 143.
11. Ts'ao Kuo-ch'ing, *Chung-kuo ts'ai-cheng wen-t'i yü li-fa* (Shanghai, 1947), pp. 182, 188–89.
12. Ibid., pp. 192–93.
13. Ts'ai-cheng-pu, *Ti-san-tz'u ch'üan-kuo ts'ai-cheng hui-i hui-pien,* pt. 2, pp. 108–12.
14. These included telegraphic and telephone services, railways, etc. See Ch'en T'ien-hsi, *Tai Chi-t'ao hsien-sheng pien-nien ch'üan-chi* (Taipei, 1958), passim.
15. Ibid.
16. Ibid.
17. Ch'en T'ien-hsi, *Tai Chi-t'ao hsien-sheng ti sheng-p'ing* (Taipei, 1968), pp. 427–503; idem, *Tai Chi-t'ao hsien-sheng pien-nien ch'üan-chi* (Taipei, 1958).
18. Ch'en T'ien-hsi, *Tai Chi-t'ao hsien-sheng pien-nien ch'üan-chi.*
19. Wang Te-fu, *Hsin-hsien-chih chih chien-t'ao yü kai-chin* (Chungking, 1944), pp. 1–38.
20. Ibid.
21. Ibid., table 6.
22. KMT, Bureau of Statistics, *Chung-kuo Kuo-min-tang tang-wu t'ung-chi chi-yao, 1944* (Chungking, 1944), p. 57, table 59.

23. Wang Te-fu, *Hsin-hsien-chih chih chien-t'ao yü kai-chin*, pp. 1–38.

24. Liu Chih-fan, "Hsin-hsien-chih chih shih-shih wen-t'i," in Kuang-tung sheng-cheng-fu, *Hsin-hsien-chih yen-chiu* (n.p., 1940), pp. 86–93.

25. Chang Ch'ün, *Chang Yüeh-chün hsien-sheng tsai Ch'uan yen-lu hsüan-chi* (Taipei, 1968), pp. 152–53.

26. Hsing-cheng-yüan, *Hsing-cheng ts'an-k'ao t'ung-chi tzu-liao* (Chungking, 1944); Nei-cheng-pu, *Ti-san-tz'u ch'üan-kuo nei-cheng hui-i pao-kao-shu*, "Report by the Deputy Minister of Interior," p. 71.

27. Nei-cheng-pu, *Shen-hsüan hsien-chang* (Nanking, 1929), pp. 1–4.

28. Ch'en T'ien-hsi, *Tai Chi-t'ao hsien-sheng ti sheng-p'ing*, pp. 496–97.

29. Hsing-cheng-yüan, *Hsing-cheng-yüan kung-tso pao-kao* (Chungking, 1942), *nei-cheng* pp. 1–3; Tang-cheng kung-tso k'ao-he wei-yüan-hui, *Tang-cheng kung-tso k'ao-he wei-yüan-hui san shih-nien san-shih-i-nien-tu ko sheng cheng-wu k'ao-ch'a pao-kao tsung-p'ing* (n.p., 1942), *Hu-nan sheng*.

30. Wang Te-fu, *Hsin-hsien-chih chih chien-t'ao yü kai-chin*, pp. 1–38.

31. Ibid.; Interview with Mr. Cheng-hsing Ch'i, May 6, 1976, concerning the situation in Kiangsi.

32. Thus, Governor Wu T'ieh-ch'eng of Kwangtung testified in 1939 that of the *hsien* magistrate appointments he made during his tenure, only 10 percent were his own choices; the rest were forced upon him by other powerful figures. See Chu Cheng-sheng, *Li Han-hun chiang-chün jih-chi* (Hong kong, 1975), vol. 1, pt. 1, p. 239. His successor, Governor Li Han-hun also complained in 1940 that he felt enormous pressure in personnel matters and said in 1943 again that "*hsien* magistrate appointments were the most troublesome matter to handle." Ibid., vol. 1, pt. 1, p. 261, and pt. 2, p. 49.

33. Li Tsung-huang, *Hui-i-lu*, vol. 1, p. 238.

34. Ssu-ch'uan sheng-cheng-fu, *Ssu-ch'uan sheng min-cheng t'ung-chi* (n.p., 1941), p. 13.

35. In Chekiang, for instance, *hsien* cadres were paid only one-quarter of the salaries of provincial cadres. See Huang Shao-hung, *Wu shih hui i*, pp. 441–44; Hu-nan sheng-cheng-fu, *Hu-nan sheng sa-nien-tu tang-cheng-chün lien-ho shih-ch'a-tsu shih-ch'a ko-hsien tsung-chien-t'ao* (n.p., 1942), pp. 16–19.

36. Nei-cheng-pu, *Ti-san-tz'u ch'üan-kuo nei-cheng hui-i pao-kao-shu*, p. 98; Chang Ch'ün, *Tsai Ch'uan yen-lun hsüan-chi*, pp. 371–77; Ssu-ch'uan sheng-cheng-fu, *Ssu-ch'uan sheng min-cheng t'ung-chi*, p. 13.

37. In Szechwan, during 1936–40, out of a total of 125 *hsien* magistrates, 52 had served for less than six months, and another 23 had served for less than twelve months. In 1940 alone, some 93 *hsien* magistrates were removed from office; Ssu-ch'uan sheng-cheng-fu, *Ssu-ch'uan sheng min-cheng t'ung-chi*, passim.

38. Wu Ting-ch'ang, *Hua-hsi hsien-pi hsü-pien* (Kweiyang, 1943), pp. 37–43.

39. Nei-cheng-pu, *Ti-san-tz'u ch'üan-kuo nei-cheng hui-i pao-kao-shu*, p. 100.

40. *Ti-san-tz'u ch'üan-kuo ts'ai-cheng hui-i hui-pien*, pt. 3, p. 67.

41. Ibid., pt. 2, pp. 91–102.

42. For description of very poor training in Szechwan, see *Tang-cheng kung-tso*

k'ao-he wei-yüan-hui san-shih-nien san-shih-i-nien-tu ko sheng cheng-wu k'ao-ch'a pao-kao tsung-p'ing (n.p., 1942).

43. Ssu-ch'uan sheng-cheng-fu, *Ssu-ch'uan sheng min-cheng t'ung-chi*, p. 36.

44. Hu-nan sheng-cheng-fu, *Hu-nan sheng sa-nien tu tang-cheng-chün lien-ho shih-ch'a-tsu shih-ch'a ko-hsien tsung-chien-t'ao*, p. 22.

45. Sun Fo's speech on April 3, 1944, translated in *Amerasia Papers*, vol. 1, no. 91, pp. 535–50.

46. For a general discussion of these regimes, see C. Martin Wilbur, "Military Separatism and the Process of Reunification Under the Nationalist Regime, 1922–1937," in *China in Crisis*, ed. Ho Ping-ti and Tsou Tang (Chicago, 1968), vol. 1, bk. 1, pp. 203–63; For some case studies of regimes in southwestern China, see Diana Lary, *Region and Nation: The Kwangsi Clique in Chinese Politics, 1925–1937* (Cambridge, Mass., 1974); Robert A. Kapp, *Szechwan and the Chinese Republic: Provincial Militarism and Central Power, 1911–1938* (New Haven, Conn., 1973); and John Christopher S. Hall, *The Yünnan Provincial Faction, 1927–1937* (Canberra, Australia, 1976).

47. Kung-chuan Hsiao, *Rural China: Imperial Control in the Nineteenth Century* (Seattle, Wash., 1960).

48. For some relevant discussions, see Wang Gunwu, "Nationalism in China Before 1949," in *China: The Impact of Revolution—A Survey of Twentieth Century China*, ed. Colin Mackerras (Essex, England, 1976), pp. 46–58; Joseph R. Levenson, "The Province, the Nation, and the World: The Problem of Chinese Identity," in *Approaches to Modern Chinese History*, ed. Albert Feuerwerker, Rhoads Murphey, and Mary Wright (Berkeley, Calif., 1976), pp. 268–88.

49. Franz Michael, "Military Organization and Power Structure of China During the Taiping Rebellion," *Pacific Historical Review* 18, no. 4 (November, 1949):478–83.

50. John Fincher, "Political Provincialism and the National Revolution," in *China in Revolution: The First Phase, 1900–1913*, ed. Mary C. Wright (New Haven, Conn., 1968), pp. 185–226.

51. For occasional exceptions, see Donald G. Gillin, *Warlord: Yen Hsi-shan in Shansi Province* (Princeton, N.J., 1967); Lary, *Region and Nation;* and Gavan McCormack, *Chang Tso-lin in Northeast China, 1911–1928* (Stanford, Calif., 1977).

52. Chang Hsiao-mei, *Ssu-ch'uan ching-chi ts'an-k'ao tzu-liao* (Shanghai, 1939), pts. b, c.

53. Chang Ch'ün, *Tsai Ch'uan yen-lun hsüan-chi*, pp. 23–24, 253–55; For general discussion, see Kapp, *Szechwan and the Chinese Republic.*

54. *Amerasia Papers*, vol. 2, no. 259, pp. 1359–63.

55. KMT, Bureau of Statistics, *Tang-cheng ch'ing-pao* (n.p., 1945–46), entry of August 14, 1945.

56. Chang Ch'ün, *Tsai Ch'uan yen-lun hsüan-chi*, p. 29.

57. Ibid., p. 219.

58. Ibid., pp. 308–9, 371–77.

59. Joseph F. Esherick, *Lost Chance in China, The World War II Dispatches of John S. Service* (New York, 1974), p. 132.

60. For a general discussion of power distribution in the provinces, see KMT, Central Executive Committee, *Chung-yang hsün-lien-t'uan tang-cheng hsün-lien-pan kung-tso t'ao-lun tzu-liao hsüan-lu tseng-pien* (Chungking, 1943), passim. For discussion of power distribution by province, see: for Kwangtung—Li Han-hun, "Meng hui chi," *Ch'un ch'iu,* no. 354 (April 1, 1972):30–33; for Kwangsi—Huang Hsü-ch'un, "Pa-nien k'ang-chan hui-i-lu," *Ch'un ch'iu,* no. 81 (November 16, 1960):2–4; for Anhwei, Kiangsu, Shantung—KMT, Bureau of Statistics, *Tang-cheng ch'ing-pao;* for Anhwei, Hupei—Nei-cheng-pu, *Ti-san-tz'u ch'üan-kuo nei-cheng hui-i pao-kao-shu.*

61. Tung-tsu Ch'u, *Local Government in China Under the Ch'ing* (Stanford, Calif., 1969), pp. 168–69, 180–92.

62. Fei Hsiao-tung, *China's Gentry* (Chicago, 1953), p. 81.

63. A. Doak Barnett, *China on the Eve of Communist Takeover* (New York, 1966), p. 136.

64. William Hinton, *Fanshen: A Documentary of Revolution in a Chinese Village* (New York, 1966), pp. 46–54; Barnett, *Communist Takeover,* pp. 103–54.

65. Feng Ho-fa, *Chung-kuo nung-ts'un ching-chi tzu-liao* (reprint ed., Taipei, 1978), pp. 836–37. Feng's data on the Chengtu plains showed that 5 percent of farmers controlled 43 percent of the land (pp. 163–65). His data on various parts of China indicated that absentee landlords usually had much larger holdings than landlords who stayed in their native places, and that the tenancy rate was about 40 percent of rural labor (pp. 102–3, 129–31).

66. Tung-tsu Ch'u, *Local Government,* p. 170.

67. Ibid., p. 171.

68. For some indications of the intrusion of outsiders into the gentry, see the biographies of gentry members in Yung-teh Chow, *Social Mobilization in China: Status Careers Among the Gentry in a Chinese Community* (New York, 1966); Feng Ho-fa, *Chung-kuo nung-ts'un ching-chi tzu-liao,* pp. 836–37.

69. Fei Hsiao-tung, *China's Gentry,* pp. 173–202; Also C. K. Yang, *A Chinese Village in Early Communist Transition* (Cambridge, Mass., 1959), pp. 109–14; and C. Martin Wilbur, "Military Separatism and the Process of Reunification Under the Nationalist Regime, 1922–1937," in Ho Ping-ti and Tang Tsou, ed., *China in Crisis* (Chicago, 1968), vol. 1, bk. 1, pp. 204–8.

70. Wu Ting-ch'ang, *Hua-hsi hsien-pi hsü-pien* (Kweiyang, 1943), pp. 74–77; For a revealing portrait of the viciousness of a commander of public safety of a county and the violence that pervaded the affairs of that county, see Fei Hsiao-tung, *China's Gentry,* pp. 242–68; For an interesting discussion of one particular aspect of secret society activities, see Jonathan Marshall, "Opium and the Politics of Gangsterism in Nationalist China, 1927–1945," *Bulletin of Concerned Asian Scholars* 8, no. 3 (July–September, 1976):19–48.

71. Chang Hsiao-mei, *Ssu-ch'uan ching-chi ts'an-k'ao tzu-liao* (Shanghai, 1939), A-26; Tai Chi-t'ao also reported that 70 to 80 percent of formerly

public-owned land in many localities was sold in the decade of 1914–24 to private citizens, contributing to the rise of new landlords and the erosion of the county tax base; see Ch'en T'ien-hsi, *Tai Chi-t'ao hsien-sheng wen-ts'un* (Taipei, 1958), vol. 1, p. 25.

72. Feng Ho-fa, *Chung-kuo nung-ts'un ching-chi tzu-liao*, pp. 824–35; Chang Hsiao-mei, *Ssu-ch'uan ching-chi ts'an-k'ao tzu-liao*, M-1-16, M-48.
73. Wu Ting-ch'ang, *Hua-hsi hsien-pi* (Kweiyang, 1940), p. 112; Also his *Hua-hsi hsien-pi hsü-pien*, pp. 77–78.
74. Chu Cheng-sheng, *Li Han-hun chiang-chün jih-chi* (Hong kong, 1975), vol. 1, pt. 1, passim.
75. Ch'en Kuo-fu, *Ch'en Kuo-fu hsien-sheng ch'üan-chi* (Taipei, 1952), vol. 5, p. 192.
76. Li Tsung-huang, *Li Tsung-huang hui-i-lu* (Taipei, 1972), vol. 3, p. 230.
77. Lary, *Region and Nation*, pp. 177–78.
78. Li Tsung-huang, *Hui-i-lu*, vol. 4, pp. 94–95.
79. Ibid., vol. 4, pp. 93–94, 98.
80. Ibid., vol. 4, p. 97.
81. Ibid., vol. 4, pp. 102–5.
82. CKS, *Chiang tsung-t'ung chi* (Taipei, 1960), vol. 1, p. 1330; Paul K. T. Sih, *The Strenuous Decade: China's Nation-Building Efforts, 1927–1937* (New York, 1970), p. 103.
83. Kuo Huan, *Chan-shih t'ien-fu cheng-li wen-t'i* (Chungking, 1942), pp. 1–8; Hsü Chien-nung, *Tsui-chin Ssu-ch'uan ts'ai-cheng lun* (Chungking, 1940), pp. 98–100.
84. Chu Tzu-shuang, *Chung-kuo Kuo-min-tang liang-shih cheng-ts'e* (n.p., 1944), pp. 81–82.
85. Ibid., pp. 65–66.
86. Hsü K'an, *Liang-shih wen-t'i* (n.p., 1942), p. 7.
87. Kuo Huan, *Chan-shih t'ien-fu cheng-li wen-t'i*, pp. 14–20.
88. Hsü K'an, *Liang-shih wen-t'i*, pp. 8–11.
89. Chu Tzu-shuang, *Liang-shih cheng-ts'e*, pp. 53–76.
90. Ts'ao Kuo-ch'ing, *Chung-kuo ts'ai-cheng wen-t'i yü li-fa* (Shanghai, 1947), pp. 30–31.
91. Ts'ai-cheng-pu, *Ts'ai-cheng nien-chien hsü-pien* (Chungking, 1942), pp. 81–82; Hsü Chien-nung, *Tsui-chin Ssu-ch'uan ts'ai-cheng lun*, pp. 119–20.
92. Arthur N. Young, *China's Wartime Finance and Inflation, 1937–1945* (Cambridge, Mass., 1965), p. 22.
93. Ts'ao Kuo-ch'ing, *Chung-kuo ts'ai-cheng wen-t'i yü li-fa*, p. 33.
94. Among the provinces, Kweichow seemed to offer the worst case, as its land tax had been collected since the late Ch'ing dynasty on the basis of households and not on land ownership at all. In 1936, Kweichow's land tax was less than one-thirtieth of that of Kiangsu. See Fang Hsien-t'ing, ed., *Chan-shih Chung-kuo ching-chi yen-chiu* (Chungking, 1941), pp. 162–65.
95. Hsü Chien-nung, *Tsui-chin Ssu-ch'uan ts'ai-cheng lun*, pp. 90–196; Chang Ch'ün, *Tsai Ch'uan yen-lun hsüan-chi*, pp. 275–77.
96. "Liang-shih-pu san-shih-nien tu kung-tso ch'eng-chi k'ao-ch'a pao-kao

tsung-p'ing,'' in *Tang-cheng kung-tso k'ao-he wei-yüan-hui san-shih-nien-tu chung-yang ko chi-kuan kung-tso ch'eng-chi k'ao-ch'a pao-kao tsung-p'ing* (n.p., n.d.).

97. For a discussion of the *t'an k'uan* system, see Hsi-sheng Ch'i, *Warlord Politics in China, 1916–1928* (Stanford, Calif., 1976), p. 166.

98. Hsü K'an, *Hsü K'o-t'ing hsien-sheng wen-ts'un* (Taipei, 1970), pp. 200–203.

99. Ibid.

100. Hu-nan sheng-cheng-fu, *Hu-nan sheng sa-nien-tu tang-cheng-chün lien-ho shih-ch'a-tsu shih-ch'a ko-hsien tsung-chien-t'ao* (n.p., 1942), pp. 64–65.

101. Hsü K'an, *Wen-ts'un*, pp. 151–53; idem, *Liang-shih-pu sa-san-nien-tu kung-tso kai-k'uang* (Chungking, 1945), pp. 7–8.

102. Hsü K'an, *Wen-ts'un*, p. 198.

103. Hu-nan sheng-cheng-fu, *Hu-nan sheng sa-nien-tu tang-cheng-chün lien-ho shih-ch'a-tsu shih-ch'a ko-hsien tsung-chien-t'ao,* pp. 64–65; Hsü K'an, *Wen-ts'un,* pp. 131–32.

104. Hsü K'an, *Wen-ts'un,* pp. 131–32; Even when the provincial governor himself was a powerful regional general, he would not be immune from pressures from other armies. See Chu Cheng-sheng, *Li Han-hun chiang-chün jih-chi,* vol. 1, pt. 1, p. 292, and pt. 2, pp. 1–2.

105. KMT, Central Executive Committee, *Chung-yang hsün-lien-t'uan tang-cheng hsün-lien-pan kung-tso t'ao-lun tzu-liao hsüan-lu tseng-pien,* pp. 52–54; Chu Tzu-shuang, *Liang-shih cheng-ts'e,* p. 96.

106. Ching-chi-pu, *K'ang-chan shih-ch'i chih Chung-kuo ching-chi* (Hong kong, 1968 reprint), pp. 1121–22.

107. Hsü K'an, *Wen-ts'un,* p. 124.

108. Huang Shao-hung, *Wu shih hui i,* pp. 447–49.

109. Hsü K'an, *Wen-ts'un,* pp. 126–27.

110. Ibid., pp. 105–19; Hsü K'an, *Tsui-chin chih liang-cheng* (n.p., 1942), pp. 4–5.

111. Nung-lin-pu, *K'ang-chan ssu-nien lai chih nung-yeh* (Chungking, 1941), pp. 1–2.

112. Chu Tzu-shuang, *Liang-shih cheng-ts'e,* pp. 4, 7–10.

113. Ibid.

114. Hsü K'an, *Wen-ts'un,* pp. 187–90.

115. Young, *China's Wartime Finance and Inflation,* p. 26.

116. On June 20, 1941, Teng Hsi-hou reported that Szechwan's total grain output was 130 million *tan,* and its grain contribution was 12 million *tan.* See *Ti-san-tz'u ch'üan-kuo ts'ai-cheng hui-i hui-pien,* pt. 1, p. 32.

117. The Chargé in China, Atcheson, to the Secretary of State: no. 1201, May 19, 1943, 893.00/15033; no. 1485, August 18, 1943, 893.00/15112; all in *Foreign Relations of the United States, Diplomatic Papers: 1943, China* (Washington, D.C., 1957), pp. 238–40, 316–17; The Ambassador in China, Gauss, to the Secretary of State, no. 1637, September 29, 1943, 893.00/15141, *Foreign Relations, 1943, China,* pp. 344–45.

118. The Chargé in China, Vincent, to the Secretary of State, no. 1173, May 12, 1943, 893.00/15026, ibid., pp. 233–36.

119. John Service memo, dated November 5, 1942, in Esherick, *Lost Chance in China*, pp. 12–13.

120. The Ambassador in China, Gauss, to the Secretary of State, no. 721, November 13, 1942, 893.48/3069, *Foreign Relations of the United States, Diplomatic Papers: 1942, China* (Washington, D.C., 1956), p. 253; no. 933, February 15, 1943, 893.48/4008, *Foreign Relations, 1943, China*, pp. 208–9.

121. Chang Ch'i-yün, *K'ang Jih chan-shih* (Taipei, 1966), pp. 337–39.

122. Ping-i-pu, *K'ang-chan pa-nien lai ping-i hsing-cheng kung-tso tsung-pao-kao* (Chungking, 1945), pp. 5–8.

123. Ibid.

124. During the last years of war, such stipends constituted about three-fifths of Szechwan's annual provincial governmental budget. See Chang Ch'i-yün, *K'ang Jih chan-shih*, pp. 342–45.

125. Chang Ch'ün, *Tsai Ch'uan yen-lun hsüan-chi*, pp. 275–77.

126. According to Theodore White, a kidnapped recruit was sold for C$50,000 to C$100,000 per head in the Ch'engtu black market. See Theodore H. White and Annalee Jacoby, *Thunder Out of China* (New York, 1946), p. 274.

127. Hu-nan sheng-cheng-fu, *Hu-nan sheng sa-nien-tu tang-cheng-chün lien-ho shih-ch'a-tsu shih-ch'a ko-hsien tsung-chien-t'ao*, pp. 78–82.

128. Chang Ch'ün, *Tsai Ch'uan yen-lun hsüan-chi*, p. 137; Ts'ui Ch'ang-cheng, *Hsien chieh-tuan chih cheng-ping wen-t'i* (Chungking, 1939), pp. 1–11.

129. Chang Ch'i-yün, *K'ang Jih chan-shih*, pp. 342–43; White and Jacoby, *Thunder Out of China*, pp. 132, 275.

130. Ping-i-pu, *K'ang-chan pa-nien lai ping-i hsing-cheng kung-tso tsung-pao-kao*, pp. 46–47.

131. Cheng Tzu-ming, *Chung-kuo hsien-hsing ping-i chih-tu* (Hong kong, 1938), passim.

132. Ch'in Te-shun, *Chin Te-shun hui-i-lu* (Taipei, 1967), pp. 192–93.

133. Chang Ch'ün, *Tsai Ch'uan yen-lun hsüan-chi*, pp. 95–96.

134. Huang Hsü-ch'u, ''Pa-nien k'ang-chan hui-i-lu,'' *Ch'un ch'iu*, no. 82 (December 1, 1960):6–7.

135. Arthur N. Young, *China and the Helping Hand, 1937–1945* (Cambridge, Mass., 1963), p. 302.

136. Nei-cheng-pu, *Ti-san-tz'u ch'üan-kuo nei-cheng hui-i pao-kao-shu*, pp. 116–17.

137. Chang Ch'i-yün, *K'ang Jih chan-shih*, pp. 342–43.

138. Ho Ying-ch'in, *Wartime Military Report*, vol. 2, p. 45.

139. Hsü Kao-yang, *Kuo-fang nien-chien* (Hong kong, 1961), pt. 2, *chün-shih*, pp. 35–36.

140. Chang Ch'ün, *Tsai Ch'uan yen-lun hsüan-chi*, p. 213.

141. Ping-i-pu, *K'ang-chan pa-nien lai ping-i hsing-cheng kung-tso tsung-pao-kao*, p. 52.

142. Ts'ai-cheng-pu, *Chung-kuo ts'ai-cheng nien-chien, 1948* (Nanking, 1948), sec. 3, pp. 98–101.

143. Albert Feuerwerker, *Economic Trends in the Republic of China, 1912–1949* (Ann Arbor, Mich., 1977), table 20, pp. 82–83.

144. Ts'ai-cheng-pu, *Chung-kuo ts'ai-cheng nien-chien, 1948,* sec. 3, pp. 98–101.

145. Between 1937 and July, 1942, four government banks created the credit for the government: the Bank of China, Bank of Communications, the Farmers' Bank, and the Central Bank. After July, 1942, the Central Bank became the only one to make advances to the government. Together, they advanced to the government (in C$ million): 1,195 in 1937–38; 853 for the second half of 1938; 2,311 for 1939; 3,834 for 1940; 9,443 for 1941; 20,082 for 1942; 40,857 for 1943; 140,091 for 1944; and 1,043,257 for 1945. See Chia Shih-i, *Min-kuo ts'ai-cheng ching-chi wen-t'i ching-hsi-kuan* (Taipei, 1954), p. 8; In percentages, the amounts of deficit of the national government covered by these bank advances were 37 percent in 1937, 71 percent in 1938, 79 percent in 1939, 70 percent in 1940, 81 percent in 1941, 60 percent in 1942, 50 percent in 1943, 52 percent in 1944 and 68 percent in 1945. See Young, *China's Wartime Finance and Inflation,* pp. 20, 33.

146. Young, *China's Wartime Finance and Inflation,* p. 161.

147. Feuerwerker, *Economic Trends in the Republic of China, 1912–1949,* p. 90; Chia Shih-i, *Min-kuo ts'ai-cheng ching-chi wen-t'i ching-hsi-kuan,* p. 8.

148. Fang Hsien-t'ing, *Chan-shih Chung-kuo ching-chi yen-chiu,* pp. 162–64.

149. In the vast area encompassing the thirteen provinces that were to remain wholly or partially under government control in the war, there were only 279 factories that utilized machine power or employed more than thirty workers each. In terms of productivity, this vast area's electric power output was 3 percent, textiles 1 percent, and flour 2 percent of the national total in 1937. See Ching-chi-pu, *K'ang-chan shih-ch'i chih Chung-kuo ching-chi,* p. 1319.

150. Chang Kia-ngau, *The Inflationary Spiral: The Experience in China, 1939–1950* (New York, 1958), pp. 213–14.

151. Ching-chi-pu, *K'ang-chan shih-ch'i chih Chung-kuo ching-chi,* pp. 1320–24.

152. Young, *China and the Helping Hand,* p. 117.

153. Ching-chi-pu, *K'ang-chan shih-ch'i chih Chung-kuo ching-chi,* pp. 456, 459, 463, 1237–44.

154. Mr. Donald M. Nelson to President Roosevelt, December 20, 1944, 033.1193 Nelson, Donald M/1-1245, *Foreign Relations of the United States: Diplomatic Papers, 1945, China* (Washington, D.C., 1969), pp. 287–95.

155. Ching-chi-pu, *K'ang-chan shih-ch'i chih Chung-kuo ching-chi,* p. 278.

156. Ts'ai-cheng-pu, *Chung-kuo ts'ai-cheng nien-chien, 1948,* sec. 3, pp. 98–101.

157. Chu Ssu-huang, *Min-kuo ching-chi shih* (Shanghai, 1948), pp. 421–22; Young, *China's Wartime Finance and Inflation,* pp. 75–77.

158. Chia Shih-i, *Min-kuo ts'ai-cheng ching-chi wen-t'i ching-hsi kuan,* p. 6.

159. Young, *China and the Helping Hand*, p. 148.
160. Ibid., p. 207.
161. The Ambassador in China, Gauss, to the Secretary of State, no. 732, June 22, 1942, 893.51/7502: Telegram, *Foreign Relations, 1942, China*, pp. 524–26.
162. Mr. Harry Dexter White to the Assistant Secretary of State, July 10, 1943, 893.5151/943, *Foreign Relations, 1943, China*, pp. 423–24; U.S. Department of State, *The China White Paper* (Stanford, Calif., 1967), pp. 485–88.
163. Young, *China and the Helping Hand*, pp. 321–25.
164. Ibid., app. 2, p. 441.
165. Feuerwerker, *Economic Trends in the Republic of China, 1912–1949*, p. 91.
166. The Ambassador to China, Gauss, to the Secretary of State, no. 1334, November 16, 1942, 893.00/14900: Telegram; no. 1486, December 12, 1942, 893.00/14909: Telegram; both in *Foreign Relations, 1942, China*, pp. 254–55, 260–63.
167. Ibid.
168. Chang Wei-ya, *Chung-kuo huo-pei ching-jung lun* (Taipei, 1952), pp. 157–58.
169. The Consul at Kunming, Ringwalt, to the Secretary of State, A-10, March 9, 1944, 893.5151/990: Airgram, *Foreign Relations, 1944, China*, pp. 374–75.
170. Memorandum by the Assistant to the Division of Far Eastern Affairs, Atcheson, April 7, 1943, 893.00 P.R. Yunnan/166, *Foreign Relations, 1943, China*, pp. 45–46.
171. The Chargé in China, Atcheson, to the Secretary of State, no. 1354, August 2, 1943, 893.5151/953: Telegram, *Foreign Relations, 1943, China*, pp. 440–41; Ching-chi-pu, *K'ang-chan shih-ch'i chih Chung-kuo ching-chi*, pp. 51–53.
172. Ts'ai-cheng-pu, *Chung-kuo ts'ai-cheng nien-chien, 1948*, sec. 3, pp. 98–101.
173. *Chinese Statistical Yearbook, 1948* (Nanking, 1948), pp. 228–31.
174. For a good discussion of these factors, see Chang Kia-ngau, *The Inflationary Spiral*, chap. 10.
175. Ts'ai-cheng-pu, *Chung-kuo ts'ai-cheng nien-chien, 1948*, sec. 3, pp. 98–101.
176. Young, *China's Wartime Finance and Inflation*, table 34, p. 303.
177. Despatch 293, April 12, 1945, American Embassy in Chungking, 893.51/4-1245, *Foreign Relations, 1945, China*, pp. 1067–72.
178. Ching-chi-pu, *K'ang-chan shih-ch'i chih Chung-kuo ching-chi*, pp. 618–69; Young, *China and the Helping Hand*, app. 1, p. 436.
179. Young, *China and the Helping Hand*, pp. 303–4.
180. For texts of these laws, see Ching-chi-pu, *K'ang-chan shih-ch'i chih Chung-kuo ching-chi*, pp. 641–47.
181. Ibid.
182. *Ti-san-tz'u ch'üan-kuo ts'ai-cheng hui-i hui-pien*, pt. 2, p. 28.
183. Ching-chi-pu, *K'ang-chan shih-ch'i chih Chung-kuo ching-chi*, pp. 623–24; Young, *China's Wartime Finance and Inflation*, app. B, table 51, p. 351.
184. The Chargé in China, Atcheson, to the Secretary of State, no. 1294, July 25,

1943, 893.5017/132: Telegram, *Foreign Relations, 1943, China*, p. 438.

185. *Statistical Service*, monthly, published by Nankai University, Institute of Economics, (Chungking), May, 1944.

186. *Ti-san-tz'u ch'üan-kuo ts'ai-cheng hui-i hui-pien*, pt. 3, p. 67.

187. Chu Tzu-shuang, *Liang-shih cheng-ts'e*, pp. 45–52, text of Chiang's speech to the Third National Conference on Finance.

188. CKS, *Chiang tsung-t'ung chi*, vol. 2, pp. 1406–8, 1434.

189. Hu-nan sheng-cheng-fu, *Hu-nan sheng sa-nien tu tang-cheng-chün lien-ho shih-ch'a-tsu shih-ch'a ko-hsien tsung-chien-t'ao*, pp. 64–65.

190. Hsü K'an, *Wen-ts'un*, pp. 200–203.

191. Ibid.

192. Ibid., pp. 151–53.

193. Wu Ting-ch'ang, *Hua-hsi hsien-pi* (Kweiyang, 1940), pp. 104–8; idem, *Hua-hsi hsien-pi hsü-pien*, pp. 7–12.

194. *Ti-san-tz'u ch'üan-kuo ts'ai-cheng hui-i hui-pien*, pt. 3, pp. 58–61.

195. Wu Ting-ch'ang, *Hua-hsi hsien-pi hsü-pien*, pp. 10–12.

196. Carsun Chang, *The Third Force in China* (New York, 1952), p. 100.

197. Li Tsung-huang, *Hui-i-lu*, vol. 4, pp. 144–45.

198. For a good account of the operations of wartime local government system, see Barnett, *China on the Eve of Communist Takeover*, pp. 103–54.

Chapter 5

1. Ch'en Hsi-hao, *Kuo-ch'ü san-shih-wu-nien chung chih Chung-kuo Kuo-min-tang* (Shanghai, 1929), pp. 145–46.

2. Ch'en Kung-po, *Ch'en Kung-po hsien-sheng wen-chi* (Hong kong, 1929), pp. 89, 301.

3. Ibid., p. 301.

4. KMT, Commission on Party History, *Chung-kuo Kuo-min-tang nien-chien, 1929* (Nanking, 1930), passim; KMT, Central Executive Committee, *Tang-yüan t'ung-chi, 1930* (Nanking, 1930).

5. KMT, Commission on Party History, *Chung-kuo Kuo-min-tang nien-chien, 1934* (Nanking, 1935), pt. 2, p. 19.

6. Chu Chia-hua, *Tang-wu shih-shih shang chih wen-t'i* (Chungking, 1940), pp. 21–24.

7. Ibid., p. 21; For a discussion of how the KMT became an elitist party, see also David Peter Barrett, "The Consolidation of Elitism in the Kuomintang, 1928–1929" (Ph.D. diss., University of Toronto, 1970).

8. Ch'en T'ien-ku, *Ch'en Tien-ku Hui-i-lu* (Hong kong, 1978), pp. 212–14.

9. Liu Shao-t'ang, *MKTS*, vol. 1, pp. 389, 414.

10. For reports on the conditions of local party organs, see Chu Chia-hua, *Tang-wu shih-shih shang chih wen-t'i*, pp. 13–15; Ch'en Kung-po, *Wen-chi*, pp. 298–99; KMT, Commission on Party History, *Chung-kuo Kuo-min-tang nien-chien, 1934*, pt. 3, pp. 239–41; Tien Hung-mao, *Government and Politics in Kuomintang China* (Stanford, Calif., 1972), p. 32; for a recent study

focusing on the conflict between the KMT's right and left over their attitudes toward local elites, see Bradley Kent Geisert, "Power and Society: The Kuomintang and Local Elites in Kiangsu Province, China, 1924–1937," (Ph.D. diss., University of Virginia, 1979).

11. Diane Lary, *Region and Nation: The Kwangsi Clique in Chinese Politics, 1925–1937* (Cambridge, Mass., 1974), pp. 178–79.

12. CKS speech, August 14, 1926, "On the Status and Responsibility of Party Members, and the Importance of Organization and Discipline," *Chiang tsung-t'ung chi,* vol. 1, pp. 475–78.

13. CKS speech, July 18, 1928, "China's Path of Reconstruction," ibid., vol. 1, p. 515.

14. CKS speech on August 14, 1926, ibid., vol. 1, pp. 475–78; on February 7, 1929, ibid., vol. 1, p. 533.

15. CKS speech to the Third National Congress of the KMT, March 5, 1929, ibid., vol. 1, pp. 536–37.

16. Ibid.

17. CKS speech to the Fourth National Congress of the KMT, November 12, 1931, ibid., vol. 1, pp. 574–76.

18. CKS speech to students of the Central Political Academy, September 14, 1929, ibid., vol. 1, p. 558.

19. Patrick Cavendish, "The 'New China' of the Kuomintang," in *Modern China's Search for a Political Form,* ed. Jack Gray (London, 1969), pp. 161, 163; For a case study, see David Tsai, "Party-Government Relations in Kiangsu Province, 1927–1932," in *Selected Papers from the Center for Far Eastern Studies,* no. 1, 1975–76 (University of Chicago, Center for Far Eastern Studies, 1976):85–118.

20. Ch'en Kung-po, *Wen-chi,* pp. 238–39.

21. Ibid., pp. 13–14; Arif Dirlik, "Mass Movements and the Left Kuomintang," in *Modern China* 1, no. 1 (January, 1975):46–74; Robert E. Bedeski, "The Tutelary State and National Revolution in Kuomintang Ideology, 1928–1931," *China Quarterly,* no. 46 (April-June, 1971):319–20; Shao Yüan-ch'ung, *Hsüan-fu i-shu* (Taipei, 1954), pp. 60, 72–73.

22. Tai Chi-t'ao, *Ch'ing-nien chih lu,* in *Tai Chi-t'ao hsien-sheng wen-ts'un tsai hsü-pien,* ed. Ch'en T'ien-hsi (Taipei, 1968), vol. 2, pp. 491–2, 502–5; For a discussion of dissension within the KMT leadership triggered by differences over mass movements and other policy issues, see John Kenneth Olenik, "Left Wing Radicalism in the Kuomintang: Teng Yen-ta and the Genesis of the Third Party Movement in China, 1924–1931," (Ph.D. diss., Cornell University, 1973).

23. Cavendish, "'New China,'" pp. 184–86.

24. For a discussion of the KMT's version of self-strengthening movement, see Jerome B. Grieder, "Communism, Nationalism, and Democracy: The Chinese Intelligentsia and the Chinese Revolution in the 1920s and 1930s," in *Modern East Asia: Essays in Interpretation,* ed. James B. Crowley, (New York, 1970), pp. 224–28; For a more benevolent evaluation of the Nanking decade, see Bedeski, "The Tutelary State," pp. 320–30.

25. KMT, Commission on Party History, *Chung-kuo Kuo-min-tang nien-chien, 1940* (Chungking, 1941), passim.

26. KMT, Bureau of Statistics, *Chung-kuo Kuo-min-tang tang-wu t'ung-chi chi-yao, 1944* (Chungking, 1944), table 3, p. 3; idem, *Chung-kuo Kuo-min-tang tang-wu t'ung-chi chi-yao, 1945,* p. 7.

27. KMT, Bureau of Statistics, *Chung-kuo Kuo-min-tang tang-wu t'ung-chi chi-yao, 1941* (Chungking, 1941), table 6, p. 6.

28. Tien Hung-mao, *Government and Politics in Kuomintang China, 1927–37* (Stanford, Calif., 1972), p. 30.

29. KMT, Bureau of Statistics, *Chung-kuo Kuo-min-tang tang-wu t'ung-chi chi-yao, 1945* (Chungking, 1945), tables 1, 2, pp. 1–2.

30. If all categories of governmental employees were included, they constituted over 45 percent of party members. See Chu Chia-hua, *Tang ti tsu-chih yü ling-tao* (Chungking, 1942), pp. 31–32.

31. KMT, Secretariat, *Chung-yang tang-pu chih-yüan lu, 1934* (Nanking, 1934); idem, *Chung-yang tang-pu chih-yüan lu, 1943* (Chungking, 1943).

32. KMT, Bureau of Statistics, *Chung-kuo Kuo-min-tang tang-wu t'ung-chi chi-yao, 1941,* table 68, p. 68.

33. KMT, Bureau of Statistics, *Chung-kuo Kuo-min-tang tang-wu t'ung-chi chi-yao, 1944,* pp. 7–8.

34. KMT, Central Executive Committee, *Ju ho tsuo hsien ti tang-wu kung-tso* (n.p., 1938), p. 3.

35. Ibid., p. 24.

36. Ch'en Fang-hsien, *Kai-chin tang-wu kung-tso i-chien* (Chungking, 1940), pp. 1–8.

37. Chang Chi, *Kai-ko tang-cheng chien-i-shu* (Chungking, 1941), as submitted by a group of CEC members under the leadership of Chang Chi in 1941.

38. Ibid., pp. 1–2.

39. The Ambassador in China, Gauss, to the Secretary of State, no. 712, November 5, 1942, 893.00/14903, *Foreign Relations of the United States, Diplomatic Papers: 1942, China* (Washington, D.C., 1956), pp. 252–53.

40. KMT, Bureau of Statistics, *Chung-kuo Kuo-min-tang tang-wu t'ung-chi chi-yao, 1941,* passim.

41. The Chargé in China, Vincent, to the Secretary of State, no. 1063, April 8, 1943, 893.00/15003, *Foreign Relations of the United States, Diplomatic Papers: 1943, China* (Washington, D.C., 1957), pp. 221–22.

42. CKS, *Kai-chin tang-wu cheng-chih chih t'u-ching yü fang-chen* (n.p., 1943), address to the 10th Plenum of the KMT, November 23, 1942.

43. Chu Chia-hua, *Tang ti tsu-chih yü ling-tao* (Chungking, 1942), pp. 33–35.

44. KMT, Bureau of Statistics, *Chung-kuo Kuo-min-tang tang-wu t'ung-chi chi-yao, 1941,* table 2, p. 2; idem, *Chung-kuo Kuo-min-tang tang-wu t'ung-chi chi-yao, 1944,* passim.

45. *Ko sheng shih lu tang-pu tsu-chih k'o(ku)-chang hui-i chi-yao* (n.p., n.d.), pp. 64–65; KMT, Bureau of Statistics, *Chung-kuo Kuo-min-tang tang-wu t'ung-chi chi-yao 1944,* p. 1.

46. *Ko sheng shih lu tang-pu tsu-chih k'o(ku)-chang hui-i chi-yao,* pp. 55–56.

47. Ibid.

48. Tien Hung-mao, *Kuomintang China*, p. 83.

49. During the war, the party's share was reduced to less than one percent of the national budget even as it experienced increases in membership and scope of activities. See Ts'ai-cheng-pu, *Chung-kuo ts'ai-cheng nien-chien, 1948* (Nanking, 1948), sec. 3, pp. 98–101.

50. Ch'en Fang-hsien, *Kai-chin tang-wu kung-tso i-chien*, pp. 1–8; *Tang-cheng hsün-lien-pan tang-wu kung-tso jen-yüan t'an-hua-hui chi-lu* (n.p., 1939), minutes of conference on February 18, 1939.

51. KMT, Bureau of Statistics, *Tang-cheng ch'ing-pao* (n.p., 1945–46), entry of March 9, 1945.

52. Ch'en Fang-hsien, *Kai-chin tang-wu kung-tso i-chien*, pp. 1–8; KMT, Bureau of Statistics, *Tang-cheng ch'ing-pao*, entry of March 9, 1945.

53. KMT, Department of Organization, *Chu pu-chang tsui-chin tui-yü tang-wu kung-tso t'ung-chih chih chih-shih* (Chungking, 1942), pp. 2–3.

54. Wang Cheng, "The Kuomintang: A Sociological Study of Demoralization," (Ph.D. diss., Stanford University, 1953), pp. 30–36.

55. KMT, Bureau of Statistics, *Chung-kuo Kuo-min-tang tang-wu t'ung-chi chi-yao, 1941*, table 41, p. 41.

56. Tang-cheng hsün-lien-pan, *Tang-cheng hsün-lien-pan ti-ssu-nien hsün-lien shih-lu* (n.p., 1942), pp. 1–14; *Chung-yang hsün-lien-t'uan t'uan-k'an*, no. 115 (February 25, 1942):2–3; In 1944, the number of party workers trained on the national level and local level constituted 5.6 percent and 4 percent, respectively, of the total trained in that year. See KMT, Bureau of Statistics, *Chung-kuo kuo-min-tang tang-wu t'ung-chi chi-yao, 1944*, tables 56, 60, pp. 54, 58.

57. KMT, Bureau of Statistics, *Chung-kuo Kuo-min-tang tang-wu t'ung-chi chi-yao, 1941*, table 65, p. 65.

58. For an assessment of this organ, see Paul M. A. Linebarger, *The China of Chiang Kai-shek* (Boston, 1943), p. 131.

59. KMT, Department of Organization, *Chu pu-chang tsui-chin tui-yü tang-wu kung-tso t'ung-chih chih chih-shih* (1942), p. 5; KMT, Control Commission, *Tang-yüan chien-ch'a-wang* (Chungking, 1941), pp. 1–16.

60. KMT, Bureau of Statistics, *Chung-kuo Kuo-min-tang tang-wu t'ung-chi chi-yao, 1944*, table 91, p. 89; For 1945 data, see KMT, Bureau of Statistics, *Chung-kuo Kuo-min-tang tang-wu t'ung-chi chi-yao, 1945*, table 61, p. 61.

61. KMT, Department of Organization, *Chu pu-chang tsui-chin tui-yü tang-wu kung-tso t'ung-chih chih chih-shih*, pp. 10–11.

62. *Chung-yang ko chi-kuan hsiao-tsu hui-i t'ao-lun-hui Wu mi-shu-chang chiang-hua chi-lu* (Chungking, 1944), August 18, 1944.

63. KMT, Department of Organization, *Chu pu-chang tsui-chin tui-yü tang-wu kung-tso t'ung-chih chih chih-shih*, p. 16.

64. Ibid., pp. 10–11.

65. Huang Hsü-ch'u, "Kwang-hsi yü chung-yang nien-yü-nien lai pei-huan li-ho i-shu," *Ch'un ch'iu*, no. 135 (February 16, 1963):9–13.

66. *Chung-kuo chih ming-yün*, particularly chap. 7, in CKS, *Chiang tsung-t'ung*

chi, vol. 1, pp. 164–65.

67. Andrew Nathan, *Peking Politics: 1918–1923, Factionalism and the Failure of Constitutionalism* (Berkeley, Calif., 1976), p. 32.

68. Ibid.

69. In the 1920s, the KMT popularized the slogan, "There should be no party outside the KMT, nor should there be any faction within the KMT." This myth of iron-clad discipline and unity discouraged any honest and objective discussion of factional activities by KMT leaders.

70. Professor William Tung, who was a longtime member of the KMT, related a conversation with Ch'en Li-fu in 1968 when the latter stoutly denied that the C.C. faction ever existed. See William L. Tung, *Revolutionary China: A Personal Account, 1926–1949* (New York, 1973), pp. 130–34.

71. Kan Kuo-hsün, "Chui ssu Liu Chien-ch'ün ping shih Lan-i-she," *Chuan-chi wen-hsüeh* 20, no. 3 (September, 1972):17–22.

72. Tien Hung-mao, *Kuomintang China*, p. 57.

73. T'ang-jen, *Shih-nien nei-chan* (Hong kong, 1964), pp. 60–66.

74. For relevant discussions of the C.C. faction's prewar activities, see Tien Hung-mao, *Kuomintang China*, pp. 47–52; Lloyd E. Eastman, *The Abortive Revolution: China Under Nationalist Control* (Cambridge, Mass., 1974), pp. 83–84, 305; See also idem, "The Kuomintang in the 1930s," in Charlotte Furth, ed., *The Limits of Change: Essays on Conservative Alternatives in Republican China* (Cambridge, Mass., 1976), pp. 196–200.

75. Chiang Shang-ch'ing, *Cheng-hai mi-wen* (Hong kong, 1966), pp. 68–84.

76. Ibid.

77. For a discussion of the origins and development of this faction, see Tien Hung-mao, *Kuomintang China*, pp. 65–71.

78. Howard L. Boorman and Richard C. Howard, ed., *Biographical Dictionary of Republican China* (New York, 1970), entries on Huang Fu, Chang Ch'ün, and Yang Yung-t'ai; Lei Hsiao-ch'in, "Yang Yung-t'ai lung she ch'i lu," *Chung wai tsa chih* 9, no. 3 (March, 1971):19–23.

79. CKS, *Chün-shih wei-yüan-hui wei-yüan-chang Nan-ch'ang hsing-ying ch'u-li chiao-fei sheng-fen cheng-chih kung-tso pao-kao* (n.p., 1934), December 27, 1933.

80. These themes permeate a large number of works, but for some systematic, if not entirely verifiable accounts, see Ch'en Po-ta, *Jen-min kung-ti Chiang Chieh-shih* (n.p., 1948); Chung Ch'i-sheng, *Ta ts'ai-fa Chiang Chieh-shih* (Hong kong, 1948); Eastman, *The Abortive Revolution*, pp. 83–84; T'ang-jen, *Chin-ling ch'un-meng* (Hong kong, 1964).

81. Other reputed members included Wu Ting-ch'ang (governor of Kweichow), Wang Ch'ung-hui (secretary-general of the Supreme National Defense Council and former Minister of Foreign Affairs), Chang Kia-ngau (minister of communication), Wong Weng-hao (minister of economic affairs), Ch'en Yi (secretary-general of the Executive Yüan), Tsiang T'ing-fu (director of the political affairs department of the Executive Yüan), Hsiung Shih-hui (head of the Chinese military mission to the United States and former governor of Kiangsi), and Wu T'ieh-ch'eng (secretary-general of the KMT).

82. *The Amerasia Papers: A Clue to the Catastrophe of China* (Washington, D.C., 1970), vol. 1, no. 24, pp. 231-43; The Ambassador in China, Gauss, to the Secretary of State, no. 553, Enclosure, July 30, 1942, 893.00/14876, *Foreign Relations, 1942, China*, pp. 212-26.

83. Ch'en Kuo-fu, *Su cheng hui-i* (Taipei, 1951), p. 2.

84. *Tang-cheng hsün-lien-pan tang-wu kung-tso jen-yüan t'an-hua-hui chi-lu* (n.p., 1939), passim.

85. Kao Yin-tsu, *Chung-hua-min-kuo ta-shih-chi* (Taipei, 1957), pp. 444-45.

86. Chu Chia-hua was party secretary-general since April, 1938, and concurrently the chairman of the organization department since December, 1939. In 1944, Wu T'ieh-ch'eng became secretary-general.

87. The Ambassador in China, Gauss, to the Secretary of State, no. 553 Enclosure, July 30, 1942, 893.00/14876, *Foreign Relations, 1942, China*, pp. 212-26.

88. One source estimated that by 1941, the *chung-t'ung* had about 13,000 field agents of which ten thousand were assigned to government offices in the provinces, two thousand in the central government, and one thousand in private organizations. See Ch'en Shao-hsiao, *Hei wang lu* (Hong kong, 1966), pp. 300-302.

89. The Ambassador in China, Gauss, to the Secretary of State, no. 1957, December 24, 1943, 740.0011 Pacific War/3678, *Foreign Relations, 1943, China*, pp. 391-93.

90. Chün-shih wei-yüan-hui, *Chan-ti tang-cheng wei-yüan-hui tsu-chih kang-yao* (n.p., 1940).

91. *Chan-ti(ti-hou-fang yu-chi-ch'ü) tang-cheng-chün kung-tso chih-tao kang-ling yao-mu* (n.p., 1940); KMT, Bureau of Statistics, *Chung-kuo Kuo-min-tang tang-wu t'ung-chi chi'yao, 1941*, table 10, p. 10.

92. William Tung, *Revolutionary China*, p. 241.

93. *Tang-cheng hsün-lien-pan tang-wu kung-tso jen-yüan t'an-hua-hui chi-lu*, passim.

94. *San-min-chu-i ch'ing-nien-t'uan chung-yang t'uan-pu kung-tso pao-kao* (n.p., 1941), pp. 1-5.

95. Ibid., pp. 1-5, 25-38.

96. Ibid., pp. 13-14.

97. Tang-cheng hsün-lien-pan, *Tang-cheng hsün-lien-pan tang-wu kung-tso jen-yüan t'an-hua-hui chi-lu*, passim.

98. KMT, Central Executive Committee, *Ch'üeh ting tang yü t'uan chih kuan-hsi pan-fa*, resolution passed by the standing committee of CEC, November 25, 1940; San-min-chu-i ching-nien-t'uan, *San-min-chu-i ch'ing-nien-t'uan chung-yang t'uan-pu kung-tso pao-kao* (n.p., 1943), p. 9.

99. KMT, Bureau of Statistics, *Tang-cheng ch'ing-pao*, entry of March 8, 1945.

100. KMT, Department of Propaganda, *Ch'ing-nien-t'uan ch'uang-li liu-chou-nien* (Chungking, 1944), no pagination.

101. Ch'en Shao-hsiao, *Hei wang lu* (Hong kong, 1966), pp. 127-30; T'ang-jen, *Shih-nien nei-chan*, pp. 163-80.

102. Memorandum for the Chief of the Division of Chinese Affairs, Vincent, April

29, 1944, 893.20211/15, *Foreign Relations, 1944, China*, pp. 64–65; General Tai Li also developed an American connection in 1942 through Admiral Milton Miles. This connection eventually led to the establishment of the Sino-American Cooperation Organization (SACO) which helped Tai with the training and equipment of thousands of agents. For a detailed description of SACO, see Michael Schaller, *The U.S. Crusade in China, 1938–1945* (New York, 1979), pp. 231–50.

103. The Ambassador in China, Gauss, to the Secretary of State, no. 888, July 29, 1942, 893.00/14862: Telegram, *Foreign Relations, 1942, China*, p. 211; For a detailed description of the vicissitudes of the People's Political Council, see Lawrence Nae-lih Shyu, ''The People's Political Council and China's Wartime Problems, 1937–1945'' (Ph.D. diss., Columbia University, 1972); Also the Ambassador in China, Gauss, to the Secretary of State, no. 1747, October 28, 1943, 893.00/15182, *Foreign Relations, 1943, China*, pp. 367–70.

104. Now incorporated in *World Revolutionary Elites*, ed. Harold D. Lasswell, as chap. six, ''Kuomintang and Chinese Communist Elites,'' pp. 319–455.

105. Ibid., p. 16.

106. Robert A. Dahl, ''A Critique of the Ruling Elite Model,'' *American Political Science Review* 52, no. 1 (March, 1958):463–69.

107. Wang Cheng, ''The Kuomintang,'' pp. 18–19.

108. Tien Hung-mao, *Kuomintang China*, pp. 34–39.

109. Wang Cheng, ''The Kuomintang,'' pp. 19–20.

110. Lai Ching-hu, ''Pan tang, pan pao, pan hsüeh,'' *Chuan-chi wen-hsüeh* 23, no. 1 (July, 1973):56–61.

111. Lei Hsiao-ch'in, *Sa-nien tung-luan Chung-kuo* (Hong kong, n.d.), vol. 1, p. 211.

112. Lasswell, *World Revolutionary Elites*, p. 415.

113. Harold Isaacs, *The Tragedy of the Chinese Revolution* (London, 1938), pp. 175–85; Ch'en Po-ta, *Chung-kuo ssu-ta chia-tsu* (n.p., 1946), pp. 18–29, 47–54; Robert W. Barnett, *Economic Shanghai: Hostage to Politics* (New York, 1941), p. 12; Barrington W. Moore, Jr., *Social Origins of Dictatorship and Democracy: Lord and Peasant in the Making of the Modern World* (Boston, 1966), p. 196; Mary C. Wright, ''From Revolution to Restoration: The Transformation of Kuomintang Ideology,'' *Far Eastern Quarterly* 4, no. 4 (August, 1955):515–32.

114. Of the thirty-eight bankers who were identified as leaders of the Shanghai banking world, the overwhelming majority of them were natives of Kiangsu and Chekiang. Up to 1937, these thirty-eight bankers occupied 163 positions as presidents, directors, and general managers of the area's leading banks. While in one extreme case, one person occupied leading positions in 11 different banks, the average number of banks in which each member of this group served was 4.3 banks. In addition to banks, many of them also occupied positions ranging into flour industry, cement industry, chambers of commerce, etc. For biographical data of these persons, see Saitō Tsuyoshi, *Shina-Kikō to Jinbutsu* (Tokyo, 1937); For a discussion of the so-called Ningpo gang's influence in the Shanghai financial world, also see the follow-

ing: Shang-hai t'ung-she, *Shang-hai yen-chiu tzu-liao hsü-chi*, pp. 289–304; Susan Mann Jones, "Finance in Ningpo. The Ch'ien-chuang, 1750–1880," in *Economic Organization in Chinese Society*, ed. William E. Willmott (Stanford, Calif., 1972), pp. 47–77; Susan Mann Jones, "Merchant Investment, Commercialization, and Social Change in the Ningpo Area," in *Reform in Nineteenth Century China*, ed. Paul A. Cohen and John E. Shrecker (Cambridge, Mass., 1976), pp. 41–48.

115. Saitō Tsuyoshi, *Shina-Kikō to jinbutsu*, pp. 240–62.

116. For a more detailed discussion, see Nathan, *Peking Politics*, pp. 82–90; and Hsi-sheng Ch'i, *Warlord Politics in China, 1916–28* (Stanford, Calif., 1976), pp. 158–60; After the nominal unification of the country by the KMT in 1927, the Central Bank system expanded most vigorously while the commercial banks made relatively modest gains. For discussion of individual banks and their capitalization and growth, see Paul K. T. Sih, *The Strenuous Decade: China's Nation-Building Efforts, 1927–1937* (New York, 1970), p. 145; and Shang-hai t'ung-she, *Shang-hai yen-chiu tzu-liao hsü-chi* (Shanghai, 1939), pp. 685–94; For a history of the rise and decline of traditional banks (*ch'ien-chuang*) in Shanghai and how KMT policies hastened their decline in the mid-1930s, see Andrea Lee McElderry, *Shanghai Old-style Banks (Ch'ien-Chuang), 1800–1935* (Ann Arbor, Mich., 1976).

117. Richard Clarence Bush, III, "Industry and Politics in Kuomintang China: The Nationalist Regime and Lower Yangtze Chinese Cotton Mill Owners, 1927–1937" (Ph.D. diss., Columbia University, 1978), pp. 8–10, 308–9.

118. Parks M. Coble, Jr., "The Kuomintang Regime and the Shanghai Capitalists, 1927–29," *China Quarterly*, no. 77 (March, 1979):7–10, 20–24.

119. Ibid., p. 24; For an extended discussion of this relationship, see Coble's "The Shanghai Capitalist Class and the Nationalist Government, 1927–1937" (Ph.D. diss., University of Illinois, 1975); also Eastman, *The Abortive Revolution*, pp. 228–40.

120. Li Tsung-jen, *Memoirs of Li Tsung-jen* (Boulder, Colo., 1978), pp. 264–65; The possibility of Shanghai businessmen's disinterest or uninvolvement in the 1927 anti-CCP purge is discussed in Bush, "Industry and Politics in Kuomintang China," p. 305.

121. For a description of the strategies of self-protection by Chinese cotton mill owners, see Bush, "Industry and Politics in Kuomintang China"; For a description of the conflict between the KMT and Shanghai businessmen over the control of the Chamber of Commerce, see Joseph Fewsmith, "The Emergence of Authoritarian-Corporatist Rule in Republican China: The Changing Pattern of Business Association in Shanghai" (Ph.D. diss., University of Chicago, 1980), pp. 222–69.

122. Chiang Chün-chang, *Chung-hua-min-kuo chien-kuo shih* (Taipei, 1957), pp. 226–27.

123. See John Service's analysis in *Amerasia Papers*, vol. 1, no. 102, pp. 575–91; Sun Fo's comments in ibid., vol. 1, no. 91, pp. 535–50.

124. The difficulties of defining the nature of fascism are discussed in two recent works: Alexander J. DeGrand, *The Italian Nationalist Association and the*

Rise of Fascism in Italy (Lincoln, Nebr., 1978), p. ix; A. James Gregor, *Interpretations of Fascism* (New York, 1974).

125. Liu Chien-ch'ün, *Kung-hsien i-tien cheng-li pen tang ti i-chien* (Nanking, 1931); another relevant book by Liu is *Fu-hsing Chung-kuo ko-ming chih lu* (Nanking, 1934).

126. For instance, Chu Chia-hua, *Tang ti tsu-chih yü ling-tao* (Chungking, 1942); or Teng Wen-i, *Ling-hsiu yen-hsing* (n.p., n.d.).

127. Ch'en Po-ta, *Jen-min kung-ti Chiang Chieh-shih;* Eastman, *The Abortive Revolution,* chap. 2.

128. Eastman, *The Abortive Revolution,* pp. 39–55, passim; For expanded versions of Eastman's view, see his "Fascism in Kuomintang China: The Blue Shirts," in *China Quarterly,* no. 49 (January-March, 1972):1–31; and his "The Kuomintang in the 1930s," particularly pp. 193–96; For some criticism of Eastman's use of his data base, see Maria Hsia Chang, " 'Fascism' and Modern China," *China Quarterly,* no. 79 (September-December, 1979): 555–58; My own view is that Eastman's implication of the German advisors in spreading fascism is unsubstantiated. It is certainly not true that "they virtually dominated education in the military academies by 1929," as Eastman claimed on p. 39 of his book.

129. Maria Hsia Chang, " 'Fascism' and Modern China," pp. 558, 562–63.

130. Kan Kuo-hsün, "Chui ssu Liu Chien-ch'ün ping shih Lan-i-she," *Chuan-chi wen-hsüeh* 20, no. 3 (March, 1972):17–22.

131. On the question of fascism in Japan, see Miles Fletcher, "Intellectuals and Fascism in Early Shōwa Japan," *Journal of Asian Studies* 39, no. 1 (November, 1979):39–64; Peter Duus and Daniel I. Okimoto, "Fascism and the History of Pre-War Japan: The Failure of a Concept," *Journal of Asian Studies* 39, no. 1 (November, 1979):65–76.

132. For a discussion of the similarities between Sun's ideology and pre-Fascist Italian Nationalism, and the differences between these on the one hand and Italian fascism on the other, see A. James Gregor and Maria Hsia Chang, "Nazionalfascismo and the Revolutionary Nationalism of Sun Yat-sen," *Journal of Asian Studies* 39, no. 1 (November, 1979):21–37.

133. Professor Eastman provided an interesting analysis of Tai Li's secret operations and Tai's book, *Political Spying,* and offered them as evidence of the Kuomintang's fascist orientation. See Eastman, *The Abortive Revolution,* pp. 74–77. But Tai's discussion of the duties of secret service, or even the methods of arrest and assassination (Eastman, p. 76) are probably standard materials in the manuals of similar agencies in other countries. Maria Hsia Chang maintains that violence was not glorified by the KMT, nor was it considered by the KMT as "critical or essential to man's fulfillment as a moral agent," as in Italian fascism. See Maria Hsia Chang, " 'Fascism' and Modern China," p. 567.

134. Tien Hung-mao, *Kuomintang China,* p. 71.

135. For related discussion of the KMT's conservatism, see Eastman, *The Abortive Revolution,* pp. 191–92, 205–10; Mary C. Wright, "From

Revolution to Restoration: The Transformation of Kuomintang Ideology,'' *Far Eastern Quarterly* 14, no. 4 (August, 1955):515–32.

136. Robert C. Tucker, *The Soviet Political Mind* (New York, 1971), chap. 1, pp. 3–19.

137. Ibid., p. 9.

138. Ibid.

139. William Kornhauser, *The Politics of Mass Society* (New York, 1959).

140. Tucker, *The Soviet Political Mind,* pp. 13–14.

141. For some general discussion of the role of the military in Chinese politics, see Ch'ien Tuan-sheng, "The Role of the Military in Chinese Government," *Pacific Affairs* 21, no. 3 (September, 1948):239–51; C. Martin Wilbur, "Military Separatism and the Process of Reunification Under the Nationalist Regime, 1922–1937," in *China in Crisis,* ed. Ho Ping-ti and Tang Tsou (Chicago, 1968), vol. 1, bk. 1, pp. 203–63; Harold Z. Schiffrin, "Military and Politics in China: Is the Warlord Model Pertinent?" in *Military and State in Modern Asia,* ed. Harold Z. Schiffrin (Jerusalem, 1976), pp. 107–23.

142. Kuo-fang-pu, *Lu-chün chün-kuan-tso tzu-chi-pu* (Chungking, 1944), vol. 1, *chiang-chün, chien.*

143. Joseph W. Esherick, *Reform and Revolution in China: The 1911 Revolution in Hunan and Hubei* (Berkeley, Calif., 1976).

144. For social background of military officers during the Peiyang period, see Sheridan, *Chinese Warlord,* p. 161; and Jerome Ch'en, "Defining Chinese Warlords and Their Factions," *Bulletin of the School of Oriental and African Studies* (London, 1968); For quality of education in military science in the early twentieth century, see Hu Shih, *Ting Wen-chiang ti chuan-chi* (Taipei, 1956), pp. 61–62; *Lu-chün t'ung-chi* (Peking, 1926), vol. 5, pt. 2, chap. 1; During the nineteenth century, the military profession seemed briefly to have been respectable and acceptable to the sons of good families. See Yoshihiro Hatano, "The New Armies," in *China in Revolution: The First Phase, 1900–1913,* ed. Mary C. Wright (New Haven, Conn., 1968), pp. 365–82. But Hatano's data dealt with only the "new armies" in two provinces and these new armies usually constituted a tiny minority of the armies in the nation.

145. "For the Mobilization of All the Nation's Forces for Victory in the War of Resistance," August 25, 1937, in *Selected Works of Mao Tse-tung* (Peking, 1964), vol. 2, pp. 23–29.

146. Ibid., vol. 2, p. 155.

147. CKS speech, September 10, 1935, "The Meaning of National General Mobilization," *Chiang tsung-t'ung chi,* vol. 1, p. 913.

148. Ibid.

149. Barnett, *China on the Eve of Communist Takeover,* chap. 10, pp. 103–54.

Bibliography

Chinese-Language Materials

General

Chang Ch'i-yün. *K'ang Jih chan-shih.* Taipei, 1966.
————. *Tang-shih kai-yao.* 5 vols. Taipei, 1960.
————, comp. *Kuo-chia chien-she lun-wen-chi.* Taipei, 1966.
Chang Chih-i. *K'ang-chan chung ti cheng-tang ho p'ai-pieh.* Chungking, 1939.
Chang Chin-hsin. *Chung-kuo ming-chiang-lu.* Nanking, 1947.
Chang Ch'ün. *Chang Yüeh-chün hsien-sheng tsai Ch'uan yen-lu hsüan-chi.* Taipei, 1968.
Chang Hsiao-mei. *Ssu-ch'uan ching-chi ts'an-k'ao tzu-liao.* Shanghai, 1939.
Chang Jun-ts'ang. *Min-kuo feng-yün jen-wu ch'i-t'an.* Taipei, 1962.
Chang Kan-p'ing. *K'ang Jih ming-chiang Kuan Lin-cheng.* Hong kong, 1969.
Chang Kuo-p'ing. *Pai Ch'ung-hsi chiang-chün chuan.* N.p., 1938.
————. *T'ieh-chün chiang-ling lieh-chuan.* Canton, 1938.
Chang Kuo-t'ao. *Wo ti hui-i.* Hong kong, 1971.
Chang Wei-ya. *Chung-kuo huo-pei ching-jung lun.* Taipei, 1952.
Chang Wen-shih. *Yün-nan nei mu.* Kunming, 1949.
Chao K'ang. *Min-tsu ko-ming ti yu-chi-chan.* Hankow, 1938.
Chao Tseng-ch'ou et al. *K'ang-chan chi-shih.* 4 vols. Taipei, 1961.
Ch'en Ch'i-t'ien. *Cheng-chih ch'eng-pai lun.* Hong kong, 1955.
Ch'en Ch'ing-ch'i, ed. *Chung-kuo ta-shih nien-piao.* Hong kong, 1964.
Ch'en Hsi-hao. *Kuo-ch'ü san-shih-wu-nien chung chih Chung-kuo Kuo-min-tang.* Shanghai, 1929.
Ch'en Hui. *Kuang-hsi chiao-t'ung wen-t'i.* Ch'angsha, 1938.
Ch'en Kung-po. *Ch'en Kung-po hsien-sheng wen-chi.* Hong kong, 1929.
————. *Chung-kuo Kuo-min-tang so tai-piao ti shih shen-mo?* Nanking, 1928.
Ch'en Kuo-fu. *Ch'en Kuo-fu hsien-sheng ch'üan-chi.* 10 vols. Taipei, 1952.
————. *Su-cheng hui-i.* Taipei, 1951.

Ch'en Po-ta. *Chung-kuo ssu-ta chia-tsu.* N.p., 1946.

———. *Jen-min kung-ti Chiang Chieh-shih.* N.p., 1948.

Ch'en Pu-lei. *Ch'en Pu-lei hui-i-lu.* Hong kong, 1962.

Ch'en Shao-hsiao. *Hei wang lu.* Hong kong, 1966.

———. *Yen Hsi-shan chih hsing-mieh.* Hong kong, 1970.

Ch'en Tien-hsi. *Tai Chi-t'ao hsien-sheng pien-nien ch'üan-chi.* Taipei, 1958.

———. *Tai Chi-t'ao hsien-sheng ti sheng-p'ing.* Taipei, 1968.

———. *Tai-Chi-t'ao hsien-sheng wen-ts'un.* 4 vols. Taipei, 1958.

———. *Tai Chi-t'ao hsien-sheng wen-ts'un tsai hsü pien.* 2 vols. Taipei, 1968.

Cheng Tzu-ming. *Chung-kuo hsien-hsing ping-i chih-tu.* Hong kong, 1938.

Ch'eng T'ien-fang. *Ch'eng T'ien-fang tsao-nien hui-i-lu.* Taipei, 1968.

Ch'eng T'ien-ku. *Ch'eng-T'ien-ku hui-i-lu.* Hong kong, 1978.

Chia Shih-i. *Min-kuo ts'ai-cheng ching-chi wen-t'i chin-hsi kuan.* Taipei, 1954.

Chiang Ching-kuo. *Feng yü chung ti ning-ching.* Taipei, 1973.

———. *Wo ti fu-ch'ing.* Taipei, 1959.

Chiang Chün-chang. *Chung-hua min-kuo chien-kuo shih.* Taipei, 1957.

Chiang Kai-shek (Chung-cheng). *Chiang tsung-t'ung chi.* 2 vols. Taipei, 1960.

———. *Chiang tsung-t'ung mi-lu.* 13 vols. Taipei, 1978.

———. *Chiang tsung-t'ung yen-lun hui-pien.* 24 vols. Taipei, 1956.

———. *China's Destiny and Chinese Economic Theory.* New York, 1947.

———. *Chin-hou fa-chan tang-wu ti t'u-chin.* Chungking, 1941.

———. *Chün-shih wei-yüan-hui wei-yüan-chang Nan-ch'ang hsing-ying ch'u-li chiao-fei sheng-fen cheng-chih kung-tso pao-kao.* N.p., 1934.

———. *Kai-chin tang-wu cheng-chih chih t'u-ching yü fang-chen.* N.p., 1943.

———. *Liu-chung ch'üan-hui hou tang-cheng-chün tang-ch'ien chi-wu.* N.p., 1939.

———. *Lu-shan hsün-lien chi.* N.p., n.d.

———. *Mu-ch'ien tang ti yao-wu.* N.p., 1939.

———. *Nan-yü chün-shih hui-i k'ai-hui hsün-tz'u.* N.p., 1938.

———. *O-mei hsün-lien chi.* Nanking, 1947.

———. *Ping-i jen-yüan chih yao-wu.* N.p., 1940.

———. *Soviet Union in China.* New York, 1958.

———. *Tang-cheng hsün-lien ti yao-chih.* N.p., 1939.

———. *Tsung-ts'ai tui t'ui-hsing ping-i chih hsün-shih.* Sian, 1944.

———. *Tsung-ts'ai tui-yü liang-shih wen-t'i ti hsün-shih.* N.p., 1941.

———. *T'uan-chang hsün-tz'u hsüan-tu.* 4 vols. Chungking, 1943.

———. *Tzu-fan-lu.* 6 vols. N.p., 1931.

———. *Yü-O-Wan san sheng chiao-fei ssu-ling-pu kung-tso tsung-pao-kao.* 2 vols. N.p., 1932.

Chiang Shang-ch'ing. *Cheng-hai mi-wen.* Hong kong, 1966.

Chiang Wei-kuo, ed. *K'ang Jih i wu.* 10 vols. Taipei, 1978.

Ch'ien Chia-chü, Hu Yü-chih, and Chang T'ieh-sheng, ed. *K'ang-chan ti ching-yen yü chiao-hsün.* Chungking, 1939.

Ch'in Te-shun. *Ch'in Te-shun hui-i-lu.* Taipei, 1967.

Ching-chi-pu (Ministry of Economic Affairs). *K'ang-chan shih-ch'i chih Chung-kuo ching-chi.* 3 vols. Reprint. Hong kong, 1968.

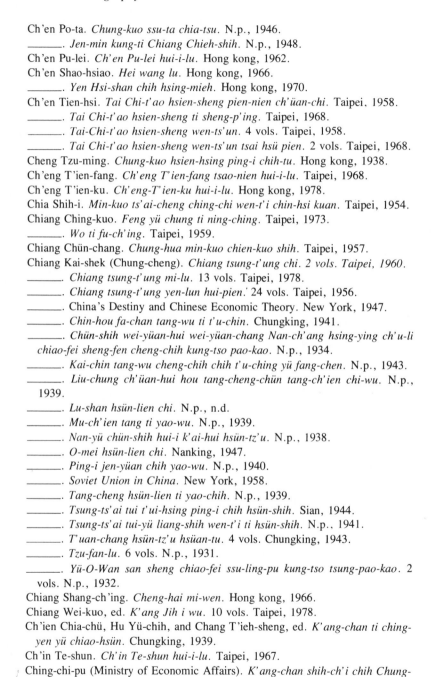

Ching-chi tzu-liao-she, ed. *T. V. Soong hao-men tzu-pen nei-mu.* Hong kong, 1948.
Ch'iu Kuo-cheng. *Shih-chiu-lu-chün hsing-wang-shih.* Hong kong, 1969.
_____. *Ta-pieh-shan pa-nien k'ang-chan chih hui-i.* Kowloon, 1970.
Chou Ch'üan. *Kuei-hsi chieh-p'o.* Shanghai, 1947.
Chou Fo-hai. *Cheng-chih p'ien.* Chungking, 1938.
_____. *Chou Fo-hai jih-chi.* Hong kong, 1955.
Chou K'ai-ch'ing. *Min-kuo Ssu-ch'uan jen-wu chuan-chi.* Taipei, 1966.
_____. *Min-kuo Ssu-ch'uan shih-shih.* Taipei, 1969.
Chou Yü-ying. *Fa-hsi-ssu-ti yü Chung-kuo ko-ming.* Shanghai, 1936.
Chu Cheng-sheng. *Ai chiang-nan.* 10 vols. Hong kong, 1962.
_____. *Li Han-hun chiang-chün jih-chi.* 2 vols. Hong kong, 1975.
Chu Ssu-huang. *Min-kuo ching-chi shih.* Shanghai, 1948.
Chung Chi-ming. *Kuan pi min fan.* N.p., 1945.
Chung Ch'i-sheng. *Ta ts'ai-fa Chiang Chieh-shih.* Hong kong, 1948.
Chung-hua pien-i-kuan. *Wei ta ti hsin Chung-kuo.* Chungking, 1939.
Chung-kuo chan-ch'ü, Chung-kuo lu-chün tsung-ssu-ling-pu. *Shou-hsiang pao-kao-shu.* Taipei, 1969.
Chung-kuo hsien-tai-shih tzu-liao pien-chi wei-yüan-hui. *Ts'ung chiu-i-pa tao ch'i-ch'i Kuo-min-tang ti t'ou-hsiang cheng-ts'e yü jen-min ti k'ang-chan yün-tung.* Shanghai, 1959.
Chung-lien ch'u-pan-she. *Chung-kuo tang-p'ai.* Nanking, 1948.
Fang Hsien-t'ing, ed. *Chan-shih Chung-kuo ching-chi yen-chiu.* Chungking, 1941.
Feng Chü-p'ei. *K'ang-chan chung ti ti-wu-lu-chün.* Hankow, 1938.
Feng Ho-fa, ed. *Chung-kuo nung-ts'un ching-chi tzu-liao.* 2 vols. Reprint. Taipei, 1978.
_____, ed. *Chung-kuo nung-ts'un ching-chi tzu-liao hsü-pien.* 2 vols. Reprint. Taipei, 1978.
Feng Tzu-ch'ao. *Chung-kuo k'ang-chan shih.* Shanghai, 1946.
Feng Yü-hsiang. *Wo so jen-shih ti Chiang Chieh-shih.* Hong kong, 1949.
_____. *Wo ti sheng huo.* 3 vols. Chungking, 1943.
Fu Ch'i-hsüeh. *Kuo-fu i-chiao kai-yao.* Taipei, 1966.
Ho Kuo-kuang. *Pa-shih tzu-shu.* Taipei, 1964.
Ho Wen-lung. *Chung-kuo t'e-wu nei-mu.* Hong kong, 1947.
Ho Ying-ch'in. *Ho shang-chiang k'ang-chan ch'i-chien chün-shih pao-kao.* 2 vols. Taipei, 1962.
_____. *Ping-i yü kung-i.* Chungking, 1940.
Hsi-an shih-pien san-i. Hong kong, 1962.
Hsieh Sen. *Tang-kuo ta-shih chi-yao.* Kweilin, 1943.
Hsü Chien-nung. *Tsui-chin Ssu-ch'uan ts'ai-cheng lun.* Chungking, 1940.
Hsü K'an. *Hsü K'o-t'ing hsien-sheng wen-ts'un.* Taipei, 1970.
Hsü Kao-yang. *Kuo-fang nien-chien.* Hong kong, 1969.
Hsü T'i-hsin. *Kuan-liao tzu-pen lun.* Hong kong, 1947.
Hsü Yung-p'ing, *Ch'en Pu-lei hsien-sheng chuan.* Taipei, 1977.
Hu Shih. *Ting Wen-chiang ti chuan-chi.* Taipei, 1956.
Hu Sung-p'ing. *Chu Chia-hua hsien-sheng nien p'u.* Taipei, 1969.

286   Bibliography

Hu Tsung-nan hsien-sheng chi-nien-chi. Taipei, 1962.
Hu Tsung-nan. *Tsung-nan wen-ts'un.* Taipei, 1963.
Hua-mei ch'u-pan kung-ssu, ed. *Chung-kuo ch'üan-mien k'ang-chan ta-shih-chi.* 2 vols. Shanghai, 1938.
Huang Shao-hung. *Wu-shih hui-i.* 2 vols. Hangchow, 1945.
Jen-min ch'u-pan-she, ed. *K'ang-Jih chan-cheng shih-ch'i chieh-fang-chün kai k'uang.* Peking, 1953.
————. *K'ang-Jih chan-cheng shih-ch'i ti Chung-kuo jen-min chieh-fang-chün.* Peking, 1953.
Jung Meng-yüan. *Kuo-tse Chiang Chieh-shih.* Peking, 1950.
Kao Yin-tsu. *Chung-hua-min-kuo ta-shih-chi.* Taipei, 1957.
Kou Chi-t'ang. *Chung-kuo lu-chün ti-san-fang-mien-chün k'ang-chan chi-shih.* Taipei, 1962.
Kuo-fang-pu (Ministry of National Defense). *Kung-fei fan-tung wen-chien hui-pien.* Taipei, n.d.
————. *Kuo-chün li-chieh chan-tou hsü-lieh-piao hui-pien.* 2 vols. Taipei, 1964.
————. *Lu-chün chün-kuan hsüeh-hsiao hsiao-shih.* 6 vols. Taipei, 1969.
————. *Lu-chun chün-kuan-tso tzu-chi-pu.* Chungking, 1944. Vol. 1.
Kuo-fang-pu, Bureau of Intelligence. *Tai Yü-nung hsien-sheng ch'üan-chi.* 2 vols. Taipei, 1979.
Kuo-fang-pu, Bureau of War History, *Chiao-fei chan shih.* 12 vols. Taipei, 1962.
————. *Chung Jih chan-cheng shih-lüeh.* 4 vols. Taipei, 1962.
————. *Fa-kuo chu Hua chün-shih ku-wen-t'uan kung-tso chi-yao.* Taipei, 1968.
————. *Jih-pen chün-shih ku-wen(chiao-kuan) tsai Hua kung-tso chi-yao.* Taipei, 1968.
————. *K'ang Jih chan-shih.* 100 vols. with individual subtitles. Taipei, 1967.
————. *Pei-fa chan-shih.* 5 vols. Taipei, 1967.
————. *Te-kuo chu Hua chün-shih ku-wen-t'uan kung-tso chi-yao.* Taipei, 1969.
Lei Hai-tsung. *Chung-kuo wen-hua yü Chung-kuo ti ping.* Hong kong, 1968.
Lei Hsiao-chin. *Sa-nien tung-luan Chung-kuo.* 2 vols. Hong kong, n.d.
Li Chien-nung. *Chung-shan ch'u-shih hou Chung-kuo liu-shih-nien ta-shih-chi.* Shanghai, 1929.
Li Hsien-liang. *K'ang-chan hui-i-lu.* Tsingtao, 1948.
Li Tsung-huang. *Hsien-cheng wen-t'i.* Chungking, 1943.
————. *Hsin-hsien-chih chiang-yen-chi.* Chungking, 1939.
————. *Li Tsung-huang hui-i-lu.* 2 vols. Taipei, 1972.
Li Tung-fang. *Chiang kung Chieh-shih hsü-chuan.* Taipei, 1976.
Liang Sheng-chün. *Chiang Li tou cheng nei-mu.* Hong kong, 1954.
Liu Chien-ch'ün. *Yin-ho i-wang.* Taipei, 1966.
Liu Chih. *Wo ti hui-i.* Taipei, 1966.
Liu Ch'ing-yang. *Pao-wei Hua-pei ti yu-chi-chan.* Sheng-huo shu-tien, 1938.
Liu Shao-t'ang. *Min-kuo ta-shih jih-chih.* 2 vols. Taipei, 1973-.
Lo Chia-lun. *Liu-shih-nien lai chih Chung-kuo Kuo-min-tang yü Chung-kuo.* Taipei, 1954.
Mao Tse-tung. *Mao Tse-tung hsüan-chi.* Ed. Chung-kung chun-yang Mao Tse-tung hsüan-chi ch'u-pan wei-yüan-hui. Peking, 1964.

Mao Tse-tung ssu-hsiang wan-sui. N.p., n.d.

P'an Shih-cheng. *Chan-shih hsi-nan.* Peking, 1946.

P'eng Tun-chih. *Ch'ing-suan Kuei-hsi.* Hong kong, 1950.

Pien Chang-wu. *Kuo-min-tang p'an-kuo t'ou-ti yao-yüan kai-kuan.* Changchiak'ou, 1949.

San-nien lai chih Ho-pei tang-wu. N.p., 1939.

Shang-hai t'ung-she. *Shang-hai yen-chiu tzu-liao hsü-chi.* Shanghai, 1939.

Shao Yü-lin. *Sheng-li ch'ien-hou.* Taipei, 1967.

Shao Yüan-ch'ung. *Hsüan-fu i-shu.* 2 vols. Taipei, 1954.

Shen I-yün. *I-yün hui-i.* Taipei, 1968.

Shih-chien hsüen-she, ed. *Jih-chün tsai Chung-kuo fang-mien chih tso-chan chi-lu.* 4 vols. Taipei, 1960.

Shu-pao chien-hsün-she. *Kuo-min-tang liu-chieh chung-wei ko p'ai-hsi ming-tan.* Nanking, 1945.

Sun Yat-sen. *Kuo-fu ch'üan-chi.* 6 vols. Taipei, 1961.

Tai Chi-t'ao. *Ch'ing-nien chih lu.* Shanghai, 1928.

T'ang En-po hsien-sheng chi-nien-chi. Taipei, 1964.

T'ang-jen. *Ching-lin ch'un-meng.* Hong kong, 1964.

———. *Shih-nien nei-chan.* Hong kong, 1964.

T'ao Chü-yin. *Chiang Pai-li hsien-sheng chuan.* Shanghai, 1948.

———. *Chiang Pai-li p'ing-chuan.* Hong kong, 1963.

Teng Wen-i. *Ts'ung-chün pao kuo chi.* Taipei, 1979.

Ting Wang, ed. *P'eng Te-huai wen-t'i ch'üan-chi.* Hong kong, 1969.

Ts'ai-cheng-pu. *Ti-san-tz'u ch'üan-kuo ts'ai-cheng hui-i hui-pien.* 1941. Reprint. Taipei, 1972.

Ts'ai T'ing-k'ai. *Ts'ai T'ing-k'ai tzu-chuan.* Hong kong, 1946.

Ts'ao Chü-jen. *Chiang Ching-kuo lun.* Hong kong, 1953.

———. *Hung cha hsia ti nan Chung-kuo.* N.p., n.d.

Ts'ao Kuo-ch'ing. *Chung-kuo ts'ai-cheng wen-t'i yü li-fa.* Shanghai, 1947.

Wang Chien-min. *Chung-kuo Kung-ch'an-tang shih-kao.* 3 vols. Taipei, 1965.

Wu Hsiang-hsiang. *Ch'en Kuo-fu ti i-sheng.* Taipei, 1971.

———. *Min-kuo pai-jen chuan.* 4 vols. Taipei, 1971.

———. *Ti-erh-tz'u Chung Jih chan-cheng shih.* 2 vols. Taipei, 1973.

Wu T'ieh-ch'eng. *Wu T'ieh-ch'eng hui-i-lu.* Taipei, 1968.

Wu Ting-ch'ang. *Hua-hsi hsien pi.* Kweiyang, 1940.

———. *Hua-hsi hsien pi hsü-pien.* Kweiyang, 1943.

Yi Hsün. *Chiang tang cheng-hsiang.* N.p., 1949.

Yü Liang. *K'ung Hsiang-hsi.* Hong kong, 1955.

Yu-lien ch'u-pan-she. *P'eng Te-huai.* Hong kong, 1969.

Bureau of Investigation Archives (Hsin-tien, Taiwan)

Chang Ch'ang-keng. *Chan-ti tang-wu kung-tso ti li-lun yü shih-chien.* Ninth war zone, 1942.

Chang Ch'iang. *Tang ti tsu-chih yü hsün-lien wen-t'i.* Chungking, 1943.

Chang Pao-shu. *Chung-kung tsai Ho-pei huo-tung chi-shih.* N.p., 1940.

Chang T'ung-ts'ai. *Fen ch'ü lien-ping hui-i chi-lu-pu*. Yenan, 1945.

Chang Wei-han. *Ko sheng shih-shih hsin-hsien-chih chih chien-t'ao*. Chungking, 1944.

Chang Yüan-shou. *Min-ping kung tso hsüan chi*. CCP Central China Bureau, 1942.

Ch'en Ch'eng. *Pa-nien k'ang-chan ching-kuo kai-yao*. Nanking, 1946.

―――. *Ti-erh-ch'i k'ang-chan kuan-yü cheng-hsün kung-tso chih chih-shih*. N.p., 1938.

―――. *Tsui-chin chün-cheng chung-hsin kung-tso*. N.p., 1945.

Ch'en I-hsin. *Chung-kung tsai Ho-pei chih mien-mien kuan*. Lin-hsien, Honan, 1940.

Chiang K'e-fu. *K'ang Jih keng-chü-ti Lu-hsi-pei ch'ü*. N.p., 1939.

Chiao-kung ti li-lun yü shih-chi. N.p., 1928.

Ch'iao Ming-li. *Ho-pei min-chün li-shih kai-yao*. N.p., 1941.

―――. *Ho-pei min-chün tso-chan ching-kuo kai-yao*. N.p., 1941.

Chieh-fang jih-pao. *Kuo-min-tang tang-cheng-chün yao-yüan p'an-kuo t'ou-ti kai-kuan*. Yenan, n.d.

Chin-Chi-Lu-Su ko sheng pu-hsing shih-chien. N.p., n.d.

Chou En-lai. *K'ang-chan ti hsin-hsing-shih yü hsin-ts'e-lüeh*. Hankow, 1938.

Chu Teh. *I-nien yü i lai Hua-pei ti k'ang-chan*. Yenan, 1938.

―――. *Ti-pa-lu-chün*. Yenan, 1938.

Chung-kuo Kuo-min-tang, Bureau of Statistics. *Chung-kung chih chün-tui tsu-chih yü yün-yung*. Chungking, 1940.

―――. *Chung-kuo Kung-ch'an-tang wu-li t'ung-chi*. Chungking, 1940.

―――. *Chung-kuo Kuo-min-tang tang-wu t'ung-chi chi-yao*. Chungking, 1941–45, annual reports.

―――. *Chung-kuo Kuo-min-tang tang-yüan tiao-ch'a shou-ts'e*. N.p., n.d.

―――. *Kung-fei tsai lun-hsien-ch'ü nei chih huo-tung chi pen tang ying-yu chih tui ts'e*. N.p., 1939.

―――. *Pa-lu-chün tsui-chin tsai Ho-pei huo-tung chi-shih*. N.p., n.d.

―――. *Tang-cheng, ch'ing-pao*. N.p., 1945–46.

―――. *Ti-shih-pa-chi-t'uan-chün tsai Ho-pei huo-tung chi-shih*. N.p., n.d.

Ho Lung. *Cheng-chün wen-t'i*. CCP Bureau of Northwestern China, 1943.

―――. *Ho Lung tsai pien-ch'ü kao-kan-hui pao-kao*. N.p., 1944.

Ho-pei ko hsien k'ang-chan shih-lüeh. N.p., n.d.

Ho-pei min-chün tsung-chih-hui-pu. *Hsien-ke kuan-hsin Ho-pei wen-t'i ti p'eng-yu*. N.p., 1939.

Ho-pei sheng-cheng-fu. *Ho-pei sheng ti-ch'ien kai-k'uang nien-pao*. N.p., 1941.

Ho-p'ing fan Kung chien-kuo wen-hsien. Nanking, 1944.

Hsin-hsien-chih shih-shih ch'eng-chi tsung-chien-t'ao chi shih-shih ch'ing-hsing yü shih-shih ch'eng-hsü. N.p., n.d.

Hsü Shu-huai. *K'ang-ta kuei-lao*. Hankow, 1938.

Hua-nan lun-hsien ch'ü t'e-chi. N.p., n.d.

K'ang-chan chung ti cheng-ping wen-t'i. N.p., n.d.

Kao Kang. *I-chiu-ssu-wu nien pien-ch'ü ti chu-yao jen-wu ho tso-feng wen-t'i*. N.p., 1945.

Kung-lun ch'u-pan-she. *Chung-kung chih mi-mi chün-shih kung-tso.* N.p., 1941.
Kung-tang tsai Chi tang cheng shih-shih kai-k'uang. N.p., n.d.
Kuo-chi kuan-hsi yen-chiu-so. *Fei O tseng-chih yüan-shih tzu-liao hui-pien.* Taipei, 1960–.
Kuo Kung liang-tang k'ang-chan ch'eng-chi ti pi-chiao. Yenan, 1943.
Li Chin. *Chan-tou chung ti chieh-fang-ch'ü min-ping.* N.p., n.d.
Lin Piao. *Chin-nien tseng-yang lien-ping.* T'ai-hang Military District, 1944.
———. *Chin-pei yu-chi-chan-cheng chi-shih.* Ch'angsha, 1938.
Liu Chien-ch'ün. *Fu-hsing Chung-kuo ko-ming chih lu.* Nanking, 1934.
———. *Kung-hsien i-tien cheng-li pen tang ti i-chien.* Nanking, 1931.
Liu Po-ch'eng. *Pa-lu-chün pai-t'uan ta-chan t'e-chi.* N.p., 1941.
Liu Yen-te. *Cheng-tun san-feng ts'an-k'ao ts'ai-liao.* Yenan, n.d.
P'eng Te-huai. *San-nien lai ti k'ang-chan.* N.p., 1940.
San-min-chu-i ch'ing-nien-t'uan. *San-min-chu-i ch'ing-nien-t'uan chung-yang t'uan-pu kung-tso pao-kao.* N.p., 1941, 1943, annual reports.
Shan-hsi sheng-cheng-fu. *Shan-hsi sheng-cheng-fu kung-tso pao-kao.* N.p., 1942, 1943, annual reports.
Shan-tung pao-an ti-liu-lü. *Shan-tung pao-an ti-liu-lü huo-tung kai-k'uang chi ch'i huan-chin.* N.p., 1944.
Shan-tung sheng ti-shih-san-ch'ü. *Shan-tung sheng ti-shih-san-ch'ü k'ang-chan chi-shih.* N.p., 1940.
Sheng-huo shu-tien, ed. *Chung-kuo ti-hou k'ang Jih min-chu keng-chü-ti kai-k'uang.* Yenan, 1944.
———, ed. *Pao-wei Hua-pei ti yu-chi-chan.* Yenan, 1938.
Ssu-ch'uan sheng-cheng-fu. *Ssu-ch'uan sheng kai-k'uang.* N.p., 1939.
———. *Ssu-ch'uan sheng min-cheng t'ung-chi.* N.p., 1941.
T'ang Chung. *K'ang-chan pi-chi.* N.p., n.d.
Wan Tzu-ling. *Ho-pei ti kung-tang ho shih-pa-chi-t'uan-chün.* N.p., n.d.
Wang Wei-wen. *K'u-ts'eng en-kan ti Ho-pei min-chün.* Chungking, 1939.
Wo-men tsen-yang tsai ti-hou ch'eng-li k'ang-Jih cheng-ch'üan. N.p., 1939.
Yeh Chien-ying. *Yeh Chien-ying k'ang-chan yen-lun chi.* Chungking, 1940.
Yeh Ch'ing. *Tang-p'ai wen-t'i.* Chungking, 1939.
Yeh Ch'u-ch'ang. *Tang-wu shih-shih shang ti wen-t'i.* Chungking, 1940.
Yü Chien-nung. *Ho-pei chien-wen chi-shih.* N.p., 1942.
Yü Hou. *Shan-pei hung-chün ch'üan-mao.* Shanghai, 1938.
Yün-nan sheng tang-pu yüan-ko. N.p., n.d.

Kuomintang Party Archives (Taipei, Taiwan)

An-hui sheng-cheng-fu. *An-hui sheng hsing-cheng kung-tso chien-t'ao.* N.p., 1942.
Chan-ch'ü hsien-cheng ch'in-hsing t'ung-chi. N.p., n.d.
Chan-ti (ti-hou-fang yu-chi-ch'ü) tang-cheng-chün kung-tso chih-tao kang-ling yao-mu. N.p., 1940.
Chang Chi. *Kai-ko tang-cheng chien-i-shu.* Chungking, 1941.
Chang Chih-chung. *Chün-shih-wei-yüan-hui cheng-chih-pu kung-tso kai-k'uang.* Chungking, 1945.

————. *I-erh-pa Sung-Hu chan-i hui-i-lu.* N.p., 1946.

Chang Chüeh-wu. *Sung-Hu k'ang Jih k'ang-chan so-te chih ching-yen yü chiao-hsün.* Nanking, 1932.

Chang Li-sheng. *Nei-cheng-pu sa-san-nien-tu kung-tso kai-k'uang.* Chungking, 1944.

Ch'en Cheng. *Ti-i wai-wu yü fu-hsing min-tsu.* Nanking, 1936.

Ch'en Fang-hsien. *Kai-chin tang-wu kung-tso i-chien.* Chungking, 1940.

Ch'en I-hsin. *Kai-chin Ho-pei sheng tang-wu i-chien-shu.* N.p., 1940.

Ch'en Yin-kuang. *Tang-ch'ien wo kuo nung-ts'un ching-chi wen-t'i.* Chungking, 1944.

Chia Ching-te. *Ch'üan-hsü-pu sa-san-nien kung-tso pai-kao.* Chungking, 1944.

Chiang-hsi sheng-cheng-fu. *Chiang-hsi sheng yün-shu kai-k'uang.* N.p., 1941.

Chieh-shou ch'u-li ti-wei wu-tzu ch'ing-ch'a-t'uan. *Chieh-shou ch'u-li ti-wei wu-tzu ch'ing-ch'a-t'uan kung-tso tsung-pao-kao.* Nanking, 1947.

Chou Chung-yüeh. *Nei-cheng-pu sa-nien-tu cheng-wu shih-shih pao-kao.* Chungking, 1941.

————. *Tsui-chin chih nei-cheng.* Chungking, 1943.

Chou Jung. *Chan-ti hsien-cheng ti chi ko chung-yao wen-t'i.* Ninth war zone, 1942.

Chu Chia-hua. *Tang ti tsu-chih yü ling-tao.* Chungking, 1942.

————. *Tang-wu shih shih shang chih wen-t'i.* Chungking, 1940.

Chu Tzu-shuang. *Chung-kuo Kuo-min-tang liang-shih cheng-ts'e.* N.p., 1944.

Ch'üan-kuo chün-tui tang-pu chu-ti-piao. N.p., 1943.

Ch'üan-kuo ko hsün-lien chi-kuan shou-hsün jen-yüan lei-pieh chi ch'i chieh-ts'eng. N.p., 1940.

Chung-kuo Kuo-min-tang, Central Executive Committee. *Ch'ueh ting tang yü t'uan chih kuan-hsi pan-fa.* Chungking, 1940.

————. *Chung-yang hsün-lien-t'uan tang-cheng hsün-lien-pan kung-tso t'ao-lun tzu-liao hsüan-lu tseng-pien.* Chungking, 1943.

————. *Ju ho tsuo hsien ti tang-wu kung-tso.* N.p., 1938.

————. *Ju ho tsuo hsien ti tang-wu kung-tso.* N.p., 1943.

————. *Tang-yüan t'ung-chi.* Nanking, 1930.

Chung-kuo Kuo-min-tang, Control Commission. *Tang-yüan chien-ch'a-wang.* Chungking, 1941.

Chung-kuo Kuo-min-tang, Commission on Party History. *Chung-kuo Kuo-min-tang nien-chien, 1929.* Nanking, 1930).

————. *Chung-kuo Kuo-min-tang nien-chien, 1934.* Nanking, 1935.

————. *Chung-kuo Kuo-min-tang nien-chien, 1940.* Chungking, 1941.

————. *Huang-p'u chien-chün san-shih-nien kai-shu.* N.p., n.d.

Chung-kuo Kuo-min-tang, Department of Organization. *Chu pu-chang tsui-chin tui-yü tang-wu kung-tso t'ung-chih chih chih-shih.* Chungking, 1942.

————. *Chung-kuo Kuo-min-tang tang-yüan chin shih nien lai chih fa-chan ch'ü-shih t'ung-chi-piao.* Chungking, 1940.

————. *Chün-tui tang-kung tsung-ho ti chien-t'ao yü chih-tao.* Chungking, 1940.

————. *Ju ho tsuo hao hsien ti tang-wu kung-tso.* Chungking, 1943.

————. *Ko chi tang-pu cheng-shu i-chien tse-yao.* 2 vols. N.p., 1941.

_____. *Ko sheng shih lu tang-pu tsu-chih k'o(ku)-chung hui-i chi-yao*. N.p., 1946.

_____. *Pa-nien lai chih chün-tui tang-wu*. Nanking, 1946.

_____. *Tang ti kung-tso*. Chungking, 1939.

Chung-kuo Kuo-min-tang, Department of Propaganda. *Ch'ing-nien-t'uan ch'uang-li liu-chou-nien*. Chungking, 1944.

_____. *K'ang-chan liu-nien lai chih tang-wu*. Chungking, 1943.

_____. *San-shih-nien-tu k'ang-chan chien-kuo kung-tso shih-chi*. Chungking, 1942.

Chung-kuo Kuo-min-tang, Pei-ching shih tang-pu. *Kai-tsu-p'ai chih tsung-chien-t'ao*. Peking, 1930.

Chung-kuo Kuo-min-tang, Secretariat. *Chung-kuo Kuo-min-tang jen-shih t'ung-chi chi-yao*. Nanking, 1946.

_____. *Chung-yang ko chi-kuan hsiao-tsu hui-i t'ao-lun hui Wu mi-shu-chang chiang-hua chi-lu*. Chungking, 1944.

_____. *Chung-yang tang-pu chih-yüan-lu*. Nanking, 1934; Chungking, 1940, 1941, 1943, annual editions.

_____. *Ko sheng chi-ts'eng tang-cheng ch'ing-hsin chien-piao*. Chungking, 1944.

Chung-yang lu-chün chün-kuan hsüeh-hsiao. *Chung-yang lu-chün chün-kuan hsüeh-hsiao ch'eng-li shih-wu chou-nien chi-nien-ts'e*. Chengtu, 1939.

_____. *Chung-yang lu-chün chün-kuan hsüeh-hsiao shih-kao*. 10 vols. N.p., 1936.

Chung-ching shih tang-pu. *Ch'ung-ch'ing shih tang-wu huan-ching chih shuo-ming*. Chungking, 1940.

Chün-shih wei-yüan-hui (Supreme Military Affairs Commission). *Chan-ti tang-cheng wei-yüan-hui tsu-chih kang-yao*. N.p., 1940.

_____. *Chün-tui cheng-chih kung-tso chiang-i kang-yao*. Chungking, 1940.

_____. *K'ang-chan ssu-nien*. Chungking, 1941.

_____. *Nan-ch'ang hsing-ying ch'u-li chiao-fei sheng-fen cheng-chih kung-tso pao-kao*. Nanch'ang, 1934.

_____. *Pu-tui cheng-kung jen-yüan jen-shih tung-t'ai t'ung-chi-t'u*. N.p., n.d.

_____. *Ti-erh-ch'i k'ang-chan chün-tui tang-yüan hsün-lien kang-yao*. N.p., n.d.

_____. *Ti-erh-ch'i k'ang-chan ti-i-chieh-tuan kuo-chün tso-chan chih ching-yen chiao-hsün*. Chungking, 1942.

Erh-nien lai chih Ho-pei tang-wu. N.p., 1939.

Fu-chien-sheng hsien-cheng jen-yüan hsün-lien-so. *Hsien-cheng jen-yüan hsün-lien*. N.p., 1939.

Han Ch'i-t'ung. *Chung-kuo tui Jih chan-shih sun-shih chih ku-chi, (1937–1943)*. Shanghai, 1946.

Hsien-tai-Chung-kuo chou-k'an she. *Chan-tou ti liang-nien*. Shanghai, 1939.

Hsing-cheng-yüan (Executive Yüan). *Hsing-cheng ts'an-k'ao t'ung-chi tzu-liao*. Chungking, 1944.

_____. *Hsing-cheng-yüan kung-tso pao-kao*. Chungking, 1942.

_____. *Kuo-min-cheng-fu nien-chien, 1943–44*. 2 vols. Chungking, 1946.

Hsü K'an. *Liang-shih-pu sa-san-nien-tu kung-tso kai-k'uang*. Chungking, 1945.

_____. *Liang-shih wen-t'i.* N.p., 1942.

_____. *Tsui-chin chih liang-cheng.* N.p., 1942.

Hsüeh Yüeh. *K'ang-chan hui-i-lu.* N.p., 1945.

_____. *Hsüeh Yüeh k'ang-chan shou-kao.* N.p., 1948.

Hu-nan sheng-cheng-fu. *Hsüeh chu-hsi san-nien pao-cheng.* N.p., 1942.

_____. *Hsiang-cheng liu-nien t'ung-chi.* N.p., 1942.

_____. *Hu-nan sheng sa-nien-tu tang-cheng-chün lien-ho shih-ch'a-tsu shih-ch'a ko-hsien tsung-chien-t'ao.* N.p., 1942.

_____. *Hu-nan sheng tang-wu t'ung-chi t'i-yao.* N.p., 1941.

_____. *Hu-nan sheng ti-i-ch'i shih-shih hsin-hsien-chih ko hsien ch'ou-pei hui-i chi-lu.* N.p., 1940.

Hu-pei sheng-cheng-fu. *Hu-pei sheng min-cheng t'ung-chi.* N.p., 1941.

Kan Chieh-hou. *K'ang-chan chung chün-shih wai-chiao ti chuan-pien.* N.p., 1938.

Kan-Yüeh-Ming pien-ch'ü chiao-fei ssu-ling-pu. *Kan-Yüeh-Ming pien-ch'ü chiao-fei kung-tso pao-kao chia-p'ien.* N.p., 1932.

Kuang-hsi sheng-cheng-fu. *Kuang-hsi t'ung-chi shu-tzu t'i-yao.* N.p., 1946.

Kuang-tung sheng-cheng-fu. *Hsin-hsien-chih yen-chiu.* N.p., 1940.

_____. *Kuang-tung sheng-cheng-fu kung-tso pao-kao.* N.p., 1943.

Kuo Huan. *Chan-shih t'ien-fu cheng-li wen-t'i.* Chungking, 1942.

Kwei-chou sheng-cheng-fu. *Ch'ien-cheng san-nien.* Kweiyang, 1947.

_____. *Kwei-chou sheng-cheng-fu kung-pao.* Kweiyang, 1944.

Lu-chün hsin-pien ti-san-shih-chiu-shih. *Lu-chün hsin-pien ti-san-shih-chiu-shih kai-k'uang.* N.p., 1943.

Lu-chün t'ung-chi (Lu-chün t'ung-chi chien-ming pao-kao-shu). 28 vols. Peking, 1926.

Nei-cheng-pu (Ministry of Interior). *Ko sheng shih-shih hsien ko-chi tsu-chih kang-yao ch'eng-chi tsung-pao-kao t'i-yao.* Chungking, 1943.

_____. *Nei-cheng-pu t'ung-chi t'i-yao.* Chungking, 1945.

_____. *Shen hsüan hsien-chang.* Nanking, 1929.

_____. *Ti-san-tz'u ch'üan-kuo nei-cheng hui-i chi-lu chi yu kuan wen-chien.* Chungking, 1942.

_____. *Ti-san-tz'u ch'üan-kuo nei-cheng hui-i nei-cheng-pu shih-cheng pao-kao.* Chungking, 1942.

_____. *Ti-san-tz'u ch'üan-kuo nei-cheng hui-i pao-kao-shu.* Chungking, 1942.

Nung-lin-pu (Ministry of Agriculture and Forestry). *K'ang-chan ssu-nien lai chih nung-yeh.* Chungking, 1941.

Pai Ch'ung-hsi. *K'ang-chan pa-nien chün-shih kai-k'uang.* N.p., 1946.

_____. *Tang ch'ien ti liang-cheng ho ping-i.* N.p., 1942.

Ping-i-pu (Ministry of Conscription). *K'ang-chan pa-nien lai ping-i hsing-cheng kung-tso tsung-pao-kao.* Chungking, 1945.

Sai-k'e-t'e (General von Seeckt). *I-ke chün-jen chih ssu-hsiang.* Nanking, 1937.

San-min chu-i ch'ing-nien-t'uan. *Tang yü t'uan ti kuan-hsi.* N.p., 1939.

Shan-tung-sheng ti shih-san-ch'ü. *Shan-tung sheng ti shih-san-ch'ü k'ang-chan chi-shih.* N.p., 1940.

She-hui-pu (Ministry of Social Affairs). *Ch'üan-kuo jen-min t'uan-t'i t'ung-chi.* Chungking, 1944.

————. *Ch'üan-kuo jen-min t'uan-t'i t'ung-chi tsung-piao.* Chungking, 1939.

Shen Hung-lieh. *Shan-tung tang-cheng-chün chiao-shou ta-kang.* N.p., 1941.

Shen Tsung-han. *Chung-kuo liang-shih wen-t'i.* N.p., 1940.

Sheng-huo shu-tien. *Chung-kuo ching-chi nien-pao.* N.p., n.d.

Su-lien chih-yüan-chün jen-su chi chan-chi tse-yao. N.p., 1940.

Tang-cheng hsün-lien-pan. *Tang-cheng hsün-lien-pan tang-wu kung-tso jen-yüan t'an-hua-hui chi-lu.* N.p., 1939.

————. *Tang-cheng hsün-lien-pan ti i erh san ssu nien hsün-lien chi-shih.* N.p., 1942.

————. *Tang-cheng hsün-lien-pan ti-ssu-nien hsün-lien shih lu.* N.p., 1942.

Tang-cheng kung-tso k'ao-he wei-yüan-hui. *Tang-cheng kung-tso k'ao-he wei-yüan-hui san-shih-nien-tu chung-yang ko chi-kuan kung-tso ch'eng-chi k'ao-ch'a pao-kao tsung-p'ing.* N.p., n.d.

————. *Tang-cheng kung-tso k'ao-he wei-yüan-hui san-shih-nien san-shih-i-nien-tu ko sheng cheng-wu k'ao-ch'a pao-kao tsung-p'ing.* N.p., 1942.

Teng Wen-i. *Ling-hsiu yen-hsing.* N.p., n.d.

Ti-chiu chan-ch'ü liang-shih kuan-li-ch'u. *Liang-shih chi-shih.* N.p., 1940.

Ti-wu-chün ssu-ling-pu. *Sung-Hu k'ang Jih chan-i ti-wu-chün chan-tou yao-pao.* Shanghai, 1932.

Ts'ai-cheng-pu (Ministry of Finance). *Chung-kuo ts'ai-cheng nien-chien.* Chungking, 1941; Nanking, 1948, annual report.

————. *Ts'ai-cheng nien-chien hsü-pien.* Chungking, 1942.

Tseng Yang-fu. *Tsui-chin chih chiao-t'ung.* N.p., 1944.

Ts'ui Ch'ang-cheng. *Hsien chieh-tuan chih cheng-ping wen-t'i.* Chungking, 1939.

Tuan Chien-min. *Kai-chin tang-wu fang-an.* N.p., 1945.

Wang Te-fu. *Hsin-hsien-chih chih chien-t'ao yü kai-chin.* Chungking, 1944.

Wang Tung-yüan. *Kan-pu hsün-lien wen-t'i.* N.p., 1941.

Weng Wen-hao. *Ti-wei tzu-ch'an chieh-shou ch'u-li kai-k'uang.* Nanking, 1945.

Wu T'ieh-ch'eng. *Wu T'ieh-ch'eng tsai chung-yang ko chi-kuan hsiao-tsu hui-i t'ao-lun-hui chiang-hua-tz'u.* Chungking, 1944.

Yü Kuo-cheng. *Ho-pei kuei-lai.* Loyang, 1940.

Yün-nan sheng-cheng-fu. *Yün-nan sheng-cheng-fu kung-tso pao-kao.* Kunming, 1941.

English-Language Materials

Alitto, Guy. "Rural Reconstruction—Experimental Hsien and Credit Cooperatives: A General Survey." Paper delivered at a seminar on local and provincial politics in Nationalist China at Boulder, Colo., October, 1974.

U.S. Senate, Committee on the Judiciary. *The Amerasia Papers: A Clue to the Catastrophe of China.* 2 vols. Washington, D.C., 1970.

Anders, Leslie. *The Ledo Road: General Joseph W. Stilwell's Highway to China.* Norman, Okla., 1965.

Bamba, Nobuya. *Japanese Diplomacy in a Dilemma: New Light on Japan's China Policy, 1924-1929.* Vancouver, B.C., 1972.

Barnett, A. Doak. *China on the Eve of Communist Takeover.* New York, 1966.

Barnett, Robert W. *Economic Shanghai: Hostage to Politics.* New York, 1941.

Barrett, David D. *Dixie Mission: The United States Army Observer Group in Yenan, 1944.* Berkeley, Calif., 1970.

Barrett, David Peter. "The Consolidation of Elitism in the Kuomintang, 1928-1929." Master's thesis, University of Toronto, 1970.

Bienen, Henry, ed. *The Military and Modernization.* Chicago, 1971.

————. *The Military Intervenes: Case Studies in Political Development.* New York, 1968.

Boorman, Howard L., and Howard, Richard C., eds. *Biographical Dictionary of Republican China.* 4 vols. New York, 1970.

Borg, Dorothy. *The Far Eastern Crisis of 1933-1938.* Cambridge, Mass., 1964.

Boyle, John Hunter. *China and Japan at War, 1937-1945: The Politics of Collaboration.* Stanford, Calif., 1972.

Buck, David D. "The Provincial Elite in Shangtung During the Republican Period—Their Successes and Failures." *Modern China* 1, no. 4 (October, 1975):417-46.

Buhite, Russell. *Patrick J. Hurley and American Foreign Policy.* Ithaca, N.Y., 1973.

Bush, Richard Clarence, III. "Industry and Politics in Kuomintang China: The Nationalist Regime and Lower Yangtze Chinese Cotton Mill Owners 1927-1937." Ph.D. dissertation, Columbia University, 1978.

Carlson, Evans Fordyce. *The Chinese Army: Its Organization and Military Efficiency.* New York, 1940.

————. *Twin Stars of China.* New York, 1940.

Cavendish, Patrick. "The 'New China' of the Kuomintang," in *Modern China's Search for a Political Form,* ed. Jack Gray. London, 1969.

Chang, Carsun. *The Third Force in China.* New York, 1952.

Chang, Kia-ngau. *The Inflationary Spiral: The Experience in China, 1939-1950.* New York, 1958.

Chang, John K. *Industrial Development in Pre-Communist China.* Chicago, 1969.

Ch'en, Jerome. "The Left Wing Kuomintang: A Definition," *Bulletin of the School of Oriental and African Studies,* no. 25 (1962):557-73.

Cheng Wan-ming. "The Battle of Pinghsingkuan Pass." *China Reconstructs* 20, no. 4 (April, 1971):2-6.

Chennault, Claire L. *Way of a Fighter.* New York, 1949.

Chesneaux, Jean. *Peasant Revolts in China, 1840-1949.* London, 1973.

————, ed. *Popular Movements and Secret Societies in China, 1840-1950.* Stanford, Calif., 1972.

Ch'i, Hsi-sheng. *Warlord Politics in China, 1916-1928.* Stanford, Calif., 1976.

Ch'ien, Tuan-sheng. *The Government and Politics of China.* Cambridge, Mass., 1950.

————. *History of Political Institutions Under the Chinese Republic.* Shanghai, 1939.

_____. "The Role of Military in the Chinese Government." *Pacific Affairs* 21 (1948):239–51.

Chinese Communist Party, comp. *Biographies of Kuomintang Leaders.* Yenan, 1945. English translation by Harvard University Committee on International and Regional Studies, 1948.

Chinese Statistical Yearbook, 1948. Nanking, 1948.

Chow, Yung-teh. *Social Mobilization in China: Status Careers among the Gentry in a Chinese Community.* New York, 1966.

Ch'u, Tung-tsu. *Local Government in China under the Ch'ing.* Stanford, Calif., 1969.

Coble, Parks, M., Jr. "The Shanghai Capitalist Class and the Nationalist Government, 1927–1937." Ph.D. dissertation, University of Illinois, 1975.

Cohen, Paul A., and Schrecker, John E., eds. *Reform in Nineteenth Century China.* Cambridge, Mass., 1976.

Cohen, Warren. "The Development of Chinese Communist Attitudes Towards the United States, 1934–45." *Orbis* 11 (Spring, 1967):219–37.

_____. "Who Fought the Japanese in Hunan? Some Views of China's War Effort." *Journal of Asian Studies* 27, no. 1 (November, 1967):111–15.

Conroy, F. Hilary. "Japan's War in China: Historical Parallel to Vietnam?" *Pacific Affairs,* vol. 43, no. 1 (Spring, 1970):61–72.

_____. "Japan's War in China: An Ideological Sommersault." *Pacific Historical Review* 21, no. 4 (Winter, 1952):367–79.

Coox, Alvin D. "Effects of Attrition on National War Effort: The Japanese Army Experience in China, 1937–38." *Military Affairs* 32, no. 2 (Summer, 1968):57–62.

Croizier, Brian, and Chou, Eric. *The Man Who Lost China: The First Full Biography of Chiang Kai-shek.* New York, 1976.

Crowley, James B. *Japan's Quest for Autonomy: National Security and Foreign Policy, 1930–1938.* Princeton, N.J., 1966.

_____, ed. *Modern East Asia: Essays in Interpretation.* New York, 1970.

Dahl, Robert A. "A Critique of the Ruling Elite Model." *The American Political Science Review* 52, no. 1 (March, 1958):463–69.

Davies, John P. *The Dragon by the Tail.* New York, 1972.

Dawson, Raymond H. *The Decision to Aid Russia, 1941.* Chapel Hill, N.C., 1959.

DeGrand, Alexander J. *The Italian Nationalist Association and the Rise of Fascism in Italy.* Lincoln, Nebr., 1978.

Dirlik, Arif. *Revolution and History: The Origin of the Marxist Historiography in China, 1919–1939.* Berkeley, Calif., 1978.

Dorn, Frank. *The Sino-Japanese War, 1937–41: From Marco Polo Bridge to Pearl Harbor.* New York, 1974.

_____. *Walkout with Stilwell in Burma.* New York, 1971.

Eastman, Lloyd E. *The Abortive Revolution: China Under Nationalist Rule, 1927–1937.* Cambridge, Mass., 1974.

Easton, David. *A Systems Analysis of Political Life.* New York, 1965.

Esherick, Joseph W. *Lost Chance in China: The World War II Dispatches of John*

S. Service. New York, 1974.

————. *Reform and Revolution in China: The 1911 Revolution in Hunan and Hubei.* Berkeley, Calif., 1976.

Fang, Chin-yen. "The Sian Incident: A Prelude to the Coming of the Sino-Japanese War (1937-1945) in China." Ph.D. dissertation, American University, 1977.

Fei Hsiao-tung. *China's Gentry.* Chicago, 1953.

Feuerwerker, Albert. *The Chinese Economy, 1912-1949.* Ann Arbor, Mich., 1968.

————. *Economic Trends in the Republic of China, 1912-1949.* Ann Arbor, Mich., 1977.

Murphey, Rhoads, and Wright, Mary, eds. *Approaches to Modern Chinese History.* Berkeley, Calif., 1976.

Fewsmith, Joseph. "Authoritarian Rule in Kuomingtang China." Master's thesis, University of Chicago, 1973.

————. "The Emergence of Authoritarian-Corporatist Rule in Republican China: The Changing Pattern of Business Association in Shanghai." Ph.D. dissertation, University of Chicago, 1980.

Finer, S. E. *The Man on Horseback: The Role of the Military in Politics.* New York, 1962.

Frillmann, Paul, and Peck, Graham. *China, the Remembered Life.* Boston, Mass., 1968.

Furth, Charlotte, ed. *The Limits of Change: Essays on Conservative Alternatives in Republican China.* Cambridge, Mass., 1976.

Geisert, Bradley Kent. "Power and Society: The Kuomintang and Local Elites in Kiangsu Province, China, 1924-1937." Ph.D. dissertation, University of Virginia, 1979.

Gillespie, Richard Eugene. "Whampoa and the Nanking Decade (1924-1936)." Ph.D. dissertation, American University, 1971.

Gillin, Donald G. *Warlord: Yen Hsi-shan in Shansi Province, 1911-1949.* Princeton, N.J., 1967.

Gray, Jack, ed. *Modern China's Search for a Political Form.* London, 1969.

Gregor, A. James. *Interpretations of Fascism.* New York, 1974.

Hahn, Emily. *Chiang Kai-shek: An Unauthorized Biography.* New York, 1955.

Hall, John Christopher S. *The Yünnan Provincial Faction, 1927-1937.* Canberra, Australia, 1976.

Herring, George C. *Aid to Russia, 1941-46.* New York, 1973.

Hinton, William. *Fanshen: A Documentary of Revolution in a Chinese Village.* New York, 1966.

Ho, Ping-ti and Tsou, Tang, eds. *China in Crisis.* 2 vols. Chicago, 1968.

Hsiao, Kung-chuan. *Rural China: Imperial Control in the Nineteenth Century.* Seattle, Wash., 1960.

Hsieh, Chiao-min. *China: Ageless Land and Countless People.* Princeton, N.J., 1967.

Hsüeh Chün-tu. *Revolutionary Leaders of Modern China.* New York, 1971.

Isaacs, Harold. *The Tragedy of the Chinese Revolution.* London, 1938.

Israel, John. *Student Nationalism in China, 1927-1937.* Stanford, Calif., 1966.

Janowitz, Morris. *The Military in the Political Development of New Nations.* Chicago, 1964.

———. *The New Military.* New York, 1964.

———. *The Professional Soldier.* New York, 1960.

Johnson, Chalmers A. *Peasant Nationalism and Communist Power: The Emergence of Revolutionary China, 1937-1945.* Stanford, Calif., 1961.

———. *Revolutionary Change.* Boston, Mass., 1966.

Jones, Susan Mann. "The Ningpo *Pang* and Financial Power in Shanghai." In *The Chinese City Between Two Worlds,* Mark Elvin and Skinner, G. William, eds., pp. 73-96. Stanford, Calif., 1974.

Jordon, Donald A. *The Northern Expedition: China's National Revolution of 1926-1928.* Honolulu, 1976.

Kahn, B. Winston. *Doihara Kenji and the North China Autonomy Movement, 1935-36.* Temple, Ariz., 1973.

Kapp, Robert A. *Szechwan and the Chinese Republic: Provincial Militarism and Central Power, 1911-1938.* New Haven, Conn., 1973.

Kataoka, Tetsuya. *Resistance and Revolution in China: The Communists and the Second United Front.* Berkeley, Calif., 1974.

Kornhauser, William. *The Politics of Mass Society.* New York, 1959.

Kotenov, Anatol M. *The Chinese Soldier.* Shanghai, 1937.

Lai, Jeh-hang. "A Study of a Faltering Democrat: The Life of Sun Fo, 1891-1949." Ph.D. dissertation, University of Illinois at Urbana-Champaign, 1976.

Lary, Diana. *Region and Nation: The Kwangsi Clique in Chinese Politics, 1925-1937.* Cambridge, Mass., 1974.

Lasswell, Harold D. *World Revolutionary Elites.* Cambridge, Mass., 1965.

Leighton, Richard M. *Global Logistics and Strategy.* 2 vols. Washington, D.C., 1955.

Li, Lincoln. *The Japanese Army in North China, 1937-1941: Problems of Political and Economic Control.* Tokyo, 1975.

Li, Tsung-jen. *The Memoirs of Li Tsung-jen.* Boulder, Colo., 1978.

Liang, Chin-tung. *General Stilwell in China, 1942-1944: The Full Story.* New York, 1972.

Lindsay, Michael. *The Unknown War: North China, 1937-1945.* London, 1975.

Linebarger, Paul M. A. *The China of Chiang Kai-shek.* Boston, Mass., 1943.

Liu, F. F. *A Military History of Modern China, 1924-1949.* Princeton, N.J., 1956.

Loh, Pichon P. Y. *The Early Chiang Kai-shek: A Study of His Personality and Politics, 1887-1924.* New York, 1971.

———. *The Kuomintang Debacle of 1949: Collapse or Conquest?* Lexington, Mass., 1965.

MacCloskey, Monro. *Rearming the French in World War II.* New York, 1972.

McCormack, Gavan. *Chang Tso-lin in Northeast China, 1911-28.* Stanford, Calif., 1977.

Mackerras, Colin, ed. *China: The Impact of Revolution—A Survey of Twentieth Century China.* Essex, England, 1976.

McElderry, Andrea Lee. *Shanghai Old-style Banks (Ch'ien-chuang), 1800-1935.* Ann Arbor, Mich., 1976.

Mao Tse-tung. *Selected Works of Mao Tse-tung.* Peking, 1964.

Miles, Milton. *A Different Kind of War.* New York, 1967.

Moore, Barrington, Jr. *Social Origins of Dictatorship and Democracy: Lord and Peasant in the Making of the Modern World.* Boston, 1966.

Morley, James William. *Japan's Road to War.* New York, 1976.

Nathan, Andrew J. *Peking Politics, 1918–1923: Factionalism and the Failure of Constitutionalism.* Berkeley, Calif., 1976.

Olenik, John Kenneth. "Left Wing Radicalism in the Kuomintang: Teng Yen-ta and the Genesis of the Third Party Movement in China, 1924–1931." Ph.D. dissertation, Cornell University, 1973.

Payne, Robert. *Chiang Kai-shek.* New York, 1969.

Peattie, Mark R. *Ishiwara Kanji and Japan's Confrontation with the West.* Princeton, N.J., 1975.

Peck, Graham. *Two Kinds of Time.* Boston, 1950.

Pepper, Suzanne. *Civil War in China: The Political Struggle, 1945–1949.* Berkeley, Calif., 1978.

Pratt, John Thomas. *War and Politics in China.* Reprint. Freeport, N.Y., 1971.

Romanus, Charles F., ed. *Stilwell's Personal File, China, Burma, India: 1942–1944.* 5 vols. Wilmington, Del., 1976.

Romanus, Charles F., and Sunderland, Riley. *Stilwell's Command Problems.* Washington, D.C., 1956.

_____. *Stilwell's Mission to China.* Washington, D.C., 1953.

_____. *Time Runs Out in CBI.* Washington, D.C., 1958.

Rosinger, Lawrence K. *China's Wartime Politics, 1937–1945.* Princeton, N.J., 1944.

Ruppenthal, Roland G. *Logistical Support of the Armies.* 2 vols. Washington, D.C., 1955.

Schaller, Michael. *The U.S. Crusade in China, 1938–1945.* New York, 1979.

Schiffrin, Harold Z. *Sun Yat-sen and the Origin of the Chinese Revolution.* Berkeley, Calif., 1968.

_____, ed. *Military and State in Modern Asia.* Jerusalem, 1976.

Selden, Mark. *The Yenan Way in Revolutionary China.* Cambridge, Mass., 1971.

Selle, Earl. *Donald of China.* New York, 1948.

Seps, J. Bernard. "German Military Advisors and Chiang Kai-shek, 1927–1938." Ph.D. dissertation, University of California at Berkeley, 1972.

Service, John S. *The Amerasia Papers: Some Problems in the History of U.S.-China Relations.* Berkeley, Calif., 1971.

Sheridan, James E. *China in Disintegration: The Republican Era in Chinese History, 1912–1949.* New York, 1975.

_____. *Chinese Warlord: The Career of Feng Yü-hsiang.* Stanford, Calif., 1966.

Shewmaker, Kenneth E. *Americans and Chinese Communists, 1927–1945: A Persuading Encounter.* Ithaca, N.Y., 1971.

Shirley, James. "Political Conflict in the Kuomintang: The Career of Wang Ching-wei to 1932." Ph.D. dissertation, University of California at Berkeley, 1964.

Shyu, Lawrence Nae-lih. "The People's Political Council and China's Wartime Problems, 1937-1945." Ph.D. dissertation, Columbia University, 1972.
Sih, Paul K. T., ed. *The Strenuous Decade: China's Nation-Building Efforts, 1927-1937*. New York, 1970.
_____. *Nationalist China During the Sino-Japanese War, 1937-1945*. Hicksville, N.Y., 1977.
Spence, Jonathan. *To Change China: Western Advisors in China, 1620-1960*. Boston, 1969.
Stratton, Roy. *SACO: The Rice Paddy Navy*. New York, 1950.
Stuart, J. Leighton. *Fifty Years in China: The Memoirs of John Leighton Stuart*. New York, 1954.
T'ang, Leang-li. *Wang Ching-wei: A Political Biography*. Peiping, 1931.
Thompson, James C., Jr. *While China Faced West: American Reformers in Nationalist China, 1928-1937*. Cambridge, Mass., 1969.
Tien, Hung-mao. *Government and Politics in Kuomintang China: 1927-1937*. Stanford, Calif., 1972.
Timperly, H. J. *What War Means: Japanese Terror in China*. N.p., 1938.
Ting, Yueh-hung Chen. "The Intellectuals and the Chinese Revolution: A Study of the China Democratic League and Its Components, 1939-1949." Ph.D. dissertation, New York University, 1978.
Toland, John. *The Rising Sun: The Decline and Fall of the Japanese Empire, 1936-1945*. New York, 1970.
Tong, Hollington K. *Chiang Kai-shek*. Taipei, 1953.
Tsou, Tang. *America's Failure in China, 1941-1950*. 2 vols. Chicago, 1963.
Tuchman, Barbara W. *Stilwell and the American Experience in China, 1911-1945*. New York, 1970.
Tucker, Robert C. *The Soviet Political Mind*. New York, 1971.
Tung, William L. *Revolutionary China: A Personal Account, 1926-1949*. New York, 1973.
United States Department of State. *The China White Paper*. 2 vols. Stanford, Calif., 1967.
_____. *Foreign Relations of the United States, Diplomatic Papers, 1937*. 5 vols. Washington, D.C., 1954, vols. 3 and 4, "The Far East."
_____. *Foreign Relations of the United States, Diplomatic Papers: 1942, China*. Washington, D.C., 1956.
_____. *Foreign Relations of the United States, Diplomatic Papers: 1943, China*. Washington, D.C., 1957.
_____. *Foreign Relations of the United States, Diplomatic Papers: 1944*. 7 vols. "China." Vol. 6. Washington, D.C., 1967.
_____. *Foreign Relations of the United States, Diplomatic Papers: 1945*. 9 vols. "The Far East: China." Vol. 7. Washington, D.C., 1969.
United States Office of Strategic Services. *The Guerrilla Front in North China*. Washington, D.C., 1943.
Utley, Freda. *Japan's Gamble in China*. N.p., 1938.
Van Slyke, Lyman P. *Enemies and Friends: The United Front in Chinese*

Communist History. Stanford, Calif., 1967.

——, ed. *The Chinese Communist Movement: A Report of the United States War Department*. Stanford, Calif., 1968.

Vladimirov, P. P. *China's Special Area, 1942–1945*. New Delhi, 1974.

Wang, Cheng. "The Kuomintang: A Sociological Study of Demoralization." Ph.D. dissertation, Stanford University, 1953.

Wedemeyer, Albert C. *Wedemeyer Reports!* New York, 1958.

Wei, William. "The KMT in Kiangsi: The Suppression of the Communist Bases, 1930–1934." Ph.D. dissertation, University of Michigan, 1978.

White, Theodore H., ed. *The Stilwell Papers*. New York, 1962.

White, Theodore H., and Jacoby, Annalee. *Thunder Out of China*. New York, 1946.

Wilbur, C. Martin, and Lien-ying How, Julie, eds. *Documents on Communism, Nationalism, and Soviet Advisors in China, 1918–1927*. New York, 1956.

Wilbur, C. Martin. *Sun Yat-sen: Frustrated Patriot*. New York, 1976.

Willmott, William E., ed. *Economic Organization in Chinese Society*. Stanford, Calif., 1972.

Woodhead, H. G. W., ed. *The China Year Book, 1929–30*. Shanghai, 1930.

Wright, Mary C., ed. *China in Revolution: The First Phase, 1900–1913*. New Haven, Conn., 1968.

Wu, Tien-wei. *The Sian Incident: A Pivotal Point in Modern Chinese History*. Ann Arbor, Mich., 1976.

Yang, C. K. *A Chinese Village in Early Communist Transition*. Cambridge, Mass., 1959.

Young, Arthur N. *China and the Helping Hand, 1937–1945*. Cambridge, Mass., 1963.

——. *China's Nation-Building Effort, 1927–1937: The Financial and Economic Record*. Stanford, Calif., 1971.

——. *China's Wartime Finance and Inflation, 1937–1945*. Cambridge, Mass., 1965.

Japanese-Language Materials

Aoi Shinichi, ed. *Taiheiyō sensō*. Pt. 2. In *Taiheiyō sensō shi*, edited by Rekishigaku Kenkyukai. Tokyo, 1976.

Bōeichō Bōei Kenkūjo Senshishitsu. *Daihonkan Rikusōbu*. 7 vols. Tokyo, 1973.

——. *Hokushi no chiansen*. 2 vols. Tokyo, 1971.

——. *Honkon Chōsa sakusen*. Tokyo, 1971.

——. *Ichigō Sakusen (1) Kōnan no kaisen*. Tokyo, 1967.

——. *Ichigō Sakusen (2) Konan no kaisen*. Tokyo, 1967.

——. *Ichigō Sakusen (3) Keisei no kaisen*. Tokyo, 1969.

——. *Kaigun gunsembi*. 5 vols. Tokyo, 1975.

——. *Kaigun Shōgō sakusen*. 2 vols. Tokyo, 1972.

——. *Kaijō goei sen*. Tokyo, 1971.

——. *Kantōgun*. Tokyo, 1969.

——. *Rikugun gunju dōin*. Tokyo, 1970.

————. *Shina jihen Rikugun sakusen.* 3 vols. Tokyo, 1976.

————. *Shōwa jūshichi-hachinen no Shina Hakengun.* Tokyo, 1972.

————. *Shōwa nijūnen no Shina Hakengun.* 2 vols. Tokyo, 1973.

Eguchi Keiichi, ed. *Manshu jihen.* In *Taiheiyō sensō shi,* edited by Rekishigaku Kenkyukai. Tokyo, 1976.

Fujii Matsuichi, ed. *Sanfuranshisuko Kōwa.* In *Taiheiyō sensō shi,* edited by Rekishigaku Kenkyukai. Tokyo, 1976.

Fujimoto Haruki. *Ishiwara Kanji.* Tokyo, 1964.

Fujiwara Akira. *Gunjishi.* Tokyo, 1961.

————, ed. *Taiheiyō sensō.* Pt. 1. In *Taiheiyō sensō shi,* edited by Rekishigaku Kenkyukai. Tokyo, 1976.

Hata Ikushito. *Nitchō sensōshi.* Tokyo, 1961.

Hatano Ken'ichi. *Gendai Shina no seiji to jinbutsu.* Tokyo, 1937.

Hattori Teishiro. *Daitōa sensō zenshi.* Tokyo, 1957.

Horiba Katsuo. *Shina jihen senō shidō.* 2 vols. Tokyo, 1962.

Imai Seiichi, ed. *Nitchu sensō.* Pt. 1. In *Taiheiyō sensō shi,* ed. Rekishigaku Kenkyukai. Tokyo, 1976.

Imai Takeo. *Shina jihen no kaisō.* Tokyo, 1964.

————. *Shōwa no bōryaku.* Tokyo, 1967.

Inaba Masao. *Okamura Jeiji Taishō shiryō—senjō kaisō hen.* Tokyo, 1970.

Kodama Kenji. *Chūgoku Kaisōroku.* Tokyo, 1952.

Nakamura Takafusa, ed. *Kokka sōdoin.* 1970. In *Gendaishi shiryo.* Tokyo, 1962-.

Narusawa Yonezō. *Ishiwara Kanji.* Tokyo, 1969.

Nippon Kokusai Seiji Gakukai, ed. *Taiheiyō sensō e no Michi.* 8 vols. Tokyo, 1963.

Saitō Tsuyoshi. *Shina-Kikō to Jinbutsu.* Tokyo, 1937.

Sanematsu Yuzuru, ed. *Taiheiyō sensō.* 5 vols. (1970). In *Gendaishi shiryō.* Tokyo, 1962-.

Satō Kenryō. *Tōjō Hideki to taiheiyō sensō.* Tokyo, 1964.

Satō Shunzō. *Shina no kokunai tōsō.* Tokyo, 1941.

Shigemitsu Mamoru. *Shōwa no dōran.* 2 vols. Tokyo, 1952.

Teradaira Tadasuke. *Rokōkyō jihen.* Tokyo, 1970.

Tōa Kenkyujo. *Jūkei Seiken no Seijō.* Tokyo, 1943.

————. *Kokumintō Shina no kyoiku seisaku.* Tokyo, 1941.

Tōa Mondai Chosakai. *Saishin Shina Yōjin-bo.* Osaka, 1941.

Togawa Isao. *Shōwa gaikō shi.* Tokyo, 1962.

Tsunoda Jun, ed. *Nitchu sensō.* 4 vols. 1965. In *Gendaishi shiryō.* Tokyo, 1962-.

Uemura Shinichi. *Nikka jihen.* In *Nihon gaiko shi,* vol. 20, ed. Kajima Institute of International Peace. Tokyo, 1971-.

Yamaguchi Jūji. *Higenki no Shōgun: Ishiwara Kanji.* Tokyo, 1952.

Yoshioka Bunroku. *Gendai Shing Jinbutsu ron.* Tokyo, 1938.

Yoshizawa Kenkichi. *Gaikō rokujū-nen.* Tokyo, 1958.

Journals and Periodicals

American Political Science Review

Bulletin of Concerned Asian Scholars
Bulletin of the School of Oriental and African Studies, University of London
China Quarterly
China Reconstructs
China Weekly Review
Chinese Republican Studies Newsletter
Chuan-chi wen-hsüeh
Ch'un ch'iu
Chung-wai tsa-chih
Chung-yang hsün-lien-t'uan t'uan-k'an
Far Eastern Quarterly
Journal of Asian Studies
Kuo-wen chou-pao
Military Affairs
Ming pao (monthly)
Modern China
North China Herald
Pacific Affairs
Pacific Historical Review
Selected Papers from the Center for Far Eastern Studies, University of Chicago
Statistical Service, Nankai University

Index